POVERTY AND POLICY IN IRELAND

Poverty and Policy in Ireland

Edited by
Brian Nolan and Tim Callan

GILL & MACMILLAN

Published in Ireland by
Gill & Macmillan Ltd
Goldenbridge
Dublin 8
with associated companies throughout the world

© Brian Nolan and Tim Callan 1994
0 7171 2017 1
Print origination by Seton Music Graphics Ltd, Bantry, Co. Cork
Printed in Ireland by ColourBooks Ltd, Dublin

To our parents:
Nancy, Stan, Imelda and Paddy

Contents

List of Diagrams

List of Tables

Contributors

Richard Breen is Professor of Sociology, Director of the Centre for Social Research, and Executive Director of the Northern Ireland Regional Research Laboratory at the Queen's University, Belfast. His research interests are in labour market issues, stratification, mathematical sociology, and statistics. Between 1980 and 1991 he was a senior research officer at the Economic and Social Research Institute, where his publications included studies of labour market programmes, co-education, crime, and the transition from education to the labour market.

Tim Callan is a senior research officer at the Economic and Social Research Institute. His research interests include poverty and income distribution, labour market issues, and the analysis of tax and social welfare policies. His publications include studies of tax and welfare reform, women's labour market participation, and studies of poverty and income distribution in a national and international context. He has a D.Phil. in economics from the University of Oxford.

Brian Nolan is a research professor at the Economic and Social Research Institute. He was previously a senior economist at the Central Bank of Ireland. His publications include studies of the distribution of income, poverty, tax and social welfare policy, wealth, low pay, health economics, and socio-economic health inequalities. He completed a Ph.D. in economics at the London School of Economics.

Ciarán J. O'Neill is currently studying for a Ph.D. at the Sloan School in the Massachusetts Institute of Technology. He was previously a research assistant at the Economic and Social Research Institute, where he worked on the analysis of tax and social welfare policies.

David B. Rottman is a senior staff associate at the National Center for State Courts, Williamsburg, Virginia, where his research interests involve comparative studies of courts as organisations, civil litigation, and disparities in criminal sentences. Between 1975 and 1992 he was a senior research officer at the Economic and Social Research Institute. Publications from that period include articles and book chapters interpreting social change in Ireland, ESRI monographs on crime trends and social class inequalities, and NESC reports analysing redistribution through public social expenditure and evaluating criminal justice policy. He has a Ph.D. in sociology from the University of Illinois.

Brendan J. Whelan is a research professor and head of the Survey Unit at the ESRI. He holds degrees in economics from University College, Dublin, and in statistics from the London School of Economics. His main research interests relate to survey design and methodology, labour market issues, and poverty. He designed and developed the ESRI's random sampling system, RANSAM.

Christopher T. Whelan is a research professor at the Economic and Social Research Institute. He is a joint author of *Understanding Contemporary Ireland* (1990), joint editor of *The Development of Industrial Society in Ireland* (1992), and editor of a forthcoming volume, *Values and Social Change in Ireland*, to be published by Gill & Macmillan. His other publications include a number of ESRI monographs and journal articles in the areas of work, unemployment, poverty, and social mobility. He has a Ph.D. in sociology from London University.

James Williams is a research officer at the Economic and Social Research Institute, where his interests include survey techniques, geographical information systems, regional development, and poverty. He has previously held research and planning positions in University College, Dublin, and Bord Fáilte. He holds postgraduate degrees in economics and geography.

Preface

This book is about poverty in Ireland and what can be done to tackle it. It is not surprising, given the scale of our economic difficulties and particularly the level of unemployment, that the focus of attention on poverty and policy has been particularly intense in Ireland in the late 1980s and early 1990s. Poverty is an emotive word and an emotive issue, and there has been a vigorous debate about the extent and nature of poverty and about the ways in which our state and society should respond. Recent research carried out in the Economic and Social Research Institute has contributed to this debate across a wide range of areas, from the measurement of poverty to the operation of the labour market, the impact of unemployment, the role of education and training, the persistence of poverty over time and across generations, the rigidities of the social class structure, aspects of disadvantage such as physical and psychological ill health, and the structure and effects of the tax and social welfare systems. Much of this research has been based on the large-scale household survey carried out by the ESRI in 1987, which was specially designed to allow such topics to be examined. The objective of this volume is to bring together and present a synthesis of the key findings of this research and to bring out the implications for policy.

This is done in a form that is intended to be accessible to a wide readership rather than aimed primarily at a narrow academic audience. The level of interest in the topic and its importance make this both necessary and particularly worth while: necessary if the research is to make as great a contribution to the debate as possible, and worth while in that there is—we hope—every prospect that it will be widely used if made available in that form. For this reason we have tried to avoid reliance on academic jargon, footnotes, discussion of statistical methodology, and the more arcane topics. (Hopefully this will whet the appetite of some readers, who can pursue the more detailed studies on which the various chapters are based.) The aim is that the content of this volume be of value not only to an academic audience but to all those interested in understanding the nature of poverty in Ireland and the options for coping with it as a society.

This, we hope and believe, is an important contribution to understanding poverty in Ireland and responding to it. It is all too easy for discussion about poverty to become a dialogue of the deaf, with participants equally convinced that they occupy the high moral ground. As in other areas, while research does not point to easy answers it can provide a more informed basis for policy choices. The book comprises chapters written by different authors on specific topics relating to poverty and policy, together with an introduction, conclusion and linking commentary by the editors. The contributors share neither a common disciplinary background—some are economists, some sociologists—nor a common political or ideological stance. The common ground is a belief in the importance of the problem and in the value of research on poverty firmly grounded in empirical analysis. Each contribution aims to enhance our understanding of a particular facet of poverty and policy, so that the volume as a whole provides a much more rounded picture than has been available up to now.

We are grateful to our ESRI colleagues John FitzGerald, Damian Hannan, Philip O'Connell and Jerry Sexton for guidance when drawing on their work. We also greatly appreciate the support we have received throughout the programme of research from the Director of the Institute, Kieran Kennedy, and the advice and encouragement provided at different stages by Tony Atkinson (University of Cambridge). The research programme was made possible by the efforts of all those involved in the 1987 household survey: Damian Hannan and Brendan Whelan, whose brainchild it was, the ESRI Survey Unit staff and interviewers, and the respondents, who we hope will see this volume as some evidence of the value of responding.

The support staff of the ESRI have been unfailingly helpful throughout the project, and we would like to acknowledge in particular the assistance of Maura Rohan, for providing such a comprehensive library service, and Pat Hopkins, for speedy copying of various drafts.

The financial support provided for our survey and various elements of the research by the Combat Poverty Agency, the Department of Social Welfare and the EC Commission is gratefully acknowledged.

PART I

INTRODUCTION

1 Context and Objectives

TIM CALLAN AND BRIAN NOLAN

Poverty, for long seen as a marginal issue, is moving towards centre stage in Ireland. This partly reflects the impact of slow economic growth in the 1980s on unemployment and living standards. It also arises, however, from the growing realisation, here as elsewhere, that neither economic growth alone nor transfers through the social welfare system offer the panacea. It can no longer be comfortably assumed that economic growth will cascade or even trickle down to the poor, with the social welfare system picking up the few stragglers in danger of being left behind. Fundamental issues, therefore, have to be faced, based on the acknowledgment that poverty, far from being a problem for a small number at the margins of society, is a product of economic and social structures affecting everyone.

Ireland now has one of the highest rates of unemployment in the developed world, and the prospects are that very high unemployment rates will persist through the rest of the 1990s. The consequences for the individuals, families and communities affected are often severe. At the same time, changing patterns of household formation, particularly the growing numbers of lone-parent families, have posed new problems. An increased awareness of these problems, and particularly of the need to 'do something' about unemployment, has been reflected in recent opinion polls and media discussion, and it appears in voting behaviour. Despite this, a coherent strategy to tackle poverty on the scale required has yet to emerge, and any such strategy faces major obstacles.

The worst effects on the public finances of the fiscal expansion funded by borrowing of the late 1970s and early 1980s have been overcome, but the legacy of debt will continue to constrain Government freedom of action. Although resource transfers from the European Community will be substantial, this reflects a recognition that the 1992 programme of opening up the single market will have costs as well as

3

benefits for Ireland. Awareness of the problem is not enough: particularly in what may well continue to be difficult economic circumstances internationally, making serious inroads into poverty poses a formidable challenge.

Without an understanding of the nature and causes of poverty it is unlikely that this challenge can be met. Research therefore has an important role to play in tackling what many now regard as the central problem facing Irish society. A wide range of studies on poverty and related topics has been undertaken at the Economic and Social Research Institute in recent years, much of it based on a specially designed household survey carried out in 1987, with the results published by the ESRI or in academic journals or contained in reports to Government departments, the European Commission, and other interested parties. The objectives of this book are to bring together what has been learnt in the course of this research about the extent, nature and causes of poverty and about framing policies to combat it, and to make these findings available to a wide audience.

The book comprises chapters written by different authors on specific topics that they have studied in some depth, together with this introduction and a concluding chapter. The research involved relies for the most part on analysis of the type of data obtained in large-scale surveys, principally the 1987 ESRI household survey. In the social sciences generally, but particularly in research on poverty, there is something of a tension between research employing case-study or ethnographic methodologies, where a small group, community or area is intensively observed and studied, and that based on representative statistical samples from large-scale questionnaire-based surveys. The relationship between the two approaches has been well put by Wilson and Ramphele (1989, 15):

Each is periodically driven to distraction by the other. But each badly needs the other in order to avoid the Scylla of assuming that a particular case study is typical of a whole population and the Charybdis of asserting that what has been enumerated (and statistically analysed) is necessarily the whole (or even the most important part) of the truth.

Townsend (1979) has shown, in presenting results from his large-scale survey of the UK, that the picture of poverty that emerges from such research does not have to be one-dimensional. Our own survey follows his emphasis on measuring many aspects of people's circumstances other than income, including various aspects of deprivation as well as attitudes and subjective assessments of their situation. We recognise the important role case studies can play in bringing out what the experience of poverty involves; the recent Combat Poverty Agency publication *Telling It Like It Is* (O'Neill, 1992), presented from the perspective of those affected by poverty, is a particularly evocative example. To form an overall picture of poverty in its societal and structural context, however, statistical analysis of nationally representative samples—on which this volume concentrates—is essential.

The availability of data from a household survey specifically designed for the purpose has greatly enhanced the ability of research to throw light on the nature of poverty and the effects of different policy options. In the late 1960s and early 1970s, when poverty in Ireland as in many other developed countries was being 'rediscovered', Ó Cinnéide in his influential study (1972) had to rely on data from various sources to try to piece together a picture of the extent of poverty and who was most at risk. Then, as now, the topic was a contentious and highly charged one, and current debates about the meaning, measurement and extent of poverty, and about the appropriate response, in many ways echo reactions at that time. The divides persist, for example, between those who see poverty as self-evidently relative and those who regard this as equating poverty with inequality, and between those who see increasing social welfare payments as part of the solution and those who see them as part of the problem. (For a flavour of recent debates see the report of the Commission on Social Welfare and the critique by Dowling (1986); Barrett (1989); successive pre-budget submissions by the Combat Poverty Agency (e.g. 1989, 1991) and the Conference of Major Religious Superiors (e.g. 1991, 1992a); Tansey (1991); and McCarthy (1993).) While it would be unrealistic to expect that research alone can produce a meeting of minds on these value-laden issues, it can at a minimum provide the basis for a better-informed debate about policy choices. As has been seen elsewhere, though, it can also significantly influence the terms on which the debate about poverty and policy is conducted, and the seriousness with which it is taken.

It is worth spelling out at this early stage the general approach adopted here to the key issue of what poverty means and how it is to be measured. Poverty is taken to be a social construct, in the sense that it refers to the failure to meet minimum social needs as they are seen in a particular society at a particular time. The scope for legitimate disagreement about precisely where to locate a meaningful poverty line and how to measure poverty is recognised, however, so findings that hold across a variety of poverty definitions—for example the impact of unemployment on incomes and living standards—are emphasised. This emphasis is intended to focus attention primarily on what has been learnt about the nature and causes of poverty rather than on the inevitably more contentious issues of definition and precise measurement, on which agreement is much less likely. This approach has recently been advocated both by economists and sociologists concerned with the conceptualisation and measurement of poverty. As Lee Rainwater, a leading American sociologist, puts it (1990, 1), rather than search for a single socially validated poverty line 'it is more useful both for descriptive and policy purposes to examine the continuum of lower incomes and their correlates.' The proof of the pudding is in the eating, and the value of this approach is best judged after seeing the strength of the conclusions—described in the course of the book—that it allows.

1.1 STRUCTURE AND CONTENT

In the remainder of this introductory chapter a brief outline of the content of the book is given, so that the reader has an initial picture of how the pieces fit together. The chapters, written by different authors on specific topics, are grouped into six parts, with an editorial commentary at the beginning of each part providing the links.

Part I consists of this introductory chapter and chapter 2, which provides the necessary foundation for the remainder of the volume by addressing the core issue of what one means by 'poverty' and how it is to be measured. This makes clear the ambiguities and uncertainties that surround the term and the concept. The way in which notions of acceptability and adequacy are related to the standard of living of the society in question, and how this affects the search for a satisfactory method of measuring poverty, is discussed. Different people use the term 'poverty' to mean different things in different circumstances: does this mean that 'poverty is in the eye of the beholder' and that no consensus is possible about what poverty means? If poverty is seen in terms of relative rather than absolute standards, does this mean that 'the poor always ye have with you'? These issues are explored, and the approach taken here to defining and measuring poverty is spelt out.

Having dealt with the problems of definition and measurement of poverty at a general level, part II moves on to the description of the situation in Ireland as revealed by recent research. On the basis of information on a large sample of households obtained in the survey carried out by the ESRI in 1987, the extent and nature of poverty is analysed. The numbers falling below relative income poverty lines is examined, with particular attention paid to those who are in addition experiencing what would be widely regarded as rather basic forms of deprivation. The types of household that are most at risk, how this compares with other countries and how it has been changing over time are discussed. Those in poverty at a particular time are not all destined to be in poverty in the long term: there is some mobility over time in and out of poverty. Using information on the same set of individuals and households for 1989, the extent to which those who were in poverty at the beginning of the period have been able to escape by the end, and the factors that trigger such 'escapes', are also examined.

This analysis allows the major causes of poverty to be identified, and it is on these that part III focuses. The impact of the dramatic rise in unemployment in the 1980s on individual and household incomes and living standards is described, with particular emphasis on the situation of the long-term unemployed. Low pay is another factor often seen as an important contributor to poverty, although the complexity of the relationship between low pay and poverty—also examined in part III— may not be generally appreciated. The underlying structure of poverty in its relationship with social class, and the crucial role of education in linking socio-economic background and current class and patterning the risk of poverty, are then examined.

In part IV some specific aspects of disadvantage are considered. The relationships between unemployment, poverty and psychological distress, and between socio-economic status and morbidity or 'premature' mortality, are discussed. The impact of such differentials in ill health on the use of health services by different income and socio-economic groups and the extent to which the distribution of usage corresponds to that of 'need' are analysed. Turning to poverty and sex inequality, the relevance of the phenomenon of 'feminisation of poverty', widely discussed elsewhere, is assessed. Trends in the extent and nature of women's participation in the labour market and in their earnings and the differences between men's and women's earnings are also analysed.

The assumption implicit in most analyses of poverty—including most of this book—is that all members of a particular household or family share a common standard of living; the likelihood that this leads to neglect of a substantial number of women and children in 'hidden poverty' is also considered. The final chapter in part IV looks at poverty from a spatial perspective, and addresses questions such as whether the poor are clustered together in particular 'black-spots' and how areas with particularly high poverty rates might best be identified with the type of information available from, most importantly, the census of population.

Part V concentrates on policies aimed at tackling poverty. First, the performance of the tax and social welfare systems in providing support to those on low incomes and in alleviating poverty is analysed. The way in which the tax and social welfare systems, especially in combination, create poverty and unemployment 'traps' is also considered, and the options for reform are assessed in terms of the extent of gains and losses and who would win and lose, the effects on incentives, and overall costing and financing. Reforms investigated include those suggested by the Commission on Taxation and the Commission on Social Welfare, as well as more radical strategies that aim to integrate the tax and benefit systems or provide a guaranteed 'basic income' to all. Income support plays a vital role in alleviating poverty, but, particularly given the scale of unemployment, it cannot be the solution. The effectiveness of labour market schemes that have been intended to promote employment and assist the long-term unemployed is examined and their weaknesses identified. Some key aspects of the European Community dimension to tackling poverty are then considered, focusing on the anti-poverty programmes of pilot development projects, social policy at EC level, and the structural funds being made available to promote 'economic and social cohesion'.

Finally, part VI provides an overview of what has been learnt from the research described in the individual contributions about the nature and causes of poverty, and highlights their implications for developing effective policies to tackle it. This is set against the prospects for economic growth, unemployment, demographic composition, and household formation patterns in the next decade or so, as well as the EC context against which domestic policy will operate. Particular emphasis is given to policies designed to address the structural causes of poverty, in particular to the ways in which education and training policies could reduce the obstacles facing those from disadvantaged backgrounds, and to reform of the tax and benefit systems. Given the prospect that long-term unemployment at high levels will persist, the types of targeted measures that could assist the long-term unemployed are also discussed. It will come as no surprise that research is also seen as having a contribution to make, and the major gaps in our knowledge about the evolution of poverty in Ireland are highlighted.

2 The Meaning and Measurement of Poverty

TIM CALLAN AND BRIAN NOLAN

Perhaps the most important challenge facing research on poverty is how to deal with the ambiguities and confusions associated with the term and concept: how to define and measure poverty in a way that is valid, meaningful in the context, and valuable for policy-making. This problem arises because poverty is a rather loose and ill-defined term, both in common usage and academic application. In this chapter the issues this raises are discussed and the implications for how we should approach the measurement of poverty in Ireland are set out. It is worth making clear at the outset that searching for a unique, objective, scientific measure of poverty on which everyone can agree is not, in our view, likely to be fruitful and has certainly not been successful anywhere else. This is not to be taken as a counsel of despair—rather the opposite: research on poverty can be a great deal more productive if it does not chase that will-o'-the-wisp.

This chapter first discusses what poverty in a country like Ireland means. It then describes various approaches to measuring poverty that have been suggested and applied internationally. Some issues that arise whatever approach is used are then discussed. Previous research on measuring poverty in Ireland is briefly reviewed. Finally, the general strategy to be employed here, underlying the findings presented in the remainder of the book, is set out.

2.1 THE MEANING OF POVERTY

Views differ on what poverty means and how widespread it is in many countries, and Ireland is no exception. What appears to be generally accepted is the notion that poverty is a condition that is unacceptable. Indeed it is precisely because of the moral or ethical connotations—

because applying the term evokes an imperative to action—that the use of the term is so hotly debated. Since the alleviation of poverty is generally accepted as one of the central objectives of economic and social policy, how the term is to be applied, how many and who are to be considered poor, will be of central importance.

In many countries people struggle to survive, to avoid starvation. In the circumstances prevailing in many 'Third World' countries it makes sense to think of poverty as an inability to obtain sufficient nutrition, clothing and shelter to survive or maintain physical health. What is often termed an 'absolute' conception of poverty is clearly of critical relevance for much of the world's population. In developed economies, however, with much higher average living standards, ensuring that everyone has an absolute minimum in nutrition, clothing and housing—though still relevant—would not generally be seen as sufficient to eradicate poverty. In a society at Ireland's stage of development, being able to 'keep body and soul together' is not enough to avoid poverty, and the fact that most Irish people have shelter and few die of starvation does not mean that there is little or no poverty here.

Compared with most of those living in the Third World, even the least prosperous in Ireland are quite rich; this is not, however, the standard of comparison that most people apply when they talk of poverty. What is seen as constituting poverty is influenced by the general socio-economic conditions of the society in question. What is considered 'adequate' will therefore differ across countries and change over time: people do not apply the standards of the 1890s to the 1990s, or those of Ethiopia to Ireland. To take a simple example, a few generations ago not many Irish households had running hot and cold water, and its absence would not have been seen as indicating poverty. Now, when most households do have running water, it is regarded as a necessity. What are generally perceived as 'needs' change over time and differ across societies. Poverty is, in that sense, relative.

This is not a 'new' definition of poverty being imposed by academics or those of particular political or ideological leanings. Poverty has always been defined in relation to the standards with which people in a particular time and place are familiar. This was put with admirable clarity by Adam Smith, in a much-quoted passage, when he wrote that 'necessaries' included 'not only the commodities which are indispensably necessary for the support of life, but what ever the custom of the country renders it indecent for creditable people, even the lowest orders, to be without.' The examples he gives are leather shoes and linen shirts—neither essential for survival, but in late eighteenth-century England 'the poorest creditable person would be ashamed to appear in public without them.' What are seen as 'needs' are thus inevitably socially determined. As Sen (1983) emphasises, it is in the notion of shame that the core of the concept of poverty is to be found: the absence of resources puts people in a situation where they cannot live with dignity in their society.

The fact that the term 'poverty' is used in different senses in different circumstances makes it all the more essential to try to clarify the underlying concept. It could be argued, of course, that some other term should be used in the context of a developed country—such as 'relative deprivation', for example—with 'poverty' reserved for those unable to meet basic needs in the Third World. However, even in the Third World poverty is widely used to describe conditions that, though desperate, are above minimum subsistence level. The layers of meaning attached to the term reflect the complexity and depth of the underlying concept, and the challenge this poses would still have to be faced with a different term. It seems preferable to try to tease out what people mean when they talk of 'poverty' in a country like Ireland, and use this as the foundation for measurement.

Perhaps the most influential attempt to spell out a definition of poverty that has general applicability is that of Peter Townsend (1979, 31):

> Individuals, families and groups in the population can be said to be in poverty when they lack the resources to obtain the type of diet, participate in the activities and have the living conditions and amenities which are customary, or at least widely encouraged, or approved, in the societies to which they belong. Their resources are so seriously below those commanded by the average individual or family that they are, in effect, excluded from ordinary living patterns, customs and activities.

This emphasis on participation versus exclusion serves to make explicit the relative nature of the concept and has been widely adopted—for example by the European Community—in much of the recent discourse on poverty in developed countries. There are some dissenting voices, who see poverty as primarily an absolute notion; but the dominant view appears to be that expressed by Piachaud (1987, 148): 'Close to subsistence level there is indeed some absolute minimum necessary for survival but apart from this, any poverty standard must reflect prevailing social standards: it must be a relative standard.'

It has been convincingly argued that the notion of a fixed absolute poverty standard, applicable to all societies and all times, is a chimera, given the extent to which judgment must be exercised in arriving at even such a basic element as nutritional 'needs' and the way in which the goods required to allow basic needs to be met will differ across societies. In practice, poverty standards that have aimed at measuring 'absolute' poverty in developed countries have been heavily influenced by prevailing conditions and expenditure patterns in the society in question. Their distinguishing feature is not the way in which the standard is set initially but how it is adjusted over time. 'Absolute' standards can be adjusted over time simply in line with the increase in consumer prices, so that—notionally at least—they represent the same standard of living. Such a measure certainly has value, as will be demonstrated later. However, over any prolonged period where real incomes are rising it will lose contact with the reality of expectations and perceptions of 'need', and therefore with what people see as poverty. This has to be taken into account in defining and measuring poverty, though it need not mean that 'absolute' living standards become irrelevant.

Focusing again on Townsend's definition, it must be emphasised that it sees poverty not simply as exclusion but as exclusion due to lack of resources. It is possible for people to be at a low level of consumption even though they have the resources to participate fully. The converse is also true, however: people may be at very low income levels but able to avoid deprivation, at least temporarily, for example by drawing on savings or relying on help from others. While this has major implications for measuring poverty, which will be discussed below, here it is the conceptual implications that are to be stressed. For some people, concern about poverty is related simply to actual levels of living; and how people are managing to avoid deprivation and exclusion is not a central concern. Others have argued from the perspective of rights, however, that people are entitled as citizens to a minimum income to enable them to participate fully in their society. In practice the two notions—focused on standards of living versus minimum rights—are often confused, but the distinction may be important both in measuring poverty and in considering responses to it. Townsend's definition could be seen as incorporating both conceptions, involving both exclusion and the resource constraint, though this may not be what was intended. The implications will be explored in discussing the various approaches to measuring poverty, in the next section, and in implementation for Ireland in chapters 3–5.

2.2 MEASURING POVERTY

Various approaches to measuring poverty have been applied in developed countries, none of which is entirely satisfactory. A brief review of these methods will help to clarify the way in which the concept has been interpreted in practice, and provides the starting-point for analysing poverty in Ireland. (For a more detailed review see Callan and Nolan, 1991.)

Budget standards
If poverty is seen as inability to afford 'necessities', one obvious way to set an income poverty line is to specify the set of goods and services that are considered the minimum necessary, and see how much it costs to buy them. Known as the 'budget standard approach', this was the method adopted in much of the early research on poverty in Britain and elsewhere, and still provides the basis for the official poverty line in use in the United States. It begins with food needs, specifying and costing an adequate diet, drawing on nutritional studies. Other elements, such as food and clothing, can then be specified explicitly and costed, or non-food expenditure can simply be taken into account by multiplying the 'necessary' food expenditure by a factor. Rowntree, in his early British studies, used the former method, whereas the US official poverty line uses the latter. The US line was set in 1965 by multiplying food costs for a family of three or more people by a factor of 3, reflecting the fact that such families spent on average about one-third of their total income on food at that time. This poverty line has been adjusted over time in line with the consumer price index, and is a good example of the 'absolute' approach in practice, being intended to represent—as Sawhill (1988) puts it—the cost of a fixed basket of goods and services that are believed to constitute the bare necessities of life.

Closer examination reveals the extent to which judgments and elements of relativity underlie such budget standards. Even for food, nutritional studies do not provide a precise estimate of what is 'needed' to survive; physical efficiency declines with falling intake at a rate that varies among individuals and locations. The necessary diet is generally related to usual eating habits in the society in question rather than an ideal nutrition-maximising one. For other expenditures, and to an extent for food as well, 'needs' as defined by experts will be based on what are in effect social rather than scientific criteria, and with a substantial degree of arbitrariness. In addition, most budget standards allow for expenditure on non-necessities and for the fact that consumers do not allocate their expenditure optimally across the items in the budget to reach the experts' minima, again introducing judgment and arbitrariness. Where budget standards rely on actual household expenditure patterns—to derive the target share of food in total expenditure, for example—the relativity and circularity involved become even more obvious. Needs, to a large extent, are determined by actual expenditure patterns of the poor or of the society as a whole.

The budget standard approach cannot therefore be seen as providing a scientific basis for a poverty line measuring the income required to meet an immutable set of 'needs': it is not in that sense an 'absolute' line. It can serve as the basis for a line that is held fixed in real terms over time, as in the American instance—though there is no reason why such a fixed standard should necessarily be based on that approach. This serves to make clear why the real choice is not between a scientific, absolute, unchanging poverty standard and a relative one: instead the issue is whether the poverty line should be held fixed over time or rise as the general standard of living rises.

Social welfare rates as poverty lines
Much of the empirical work on measuring poverty in developing countries has taken as its benchmark the rates of income support provided by the social welfare system. The rate of support given by the safety-net scheme is taken to be, in some sense, an 'official' poverty line. This may reflect the belief that these rates represent either expert views or a consensus about the minimum acceptable level of income in that society. It is difficult to accept either interpretation, however. While levels of support may originally have borne some relation to the costs of what were seen as minimum needs, both these levels and their adjustment over time are the product of a complex political process influenced by many other factors. Levels of support are affected by changing standards of living over time, rising more or less rapidly than other incomes in a manner that reflects neither expert views nor those of the electorate, for whom they constitute but one issue among many. They cannot then be afforded the status of 'expert' or 'consensual' poverty lines.

The appeal of reliance on social welfare rates as a benchmark is practical rather than conceptual, in that information on these rates is readily available. Their use as poverty lines gives rise to obvious anomalies, however. Most obviously, increasing social welfare rates could lead to a rise in measured poverty, since the poverty line also rises. Comparisons across countries could likewise show more poverty where social welfare rates are relatively generous. Even more fundamentally, as Sen points out (1983), social welfare rates reflect a number of influences, including the state of the public finances, but the fact that elimination of some specific deprivation might be seen as impracticable does not change the fact of that deprivation: 'inescapable poverty is still poverty.'

Seeing how many people fall below the social welfare system's safety net does serve a valuable function, in allowing the performance of the system in meeting its own objectives (or one of them) to be measured. As a measure of poverty this is fundamentally inadequate, however: what is needed is a benchmark independent of the social welfare system against which the effectiveness of that system in reducing poverty can be assessed.

Subjective poverty lines

If the poverty line is to be based on prevailing social standards, one apparently straightforward approach is to ask people their views about the minimum income needed. Poverty lines intended to reflect a social consensus about minimum income needs have been derived from survey responses in a number of different ways, and these have been termed 'subjective' or 'consensual' poverty lines. For example, people may be asked what they would regard as the minimum they would need 'to make ends meet,' or what income levels they would consider to be 'very bad', 'bad', and so on.

A number of difficulties with this approach can be seen. Critical assumptions are involved about the way in which responses to this type of question can be interpreted. The relationship between 'making ends meet' or the evaluations of different income levels and what respondents would regard as poverty is not clear, nor is it obvious that the terms themselves will be interpreted in the same way by different people. The way in which the poverty line is actually derived from the responses is also problematic. (A simple average across the sample is not generally used, some methods giving more weight to those 'near' the poverty line, on the basis that they are most likely to be well informed.)

Further, people's responses may be affected by what they see as the implications for them, particularly in terms of taxation. Finally, there may not in fact be a social consensus: different groups may have quite different views. The consensual approach thus appears to have serious limitations as the basis for a poverty line, though the survey responses may have an important role in exploring how the views of different groups about income adequacy are formed.

Purely relative poverty lines

If poverty is to be seen relative to the standard of living of the society in question, an alternative that has been increasingly adopted is to frame poverty lines purely and explicitly in terms of relative income, taking for example half average income as a cut-off. The rationale for this 'purely relative' approach is that those falling more than a certain distance below the average or usual income level in the society are unlikely to be able to participate fully in the life of the community.

This has been the method used in a number of recent international comparisons of poverty rates, including studies carried out for the OECD and the EC and analyses based on the Luxembourg Income Study harmonised data-base. It has significant advantages for such comparisons across countries, or over time for a particular country. It builds in relativity in a consistent manner across countries or over time, it is straightforward to apply, the data required is limited, and the interpretation of the results is transparent compared with other methods.

Obviously this method discounts entirely any improvement in the living standards of low-income groups that are shared by the rest of the population, or differences in average living standards across countries. Even if the incomes of the poor decline, no increase in poverty will be registered if incomes of the rest of the population fall by as much or more: as Sen points out, such measures thus look more credible in situations of growth than of contraction.

More generally, even among those who view poverty primarily in relative terms, there is considerable diversity of views and indeed lack of clarity about the precise nature of the relativity concerned and therefore the extent to which a purely relative income approach is satisfactory. Most would presumably be much less happy with its application over a period of recession than one of growth. Even in a steadily growing economy, do socially perceived 'needs' necessarily rise *pari passu* with average incomes, or do they lag behind when incomes grow rapidly, only to catch up as growth slows and expectations adjust to higher living standards?

We return below to the issue of how and to what extent relativity should be built into a poverty measure, having discussed the final broad approach to distinguishing the poor from the non-poor, based on indicators of deprivation.

Deprivation indicators

The approaches described so far have in common the objective of constructing an income poverty line. Such income poverty lines can also be derived from the analysis of patterns of living and deprivation in the society, along lines pioneered by Townsend in Britain in the 1970s. His aim was first to identify indicators of deprivation, i.e. items or activities that are socially prescribed necessities. Through relating deprivation 'scores'—in terms of an index composed of such items—to household resources, people with resources 'so seriously below those commanded by the average individual that they are, in effect, excluded from ordinary living patterns, customs and activities' could be identified. In this manner, the definition of poverty he proposed (quoted earlier) could be empirically implemented.

In applying this approach to data from a British household survey, Townsend selected twelve items or activities (from sixty included in the survey) as indicators of deprivation, primarily on the basis that most people had these items. Relating deprivation scores to household income, he suggested that there was an income 'threshold' below which deprivation scores 'escalated disproportionately', and that this could be taken as the poverty line.

Criticism of Townsend's procedure has been considerable, and falls under two main headings. The first relates to the way the income threshold was derived from deprivation scores. Apart from the technical issues involved, the proponents of a threshold have so far failed to convince empirically. Indeed some critics argue that a threshold of this kind is intrinsically implausible, with reality more accurately described as a continuum from great wealth to chronic poverty. If that is so it has major implications, beyond Townsend's particular methodology, for how poverty should be conceived and measured, as we discuss shortly.

The second area of Townsend's approach on which critics have focused is the selection of the deprivation indicators. The particular indicators used were chosen in a rather ad hoc manner, and the degree of judgment and therefore influence over the results accorded to the researcher has been questioned. An alternative approach implemented by Mack and Lansley (1985) is to ask people directly what items or activities they regard as 'necessities' and to use these views in determining which are selected as indicators of deprivation—a consensual approach rather than what Townsend would term an 'objective' one.

A more fundamental criticism argues that observed differences in living patterns may be largely attributable to differences in tastes rather than in resources, and absence of a particular item or set of items cannot therefore be taken to represent deprivation caused by resource constraints. Mack and Lansley also attempt to deal with this issue, by asking people who do not have a particular item whether this is because they cannot afford it. This is useful information, but cannot be taken entirely at face value as accurately measuring 'enforced' absence: some people at low income levels may be reluctant to admit that they cannot afford a particular item, while others at relatively high incomes may say that they cannot afford a 'necessity'.

The deprivation indicator approach thus faces many difficulties: how to select and aggregate items whose enforced absence can be taken to represent deprivation, how to take account of the role of tastes in determining living patterns, and how to derive a particular cut-off to distinguish 'the poor' from the rest of the population. It is important to note that, although Townsend used this approach to attempt to derive an income poverty line, an alternative would be to use deprivation scores themselves as the criterion for identifying the poor. The problem that then has to be faced, of course, is how to choose a particular score on a deprivation index as the cut-off. Unless income is also taken into account, it will also mean that some people with relatively high incomes will probably be counted as poor. Further, simply adding together different deprivation indicators into an overall index may be questionable. It implicitly assumes that poverty is one-dimensional, which may not be an accurate reflection of reality. Poverty may rather be multidimensional, in the sense that households may for example be 'food-poor' but not 'housing-poor', or vice versa. It may then be preferable to assess whether households are deprived across dimensions rather than masking such differences by aggregation into a single index. (There are obvious parallels here with the 'basic needs' approach widely advocated in a Third World context, where the emphasis is on assessing the extent to which different dimensions of need—food, housing, health care, etc.—are being met.)

While acknowledging these difficulties and complexities, we feel that examination of direct measures of deprivation nonetheless has a great deal to offer in the analysis of poverty, complementing other approaches that focus on resources.

2.3 OTHER ISSUES IN MEASURING POVERTY

Household size

Apart from the crucial question of how a poverty line can be set, a number of other important issues have to be faced in measuring poverty. First, how are the differing needs of families or households of different size and composition to be taken into account in comparing welfare? One straightforward way, if income is the measure of welfare, would be to divide household income by the number of household members. However, household income per capita does not take into account the fact that there may be economies of scale in consumption—'two can live as cheaply as one'—for people living together, particularly for items such as housing and food. The 'needs' of different types of people, most obviously children versus adults, may also differ.

The standard procedure is to use a set of 'adult equivalence scales', designed to bring households to a common basis for comparison. If the household head is attributed a value of 1 equivalent unit, such scales might give each of the other adults in the household a value of 0.7 and each child a value of 0.4. 'Equivalent income' is then calculated by dividing household income by the number of equivalent units in the household. A couple with two children would count as (1 + 0.7 + 0.4 + 0.4) = 2.5 equivalent units. If their income was £200 a week they would then have equivalent income of £200 ÷ 2.5 = £80. This is considerably higher than income per capita, which is £200 ÷ 4 = £50, showing the extent to which it is being assumed that they benefit from living together and the lower needs of children.

Some of the poverty line methods themselves produce different lines for different household types, for example the consensual income line approach. The 'official' method simply takes the relativities incorporated in social welfare rates. In the purely relative line approach, equivalence scales have to be imposed from external information. Although there is an extensive research literature on the topic internationally, no entirely satisfactory method for estimating or deriving equivalence scales has been identified: as the Canadian statistical office recently concluded, 'the construction of equivalence scales is, however, an unsettled matter, depending on judgements of an essentially arbitrary character.' This is very important, because the actual scales produced by different methods vary substantially, and the scales used can have a major impact on both the size and composition of the low-income population. There is a clear need, then, to examine the sensitivity of results to the equivalence scales employed.

Recipient unit
The second general question in measuring living standards is which recipient or sharing unit is most appropriate: the individual, family, or household. To concentrate solely on an individual's own resources in assessing welfare when he or she is living with others would be extreme: all children and many married women have no income. Most research on poverty is devoted to what may be seen as the other extreme, using the household as recipient unit and assuming that all members of a particular household share a common standard of living. Some focus instead on the narrower nuclear family, of single person or couple and dependent children, if any. This involves the assumption of no sharing between, for example, an elderly person and the adult son with whom he or she is living, or between someone in their twenties who is earning and the parents with whom they still live. Very little is known about the extent of income sharing within households or families, and it is not clear if the use of either gives an accurate picture of living standards of individual members. Again, an assessment of sensitivity of results is important.

Income concept and measuring resources or living standards
The most common approach in measuring poverty has been to use household (equivalent) disposable income as the welfare or resources measure. Some studies instead compare household expenditure with the poverty line. Income may understate living standards to the extent that people can draw on savings or borrow, and it is argued that consumption is therefore a better measure. At a conceptual level, this obviously goes back to the distinction drawn earlier between a concern with living standards versus rights to resources: the appropriate indicator depends on which one is trying to measure.

However, the choice between income and consumption is also influenced by practical considerations, use of expenditure being advocated on the grounds that it is better measured in surveys than income. Both in fact have limitations. Expenditure data in surveys usually relates to a short period, often a fortnight, and may therefore be distorted by exceptional purchases and by some types of expenditure, such as alcohol and tobacco, known to be subject to understatement. Incomes from particular sources, such as self-employment and investments, are likewise known to be subject to understatement in surveys. The nature of the data available, as well as the conceptual framework, must therefore influence the way it is used in measuring poverty.

Leaving aside data reliability, both current expenditure and disposable income have limitations as measures of consumption and of resources available for consumption, respectively. Neither takes into account goods and services provided free or at subsidised prices by the state to some or all households or by private employers, such as education, health care, or housing. Clearly these goods and services affect economic well-being, but the difficulties in trying to value them and take them into account in measuring poverty are many. This is illustrated by the fact that ten alternative official poverty measures are published in the United States, involving different choices about the extent to which non-cash benefits are included in income and how they are valued.

Current income aims to measure resources available for consumption without depletion of savings or other assets, but may fail to capture the influence of assets not producing a stream of income but affecting command over resources. The most important example is housing: those who own their own houses have considerably greater consumption potential than those on the same income who must pay for housing. This could be taken into account by imputing the implicit rent on owner occupation and adding it to cash income, or by focusing on income net of housing costs. Both these approaches have been adopted but pose problems, both conceptual and empirical. Valuation of imputed rent is difficult where owner occupation dominates and the private rented sector is very limited, while income net of housing costs abstracts from differences in the choices made by different households about housing expenditure as well as differences in constraints.

Accounting period
The period over which income (or expenditure) should be measured is another important choice to be made in applying income poverty lines. Quite different results may be produced depending on whether income is measured over a week, a month, a year, several years, or even a lifetime. Recent evidence from panel studies following a particular group over time shows considerable income mobility. People on low income this week may not stay there long, and using annual incomes might give a rather different picture of the extent and composition of the low-income population. There is no 'correct' period: different periods allow different questions to be addressed, and short-term poverty is of interest in itself even if many of those experiencing it move in and out of poverty over time. The availability of panel data has, however, led to a realisation of the importance of seeing poverty in a dynamic rather than purely static context, and distinguishing more mobile groups from those likely to be poor in the longer term.

Summary measures of poverty

Finally there remains the issue that has in fact preoccupied much of the recent literature on poverty measurement, namely how best to summarise the extent of poverty—given a poverty line—in a summary measure. It is obviously helpful, for example, if it is possible to conclude that poverty has gone up or down by x per cent, but this requires an aggregate measure. Sen (1976) highlighted how the traditional headcount measure—simply counting the numbers below the poverty line—could be misleading: the percentage below the line could fall slightly while those remaining below it suffer a substantial fall in income, and this would register unambiguously as a fall in poverty. This spawned a substantial literature, and various measures have been proposed that take into account not only the numbers below the line but also the depth of their poverty, some of which have particularly attractive properties.

2.4 PREVIOUS RESEARCH ON POVERTY

It is useful to briefly review previous research on poverty in Ireland against the background of this general outline of methods applied in developed countries, before setting out the broad strategy employed in this book. The key Irish study in what has been termed the 'rediscovery of poverty' was Ó Cinnéide's presentation (1972) to the Kilkenny Conference on Poverty. He had to piece together information from a variety of sources on the income position of different groups. The poverty line applied was close to the means-tested rates paid at the time in the UK, significantly above corresponding Irish rates. About 24 per cent of the population was thought to have income below this level, on the basis of the piecemeal data available.

The first source that provided comprehensive information on incomes for a representative national household sample was the 1973 household budget survey (HBS) carried out by the Central Statistics Office. This was the basis for studies of poverty by FitzGerald (1981), Rottman, Hannan, et al. (1982), and Roche (1984). All three applied poverty lines derived from social welfare rates, though differing in detail. Roche used the 1973 unemployment assistance rates and those rates plus 20 per cent and plus 40 per cent as poverty lines, and found 10, 15 and 23 per cent of households, respectively, below these three lines. FitzGerald in effect applied a line based on the real value of old age pensions payable when she was writing (in 1980), which she argued 'corresponds roughly to our current perception of what it means to be poor.' About 30 per cent of the households in the 1973 HBS were below that level. Rottman, Hannan et al. looked at lines based on unemployment benefit rates in 1973, and found 7 per cent of households at or below benefit level and 20 per cent below benefit plus 40 per cent, the latter being the line to which most attention was paid.

The second full-scale national budget survey was carried out in 1980 and formed the basis for Roche's study of poverty (1984), including trends between 1973 and 1980. The three poverty lines used were those from his earlier analysis of 1973, adjusted to 1980, taking into account the increase in prices and real national income over the period. Applying these to 1980, he found a substantial fall in the percentage of households below the lines, with 4 per cent below the lowest one, 7 per cent below the middle one, and 12 per cent below the highest line.

Previous research measuring the extent of poverty has thus relied on the 'official' approach to deriving poverty lines, but within this common approach there has been a good deal of diversity in the actual choice of line. This illustrates one of the problems with that method adverted to earlier, that very often the social welfare system does not define an unambiguous 'minimum', leaving considerable scope for judgment about the appropriate rate to select, whether the basic rate or some multiple should be used, and so on. More fundamentally, the approach is severely flawed as a basis for making comparisons over time or across countries, for the reasons set out earlier: it is suitable for assessing the performance of the social welfare system in its own terms, but does not provide independent standards of 'adequacy'.

While there are significant differences between these studies in poverty standards and estimates of the overall extent of poverty, there is much greater agreement on the characteristics of those at low incomes. Ó Cinnéide highlighted the importance of four groups—the elderly, farmers, the unemployed or ill, and low-paid employees—who accounted for over 90 per cent of the total estimated number of poor. While the 1973 HBS provided a much more satisfactory data-base, the analysis by Roche, FitzGerald and Rottman, Hannan et al. in fact broadly confirmed this emphasis. Employees with large families were seen to make up a larger proportion of the poor as the poverty line was raised. Some small groups that did not constitute a significant proportion of the poor but nonetheless faced a very high risk of being in poverty were also identified, such as lone parents.

Roche's analysis of the 1980 HBS showed some striking changes in the risk of poverty and composition of the poor compared with

1973. The risk of being in poverty for households headed by an elderly person fell sharply, while that for households with children rose substantially. The risk facing households with an unemployed head remained high, and as the unemployment rate rose this group accounted for an increased proportion of the poor. Farm households remained at high risk and formed a substantial proportion of the poor in both years.

2.5 THE STRATEGY ADOPTED HERE

This review of the methods applied to measure poverty internationally and in previous research on Ireland has shown that there is no consensus on the best approach, nor indeed any sign of such a consensus emerging. No single satisfactory and convincing method of setting a poverty line that is 'objective' and appropriate for all purposes is available. Indeed, given the absence of a consensus about what poverty means, it is difficult to see how this would be possible. Piachaud (1981) likened the search for an objective or scientific method of setting a poverty line that could command universal acceptance to the quest for the Holy Grail; since the Grail was eventually found, a more appropriate analogy might well be the search for the philosopher's stone, which would turn base metal to gold.

This does not mean that research on poverty is a waste of time and must be abandoned. The reality of poverty exists, policy must still be formulated, and research can play a vital role. The approach adopted in the present study is to explicitly acknowledge the uncertainty and absence of consensus on where to locate a poverty line and how to measure poverty, and place most emphasis on findings that do not depend on a precise location of the line or measurement approach. It will be seen in the course of the various contributions that without concentrating on a particular line a great deal may still be learnt about the nature and meaning of poverty, the characteristics of those in or on the margins of poverty, and the effects of anti-poverty policy.

This general approach is very much in keeping with that recently advocated by Atkinson (1987) and Foster and Shorrocks (1988), who argue that the diversity of possible judgments about the specification of the poverty line and the choice of poverty measure should be acknowledged and taken into account in the measurement procedures adopted. While this may permit less all-embracing conclusions, it does offer the prospect of unambiguous conclusions in certain circumstances. Such conclusions, holding across a variety of poverty lines and measures, can then command much more widespread acceptance than those that are dependent on a particular line and measure. Equally importantly, ambiguous results that do depend on the line or measure chosen can be recognised as such.

The data available to us, described in the following chapters, is extremely unusual in allowing a number of different approaches to deriving poverty standards to be implemented. Echoing Piachaud (1987), while each has limitations, each has something to contribute. The most appropriate approach may vary not only with the underlying concept of poverty one has in mind but also with the specific question to be addressed. For example, it may be possible to approach the question 'Has poverty increased over time in Ireland?' in particular ways. These need not produce answers to the questions 'How many people are poor in Ireland today?' or 'What does it mean to be poor in Ireland today?' or 'How effective are social welfare transfers in alleviating poverty in Ireland?', for which different approaches might be more productive. It is worth sketching out here the main approaches employed in this book and the thinking behind the choices made, both discussed more fully in the relevant chapters.

We begin then by applying a set of income poverty lines, in chapter 3. These are constructed using the purely relative approach rather than alternative methods of deriving income lines, because of the advantages of that approach for making transparent comparisons across countries or over time. To assess the sensitivity of the results to the precise location of the line, a set of lines is used representing 40, 50 and 60 per cent of average income. The difference made by varying the equivalence scales is also analysed. Because of the limitations of the head-count as a summary measure, alternative aggregate measures taking into account the depth of poverty for those falling below the lines are also used. In looking at trends over time, the change in numbers falling below the purely relative income lines and in the more sophisticated aggregate measures from the early 1970s to the late 1980s is discussed.

While 'needs' may be seen as primarily socially determined, the background against which such changes in purely relative income positions take place, in terms of real income growth, may also affect one's assessment of the period. These changes are therefore put in context by also looking at what was happening to average real incomes over the period. Comparisons with other EC countries are made, primarily on the basis of the numbers falling below purely relative lines in each, but it is also interesting to see what happens to the comparative picture when one line is applied across all the countries, and this is taken up both in the next chapter and in chapter 18.

Focusing simply on income, though the most common practice in poverty studies in developed countries, has limitations, as discussed in this chapter. On the other hand, concentrating on direct measures of exclusion does not offer a satisfactory alternative as a measure of poverty. This is both because of the many difficulties that must be faced in trying to construct valid and reliable indicators of deprivation and because such measures do not incorporate the other central element in the widely adopted definition of poverty, namely the resource constraint. We therefore explore how to use deprivation indicators together with income in order to capture both elements, exclusion and resource constraint. To do so, as chapter 4 describes, new methods of identifying appropriate deprivation indicators are developed. To understand the relationship between deprivation and current income, we also take into account ability to draw on savings and call on networks of social support. All this makes possible a more rounded picture of the position of different groups than provided by income alone.

Previous research on poverty has employed social welfare rates as the basis for setting poverty lines, often using some multiple of these rates, such as 120 or 140 per cent. We do not follow this approach, because of the disadvantages of the method discussed earlier. However, that discussion made clear that looking at the numbers falling below social welfare safety-net levels does serve a distinct and valuable purpose in allowing the effectiveness of the system in bringing people up to its own minimum income target to be measured. An analysis of the numbers falling below safety-net income levels is therefore presented here, not as a measure of poverty but, in chapter 15, in the context of measuring the effectiveness of the social welfare system.

This chapter has sought to clarify the issues involved in attempting to define and measure poverty. We now move to the findings of recent research by the Economic and Social Research Institute based on the broad strategy described here.

PART II

POVERTY IN IRELAND

To analyse the cause of poverty, it is necessary first to be able to measure its extent and to identify the groups most affected by it. The chapters in this section provide a profile of poverty in contemporary Ireland, based on measures that take account of divergences in views about what constitutes poverty. Taken together, they show that many useful findings about trends in poverty and the groups most affected by it hold over a wide range of poverty line standards.

The most commonly used methods of measuring poverty, as discussed in part I, are based entirely on income information. Basic results on the numbers of people falling below widely used poverty line income thresholds are set out in chapter 3. These simple methods have the advantage of allowing comparisons over time, and across countries. For example, it is found that the percentage of households below half average income is higher in Ireland than in our richer EC partners but lower than in Portugal or Greece. Trends over time are discussed using surveys with similar income information from 1973, 1980, and 1987.

Current income has limitations as an indicator of household welfare, and the Economic and Social Research Institute's 1987 survey gathered a range of other information on living patterns, savings, and other assets, and people's views about their own situation, which can supplement income-based measures. Chapter 4 shows how this information can be used to provide a more comprehensive picture of poverty. Households at low income levels and clearly experiencing what would be widely regarded as deprivation are identified. Some of those at low incomes are apparently not experiencing such deprivation, primarily because they have some other resources to fall back on and have not been at those low incomes over a long period. A substantial number are seen to be experiencing deprivation of a basic sort—even if the criteria for measurement of deprivation are made stringent. The type of

27

indicators of deprivation used—for example, whether people can afford new rather than second-hand clothes, or a warm overcoat—provides, a concrete and evocative basis for directly identifying deprivation and exclusion.

Armed with these alternative measurement tools it is possible to identify which individuals and households are most likely to experience poverty. This is essential if the major causes of poverty are to be identified and policy is to be directed towards those in greatest need. Chapter 5 deals with this important topic. It shows which groups are most at risk of poverty in Ireland, how this compares with other countries, and how it has been changing over time. Major changes in the make-up of the poor over time are emphasised, the position of the elderly having improved but with unemployment playing a much more important role than in the early 1970s. Those of working age, and consequently children, are now much more likely to be affected. This mirrors trends in other western countries; but since unemployment has risen to very high levels in Ireland the impact has been much more pronounced here than elsewhere. It poses particular challenges for policy, since the target groups can no longer be taken as divorced from the labour market: anti-poverty strategies must now take account of labour market effects, and policies affecting the labour market form a key element in strategies to combat poverty.

Any profile of poverty must take into account the fact that those in poverty at a particular time are not all destined to be in poverty over the long term. Just as individuals move into and out of unemployment, there is some mobility over time into and out of poverty: indeed, flows into and out of unemployment are one of the main factors affecting such mobility. It is important, therefore, to distinguish between long-term and short-term poverty, a task undertaken in chapter 6. To make this distinction, information on the same set of individuals and households at two points in time, and on their experiences in the intervening period (an average of about eighteen months), is used. This allows the 'dynamics' of households' situations to be tracked, and reveals the extent to which those in poverty at the beginning of the period have been able to escape by the end. It is particularly valuable not only in measuring the extent of this type of mobility but also in identifying the factors that trigger such escapes and distinguish the 'escapers' from those who remain in poverty.

3 Income Poverty in Ireland

TIM CALLAN AND BRIAN NOLAN

Most methods of measuring poverty define an income level as a 'poverty line'; those with incomes below that line are considered to be 'poor' and those above the line are not. But the circumstances of households just below any given income level will often be similar to those of households just above that level. This suggests that it may be helpful to regard poverty as not simply an 'all or nothing' phenomenon. Measures that recognise this, by showing the extent of poverty at different cut-offs and taking into account the depth of poverty at any given cut-off, would therefore be desirable. Furthermore, as our review in the previous chapter indicated, there are various methods of defining a poverty cut-off, and the income levels they suggest as poverty lines can diverge considerably. Thus, even if it were agreed that poverty was an 'all or nothing' phenomenon, there could be widespread disagreement about the precise level and structure of the poverty-line income. Recognition of this uncertainty would argue for consideration of measures of poverty at different income cut-offs.

Measuring poverty in terms of income alone also has limitations, and in the next chapter we examine the potential for supplementing income information with data on indicators of deprivation. In this chapter, however, we concentrate on what can be learnt from the application of income poverty lines.

A simple approach, based on relative-income poverty lines, is particularly valuable in taking account of the scope for disagreement about the level and structure of the poverty line. The relative poverty line method, described in section 3.1, allows the use of different income cut-offs, so that the results for differing levels of income can be explored. Similarly, the method allows for differing adjustments for family size, so that the sensitivity of the results to differing equivalence scales can be examined. This simple approach can therefore provide basic information on the numbers of households and individuals below particular income levels (section 3.2). Because the information required to implement this approach is restricted to income, it is possible to obtain comparable results using different data sources. Thus comparisons over time (with results derived from the Central Statistics Office's household budget survey) and some comparisons across countries (with results from studies of EC countries and some others) are possible, and are presented and discussed in sections 3.3 and 3.4, respectively. The possible implications of non-cash incomes (such as education or health services provided free) for the measurement of income poverty are considered in section 3.5. The main findings are drawn together in the concluding section.

3.1 RELATIVE POVERTY LINES: METHODS

The first step in constructing a relative-income poverty line is to adjust the income of each household to reflect its size and composition. One way of doing this is simply to calculate average income per head for each household. But this does not take account of the fact that adults are thought to have greater needs than children; nor does it recognise the fact that 'two can live more cheaply than one' because of economies of scale in accommodation costs, cooking, and heating.

The precise degree to which households benefit from economies of scale and the relative needs of adults and children of different ages have been extensively studied in many countries, but no consensus has emerged. As noted in chapter 2, this makes it essential to examine the sensitivity of poverty measures to the equivalence scales used. In this chapter we present results based on three different scales, ranging from one that makes very generous allowance for the needs of children to one that is much less generous. Each of the scales takes a value of 1 for a single-person household, or for the first adult in larger households, with the following values for additional members:

Scale A: 0.7 for other adults, and 0.5 for children. This is the scale used in O'Higgins and Jenkins's (1990) estimates of relative poverty in EC countries.

Scale B: 0.6 for other adults, and 0.4 for children. This is close to the scale implicit in UK rates of income support (formerly supplementary benefit), widely used in studies of poverty there.

Scale C: 0.66 for other adults, and 0.33 for children. This is close to the scale implicit in rates of unemployment assistance in Ireland, when child benefit payments are also taken into account.

The well-being of each household is then represented by its 'adult equivalent income', i.e. total income divided by the number of 'adult equivalents' as defined by the equivalence scale.

A purely relative poverty line is simply a particular proportion of mean or median income. The most commonly chosen lines are half of mean or median income; but there is no strong reason why either of these thresholds should be regarded as 'the' poverty line. Our approach, in line with that of Atkinson (1987), Foster and Shorrocks (1988), and O'Higgins and Jenkins (1990), among others, has been to examine a number of relative income cut-offs. We look at the most commonly employed relative poverty line of 50 per cent of mean income, but also at lower and higher cut-offs at 40 and 60 per cent of mean income.

Current disposable income per adult equivalent is the measure of resources used throughout most of this chapter. This measure reflects net pay from employment or self-employment (after the deduction of income tax and PRSI contributions) as well as social welfare payments, private pensions, and income from investment and property. This is the measure of resources most commonly used in the analysis of poverty, but wider measures may also be relevant. In this chapter we also briefly consider the effects of using annual rather than current income as a measure of resources; the next chapter deals in depth with the relationship between income, wider resources, and directly measured deprivation of basic necessities.

3.2 RELATIVE POVERTY LINES: RESULTS FOR 1987

The overall incidence of income poverty is very sensitive to the precise location of the poverty line, as shown by table 3.1. No more than 10 per cent of households fell below 40 per cent of mean equivalent income in the 1987 survey, but about three to four times that number fell below the 60 per cent cut-off, the highest one examined here. Since there is no strong a priori reason to choose any one of these lines as 'the' indicator of poverty, it is useful to put the actual income levels corresponding to these cut-offs into perspective. For a single person the income cut-off for the 40 per cent line was between £32 and £34.50 per week in 1987, depending on the equivalence scale. This was close to the lowest rates of social welfare support payable at the time: £33 per week for supplementary welfare allowance or short-term unemployment assistance in rural areas. The 50 per cent line corresponds to an income of between £40 and £43 per week for a single person, roughly equal to the maximum flat-rate unemployment benefit. The income cut-off for the 60 per cent line, at about £50 per week, lies between the maximum rates for non-contributory and contributory old age pensions (just under £46 and just over £53, respectively).

About 20 per cent of households, therefore, had equivalent incomes between about £33 and £50 per week. For larger households, the gap in terms of actual incomes could be substantially greater; for example, the cut-offs corresponding to the 40 and 60 per cent lines would be about £100 and £150, respectively (under equivalence scale C).

TABLE 3.1   *Households below relative-income poverty lines, 1987*

	Equivalence scale		
Cut-off as a proportion of mean equivalent disposable income	A	B	C
40%	10.0	8.9	7.5
50%	18.9	18.5	17.5
60%	29.0	30.5	30.0

Table 3.1 also shows, however, that the numbers of households falling below relative-income poverty lines do not vary a great deal across the different equivalence scales. Results for a scale that gives still greater weight to adults (0.7) and less to children (0.3) are almost identical to those for scale C. To facilitate comparisons with the household budget survey, a child is defined here as aged under fourteen. Alternative definitions, including as children all those engaged in full-time education, or providing for age-related equivalence scales, were also employed in analysing the ESRI data-set. Again the overall levels of poverty were found to be similar.

While poverty is often measured on a household basis, it is the number of people in poor households that is of primary interest. Table 3.2 shows that a higher proportion of people than of households are found to have incomes below each of the cut-offs. This means that the poor households, on average, contain more members than non-poor households. For equivalence scales that attribute greater

TABLE 3.2 *Households and persons below relative-income poverty lines, 1987*

Cut-off as a proportion of mean equivalent disposable income (equivalence scale C)	Households	Persons
40%	7.5	8.2
50%	17.5	19.8
60%	30.0	31.4

needs to children, this phenomenon is even more marked; but the general point holds true across all the equivalence scales used here: poor households are larger than average. The main reason for this is the extent of poverty among the unemployed, many of whom have child dependants, as will become clear when we consider the composition of the poor in chapter 5.

In presenting the results of this research, we found that many people had in mind a higher poverty line income than the cut-offs used in this chapter but were surprised to find that so many households and individuals fell below a lower income cut-off. For example, a person might believe that anyone with an income below £50 per week (per adult equivalent) was poor but find it difficult to accept that close to a million people fell below this line. Explaining such perceptions of where the poverty line lies, and how many people fall below it, raises questions that bring us outside our present focus on the reality of low incomes and poverty. But part of the explanation may lie in a perception that all those with incomes below such levels are experiencing similar deprivation—a perception that the analysis in the next chapter will show to be false.

These relative poverty lines, based on current income, give us a snapshot of the low-income population. But we may be particularly concerned with households that find themselves below such income cut-offs over a prolonged period. In principle it would be possible for many households to experience low income for a short period but much fewer households to experience low income for a long duration. This dynamic aspect of poverty will be investigated in chapter 6. Some insights can be gained, however, by considering relative poverty line measures applied to estimates of annual rather than current income. Such estimates can be obtained from the ESRI data-set, because information was gathered on employment and unemployment experience, pay and social welfare benefits over the twelve months before the date of interview. Relative-income poverty lines applied to annual incomes show similar levels of poverty to those for current incomes. These results also suggest rather limited short-term movement in incomes across poverty lines. The high degree of long-term unemployment is one of the main factors behind this situation.

Thus far, poverty status has been determined purely at household level: all members of a given household are regarded as poor if household income falls below the threshold, and not poor if household income is above the threshold. This approach is the most usual in poverty analysis, but it assumes implicitly that income is fully shared within the household. Actual income sharing patterns are difficult to measure in large-scale surveys, but small-scale investigations suggest a need to examine the sensitivity of poverty measures to alternative income-sharing assumptions. Some evidence on the degree of sharing between husband and wife is considered in chapter 14, in the context of overall patterns of financial management. Here we consider the assumption that income is fully shared within narrow family units, comprising an adult or couple together with children who have not completed full-time education. For convenience, we refer to this unit as the 'tax unit'.

Analysis at tax unit level finds that at the 50 per cent and 60 per cent cut-offs, a higher proportion of people fall below the poverty threshold than under household-based analysis. Thus, households that are above the poverty line but contain tax units with incomes below the corresponding threshold are more common than households below poverty thresholds but containing tax units with incomes above the corresponding poverty line. There is no difference at the 40 per cent line, however, and the differences at the higher lines are not very substantial. Thus the overall picture of relative poverty presented by the household-based analysis seems quite robust with respect to changes in the income-sharing assumption between these two extremes.

We noted in chapter 2 that expenditure has been proposed as an alternative measure of resources for poverty analysis. The main advantages claimed for it is that it appears to be more reliably measured than income in many household budget surveys, and that it may provide a better proxy for long-term or 'permanent' income, because individuals seek to smooth their consumption patterns over time. As against this, expenditure figures in such surveys may be distorted by occasional purchases; and, more fundamentally, it is not clear that low expenditure is a better indicator of low command over resources than low income.

However, it is of interest to compare the results of relative poverty methods applied to household expenditure rather than income.

Eurostat (1990) estimates that 17.4 per cent of Irish households fell below 50 per cent of average equivalent expenditure in 1987. This is within 1.5 percentage points of the corresponding figure for income-based poverty, using either the ESRI data-set or the HBS data-set. The expenditure-based figures also show that poor households are larger than average in the late 1980s.

3.3 RELATIVE POVERTY LINES: TRENDS OVER TIME

The information required by relative poverty line methods is also available from the 1973 and 1980 household budget surveys. Thus we can obtain comparable results for relative-income poverty in those years, and seek to identify trends in poverty over that period. Basic head-counts of poverty for households and persons at the 50 per cent line are set out in table 3.3.

TABLE 3.3   *Trends in relative poverty at 50% line, 1973, 1980, 1987*

Equivalence scale	Year & data source		
	1973 HBS	1980 HBS	1987 ESRI
	Percentage of households		
A	18.2	17.2	18.9
B	17.9	17.6	18.5
C	17.7	16.8	17.5
	Percentage of persons		
A	17.8	19.2	22.9
B	15.9	17.4	21.2
C	14.8	16.2	19.8

The proportions of households below 50 per cent lines changed by less than one percentage point over the 1973–87 period, with the changes in the sub-periods 1973–80 and 1980–87 also being relatively small. But the proportion of persons living in households below this cut-off rose substantially between 1973 and 1987. The increase in the 1973–80 sub-period was followed by an even greater increase between

1980 and 1987. These trends held for all three equivalence scales. Similar trends can also be identified at the 60 per cent line, for each equivalence scale: the proportion of people falling below this line also rose by something in the region of five percentage points.

Trends at the 40 per cent line are also similar for the 1973–80 period but at some equivalence scales show a decline in the proportion of people below the line in the later sub-period. The general pattern shown by these head-count measures, therefore, is one of an increasing proportion of people being found in a relatively stable proportion of poor households. This reflects an increase in the size of poor households relative to the average size.

Some additional insights into trends in poverty in the 1980s can be gained from recent EC estimates applying expenditure-based relative poverty lines to the 1980 and 1987 household budget surveys and from Nolan's analysis (1991a) of the 1987 HBS. The EC figures for 1980 and 1987 show a one percentage point increase in the proportion of people falling below the 40 and 50 per cent lines, accompanied by a decline in the proportion of households falling below the line. Income-based estimates from the 1980 and 1987 household budget surveys suggest an increase of two percentage points in the proportion of people below the 50 per cent line. This compares with an increase of about twice that magnitude suggested by the ESRI data.

A major factor contributing to the difference between the income-based figures produced by the two data-sets is that the ESRI survey estimated farm income for the calendar year 1986, whereas farm income in the HBS refers to the calendar year 1987. Farm income was at a very low ebb in 1986 but recovered substantially in 1987. Despite such differences, an increase in the proportion of people in poverty at the 50 per cent cut-off is indicated by income-based estimates using either data source, as well as by the expenditure-based estimates.

While head-counts of poverty (in terms of households or persons) have the obvious attraction of simplicity, they have several deficiencies, as outlined already in chapter 2. There are good reasons, therefore, to consider more sophisticated measures that take into account the depth of poverty and the distribution of income among those below the poverty line in assessing trends in poverty. Foster, Greer and Thorbecke (1984) proposed a number of measures that are particularly useful in this context. They combine information on the proportion of individuals (or households) in poverty and on the gap between each poor person's income and his or her poverty line income. The information on the 'income gaps' is summarised by taking the average gap, as a proportion of the poverty line, for all poor individuals; this can then be multiplied by the proportion of persons in poverty to provide a 'per capita income gap' that combines information on the extent and depth of poverty.

If we wish also to place a higher weight on the welfare of the poorest individuals (i.e. those with the greatest income gaps) this can be done by squaring the income gaps (as a proportion of the poverty line) before taking the average across all poor individuals, and multiplying by the proportion of persons in poverty. This measure is called a 'distributionally sensitive' one.

TABLE 3.4 *Depth-sensitive and distribution-sensitive measures of poverty, 1973, 1980, 1987*

	Year & data source		
Cut-off as proportion of mean	1973	1980	1987
equivalent income	HBS	HBS	ESRI
	Depth-sensitive measure: per person income gap		
40%	0.018	0.027	0.030
50%	0.036	0.046	0.054
60%	0.062	0.074	0.087
	Distribution-sensitive measure		
40%	0.009	0.016	0.021
50%	0.015	0.023	0.029
60%	0.026	0.034	0.041

Results for these more sophisticated summary measures of poverty are shown in table 3.4, drawn from Callan, Nolan, et al. (1989). Since the general trend of these results is not affected by the equivalence scale, results are reported here for one equivalence scale only (scale C). These results show a consistent increase in poverty between 1973 and 1980 and between 1980 and 1987. Even at the 40 per cent line, where simpler head-count measures suggested a decline in poverty, measures that take the depth and distribution of poverty into account show an increase in poverty between 1980 and 1987.

A major difference between the two sub-periods must be borne in mind when interpreting these results. Real incomes per adult equivalent grew by an average of about 11 per cent between 1973 and 1980 but fell slightly between 1980 and 1987. This implies that the real value of the poverty lines in 1980 are correspondingly higher than the 1973 values, but the real value of the 1987 relative poverty lines are less than those of the 1980 lines. The measures of relative poverty reported here do not take this fact into account, but it may be regarded as highly significant additional information: not only do we find an increase in the extent of relative poverty between 1980 and 1987 but the living standards of those measured as poor were declining over this period.

This is not to argue for an 'absolute' or fixed standard for the measurement of trends in poverty. In a longer-term context of sustained growth, any fixed standard will go out of date as living standards and expectations rise. Relative-income poverty lines avoid this pitfall and can be clearly interpreted; but for a complete picture they must be combined with information on the evolution of real income levels and living standards.

3.4 INTERNATIONAL COMPARISONS

Somewhat similar issues arise in the context of international comparisons of rates of poverty. Should the focus be on poverty measured by some fixed standard that does not vary across countries, or on poverty measured by national standards, which will vary in real value across countries? The appropriate framework will depend on the questions being asked. If the interest is in guiding the allocation of development aid between Third World countries, for example, a fixed standard may be deemed appropriate. But in comparing rates of poverty for developed countries, a national standard of comparison is often regarded as more appropriate: what is of interest is the proportions of the population that are excluded by lack of resources from participating in the ordinary living patterns of their society.

There are considerable difficulties in obtaining fully comparable data across countries. A number of recent studies have, however, produced comparable estimates of relative poverty rates for EC countries. Table 3.5 reports results for income-based and expenditure-based lines drawn from these studies, using a consistent equivalence scale (scale A). Poverty lines were based on 50 per cent of average equivalent household income or expenditure in each country. The countries are listed in the table in increasing order of relative-income poverty. The lowest rates were found in Belgium, the Netherlands, and Germany, with the

UK, Italy and Denmark having somewhat higher rates in 1985. At the other extreme we find that Greece and Portugal had the highest rates of poverty, with Ireland and Spain also having high rates. Similar analysis on an expenditure basis shows that Portugal still has the highest rate of poverty, with Ireland, Greece and Spain still having high rates. Germany, Belgium and the Netherlands are still found to have low rates of poverty. But poverty rates on an expenditure basis for some of the intermediate countries (the UK, Italy, and Denmark) put them in rather different positions in the ranking.

TABLE 3.5 *Percentage of persons below half national average equivalent income and expenditure, EC countries, 1985*

Country	Income line	Expenditure line
Belgium	7.2	5.9
Netherlands	7.4	11.4
Germany	8.5	9.9
Italy	11.7	15.5
UK	12.0	18.2
Denmark	14.7	8.0
France	17.5	15.7
Spain	20.0	18.9
Ireland	**22.9**	**19.5**
Greece	24.0	18.4
Portugal	28.0	32.7

Note: Estimates are based on data for nearest available year.

Sources: Income: O'Higgins and Jenkins (1990), table 1, except for Ireland, for which Callan, Nolan, *et al.* (1989), table 5.4. Expenditure: Eurostat (1990), table B7.

The general pattern shown by both income-based and expenditure-based estimates suggests that Ireland has more relative poverty than member-states at higher levels of GNP per head. Portugal, on the other hand, which has a lower level of GNP per head than Ireland, has a higher rate of relative poverty. Despite some methodological differences, comparison with published results for non-EC countries (Buhman et al., 1988) suggests that Ireland also has a higher proportion of people below half median income than Sweden, Norway and Switzerland but lower than the United States.

In interpreting these results, as with the interpretation of trends in poverty, information on the average levels of income on which relative poverty measures are based is obviously significant. It must be recognised that being relatively poor in a richer country means something different from being relatively poor in a country with a lower average standard of living. Such considerations may be of particular relevance in the EC context, in guiding the allocation of Community efforts to reduce poverty. A poverty measure based on Community-wide income or expenditure rather than country-specific measures may be of interest in this context. This introduces additional complications, such as the appropriate exchange rate used to convert national incomes or expenditures into a common currency. Eurostat (1990) reports poverty rates based on half average expenditure in the EC, using purchasing power parity conversions. About 21 per cent of the Irish population is found to be below this standard. This poverty rate is lower than that for Portugal, Greece or Spain but higher than other countries. Very low rates are found in the Benelux countries and Denmark, with the German rate also being well below 10 per cent.

3.5 IMPACT OF NON-CASH BENEFITS

So far the analysis has concentrated on cash income as a measure of resources. But households also differ in the extent to which they receive non-cash benefits. The treatment of non-cash benefits in poverty studies raises many complex issues, reflecting the nature of the poverty lines used and the institutional structure of the society concerned.[1] In the United States, where state provision of in-kind benefits is highly targeted on low-income households, the treatment of such benefits has been the subject of much recent debate. In the UK, by contrast, the fact that health care and education have been provided free to all is seen as justifying their omission from measures of 'needs' and 'resources' in determining poverty status. The existence of such international differences must be borne in mind in interpreting the results of international comparative work on poverty, such as those reported in the previous section.

In the context of national applications of relative poverty lines, two key issues arise. Do non-cash benefits substantially improve the relative position of those on low cash incomes, so that calculations that exclude non-cash income are likely to overstate relative poverty in terms of wider resources? And does the distribution of non-cash income substantially alter the ranking of household welfare, so that the composition of the poverty population is altered?

There are substantial theoretical and empirical problems that make it difficult to obtain clear-cut answers to these questions; but the evidence we have been able to bring to bear on these issues suggests that the analysis of cash incomes is a good starting point. For example, it is clear that families with children receive substantial benefits in the form of free or subsidised education. But this has implicitly been taken into account in the equivalence scales that are used to adjust income to take differences in needs into account. If the benefits of free education were to be attributed to these households, the equivalence scales would also have to reflect the educational needs of children, leading to similar if not identical overall results in terms of poverty analysis.

State provision of free health care services raises complex issues regarding the valuation of eligibility for services. Despite intensive investigation of these issues in the US context, no consensus has emerged. In the Irish context, given that at the time of the 1987 survey a large element of hospital care was available free to most of the population, a key point to bear in mind is that those on low gross incomes were entitled to free GP services under the medical card scheme. Evidence on the distribution of these benefits is discussed in chapter 12.

Substantial non-cash incomes also arise from the implicit (or imputed) rental income of owner-occupiers and from the provision of local authority housing at rents below fully economic levels. Once again the general issue of valuing non-cash incomes in cash terms arises. An alternative approach, often applied in the UK, is to examine income net of housing costs (rent or the interest payments on a mortgage), as a better measure of 'net resources' available for other purposes. This has the disadvantage that it regards households that choose to spend a high proportion of their income on housing as worse off than identical households that allocate their spending in other ways; but it does help to put households with a non-cash income (from owner-occupation or an effective rent subsidy from the local authority) on a similar footing to households without such a non-cash income.

Aggregate results for this income concept are very close to those for disposable cash incomes reported here. Nevertheless, some change in composition of the poverty population might be expected at the margins. Both local authority housing and medical cards are means-tested on the basis of gross income: this could alter the ranking in terms of economic welfare of households dependent on PAYE income as against untaxed short-term social welfare payments. Owner-occupiers, particularly those without large outstanding mortgages, would also tend to be better placed: a strong life-cycle element could be expected here, with older persons more likely to own their homes outright.

Some of the impact of non-cash benefits will become clear from the analysis in the next chapter—for example the fact that the link between low income and housing deprivation has been substantially weakened by policy interventions. Direct information on indicators of deprivation will also show how some households fare better than others on the same cash income level, whether because of receipt of non-cash benefits or for other reasons.

3.6 CONCLUSIONS

Relative-income poverty lines can be used to explore the sensitivity of measures of poverty to the level of the poverty line, and its structure as between different types of household. We have seen that in Ireland, as in many other countries, the number of households and people measured as poor is very sensitive to the exact level of the cut-off. Fewer than 10 per cent of households fall below 40 per cent of average equivalent income, with about 18 per cent below half mean income and close to 30 per cent below 60 per cent of average income. But many features of poverty were found not to depend on the level of the poverty line, or on its structure. In 1987 poor households were consistently found to be larger than the average. From 1973 to 1980 and from 1980 to 1987 the proportion of people in poverty was found to have risen for most poverty line and equivalence scale combinations. When the depth and distribution of poverty was taken into account, relative-income poverty was found to have increased consistently between 1973 and 1980 and between 1980 and 1987. International comparisons with other developed countries, particularly those in the EC, suggest a tendency for relative poverty to be lower in countries with a higher level of GNP per head.

Relative income or expenditure measures do not, however, provide a full insight into the nature or extent of poverty. Households with the lowest measured incomes are not necessarily those suffering the greatest deprivations. Some of those with very low incomes may, for example, be farmers or other self-employed people experiencing a temporary drop in their income but with sufficient resources to maintain a high standard of living. Direct information on standard and style of living, combined with information on income, can help to indicate whether a household is suffering generalised deprivation as a result of lack of resources. It is to this approach that we turn in the next chapter.

4 Income, Deprivation, and Exclusion

TIM CALLAN, BRIAN NOLAN, AND
CHRISTOPHER T. WHELAN

Poverty status is commonly measured on the basis of income, as indeed are living standards more generally. In the previous chapter, income poverty lines were employed in analysing the situation of households in the 1987 Economic and Social Research Institute sample, and comparisons over time and across countries could be made on this basis. That analysis also looked at whether the choice of current or annual income has substantive implications for how many households are identified as falling below income poverty lines.

However, focusing simply on income has limitations, because income, current or annual, is not the sole determinant of command over resources and living standards. Some people have access to other resources, such as savings or family support, that enable them to smooth out the effects that income fluctuations would otherwise have on consumption and living standards. On the other hand, some people, far from having such resources, may have accumulated debts that mean that the impact of income fluctuations on living standards are immediate and unavoidable, if not actually magnified. For this reason it is valuable to complement income measures with direct indicators of the extent and nature of deprivation and exclusion being experienced by households.

This also allows us to address some central questions about how poverty is best conceptualised and measured, which were among those highlighted in the discussion of the meaning and measurement of poverty in chapter 2. The general reliance in developed countries on income poverty lines for measuring poverty has been strongly criticised by Ringen (1987, 1988), on the basis that income is not a reliable measure of poverty. Here we follow through his suggestion that both income and deprivation criteria be used in identifying those who are excluded from society because of lack of resources. This provides a framework for exploring the relationship between income, wider resources, and indicators of deprivation.

The results show that employing both income and deprivation criteria rather than income alone can make a substantial difference to both the extent and composition of measured poverty. This serves to highlight the need to be clear about what one is in fact attempting to measure, with the distinction between a standard of living conception of poverty and one based on minimum rights to resources being of central importance (see Atkinson, 1987).

Section 4.1 provides some background, describing how indicators of deprivation have been used elsewhere in measuring poverty and the conceptual and measurement issues involved. Section 4.2 describes the range of information on life-styles obtained in the 1987 ESRI survey. Section 4.3 outlines the derivation of the preferred indicators of deprivation for present purposes. Section 4.4 describes the way in which income and deprivation are then combined in measuring poverty. In Section 4.5 the results are used to illuminate the relationship between deprivation, current income, and broader resources. Finally, section 4.6 considers the implications of the analysis for the conceptualisation of poverty and the use of poverty measures and for our view of the extent and nature of poverty in Ireland.

4.1 DEPRIVATION INDICATORS AND THE MEASUREMENT OF POVERTY

As discussed at length in chapter 2, poverty in developed countries has most commonly been defined as exclusion from the ordinary life of the society because of lack of resources. Townsend's classic definition (given in full in chapter 2) quite clearly incorporates both elements. In measuring poverty, however, most studies rely on income to distinguish 'the poor' from the non-poor, using the variety of methods for constructing income poverty lines also reviewed in chapter 2. A minority of poverty studies, ranging from Abel-Smith and Townsend's mould-breaking *The Poor and the Poorest* (1965) to recent research carried out for Eurostat (1990), have used expenditure as a direct measure of living standards. Sen (1979) has emphasised that the 'direct method', focusing on consumption, and the 'income method' are not two alternative ways of measuring the same thing but represent two alternative conceptions of poverty: the former identifies those whose actual consumption fails to meet (what are accepted as) minimum needs, while the latter identifies those who do not have the ability to meet those needs within the behavioural constraints (e.g. on expenditure patterns) typical in that community. Despite this clear distinction, many of the studies using income appear in fact to be taking it as a measure of living standards rather than of consumption 'possibilities'.

Reliance on income as a measure of living standards assumes that it is a reliable indicator of the economic resources available to people and that economic resources largely determine living standards. However, current or annual household income is not always a reliable indicator of household economic resources at a particular point, because income fluctuates, because households at similar income levels may have quite different levels of savings and debts, because of differences in the availability of social support networks, and because resources in the form of non-cash income—benefits and services provided by employers or the state—differ across households. The fact that income may not adequately capture differences in living standards and may not always be a reliable measure of exclusion has led to attempts to develop other indicators that could be used along with, or instead of, income. Focusing directly on expenditure is usually justified on the basis that it more accurately reflects living standards and is better measured in surveys than income (Eurostat, 1990; see also McGregor and Borooah, 1992). There are serious questions about the suitability of the information obtained in such surveys on expenditure over a short period (usually two weeks) as a measure of living standards, but the more fundamental question is what one is interested in measuring: low expenditure, low income, or both.

Ringen (1987, 1988) has argued that if poverty is defined as exclusion because of lack of resources—understood as a state of generalised deprivation—it is characterised by both a low standard of consumption and a low level of income. The poor should therefore be identified using both a consumption-deprivation and an income criterion: exclusion is to be measured directly, together with an income criterion to exclude those who have a low standard of living for reasons other than low income. This approach has the potential to measure exclusion caused by lack of resources rather than low expenditure or low income. Identifying and counting those who are excluded because of lack of resources, and analysing the evolution over time of their income and the wider resources available to them, we see as a crucial step in explaining the processes producing exclusion. It may also allow conclusions to be drawn about the minimum resources necessary to avoid such exclusion, which will be crucial to assessing the adequacy of levels of social welfare support; but that must be treated as a distinct issue, as we discuss further in the concluding section.

Townsend (1979) pioneered the direct measurement of deprivation, selecting items from a set of indicators of style of living for British households to construct a summary deprivation index. Using an index of deprivation scores, he derived an income threshold representing the point below which deprivation scores, it was tentatively suggested, 'escalated disproportionately.' In actually counting the poor, Townsend employed the income threshold alone, without reference to the deprivation scores of the households concerned. The existence of such a threshold continues to be hotly debated.

More recently, Townsend and Gordon (1989) have made use of data from a survey carried out in London in 1985–86 that covered a wider range of activities and items to construct separate summary indices of material and social deprivation. Discriminant analysis is employed to identify the income level that best separates the 'deprived' and the 'non-deprived', which they argue can be considered to be the 'poverty line'.

Mack and Lansley (1985), by contrast, adopted a 'direct' approach, which uses deprivation indicators to identify the poor. They defined poverty as 'enforced lack of socially perceived necessities'—enforced in the sense of springing from lack of resources (p. 39). Life-style items were selected for inclusion in their deprivation index on the basis of views in their sample on which ones constituted a necessity (whereas Townsend's aim was to include items that reflected 'ordinary living patterns'). To control for diversity arising simply from tastes—a major element in Piachaud's (1981) critique of Townsend—'enforced lack' of an item was taken to be where the respondent lacked the item and said they would like it but could not afford it. In assessing the numbers in poverty, they focused on those who are experiencing enforced lack of three or more out of a set of twenty-two necessities. Recognising that there may be problems with taking at face value people's own evaluations of whether absence is enforced, they also looked inter alia at the difference made by excluding those on 'high' incomes, even if they report enforced lack of three or more items, and including those on low incomes lacking three or more items, even where they said they were doing without by choice.

Mack and Lansley do not attempt to take into account the possibility that the relationship between possessions or activities and income or wider resources may vary across different types of items or different household types. Simply adding together items relating to everyday activities with those related to the possession of consumer durables or the quality of housing may also be unsatisfactory as a measure of current living standards or resource constraints.

Hagenaars (1986) makes the point that there are systematic biases in the possession of, for example, consumer durables that are related to age, household size, and stage in the family cycle. Thus absence of a particular durable item—for example a washing machine—may mean something quite different for a young single person than it does for a couple with children. Such items may therefore be inappropriate as general indicators of deprivation. More generally, aggregation of deprivation indicators into a single index implicitly assumes that poverty is one-dimensional, but this may not be an accurate reflection of reality. For example, some households may be in poor-quality housing but not otherwise experiencing deprivation, while others in good-quality housing may be experiencing a variety of other forms of deprivation. Previous studies have also failed to elucidate how the observed deprivation-income pattern comes about, how the two are in fact related, which is necessary if we are to understand the impact of income dynamics on living standards and poverty.

Our central concern in this chapter, then, is with the relationship between living patterns, income, and wider resources, and the implications for poverty measurement. Our primary objective is to take the definition of poverty as exclusion caused by lack of resources as starting point, and follow through the logic of incorporating both in a poverty measure to see what this tells us about the extent and nature of poverty in Ireland, and about the relationships involved. Having described the information available on life-styles in the 1987 survey, we proceed through the following steps:

(1) The set of items or activities on which information has been gathered is analysed, to see which can not only be taken as socially defined necessities but can also best serve as indicators of generalised deprivation or exclusion from ordinary living patterns.

(2) Using indicators of deprivation and current income, households that are both below income thresholds and apparently experiencing enforced deprivation are identified.

(3) Information on annual incomes and on savings and other assets is used to help explain the relationship between deprivation scores and current income.

4.2 THE DATA ON LIFE-STYLES AND DEPRIVATION

In the 1987 ESRI survey, in addition to the data on income and individual and household characteristics described in previous chapters, information on a range of indicators of style of living was also sought. Respondents were given a list of twenty items or activities and asked which ones they believed were 'necessities, that is things which every household (or person) should be able to have and that nobody should have to do without.' They were then asked which items they did not themselves have or avail of, and which of these they would like to have but had to do without because of lack of money. (The items selected for inclusion in the survey were for the most part taken from previous studies, such as Townsend (1979) and Mack and Lansley (1985).)

Table 4.1 lists the items and shows the overall sample responses. The more widely possessed items also tended to be more generally regarded as necessities—with, for example, a fridge, heating for the living-rooms, indoor toilet and bath or shower possessed by most and felt by nearly all respondents to be necessities. There were some notable exceptions, with most people stating that being able to save was a necessity but less than half saying they could do so, while 80 per cent of households had a television but only 37 per cent thought it was a necessity. This means that selecting items as deprivation indicators on the basis of views in the population about which are necessities (which was Mack and Lansley's approach) will not give exactly the same results as using actual possession by a majority (which was Townsend's procedure).

In addition to the twenty items in table 4.1, a further four included in the survey (but without the supplementary question whether households were doing without because they could not afford it) are used:

(1) whether there was a day during the previous two weeks when the respondent did not have a substantial meal at all—from getting up to going to bed;

(2) whether they had to go without heating during the last year through lack of money, i.e. having to go without a fire on a cold day, or go to bed early to keep warm, or light the fire late because of lack of fuel;

(3) whether the respondent has not had an afternoon or evening out in the last fortnight, 'something that costs money,' and said that this was because they had not enough money;

(4) whether the household has experienced serious debt problems, i.e

(*a*) it is currently in arrears of rent, mortgage, electricity, or gas;

(*b*) it has had to go into debt in the last twelve months to meet ordinary living expenses (such as rent, food, Christmas, or back-to-school expenses);

(*c*) it has had to sell or pawn anything worth £50 or more to meet ordinary living expenses; or

(*d*) it has received assistance from a private charity in the past year.

TABLE 4.1 *Indicators of actual style of living and socially defined necessities*

Indicator/life-style item	Percentage lacking	Percentage experiencing enforced lack	Percentage stating item is necessity
Refrigerator	5	3	92
Washing machine	20	10	82
Telephone	48	31	45
Car	38	22	59
Colour television	20	11	37
A week's annual holiday away from home	68	49	50
A dry, damp-free dwelling	10	9	99
Heating for the living-rooms when it is cold	3	2	99
Central heating in the house	45	30	49
An indoor toilet in the dwelling	7	6	98
Bath or shower	9	7	98
A meal with meat, chicken or fish every second day	13	9	84
A warm, waterproof overcoat	13	8	93
Two pairs of strong shoes	16	11	88
To be able to save	57	55	88
A daily newspaper	45	16	39
A roast meat joint once a week	24	13	64
A hobby or leisure activity	33	12	73
New, not second-hand, clothes	10	8	77
Presents for friends or family once a year	24	13	60

4.3. MEASURING DEPRIVATION

The first step in the analysis is to identify, if possible, a set of items or activities widely regarded as necessities that can be satisfactorily employed as indicators of deprivation. Callan, Nolan et al. (1989) showed that if one simply constructs an index from the twenty items in table 4.1, with a household scoring 1 for each item it does not have, mean scores vary little across the bottom three deciles of the income distribution (i.e. the bottom 10 per cent, next 10 per cent, etc.), then fall steadily as one moves up the distribution. However, there is a good deal of variability in scores within each decile, with some low-income households having most of the items and some high-income ones lacking a considerable number. (This is consistent with the pattern shown by Townsend's and Mack and Lansley's British data, as well as Mayer and Jencks's (1988) for the United States.)

Concentrating on (subjectively assessed) enforced lack, where the respondent said that he or she would like but could not afford the item, the relationship with income was stronger, but considerable variability remained. Current disposable income is clearly not the sole predictor of life-style or deprivation—as indeed one would expect, with, for example, stage in the life cycle and experiences and resources over a longer period also playing a central role.

Previous research employing deprivation indicators has generally relied on summary indices of this type, using a sub-set of items chosen on the basis of the extent to which they are possessed or regarded as necessities by most of the sample. The relationship between the different indicators has been given little attention—in effect, a single underlying dimension of deprivation has been assumed. It is clear, however, that enforced absence of particular items is of interest in this context in that this reflects what Coates and Silburn (1970) termed an interrelated network of deprivation, or, as Mack and Lansley put it, when they affect a person's way of life: the relationship between the items is therefore of central importance. The first stage in the analysis, before attempting to select items that would be appropriate as indicators of generalised deprivation, is to systematically examine the dimensions of deprivation, to see whether the items cluster into distinct groups. In order to do so, factor analysis was applied to the 24 items (concentrating on self-assessed enforced lack for the 20 items for which that was available).

The way in which factor analysis was applied and the results are described by Whelan et al. (1991) and Callan, Nolan, and Whelan (1993). It suffices to say here that they suggest it is useful to distinguish three clusters or groupings of items:

(1) a 'basic' life-style dimension, consisting of eight items such as food and clothes;
(2) a 'housing and durables' dimension, consisting of seven items related to housing quality and facilities;
(3) 'other' aspects of life-style, consisting of nine items such as social participation and leisure activities, having a car or a telephone.

The items fall into these three groups in the manner shown in table 4.2. (The results of the factor analysis were taken as a general guide in grouping items, but judgment was applied where the loadings on the two factors were similar.) The distinction between the basic and housing dimensions is extremely clear-cut and is the most important implication of the results of the factor analysis. The distinction between basic and 'other' dimensions is less clear-cut but still pronounced for many of the items.

The sample evidence thus suggests that it is useful to distinguish these three dimensions, rather than simply aggregating items across the factors into a summary index; rather different households or types of household are lacking each type, and the underlying processes may also be rather different.

Taking this into account, to select items that would be appropriate as indicators of generalised deprivation we return to the information in table 4.1 about the extent to which the various items are considered to be necessities by respondents and the extent of possession or lack in the sample. Following Mack and Lansley, we place most weight on social perception of needs. The five basic items for which this information is available are regarded as necessities by two-thirds or more of the sample. Of the remaining three basic items, it appears likely to us that 'not having a substantial meal all day' and 'having to go without heating through lack of money', and probably also going into arrears or debt 'to meet ordinary living expenses' such as food and rent, would be regarded by most people as something that everyone should be able to avoid. With the possible exception of arrears or debt to meet ordinary living expenses, then, the basic items can be taken to be socially perceived necessities. The levels of absence and enforced absence of these items are also low, with only 10 to 15 per cent or less of the sample lacking each item except the weekly roast, which 24 per cent lacked.

The items in the housing and durables dimension are overwhelmingly regarded as necessities, by 82 per cent or more, with the exception of a television set, which is something of a special case, as already discussed. They are also possessed by 80 per cent or more of the

Poverty and Policy in Ireland

TABLE 4.2 *Dimensions for life-style deprivation items*

Basic dimension	Housing & durables dimension	Other dimension
Go without heat	Bath or shower	Annual holiday away from home, not with relatives
Go without substantial meal	Indoor toilet	
	Washing machine	To be able to save some of one's income regularly
Arrears or debt		
	Refrigerator	
New, not second-hand, clothes	Colour television	Daily newspaper
Meal with meat, chicken or fish	A dry, damp-free dwelling	Telephone
		A hobby or leisure activity
A warm waterproof overcoat	Heating for the living-room when it is cold	
		Central heating
Two pairs of strong shoes		Presents for friends & family once a year
A roast or its equivalent once a week		Car
		Able to afford an afternoon or evening out in the previous two weeks

sample. The items included in the 'other' dimension, on the other hand, are regarded as necessities by much lower percentages, with the exception of being able to save regularly and a hobby or leisure activity. They are also generally possessed by a much lower percentage. Even the ability to save, so heavily regarded as a necessity, is actually possessed by only a minority of households.

For some purposes it will be valuable to look at each dimension, but here, given our objective, we concentrate on what we have termed the basic dimension. These items represent socially perceived necessities, they reflect rather basic aspects of current material deprivation, and they cluster together, which lends support to the notion that they are useful as indicators of the underlying generalised deprivation we are trying to measure. It is important to be clear about why we focus on this dimension: it is not because we wish to prescribe in a normative fashion a hierarchy in which people should satisfy their needs, or to focus exclusively on a particular set of items. Rather, the respondents' evaluations, the results of the factor analysis and the relationship between the different items and household resources lead us to believe that these are the best indicators available to us of generalised underlying deprivation.[1]

We now construct a 'basic deprivation index' based on these eight items. For the five items for which the information was available, households score 1 on the index for each item the household lacks and says they could not afford. This may be regarded as unduly stringent. As Mack and Lansley suggest, some households may have very low expectations and/or be unwilling to acknowledge or state that they could not afford such basic necessities. However, a comparison of those lacking a basic item who say that this is enforced by lack of resources with those who say they did not want the item reveals that the latter do have significantly higher incomes on average and also display levels of deprivation on the other basic items that are little different from those who possess the item, well below those stating they cannot afford the item. This suggests that, for the most part, those who say they are doing without basic items voluntarily are indeed choosing to go without. For the other three items the subjective assessments are not available, but the nature of these items suggests that lack is likely to be enforced by resource constraints in most cases, so lacking the item adds to the basic deprivation index.

The distribution of scores on this index for the sample is that 68 per cent of households score 0, 15 per cent score 1, and 17 per cent are experiencing enforced lack of two or more basic items. We now focus on the way in which these basic deprivation scores relate to current resources, and how deprivation and income may be combined to measure poverty and exclusion caused by lack of resources.

4.4 BASIC DEPRIVATION, CURRENT INCOME, AND POVERTY

Establishing who is experiencing basic deprivation, in terms of the eight-item index, should be seen as only a first stage in identifying households that could be regarded as excluded because of lack of resources. The households concerned clearly themselves regard the lack of items as enforced by lack of resources, but, as table 4.3 shows, some of those households are on relatively high incomes. We explore shortly how this comes about; but the central point to be made here is that enforcement because of lack of resources needs to relate to societal rather than simply individual standards and expectations, and needs to be taken into account directly if the poverty measure is to be fully consistent with the definition. This provides the rationale for focusing on those households that are both experiencing basic deprivation and at relatively low income levels.

TABLE 4.3 *Basic deprivation scores by equivalent income decile*

Current equivalent disposable income decile	Households with a basic deprivation index score of:	
	1 or more	2 or more
	%	%
1	17.2	21.2
2	17.9	23.4
3	16.3	18.2
4	12.5	9.4
5	8.3	7.3
6	8.9	8.4
7	6.6	5.3
8	5.6	3.2
9	3.6	2.5
10	3.1	1.2
All	100.0	100.0

In measuring low income, we use the set of relative income poverty lines derived from average equivalent disposable income in the sample as described earlier; lines going from 40 to 70 per cent of that mean are now employed. Table 4.4 shows the percentage of households in the sample falling below each of these income thresholds and reporting enforced deprivation of at least one basic item, and the percentage reporting two or more. We see that about 60 per cent of the households below each income threshold are experiencing enforced lack of at least one basic item.

Should a score of one basic item lacked suffice to indicate exclusion for current purposes? Here it is essential to emphasise that the presence or absence of a particular item in itself is not crucial. The set of items measured is intended to serve as an indicator of generalised deprivation,

TABLE 4.4   *Percentage of households below relative-income thresholds and experiencing basic deprivation*

Below relative income line	Experiencing enforced deprivation of:	
	One or more basic items	Two or more basic items
	%	%
40%	3.3	2.0
50%	9.8	6.6
60%	16.0	10.7
70%	20.9	12.7

which is the latent or underlying variable one is trying to measure. Given the way in which the basic index has been constructed—the nature of the items themselves, the fact that the factor analysis showed that they cluster together, and that only subjectively assessed enforced lack is counted—and that an income criterion is also to be applied, we would argue that even a score of 1 on that index is likely to indicate generalised deprivation.

To identify those excluded because of lack of resources, an income threshold has also to be employed. The choice of a particular figure will of its nature be rather arbitrary, and we see greater merit in looking at a range of thresholds and assessing the sensitivity of the results; exactly analogous arguments to those presented in chapters 2 and 3 in the context of using income poverty lines alone apply. However, it is possible to specify upper and lower limits to the range people might want to consider. In broad terms, such a range might be bounded by the 50 and 70 per cent relative lines. Below the 50 per cent line the income levels involved are lower than most social welfare support rates, and most of the people reporting basic deprivation are above that line. The 60 per cent line is at about the level of many of the social welfare rates at the time but below the levels recommended as 'minimally adequate' by the Commission on Social Welfare (1986). The 70 per cent line has now been introduced because it represents the upper end of the range specified by the commission as minimally adequate, and most of the households above that line, even those not very far above, are not experiencing basic deprivation.

A question included in the survey on the extent to which respondents feel they are having difficulty 'making ends meet' provides some validation of the distinction being drawn between those below the line and experiencing or not experiencing basic deprivation. Whereas 71 per cent of those below the 60 per cent income line and experiencing such deprivation said they were having extreme difficulty making ends meet, only 37 per cent of those below that income line and not experiencing basic deprivation gave that response. Those below the income line and not experiencing basic deprivation also show much lower levels of (what they regard as) enforced lack of housing and other items than do the group experiencing basic deprivation.

While the characteristics of poor households will be discussed in detail in the next chapter, it is worth mentioning here that farmers, other self-employed and the retired form a considerably smaller proportion of those below the income lines and experiencing basic deprivation than of all those below the lines, while the ill or disabled and, especially, households headed by someone in home duties form a higher proportion. This again indicates that the deprivation criterion is allowing us to distinguish between groups in rather different situations.

A number of important issues remain to be addressed. Why are some low-income households apparently not experiencing basic deprivation when a substantial proportion clearly are; and why are some higher-income households reporting such deprivation? In the next section we explore these issues, drawing on information relating to resources other than current income.

4.4 INCOME, DEPRIVATION, AND WIDER RESOURCES

The starting point in trying to understand why some of those with low current reported incomes manage to avoid basic deprivation while others experience it is the nature of the current income measures and the relationship between current and annual incomes. As discussed in chapter 3, the current income measure relates to the amount received last week (or fortnight or month) for employee income and social welfare transfers, while for income from self-employment, including farming, the weekly average amount received over a twelve-month period is used instead.

For employees and social welfare recipients, current income as measured in this way may sometimes differ from average income received by the household over the year. Social welfare recipients, particularly those away from work through unemployment or illness, may have spent much of the previous year in work, while the currently employed may have spent some time away from work. For households headed by an unemployed person below the 60 per cent income line and experiencing basic deprivation, the head has on average been away from work for longer, and spent less of the last year in work, than the heads of corresponding households not experiencing deprivation. Similarly for households headed by an employee and below that income line, those experiencing deprivation are more likely to have spent some of the past year out of work than those not experiencing deprivation. Annual income was therefore significantly higher for some of those currently on low incomes and not experiencing basic deprivation.

While annual income is relevant, the resources available to households will be influenced by their experiences over a much longer period. When income falls, some households may be able to draw on savings or to increase debt to avoid basic deprivation, at least for a time. The additional information obtained in the survey on savings and other assets—described in detail by Nolan (1991b)—is particularly helpful in exploring the importance of savings and other assets.

Table 4.5 shows the average level of reported household savings in the form of deposits in banks, building societies etc. for households below the 60 per cent income threshold and experiencing or not experiencing basic deprivation, categorised by head's current labour force status. For each labour force status the households not experiencing such deprivation have much greater savings to draw on. For example, the mean level of savings for households headed by an employee and not experiencing basic deprivation is about £1,350, compared with only £200 for households at similar levels of current (equivalent) income but experiencing such deprivation. As another indicator of resources available to the household over a longer period, the table also shows the average value of property in the form of housing (i.e. reported market value of the house less outstanding mortgage). Again, those not experiencing basic deprivation consistently have substantially higher levels of house property. Thus significant differences in longer-term income between the two groups are suggested.

It is also clear that neither those below the line and experiencing basic deprivation nor those below it and not experiencing such deprivation form a homogeneous group in terms of resources. Within each group, substantially higher levels of resources are available to the households headed by a farmer, other self-employed or retired than where the head is an employee, in home duties, sick or ill, or unemployed, with the unemployed having particularly low levels. This is reflected in the extent of enforced deprivation of life-style items other than the basic set, which is a good deal higher for the unemployed than for others. A higher percentage of the unemployed also report difficulty making ends meet.

TABLE 4.5   *Savings and assets of households below 60% income line experiencing or not experiencing basic deprivation by labour force status of head of household*

Labour force status	Mean level of savings		Net house value	
	Basic deprivation	No basic deprivation	Basic deprivation	No basic deprivation
	£	£	£	£
Employee	204	1,342	9,398	14,655
Farmer	790	2,208	19,677	27,060
Self-employed	397	2,681	22,537	29,284
Unemployed	45	442	5,335	16,460
Sick or disabled	360	1,741	12,481	19,222
Retired	832	3,052	11,034	22,364
Home duties	27	1,200	14,719	18,147
All	260	1,720	10,974	20,990

Households experiencing basic deprivation but not on low incomes
We now turn to the group of households not on low current incomes but apparently experiencing what they regard as enforced basic deprivation. About one-third of those experiencing basic deprivation are above even the 70 per cent income threshold. Most of these households are not just above the cut-offs, they are in fact distributed over the (equivalent) income distribution. This group is dominated by employees, the retired, and those in home duties, with only a small proportion headed by someone away from work through unemployment or illness. In terms of demographic characteristics—age of head, number of children—the group does not appear particularly distinctive. Similarly, the nature of the basic deprivation being experienced is not very different from the pattern for the households below the income lines.

Why then are these households, with current incomes close to or above average, nonetheless experiencing basic deprivation? Part of the explanation may again be with the fact that current income is not always a satisfactory indicator of longer-term command over resources.

Some, but only a minority, are headed by an employee who spent much of the previous year away from work, so annual income is well below that currently being received. Relatively high expenditure on housing, leaving less for other goods and services, also appears to be a factor for some of these households. Particularly among households headed by an employee, those reporting basic deprivation have much lower levels of savings and own much less valuable houses on average than households at similar income levels not experiencing basic deprivation.

This group clearly requires further investigation, though it does appear that resources over a prolonged period have a role in explaining their current living patterns. This is also indicated by the fact that over two-thirds of these households come from the manual social classes. It is not to be expected that resources would fully explain differences in living patterns, however. In the final analysis it may be necessary to accept that some households are doing without what most regard as necessities, and that they themselves consider this to be due to lack of resources, but by societal norms have relatively comfortable incomes. To what extent is this a 'puzzle' or a problem for the researcher? As Mack and Lansley (1985) put it, any study on poverty and deprivation depends on generalisations about people's needs and circumstances that will not fit every single individual. Poverty is not simply deprivation, and diversity in living patterns highlights the importance of employing an income as well as deprivation criterion in measuring what will be generally viewed as exclusion because of lack of resources.

Non-essentials and housing deprivation

Finally we may briefly consider two other issues. First, some of those at relatively low income levels and experiencing enforced basic deprivation still possess items that are not overwhelmingly regarded as necessities. Does this invalidate the contention that their deprivation is enforced? We focus on two items that tend to receive particular attention: a car and a telephone.

About 21 per cent of the households below the 60 per cent relative income threshold and experiencing basic deprivation own a car, 36 per cent have a telephone, and 12 per cent have both. Those owning a car are predominantly rural, middle-aged, and/or have children. Those having a telephone, by contrast, are more likely to be elderly and/or widowed. It would not be difficult to argue that, for many of the households involved, a car or a telephone could reasonably be regarded as a necessity—and many of these households say they regard them as such. Excluding all households that possess a car would make poverty in

Ireland largely an urban matter, and would certainly mean that almost no rural households with married middle-aged heads could be classified as poor. Similarly, excluding those with telephones would mean that a considerably smaller number of elderly people would be so classified.

Turning to the housing and housing-related items, we have seen that these are overwhelmingly regarded as necessities (the exception being the television), and only a relatively small percentage of households lack each, with an even smaller percentage regarding this as enforced. What is the relationship between housing-related deprivation, basic deprivation, and resources, and where does it fit in to the measurement of poverty? The factor analysis itself shows that housing and basic deprivation are quite frequently experienced by different households. Only 30 per cent of the households reporting enforced lack of one or more of the housing items are both below the 60 per cent income threshold and experiencing basic deprivation.

Looking at the characteristics of the remaining 70 per cent of the households experiencing enforced lack of housing items, what is striking is their distinctive demographic and geographical profile. Almost 60 per cent live in a rural area, 50 per cent are headed by a single person or a widow or widower, and 80 per cent fall into one or other of these categories. About one-third are elderly, single, or widowed. Quality of housing and housing-related durables for many of these households is probably determined by the combination of relatively low resources over a prolonged period and their marital status and location. These households report significantly lower current levels of financial strain than households below the income threshold and experiencing basic deprivation, and they also have substantially higher levels of savings.

As emphasised by Donnison (1988), housing is the sector in which welfare states have found it easiest to break the links between economic status and living standards. This may mean that in many countries, taken alone or even together with low current income, measures of housing conditions are not particularly reliable indicators of generalised exclusion arising from lack of resources. Both the processes producing poor housing conditions and the consequences of such deprivation may be distinctive. Once again this is an area for further investigation. The general point that it serves to illustrate, however, is that appropriate measures of deprivation will change over time and vary across countries if the objective is to reflect generalised deprivation and exclusion. Studying how the nature of deprivation is changing is therefore as important as studying trends in poverty if we are to see where progress is actually being made.

4.5 CONCLUSIONS

To be fully consistent with the widely accepted definition of poverty put forward by Townsend, which refers to exclusion from ordinary living standards because of lack of resources, in measuring poverty one should focus on both living standards and resource constraints. In this chapter we have looked at the implications of taking both current income and measured deprivation into account in measuring poverty. Concentrating on a limited set of items referring to basic deprivation, households experiencing such deprivation and below relative income thresholds were examined. Between 10 and 20 per cent of households were at relatively low income levels and experiencing basic deprivation, depending on the income threshold chosen, with about 16 per cent below 60 per cent of mean equivalent income and experiencing such deprivation. Households distinguished as 'poor' in this way differ to a significant extent from those simply below current income thresholds. Households headed by a farmer, other self-employed or retired person are less significant, and those headed by an ill or disabled person or someone in home duties more significant, while those with an unemployed head continue to be the most substantial group. The role of labour force experience and resources over a prolonged period, rather than simply current income, in determining current living standards was revealed by analysis of data on annual income, savings, and other assets.

Many questions are raised rather than resolved by the analysis. The 'inconsistent' groups, especially the high-income households reporting deprivation, require more consideration. Similarly the relationship between housing and resources, and its implications both for assessing the position of households experiencing housing deprivation and for policy, need to be examined further. Moving from a point in time to the analysis of changes over time would raise a further host of questions about the way in which the deprivation and income criteria could or should reflect changes in the general standard of living. All these issues arise within the framework of applying combined deprivation and resources criteria to measuring poverty.

More fundamentally, however, following through this measurement approach serves to highlight features of the definition itself. Households are only to be categorised as 'poor' if they are both at low income—however defined—and experiencing deprivation and exclusion—again, however defined. We have seen that a considerable number of households with current low incomes are not experiencing basic deprivation. Leaving aside the precise way in which deprivation is defined and measured, as well as the problems of measuring income accurately, it is clear that some households have current incomes that would not be adequate to avoid exclusion and deprivation, but manage to do so by running down accumulated resources and by borrowing and/or relying on help. Others may be able to avoid deprivation only by being particularly good managers of their limited resources.

This makes clear first of all that measuring exclusion caused by lack of resources will be informative about what constitutes an 'adequate' income, but poverty defined in this way is by no means identical to income inadequacy. It may also lead us to return to Atkinson's (1987) distinction between poverty as deprivation in terms of standard of living and poverty as concerned with minimum rights to resources. In terms of the latter, falling below the minimum adequate income level may be seen as a violation of rights even if it does not always or immediately result in deprivation.

This has obvious policy as well as conceptual and methodological implications. To give a concrete example, an analysis of panel data on American households by Ruggles and Williams (1989) showed that about one-third of those entering poverty—falling below the official poverty line—had sufficient savings to allow them to maintain their standard of living above that line through their full poverty spell, by running down savings to supplement income support. Whether or not we wish to call such households 'poor', clearly social welfare policy will be concerned to provide income support to those with inadequate incomes even if they could not (yet) be categorised as 'excluded from ordinary living patterns.'

5 Who Are the Poor?

TIM CALLAN, BRIAN NOLAN, AND
CHRISTOPHER T. WHELAN

In this chapter we focus on the characteristics of poor households. Seeing which types of household are poor is an essential step towards understanding the causes of poverty and designing policies to combat it. Using the 1987 Economic and Social Research Institute survey data and the approaches to measuring poverty discussed in previous chapters, we can analyse in detail the characteristics of the households involved and what distinguishes them from the remainder of the sample. It is particularly useful to examine how the profile of poverty has been changing over time and how the situation of different groups has been evolving, and this is explored for the 1970s and 1980s. It is also helpful to try to identify those features and trends that are common to other developed countries and those that appear to be distinctive to or more pronounced in Ireland, which we pursue using available information for other countries.

A central distinction in the analysis of the characteristics of poor households is between the concepts of risk and incidence. For any categorisation one cares to apply, the *risk* facing a particular type of household is given by the proportion of households of that type found to be in poverty. The *incidence* of poverty, on the other hand, is the proportion of all those in poverty who belong to that group. For example, suppose 50 per cent of households with an unemployed head are in poverty, and these make up 30 per cent of all poor households, then the risk of poverty for households with an unemployed head is 50 per cent, while in terms of the incidence of poverty, 30 per cent is the relevant figure. Obviously both are of interest: we will want to know which types of household face particularly high risks of being in poverty and which account for most of the poor, and the two groups need not be identical. This can arise most obviously when a relatively small group in the population faces a very high risk of being poor—the homeless or travellers, for example—but still will not constitute a large proportion of all poor households.

The characteristics on which the analysis of risk and incidence of poverty in this chapter concentrates are the size and composition of the household, the nature of the participation in the labour force by household members, particularly the household head, and social class or socio-economic background. This analysis is based firstly on the relative income poverty lines described in chapter 3. Using this type of income line, it is possible to derive comparable results from the CSO's household budget surveys of 1973 and 1980, allowing changes in the composition of those below the income lines and in the risks of income poverty for different groups to be identified. Some information for other countries is also available using this general approach, so some international comparisons are also possible on this basis.

In section 5.1 relative income lines are used to look at the situation in 1987, and trends between 1973 and 1987, for households of different size and composition. Section 5.2 uses the same approach to analyse the position of households categorised by the nature of their members' labour force participation, while section 5.3 looks at the relationship between low income and social class. In section 5.4 we go on to combine income and deprivation indicators in the manner described in chapter 4, so that the characteristics of those on low incomes and experiencing basic deprivation in 1987 can also be examined. (Since the necessary information on aspects of deprivation is not included in the household budget survey, changes over time on this basis cannot be assessed, nor are comparable figures available for other countries.) Finally, section 5.5 highlights the way in which the key findings point towards the causal processes at work, many of which are examined in the contributions in part III.

5.1 INCOME POVERTY AND HOUSEHOLD COMPOSITION

One of the most interesting characteristics to focus on is the composition of the household in terms of number of members and their ages and sex. We first of all use a simple categorisation employed by the Central Statistics Office, based on number of adults and children. Table 5.1 shows the entire 1987 ESRI sample and those below the 50 per cent relative income line classified by household composition type, as well as the risk of being below that line for each type. The equivalence scale used here, where the household head is attributed a value of 1, allows 0.66 for the 'needs' of each extra adult and 0.33 for each child.

What is most striking is the fact that households with children face a much higher risk of being below the 50 per cent line than those without children. While households consisting of a couple and one or two children face about the average risk for all households, those comprising two adults and three or four children, or more than two adults with children, have a particularly high probability of being below the 50 per cent line. (To allow comparison with the household budget surveys, a child is taken to be aged under fourteen, so some of the 'adults' in these larger households are in fact still at school and living with their parents.) When households consisting of one adult with children (included in 'others with children' in table 5.1, following the CSO's categorisation) are separately distinguished, they are seen to have a very high risk: 29 per cent are below half average income, and over two-thirds are below the 60 per cent line, by far the highest risk group at that higher line.

TABLE 5.1 *Risk and incidence of poverty (50% income line) by household composition*

Household type	Risk (percentage falling below 50% line)	Incidence (percentage of all households below 50% line)	Percentage of all households in sample
1 adult	13.2	12.5	16.6
2 adults	13.9	14.7	18.5
Other adults only	12.3	14.1	20.2
2 adults + 1 child	16.7	5.9	6.2
2 adults + 2 children	19.4	10.6	9.6
2 adults + 3 children	21.7	8.7	7.0
2 adults + 4 or more children	35.1	11.1	5.5
3 adults with children	25.5	8.8	6.0
4 adults with children	20.1	5.4	4.7
Others with children	24.9	8.1	5.7

While households with children account for 45 per cent of the sample, then, they make up 59 per cent of those below half average (equivalent) income. While this is not quite as pronounced with either the 40 per cent or the 60 per cent relative income cut-off, irrespective of the line chosen, households with children face a substantially higher risk of being below the line than those without children. It is particularly important to assess the sensitivity of this finding to the equivalence scale applied, since it could be that an alternative and perhaps equally valid scale would produce quite a different result. A range of possible scales was tested, including allowing progressively less for each additional child as family size increases or allowing the scale to vary with the age of the child (see Nolan and Farrell, 1990). This showed that larger families consistently faced a relatively high risk.

Comparing the pattern found for 1987 with that revealed by the 1973 and 1980 household budget surveys, the composition of the households below relative income lines has in fact altered dramatically over the period. Table 5.2 shows that in 1973, households with children faced about half the risk of those without children of being below the 50 per cent income line. By 1980 the gap was very much narrower, while by 1987 it had reversed, so that those with children faced almost twice the risk of those without children. Again a similar pattern is seen with the 40 per cent or 60 per cent relative lines. This reversal reflects both an improvement in the situation of households without children— a decline in their risk—and a deterioration in the situation of those with children. We have seen that 59 per cent of households below half average equivalent income in 1987 contained children: the corresponding figure in 1973 was only 32 per cent. As a consequence, the proportion of all children living in households below half average income rose from 16 per cent in 1973 to 26 per cent in 1987.

TABLE 5.2   *Risk of poverty (50% income line) by household composition type, 1973, 1980, 1987*

Household type	1973 Below line	1980 Below line	1987 Below line
	%	%	%
With children	12.5	15.0	22.9
Without children	23.3	18.6	13.1

Counterpointing the worsening situation of households with children over the 1970s and particularly the 1980s was an improvement in the position of the elderly, as can be seen by analysis of the relationship between risk and the age of the household head. In the 1987 sample, households headed by an elderly person were at relatively low risk, particularly with the 40 and 50 per cent lines. Only 8 per cent of households headed by a person aged sixty-five or over fell below the 50 per cent line, compared with 19 per cent of those with a 'non-elderly' head. The gap was less pronounced with the 60 per cent line, with a sharp rise in risk for the elderly to 22 per cent, but this was still well below average.

This contrasts sharply with the situation in 1973, when households headed by an elderly person were much more likely than others to be below the relative lines. About 31 per cent of such households were below half average equivalent income in 1973, and 44 per cent were below the 60 per cent line. This marked improvement in the relative incomes of the elderly meant that by 1987 only 11 per cent of households below half average income were headed by a person aged sixty-five or over, compared with fully 41 per cent in 1973. The elderly, who dominated in the 1960s and early 1970s, had by the late 1980s become a much smaller element in the low-income population.

This pattern of an improvement in the last two decades in the position of the elderly and an increase in the risk of poverty for families with children is not unique to Ireland: it has in fact been seen in a number of other developed countries over the same period. It has received particular attention in the United States (where the proportion of children in households below the official poverty line rose from 14 per cent in 1969 to over 20 per cent by the late 1980s), but has also been found in such disparate societies as Sweden, the Netherlands, France, and Japan (Palmer et al., 1988; Eurostat, 1990). While the factors involved are not identical across countries, improved old age and retirement pensions have been the key development for the elderly, while deteriorating economic conditions have adversely affected the position of families with children, through stagnant earnings growth (in the United States) or increased unemployment (in a number of European countries). The impact of unemployment in the Irish situation will be made clear by the analysis of the changing composition of the poor in terms of labour force status in the next section.

A major factor in the improved position of the elderly was the increase in the value of social welfare old age pensions. These rose by 107 per cent in real terms between 1973 and 1987, when average industrial earnings rose by 88 per cent in real terms and after-tax earnings grew by considerably less. As the coverage of occupational pensions widened and schemes matured, these also contributed to the improvement in the relative position of the elderly.

We now turn to the position of male versus female-headed households. The increasing percentage of poor households headed by a woman in the United States has led to much debate there about the causes and implications of the 'feminisation of poverty'—although, contrary to popular belief, this does not appear to have been a major factor in the deteriorating position of children in the 1970s and 1980s (Gould and Palmer, 1988). In the 1987 ESRI sample, female-headed households were found to face a lower risk of being below the 40 or 50 per cent relative income lines than those headed by a male, with 19 per cent of male-headed versus 11 per cent of female-headed households below half average income. With the 60 per cent line there is little difference between the two in terms of risk.

This pattern is closely related to the age-risk relationship just described: a much higher percentage of the female household heads are aged 65 or over, so the relatively low risk faced by the elderly brings down the average for this group. (Looking separately at those aged under 65 and those aged 65 and over, the risk for female-headed households is in fact lower than for male-headed ones at the 50 per cent line but higher at the 60 per cent one within both age groups.) What is particularly interesting is that female-headed households faced a much higher risk than male-headed ones in 1973: about twice as many were then below half average income, and even with the 60 per cent line there was a substantial differential in risk in favour of male-headed households. Over the 1973–87 period, therefore, the position of female-headed households improved significantly (their risk of falling below half average income declining from 30 to 11 per cent), and the differential in risk between male and female-headed households was eliminated or reversed. Once again the fact that more female household heads are elderly and that the relative position of the elderly improved substantially over the period is central to understanding this trend.

Rather than an increase in the proportion of poor households headed by a woman, then, the 1973–87 period saw a substantial decline. In this sense there has not been a 'feminisation of poverty' in the Irish situation, rather the reverse. (The same is true of Britain, as shown by Wright (1992).) This is the overall pattern for female-headed households, although, as we have seen, households comprising an adult living with dependent children—most of which are headed by a woman—face a relatively high risk of being below the relative income lines.

5.2 INCOME POVERTY AND LABOUR FORCE STATUS

We now focus on the central determinant of a household's income, namely the labour force status of its members, particularly the household head. Table 5.3 shows the risk of being below half average equivalent income by labour force status of the head, and the importance of each status type among households below that line and in the sample as a whole. The group at highest risk, unsurprisingly, is households with an unemployed head, 58 per cent of whom were below the 50 per cent line. Those headed by someone away from work through illness are at almost as high a risk. Farmer-headed households face a risk well above average. (It is important to note, as already mentioned in chapter 3, that the farm income data collected in the survey refers to the calendar year 1986, which was a particularly poor year, so the income position of farm households in the sample is particularly depressed compared with the years immediately before or after.) Households with a head who is self-employed, retired or engaged in home duties have a below-average risk, while employee-headed households have by far the lowest chance of being below the line.

TABLE 5.3   *Risk and incidence of poverty (50% income line) by labour force status of head*

Labour force status of head	Risk (percentage falling below 50% line)	Incidence (percentage of all households below 50% line)	Percentage of all households in sample
Employee	3.9	9.2	38.6
Farmer	34.9	23.9	11.8
Other self-employed	11.6	5.0	7.5
Unemployed	58.1	34.3	10.3
Ill	51.2	3.5	1.2
Retired	11.3	9.3	14.4
Home duties	11.8	7.6	11.3
Other	25.4	7.1	4.9

In 1987, 10 per cent of all households in the sample were headed by an unemployed person. Given their very high risk, however, such households accounted for 34 per cent of those below half average income. Farm households were the other substantial group among those below that line, accounting for 24 per cent. There are not many households whose head was away from work because of illness, so despite their high risk they make up only a small proportion of those below the line. Employee-headed households, on the other hand, are by far the largest group in the sample and account for 9 per cent of those below the line,

even though they face a very low risk. Households with a retired head
and where the head is engaged in home duties each also account for
about 9 per cent. A similar pattern is seen with the 60 per cent line, or
with alternative equivalence scales.

Major changes in the incidence of poverty over time, which help to
explain the trends in household composition type described in the previous section, can be seen by a comparison with the household budget
surveys of 1973 and 1980. The risk of falling below the relative income
lines facing households headed by an employee, farmer, other self-
employed or the unemployed or ill altered remarkably little over the
1973–87 period, though the risk for the retired and those engaged in
home duties fell significantly. However, there were substantial changes
in the numbers in the different categories. Most importantly, only 3
per cent of households in the 1973 survey had an unemployed head,
whereas by 1987 we have seen this figure rise to 10 per cent. (The
unemployment rate among household heads—that is, the numbers
unemployed as a percentage of household heads in the work force
rather than of all household heads—was 15 per cent by 1987.) There
was a substantial decline in the importance of farm households (from
22 to 12 per cent), while the proportion of households with a retired
head rose (from 11 to 14 per cent) and those headed by an employee
fell (from 43 to 39 per cent). Table 5.4 shows the impact that this and
other factors, such as the improvement in the relative position of the
elderly, had on which types of household were below half average
income.

TABLE 5.4   *Incidence of poverty (50% income line) by labour force status
of head, 1973, 1980, 1987*

Labour force status of head	1973	1980	1987
Employee	9.0	10.3	9.2
Farmer	26.0	25.9	23.9
Other self-employed	3.6	3.5	5.0
Unemployed	9.6	14.7	34.3
Ill	5.7	7.3	3.5
Retired	17.0	18.9	9.3
Home duties	24.6	17.4	7.6
Other	4.5	2.0	7.1

In 1973, households with an unemployed head accounted for only 10 per cent of those below the line, while the retired and those engaged in home duties together made up over 40 per cent. By 1987 the unemployed accounted for 34 per cent and the retired and those engaged in home duties made up only 17 per cent. Households headed by a farmer consistently formed about one-quarter of those below the line, while those headed by an employee were about 10 per cent throughout. The fact that many households with a retired head saw their situation improve and were in effect 'replaced' among those on low incomes by households with an unemployed head is the key factor underlying the increase in risk described earlier for households with children. It is worth noting in this context that over half the children in households below the 50 per cent line in 1987 were in households with an unemployed head; unemployment is central to the high risk of poverty facing children and to the very substantial rise in that risk over the 1970s and 1980s.

The comparative study of poverty in the EC carried out for Eurostat showed that there were significant differences across member-states not only in the extent of poverty (as measured by the percentage of households below country-specific relative lines) but also in the types of household involved. Households without an economically active member were at high risk in most countries, and the risk facing children compared with the average worsened in a majority of countries over the 1980–85 period. The comparative analysis makes clear that by the mid-1980s the relative position of children (i.e. their risk relative to the overall average) was worse and that of the elderly was better in Ireland than in most of the other member-states. Similarly, both the improvement in the situation of the elderly and the deterioration in that of families with children in the 1980s was a good deal more pronounced in Ireland than in most other countries.

The importance of differentiating not only among those of different labour force status but also among recipients of different types of social welfare payments can be seen by a comparison of risk across recipients. Households headed by someone receiving an old age pension face a lower risk of being below the relative lines than other types of recipient; but within this group those on a non-contributory pension have a significantly higher risk than recipients of contributory OAP. Indeed the latter face a much lower risk than any of the other types of recipient, with very few below half average income and only 10 per cent falling below the 60 per cent relative line. Those receiving a widow's contributory pension also have a relatively low risk, whereas about 10 per cent of households headed by someone getting non-contributory widow's or old age pension are below half average income and about 38 per cent are below the 60 per cent line. Households headed by a recipient of unemployment or disability benefit face a high risk, with about 35 per cent below the 50 per cent line and 55–60 per cent below the 60 per cent line. However, an even higher percentage of households headed by someone receiving unemployment assistance or supplementary welfare allowance are below these lines, 70 per cent falling below the 60 per cent threshold.

The precise risk figures are sensitive to the exact location of the poverty line chosen, with the 60 per cent line lying between the non-contributory and contributory old age pensions payable at the time, but the comparative pattern across the various schemes is consistent, reflecting both the relative generosity of the schemes and differences in the extent to which recipient households are dependent on the social welfare payment or have other income sources.

5.3 INCOME POVERTY AND SOCIAL CLASS

In identifying the key characteristics of low-income households, social class and socio-economic group are of central importance. The Central Statistics Office has for many years categorised occupations into socio-economic groups, each of which contains occupations considered 'generally similar as regards the level of skill or educational attainment required.' More recently, starting with the 1986 census, the CSO has also employed a social class scale, which is intended to bring together 'individuals whose market situation is such as to involve them in the use of similar resources to generate incomes and who share similar work situations and backgrounds' (O'Hare, Commins, and Whelan, 1991). The key difference between the two is that the class schema is explicitly designed to provide a ranking: thus whereas all farmers are taken together as a separate socio-economic group, they are distributed among the social classes on the basis of farm size. In each case we classify households on the basis of the occupation etc. of the household head.

Table 5.5 shows the risk and incidence of income poverty in the 1987 survey for the six social classes distinguished by the CSO. The risk of being below the 50 per cent relative line rises from less than 7 per cent for the professional and managerial classes to 18–20 per cent for the skilled and semi-skilled classes and 30 per cent for the unskilled manual class. The professional and managerial classes are thus significantly underrepresented among the poor—making up 22 per cent of all households but only 9 per cent of those below the line—while the unskilled manual class is heavily overrepresented, making up 16 per cent of the sample but 28 per cent of those below the line. Nonetheless it is worth emphasising that more than two-thirds of those below half average income are not from the unskilled manual class: low income is far from being confined to that class.

Categorisation by socio-economic group shows a similar pattern, except that farmers, taken as a group, are seen to have about the same risk overall as the semi-skilled manual social class. The socio-economic categorisation also allows a comparison to be made with the earlier household budget surveys. The main difference between 1987 and 1973 is that the proportion of households in the farmer socio-economic group is considerably lower in the latter year but their risk of being below the income poverty lines is higher, again because the year covered in the survey was a particularly bad one for farm incomes, so the importance of this group among those on low incomes did not decline.

TABLE 5.5: *Risk and incidence of poverty (50% income line) by social class*

Social class	Risk (percentage falling below 50% line)	Incidence (percentage of all households below 50% line)	Percentage of all households in sample
Higher professional	6.8	4.1	10.2
Lower professional	6.7	4.9	12.3
Intermediate non-manual	13.5	14.1	17.7
Skilled manual	19.7	27.4	23.5
Semi-skilled manual	17.7	21.5	20.5
Unskilled manual	30.0	28.1	15.8

5.4 INCOME, DEPRIVATION, AND THE CHARACTERISTICS OF THE POOR

So far in this chapter we have focused on the characteristics of the households below relative income poverty lines—the 'income-poor'. Chapter 4 showed the relevance, in measuring living standards and poverty, of also taking into account direct indicators of deprivation. Using a particular set of indicators of basic aspects of deprivation, the numbers in the sample both falling below relative lines and experiencing such deprivation were analysed. We now want to examine the characteristics of the households meeting these combined criteria, to see whether they differ from those associated simply with low income. If there are significant differences, this may help in understanding why some of those at low income levels are experiencing basic deprivation and others are not, and also point to priority groups among those on low income who are in particular need of attention in designing policy responses to poverty.

Table 5.6 compares the profile of households below the 50 per cent income line, in terms of labour force status of the head, with those below the 60 per cent income line and experiencing basic deprivation (in the sense described in chapter 4). Approximately the same number of households is involved in each case, so the comparison allows us to focus on differences in composition, rather than in numbers, produced by the application of a combined income and deprivation criterion rather than simply an income one. We see that the major difference, already mentioned in chapter 4, is that households headed by a farmer account for a much smaller proportion of those meeting the income plus deprivation criteria—only 12 per cent, compared with about a quarter of those below the 50 per cent line. Interestingly, it is not households headed by an unemployed person that are now more important: though still the largest single group, they account for about 38 per cent, whether the income or income plus deprivation criteria are applied. Households headed by an employee account for a slightly higher proportion; but it is those headed by a person engaged in home duties or in the 'other' category—many of whom are out of the labour force because of disability—that are a considerably higher proportion of those below the 60 per cent line and experiencing basic deprivation than of those below the 50 per cent line.

To highlight the differences between the categories, table 5.6 also shows the breakdown of those below the 60 per cent income line and not experiencing basic deprivation. This makes it clear that among those falling below the 60 per cent income line, households headed by a farmer or a retired person are more likely than others not to be experiencing basic deprivation, while those headed by an unemployed person or someone engaged in home duties or in the 'other' category are more likely to be experiencing such deprivation. It also makes clear, however, that across all the labour force status categories there are substantial numbers among those on low incomes who are not experiencing basic deprivation, as well as a significant proportion who are experiencing such deprivation.

TABLE 5.6 *Incidence of poverty by labour force status of head, income and combined income and deprivation criteria*

Labour force status of head	Below 50% income line	Below 60% income line, experiencing basic deprivation	Below 60% income line, not experiencing basic deprivation
Employee	8.9	11.7	16.8
Farmer	23.3	12.4	25.1
Other self-employed	4.7	2.1	7.7
Unemployed	39.0	36.5	17.5
Ill	2.9	3.2	0.9
Retired	7.5	5.6	13.0
Home duties	6.3	15.0	11.6
Other	7.4	13.5	7.4

While labour force status and income source provide part of the story, then, the relationship between current income, wider resources and deprivation is a complex one (see Callan et al., 1993). Those whose earned income fluctuates over time, such as farmers and other self-employed, may be more accustomed to 'smoothing' their consumption by saving in good times and drawing down savings or running up debts in bad. (There are also particular problems in obtaining an accurate measure of income from these sources.) For any household, though, the crucial point is that it is not simply current income that determines current living standards but also how the household got into the present position, how long it has been there, and how long it expects to remain at that income level. Some of those currently on low incomes have not been in that situation very long, and can draw down savings, borrow, or rely on help from friends and family to supplement that income and avoid basic deprivation. Others, who have been on low income for a long period or frequently experience spells of low income, are likely to have no such resources to draw on; indeed they may need to use some of their income to pay back previous borrowing, and will find it much more difficult to avoid basic deprivation.

Thus, as was seen in chapter 4, for each labour force category those on low incomes but not experiencing basic deprivation were found to have substantially higher levels of savings than those experiencing deprivation. Some of those reporting such deprivation, such as households with an unemployed head, had virtually no savings and were entirely dependent on current income, mostly from social welfare.

This highlights the importance, in trying to understand the situation of different households, of taking into account the dynamics of income over time. The implications of a dynamic rather than static perspective on poverty are further explored in chapter 6, which makes use of data from a further survey carried out by the ESRI in 1989 that followed up some of the respondents to the 1987 survey. Here our focus is on the implications for the characteristics of the households involved. Moving on from labour force status, there is little difference in household composition between those below the 50 per cent line and those below the 60 per cent line and experiencing basic deprivation. Thus the high risk facing households with children still applies, although among households without children single adults face a significantly higher risk and larger households a lower one using the combined income and deprivation criteria.

Looking at social class, however, those below the combined income and deprivation criteria are more concentrated in the manual social classes than those below the income line. Whereas 28 per cent of those below half average income are from the unskilled manual class and 77 per cent in total are from the manual classes, 33 per cent of those below the 60 per cent line and experiencing primary deprivation are from the unskilled manual class and 85 per cent are from the manual classes. Only 4 per cent of those meeting the combined income and deprivation criteria are from the professional and managerial classes. This is entirely consistent with the notion that resources over a longer period, which one would expect to be highly correlated with social class, play an important part in determining the likelihood of a low-income household experiencing basic deprivation.

5.5 CONCLUSIONS

In this chapter, some salient characteristics of poor households have been identified. Households where the head is unemployed face the highest risk or probability of being on low incomes. Largely as a consequence of the increase in unemployment during the 1980s, households with children, particularly those with three or more children, now face a high risk, much higher than in the 1970s. The position of the elderly, on the other hand, has improved substantially over the 1970s and 1980s, as the real level of social welfare old age pension was increased rapidly relative to other incomes and occupational pension schemes matured and covered more of the retired.

The result has been a major shift in the profile of households below relative income lines. The retired and elderly now make up a much smaller proportion, and the unemployed and families with children a much higher proportion, than in the early 1970s. While similar trends have been seen in a number of other developed countries, this has been exceptionally pronounced in Ireland.

Concentrating on those who are on low incomes and experiencing basic deprivation, farm households are less significant, though they still face a higher risk than employees. The unemployed, the disabled and those engaged in home duties are at highest risk, though significant numbers of employees, farm households and the retired are also experiencing basic deprivation because of lack of resources. Most of these households are from the manual social classes, and almost two-thirds contain children.

In understanding the causes of poverty and in framing policy, then, unemployment is seen to be the most important single cause of poverty, and policies aimed at reducing unemployment and improving the situation of the unemployed must receive priority. Part V considers inter alia the contribution that reform of the tax and social welfare systems could make to assisting the unemployed and other recipients, while at the same time improving incentives facing those on low incomes.

Because the elderly have little involvement in the labour market, improving their position through the social welfare system did not face the difficulties in the relationship between income support and earnings that greatly complicate the design of an effective, efficient and equitable tax and transfer system for those of working age. These problems arise particularly in providing support for children, another priority identified here. To enhance understanding of the processes at work, however, it is important to first examine the causes of poverty in more depth, which is the topic of part III, and to look at dynamic perspectives on poverty, the subject of the next chapter.

6 Poverty: Temporary or Permanent?

JAMES WILLIAMS AND BRENDAN J. WHELAN

There is a common misconception that we can talk of 'the poor', implying a simple, static dichotomy between poor and non-poor households, with those in poverty constituting a homogeneous and unchanging stock of individuals. The reality is much more complex. For some people, poverty may indeed be a long-term, almost permanent state. For others, however, it may be a more transitory phenomenon. Households or individuals may move into and out of poverty in response to a variety of events, for example changes in the employment status of household members or a change in family composition.

Comparisons of the results from independent sample surveys of the population at different times allow changes in the extent and incidence of poverty over time to be analysed. Thus chapters 3 and 5 examined trends in the incidence and risk of poverty over the period 1973–87, using the household budget surveys for 1973 and 1980 and the Economic and Social Research Institute's survey for 1987. The results showed, for example, that the position of elderly households had improved, whereas the risk of poverty among large families increased substantially. This type of comparative analysis, therefore, allows one to identify *net* changes in the structure of the incidence and risk of poverty over time. It does not, nor does it purport to, tell us anything of the changing circumstances of *particular* households over time.

In this chapter we shift the focus from these net population changes towards those at the level of the individual household, drawing on research elsewhere and analysing income mobility in Ireland for the first time. This is done on the basis of a follow-up survey that involved the re-interviewing in 1989 of a sub-set of the households in the 1987 ESRI survey. Chapter 4 has shown that a dynamic rather than static perspective is crucial to understanding the relationship between current income and living standards. By examining the nature and extent of short-term movements into and out of poverty, we further highlight the importance of adopting such a perspective in understanding poverty and in framing policy responses.

6.1 POVERTY DYNAMICS: THE INTERNATIONAL EXPERIENCE

We begin by considering some of the main findings from the international literature on changes in income and poverty status. Much of this is focused on the United States, where 'panel' survey data on the changing financial and economic circumstances of a set of families and individuals is available over a period stretching back to the late 1960s. This is from the longest-standing panel survey in the developed world, the Panel Survey of Income Dynamics (PSID) based at the International Survey Research Centre at the University of Michigan.

Only in recent years have substantive findings on the extent and correlates of poverty dynamics begun to emerge from European panel surveys, and therefore much of the overseas experience discussed here relates to the United States.

Income mobility
In terms of overall income mobility, results from the PSID over the period 1971–78 show that about 40 per cent of the sample were in the same income quintile position at the end of the period as at the beginning, with about 30 per cent moving up to a higher quintile and 30 per cent moving down to a lower one (Duncan and Morgan, 1981; Duncan, 1984). About 20 per cent had moved either up or down by more than one quintile. In a comparable study Fritzell (1990) found a remarkably similar level of economic mobility, at an aggregate level, among the Swedish population over the period 1973–80. In general, then, the evidence suggests a substantial degree of stability in income rankings.

What are the factors associated with income mobility? The overriding impression from American research is that the most important factor associated with income mobility is changes in family composition. This was particularly the case for women, where the effects of marital disruption on income status were severe. The corollary was that marriage or remarriage was found to substantially improve the economic status of women. The income status of children was strongly linked to changes in family composition: on average, a child in a household in which the parents stayed married over the period 1972–78 experienced a substantial real income increase, whereas children in families where the parents divorced or separated experienced a substantial fall. Similarly, children in households headed by a woman who was unmarried in 1972 and who remained unmarried throughout the period experienced an increase in absolute real income, but when the mother had married by 1978 a much larger real increase was observed (Duncan, 1984). Fritzell (1990) also found that family composition was extremely important in explaining income change for both men and women in Sweden.

The data from the PSID also suggests that labour market events, although not as important as changes in household composition, do have a major influence on changes in economic status. The greatest impact on household income is where the male head of household becomes unemployed. Unemployment of women (other than for households that are headed by a woman or those in which the woman is the only income earner) does not have such a significant effect on total family income. Large changes in male labour income are also experienced by those continuously at work, often associated with changes in the number of hours worked (possibly because of second jobs, overtime, or job changes). Fritzell again found roughly comparable results in his analysis of income mobility in Sweden.

In general, therefore, income mobility was found to be primarily associated with changes in family composition and, to a lesser degree, labour market events. Other characteristics, such as education and age, were found to have an effect on economic well-being and changes therein, although the latter in particular was found to impact through the labour market. These findings are best summarised by Morgan et al. (1974, 78), when they note that 'if people's own attitudes or behaviour or environment affect their economic situations, they must do it through changes in family composition or labour force participation . . . We found that changes in family composition and labour force participation so dominate changes in family well-being that nothing else seems to matter very much.'[1]

Poverty dynamics

Focusing on movements into and out of poverty, there is no definitive way in which one can measure aggregate poverty transitions. One approach is to examine the percentage of the population that is poor in one year and remains poor in the next. If poverty were an entirely structural phenomenon one would expect that 100 per cent of those who were in poverty in each year would still be in poverty in the following year. On the other hand, if it were entirely cyclical or transitory in nature (with a twelve-month cycle) then none of those in poverty in one year would be in poverty in the next. The reality is, of course, likely to be somewhere between these two extremes.

Transitions into and out of poverty in the United States over the period 1969–78 have been estimated on an adjacent-year basis by Hill (1981) and Duncan (1984), using the PSID data mentioned above. Overall, both report that the annual percentage of people who remained poor from one year to the next ranged from a low of 54 per cent to a high of 65 per cent. In other words, throughout the 1970s between 35 and 46 per cent of those who were poor in any one year had escaped from poverty by the next. Berghman and Dirven (1991) analysed panel data for the Netherlands over the period 1986–88 and found that 64 per cent of those who were poor (below the legal minimum) in 1986 had escaped from poverty one year later, while the annual escape rate for those poor in 1987 was 61.2 per cent. These year-on-year escape rates for the Netherlands are clearly considerably higher than the 1970s figures for the United States.

Another important source of information on poverty transition rates is the Survey of Income and Program Participation (SIPP) of the US Bureau of the Census. The bureau uses a threefold classification: 'poor' (below the official poverty line), 'near-poor' (in the range 100–124 per cent of the poverty threshold), and 'non-poor' (over 125 per cent of the threshold). It was found that 25 per cent of those who were poor in 1984 were above the poverty line one year later, but 44 per cent of these ended up in the 'near-poor' category. Thus only 14 per cent of those who were in poverty in 1984, as measured by the SIPP, were in an economically secure position one year later (Bureau of the Census, 1989).

To get a complete picture of annual poverty transitions one needs to look not only at poverty escape rates or *outflows* but also at the extent of *inflows* into poverty, as overall incidence is clearly a function of the balance between the two. Duncan (1984) notes that over the period 1974–78 in the United States between 3 and 4 per cent of those who were not in poverty in one year were in poverty in the following year. Berghman and Dirven suggest that comparable figures for the Netherlands were 4.8 per cent in 1986/87 and 3.8 per cent in 1987/88.

Discussion of annual poverty transition rates logically leads to a consideration of poverty duration. The study of spell length is particularly problematic, and only the PSID offers a sufficiently long run of data to capture a substantial number of completed poverty spells that have begun and ended over a reasonably long period.[2] Using data from the PSID, Bane and Ellwood (1986) examined poverty durations over the period 1970–82 and found that the majority of poverty spells are short: 45 per cent are over within one year and 70 per cent are over within three. A total of 12 per cent last more than nine years. However, if one concentrates on those people who are poor at a given point, one finds that as much as 52 per cent of those identified as being poor in a cross-sectional survey are experiencing a poverty spell of ten or more years. (Bane and Ellwood use the analogy of hospital admissions and patients: although only a small proportion of those admitted to hospital will be long-stay patients, they will account for a high percentage of total hospital days and thus of hospital patients at any time.) This focuses attention on the dual nature of the distributions of poverty duration: the majority of people who are ever poor experience only short periods of poverty, but most poor people and person-years of poverty at a given time will be accounted for by those in long-term poverty.

Adopting a slightly different approach, Duncan (1984) looked at the proportion of the population that was in poverty for various lengths of time over the period 1969–78. He found that 24 per cent were poor in one or more years over the period, 5 per cent were poor in five or more of the years in question, and 3 per cent were poor in eight or more years. A total of 0.7 per cent were poor in all ten of the years under study. There was little evidence to suggest any substantial change in the relative levels of long-term and short-term poverty over the period in question, which is somewhat surprising in view of the sluggish conditions in the American domestic economy in the middle to late 1970s compared with the earlier years.

Bane and Ellwood also examined the relationship between the onset of a poverty spell and events such as changes in income and household composition. They found that for about half of those who experienced a spell in poverty over the period 1970–82 this was preceded by a fall in the earned income of one or more household members, most often the household head. The remainder of poverty spells were preceded by non-income-related events, primarily changes in family composition. The most common of these were a child leaving home to set up his or her own household. Other important factors were a child being born into a low-income household, marital disruption, and unmarried motherhood.

The overriding finding, however, is the variety and heterogeneity of events relating to the onset of a poverty spell. The only systematic pattern to emerge from this heterogeneity is that male-head families most commonly had suffered a fall in earnings, whereas for those with female heads poverty typically begins when that family is formed, either through separation or divorce or when an unmarried woman has a child.

A particularly important aspect of the onset of a poverty spell is the extent to which it is related to the experience of previous spells in poverty. Hill (1981) examines the relative significance of 'state dependence' versus 'heterogeneity'. State dependence is the effect that poverty per se in one year has on the probability of being poor in subsequent years, implying that being poor in one period will itself increase the chance of a further poverty spell in the future, regardless of individual characteristics etc. What she calls heterogeneity effects refers to the specific characteristics of each individual—such as low levels of educational attainment or partial disability—that may in themselves increase the probability of subsequent periods of poverty. Hill's research suggests that although it is significant, the effect of state dependence is small relative to heterogeneity effects. The heterogeneity of individuals' characteristics and their role in determining subsequent spells of poverty underline the complexity of policy formulation in this area.

What of the events associated with the ending of a spell in poverty? Bane and Ellwood (1986) note that in the United States in the 1970s about half of all poverty spells were ended when the earned income of the household head increased. An increase in the earned income of another household member was associated with the ending of about a further quarter of poverty spells. The ending of the remainder was related to increases in transfers or to marriage, which was an important route out of poverty for female household heads, especially those with children. One should note, however, that marriage was not the only, or indeed the most important, way out of poverty for women: more female heads with children escaped from poverty as a result of a change in employment or income status.

Berghman and Dirven (1991), in analysing poverty-related events in the Netherlands over the period 1986–88, found that for married men changes in employment status had a substantial and significant effect on poverty status. Neither changes in marital status (marital disruption or widowhood) nor changes in the number of children living at home significantly affected the probability of changing the poverty status of married men. For married women, changes in the employment status of their husband had a more substantial and significant impact on their poverty status than changes in their own employment status. Changes in employment status were also significant and substantial for unmarried men, while for unmarried women, getting married significantly increased the probability of escape from poverty.

6.2 DYNAMICS OF INCOME AND POVERTY STATUS: THE IRISH EXPERIENCE

What can we say about changes in the income and poverty status of Irish households? In the remainder of this chapter we consider new evidence for Ireland in the light of the findings from research on income and poverty dynamics elsewhere. The analysis is based on data from the ESRI's 1987 survey of income, life-style, and usage of state services, together with information collected in 1989 from a sub-sample of the same group of households. The sample used in the 1989 round of interviewing is relatively small, and households from the agricultural sector are not included in the analysis.[3] When reweighted to adjust for differential non-response and related issues and when farm households have been excluded, we are dealing with only 767 households. This is undoubtedly smaller than desirable, and the analysis is consequently constrained in the extent to which we can disaggregate the data.

It is also important to note that low-income households in the 1987 sample were oversampled in the 1989 follow-up, to maximise the reliability of the picture it provides about whether the situation of these households had changed. The sample has been reweighted to take this into account and to represent the overall national picture, but most confidence can be placed in the results for those who were on low incomes in 1987. Since only households in existence in 1987 are covered, those that were set up between that date and 1989 are not included.

Despite these limitations and the relatively short period covered, the data allows changes in the situation of Irish households over time to be examined for the first time.

We consider in turn four aspects of short-term changes in financial well-being and poverty status. Firstly, we discuss the extent of relative or positional income change using income quintiles; secondly, we consider net changes in poverty levels in the sample over the period 1987–89; thirdly, we examine the household's subjective assessment of change in its own financial situation; and fourthly, we look at micro-level changes in poverty status and related events. For convenience we refer to the 1989 sample as phase 2 and the 1987 results for these households as phase 1.

Changes in household income, 1987–89
Just over half the sample households experienced a real increase in
equivalent income between 1987 and 1989,[4] and about three-quarters
of the sample households experienced an income change of ±15 per
cent. An alternative way of analysing changes in household income is
to consider changes in the relative position of households in the
income distribution. Table 6.1 presents details on the extent of income
mobility measured on the basis of income quintile transitions. From
this we can see that 52 per cent of households remained in the same
income quintile over the study period, 24 per cent experienced an
improvement, and 24 per cent experienced a fall in income quintile
position. Most of those that changed their relative position did so by
only one quintile.

TABLE 6.1   *Extent of relative income mobility based on quintile transitions*
for unadjusted and equivalent income among non-farm
households, 1987–89

Change, phase 1/phase 2	Unadjusted income		Equivalent income	
	Percentage	(*n*)	Percentage	(*n*)
Fall > 1 quintile	3.8	(29)	7.2	(55)
Fall 1 quintile	18.6	(143)	16.6	(127)
Unchanged	56.4	(432)	51.8	(397)
Rise 1 quintile	16.3	(125)	18.5	(142)
Rise > 1 quintile	5.0	(38)	6.0	(46)
Total	100.0	(767)	100.0	(767)

Overall, then, the great majority of households did not experience
very substantial change over the study period, either in the percentage change in their income or in their relative position in the
income distribution. This is largely as one would expect, given that
the interval between interviews was relatively short—eighteen to
twenty-four months. These results are also in line with the overall
stability found in the American and Swedish studies discussed above.
What are the most significant factors underlying income change over
the study period? First, a change in quintile position is strongly associated with a change in the number of economically active household
members. Consider, for example, households that had one economically active member in phase 1 and two or more such members in

phase 2. A total of 41 per cent of such households remained in the same quintile position over the study period, 5 per cent experienced a deterioration in quintile position, and 54 per cent experienced an improvement.

The relationship between changes in the employment status of the household head and relative position in the income distribution is also important. Just over half the households whose head changed status from employee in 1987 to unemployed in 1989 experienced a deterioration in income quintile position, the remainder staying in the same quintile position over the study period. The corollary is the strong positive relationship between a change in the employment status of household head from unemployed to employed and an improvement in the household's relative position in the income distribution. Although the number of households where the head went from unemployed to employed is particularly small, approximately one-half of these households experienced an improvement in their relative position in the income distribution, about one-third stayed in the same quintile position, and the remaining 17 per cent experienced a fall in their ranking in the income distribution.

Changes in well-being and poverty status
As a preliminary to examining changes in household poverty status, it is instructive to look at the household's subjective assessment of its financial position and changes in this position over the study period. Table 6.2 presents details on the head of household's assessment at both points of interview of the degree of difficulty the household was having in making ends meet. This is obviously conditioned by his or her personal assessment of an acceptable standard of living, intuitive equivalence scale, and the like.

Although this is entirely a subjective measure, one should note that a household's perceived ability to make ends meet is strongly related to income. For example, of the households in phase 1 that were below the 50 per cent relative income line, 54 per cent said they were having 'great difficulty' in making ends meet, and a further 30 per cent said they were having 'some difficulty'. From the table we can see that in 1987 almost 52 per cent of all households said they were experiencing 'great difficulty' or 'some difficulty' in making ends meet, and the comparable figure for 1989 was 46 per cent. Part of the reason for this apparent fall in the percentage of households experiencing difficulty may be the exclusion from the population under study of households that were set up over the period.

TABLE 6.2   *Households classified by perceived ability to make ends meet, phases 1 and 2*

Phase 1	Phase 2				
	Great difficulty/ some difficulty	A little difficulty	Fairly easily/ easily/ very easily	Total (*n*)	Total, phase 1
Great difficulty/ some difficulty	66.3	18.7	15.0	100.0 (380)	51.2
A little difficulty	36.2	33.5	30.3	100.0 (165)	22.2
Fairly easily/easily/ very easily	12.8	20.7	66.5	100.0 (197)	26.6
Total phase 2	45.4	22.5	32.1		
(*n*)	(337)	(167)	(238)		

Two-thirds of those who were experiencing great or some difficulties in 1987 continued to experience a similar degree of difficulty in 1989. A further 19 per cent of this group seems to have experienced a slight improvement, while the remaining 15 per cent (8 per cent of the total sample) by 1989 were stating that they were making ends meet fairly easily, easily, or very easily. At the other extreme we can see that just over two-thirds of those who were able to make ends meet with some relative degree of ease in 1987 were still able to do so by 1989. Noteworthy, however, is the fact that 13 per cent of this group (6 per cent of the total sample) perceive themselves as having experienced a substantial deterioration in their ability to make ends meet over the study period.

At the second round of interviewing, the head of household was also asked to say how the household's financial situation had changed over the previous eighteen months. Table 6.3 classifies households according to their ability to make ends meet in 1987 and shows how they felt the household's financial situation had changed by 1989. Almost half those who were experiencing great or some difficulty in making ends meet at the first round of interviewing felt that they had experienced a deterioration in their financial situation between 1987 and 1989, compared with an aggregate figure of 38 per cent for the population as a whole. Among those who found it easy to make ends meet at the first round of interviewing, on the other hand, an above-average percentage felt that their situation had improved by 1989.

This information on households' subjective assessments of financial well-being and changes in this assessment suggests that there is a degree of change in households' financial circumstances (or at least in the head of household's perception thereof) over the short term. For example, about 8 per cent of households were experiencing substantial difficulty at the first interview but said they had experienced a fairly substantial improvement in their financial situation by 1989. Furthermore, about 6 per cent of households were able to make ends meet with some degree of ease in 1987 but were experiencing great difficulty or some difficulty by 1989.

TABLE 6.3   *Households classified by perceived ability to make ends meet in phase 1 and perceived change in household's financial situation between phases 1 and 2*

| Make ends meet in phase 1 | Changes in financial situation between phases 1 & 2 | | | | |
	Much better/ somewhat better	Same	Somewhat worse/ much worse	Total	(n)
Great difficulty/ some difficulty	14.1	39.3	46.6	100.0	(384)
A little difficulty	20.5	41.6	37.6	100.0	(166)
Fairly easily/easily/ very easily	24.4	52.3	23.2	100.0	(197)
Total	18.2	43.2	38.5	100.0	(747)

We now turn to the measured changes in the poverty status of households, on the basis of relative income poverty lines of the kind employed in chapter 4. These relative-income poverty lines are calculated as a percentage of mean equivalent household income in the year in question, and three different lines are again used, namely 40, 50 and 60 per cent of average income. Very much the same overall poverty rates are found in the two years with the 40 and 50 per cent lines (6.5 and 15.3 per cent of households, respectively). As regards the 60 per cent line the proportion of households in poverty rose from 25 per cent in 1987 to 27 per cent in 1989. Such differences could be ascribed to sampling variances, and the point to be made is the stability in overall poverty levels. This stability in itself reinforces the often-held view (albeit an implicit one) that poverty is essentially a permanent phenomenon.

Although such cross-sectional 'snapshots' of poverty rates at two points in time provide a measure of aggregate net change in poverty levels, they say nothing of micro-level changes in the poverty status of individual households nor of the flows into and out of poverty over the period in question, which we can now examine, given the panel nature of the data. Because of the sampling design, as already noted, one can have greater confidence in the measure of the extent to which those in poverty in 1987 had escaped by 1989 than one can in the extent to which households fell into poverty.

The definition of an escape from poverty that is used here is the movement from below any poverty line in 1987 to a point above the same line by 1989. Table 6.4 presents details of the extent of such poverty escapes over the study period. Using the lowest (40 per cent) relative income line, 59 per cent of households that were in poverty in 1987 had escaped by 1989. As one increases the poverty line to the 50 and 60 per cent levels, the escape rate falls off dramatically, to 30 per cent with the highest line.

TABLE 6.4   *Extent of poverty escapes among non-farm households below poverty line, 1987*

Change in status, phase 1 to phase 2	Poverty line		
	40%	50%	60%
Percentage escaped from poverty	58.6	38.4	30.0
Percentage still in poverty	41.4	61.6	70.0
Total	100.0	100.0	100.0
n (weighted)	(50)	(117)	(192)
Overall percentage in poverty in phase 1	6.5	15.3	25.1

Extending beyond poverty escapes to look at poverty transitions among all the (non-farm) sample households over the study period, we can present a fourfold classification, as follows: (1) no poverty in either 1987 or 1989; (2) a fall into poverty over the study period; (3) an escape from poverty over the study period; (4) poverty in both 1987 and in 1989. Because we are constrained by the relatively small sample size, it is possible to discuss trends according to this fourfold classification only in respect of the 60 per cent line, for which the results are as shown in Table 6.5. Almost two-thirds of the households did not experience poverty at either round of interviewing; just under 10 per cent fell into poverty over the study period, i.e. did not experience poverty in 1987 but were below the line in 1987; a further 7.5 per cent of households escaped from poverty over the period; and the remaining 18 per cent of households were in poverty at both times.

TABLE 6.5 *Poverty status among non-farm households, 1987, 1989*

	60% line	n
	%	(weighted)
No poverty	65.3	(500)
Poverty in phase 2 only	9.6	(74)
Poverty in phase 1 only	7.5	(58)
Poverty in phase 1 & 2	17.5	(135)
Total	100.0	(767)

The reader should note that the numbers of reweighted cases in at least two of the four categories are relatively small and that, in view of the sample structure, we can have greater confidence in the data relating to poverty escapes than to that relating to those who fell into poverty over the period.

Some consideration must also be given to the prospects over the medium and long term of these changes in poverty status. For example, can one assume that the 17.5 per cent of households that were found to be in poverty in both 1987 and 1989 represent those in a state of long-term, structural poverty? The answer is no, at least not from the data available to us. The results we have presented here relate to short-term movements into and out of poverty. We do not know what the poverty status of households was either before 1987 or after 1989. Some of the households in poverty at both points of interview may indeed be experiencing long-term, structural poverty; for others it may be a shorter, perhaps two- or three-year, phenomenon. Similarly, for some of those who escape, the graduation out of poverty may be short-lived, and they may return to poverty in 1990 or later.

Furthermore, we have no information on actual duration of poverty spell. Some of those who escaped over the period 1987–89 will have ended a very lengthy spell of poverty; for others the experience of poverty in 1987 at the point of first interview may have been a short-term aberration in their longer-term status, and so the escape by 1989 was simply a return to a more normal situation. The problems presented by so-called left and right truncation of the data, as well as issues associated with duration of spell per se, can be addressed only if one has access to a relatively long run of high-quality data such as that available in the United States from the Panel Survey of Income Dynamics (PSID).

Finally, we must ask whether anything can be said about differences in the characteristics of the households that make up each of the four groups in table 6.5. We are obviously constrained by the number of cases available for analysis, but a few observations may be made. Changes in poverty status are strongly associated with changes in the number of economically active members in the household, an increase in the number of economically active household members being an important factor in escape from poverty.

Change in the employment status of the head of household is also of importance in an analysis of change in household poverty status. Over 60 per cent of households that did not experience poverty at either round of interviewing were headed by a person in employment at both points of the survey, compared with only 18 per cent for households that fell into poverty over the study period, 32 per cent for those that escaped from poverty, and 14 per cent for those that experienced poverty in both 1987 and 1989. Similarly, over one-third of households that were experiencing poverty in both 1987 and 1989 were headed by a person who was unemployed at both points of interview, compared with less than 1 per cent for households that were not experiencing poverty at either point of the survey. Households that fell into poverty over the study period were more likely than average to be headed by a person who went from an employed to an unemployed status, and households that escaped from poverty had an above-average probability of being headed by a person who went from unemployment to employment. It is worth noting, however, that such changes in the labour force status of the head of household occurred in only a small proportion of the households escaping or falling into poverty.

6.3 SUMMARY

In this chapter we have focused on the need for a dynamic rather than static perspective on poverty. The importance of adopting such a perspective has been illustrated using the research findings on poverty dynamics emerging internationally as well as the results of analysing new, though limited, data for Ireland on how the situation of particular households changes over time.

The focus of much of this research has been the United States, where a good-quality longitudinal data-set stretching back to the late 1960s, the Panel Survey of Income Dynamics, is available. In terms of overall income dynamics, the key finding to emerge from analysis of the PSID is that changes in household or family composition have the greatest effect on economic well-being. Labour force experience, although exerting a substantial influence on changes in economic status, is of secondary importance.

PSID data covering the period 1969–78 has shown that between 35 and 46 per cent of those who were poor in a given year had escaped by the next year. The corollary is that 3–4 per cent of those who were not poor in a given year had fallen into poverty by the following year. In general, the duration of poverty spells in the United States is relatively short. Bane and Ellwood (1986) found that over the period 1970–82 about 45 per cent of poverty spells were over within one year and 70 per cent were over within three years. A total of 12 per cent, however, last more than nine years. The same household may, of course, experience more than one spell. Using a different approach, not focusing on spells per se, Duncan (1984) found that over the period 1969–74, 24 per cent of the sample were poor in one or more years, 5 per cent were poor in five or more years, and 3 per cent were poor in eight or more years. Less than 1 per cent of the sample were poor in all ten of the years under study.

Looking at the Irish experience of income and poverty dynamics for the first time, short-term transitions over the period 1987–89 can be assessed using information obtained from a follow-up survey that re-interviewed some of the households that responded to the survey carried out by the ESRI in 1987. This found, not surprisingly in view of the relatively short interval, that the great majority of households experienced only a relatively minor degree of income change over the study period: over half did not change their ranking in the distribution in terms of equivalent income quintile. The most clearly identifiable factors associated with income mobility were a change in the number of economically active household members and a change in the employment status of the head of the household.

As a preliminary to examining poverty dynamics per se we saw that some households certainly experienced a major turn-around in their perceived ability to make ends meet between 1987 and 1989. About 8 per cent of sample households were experiencing great difficulty or some difficulty in making ends meet in 1987 but said they were able to do so fairly easily, easily or very easily by 1989, while 6 per cent were able to make ends meet with some relative degree of ease in 1987 but by 1989 were experiencing great difficulty or some difficulty.

Using relative-income poverty lines, we found that for those below the line in 1987, escape rates were 59 per cent with the 40 per cent line, 38 per cent with the 50 per cent line, and 30 per cent with the 60 per cent line. Of the total sample, about two-thirds had experienced no poverty at either round of interviewing, about 10 per cent had fallen into poverty over the study period, 8 per cent had escaped from poverty, and the remaining 18 per cent were experiencing poverty at both points of interview.

Thus both the subjective perceptions of ability to make ends meet and income status vis-à-vis relative poverty lines clearly suggest that there is an important dynamic aspect to poverty and deprivation. Significant numbers are escaping from poverty and are being replaced, in approximately the same proportion, by others who fall below the poverty line over the short term. The critical factor in regard to income mobility and poverty transitions in Ireland seems to be labour market conditions and related changes in employment status of the head of household, rather than changes in family composition, which in the United States appear to be the most important factor in determining economic mobility.

Although the Irish sample was small, we did not identify a significant incidence of marital break-up. Most of the compositional change involved the birth of a child or the entry of another member to the household. In the small number of cases where marital break-up did feature there were certainly specific instances of consequent hardship, but this was not manifest on a systematic or widespread basis.

Although some of the findings presented from both the international literature and the Irish data may seem to be self-evident and to accord with what one would expect a priori, they clearly have an important role to play in the poverty debate. They underline the dynamic nature of poverty and consequently have policy implications that may often be overlooked. Only by quantifying the relative extent of cyclical and structural poverty and by identifying differences in the characteristics of both groups can we hope to put forward policy prescriptions that will tackle all aspects of the problem.

PART III

CAUSES OF POVERTY

What are the factors giving rise to the profile of poverty in Ireland set out in part II? This is the theme of the three chapters in this section. An understanding of the causal factors involved is essential if poverty is to be tackled effectively, and each of the chapters contributes to our understanding of these processes.

The most important cause of poverty in Ireland today is unemployment. Chapter 7 deals with many aspects of the relationship between unemployment and poverty. The dramatic rise in unemployment in the 1980s is described, and its impact on individual and household incomes is demonstrated. The very high poverty rates experienced by households headed by a person who is unemployed, particularly if unemployed in the long term, are shown. The experiences of such households are documented not only in terms of income but also of the indicators of deprivation set out in chapter 4. The role of family size and household composition interacting with unemployment is also discussed. Trends in the late 1980s and early 1990s and prospects for the future are described.

While the risk of poverty is much lower for those in paid employment, a significant number of households in poverty are headed by employees. The relationships between employment, low pay and poverty are explored in chapter 8. The relationship between low pay and poverty is shown to be a complex one, with the overlap between low individual earnings and family or household poverty being quite limited. The extent to which individual earners fall below various low-pay thresholds is shown, and the characteristics of these people are described. A large proportion are young, and many of the remainder are married women. This means that in a majority of cases the households in which these low-paid individuals live are not mainly dependent on their earnings. Where household income is low relative to needs and the head of the household is in employment, this is generally associated with family size rather than very low earnings per se. Thus the relationship between low pay and household poverty is far from direct, a pattern also found in other countries. As a result, a national minimum wage would not have a substantial beneficial impact on low-income households, even if it did not adversely affect employment. This and other policies aimed at helping low-income working families are considered in part V.

While unemployment has a clear and direct impact on poverty, people do not have equal chances of becoming unemployed. Individuals with a working-class background are much more likely to experience unemployment than those with a parent in the professional or managerial class. The relationships between class background, educational participation and risks of poverty are explored in chapter 9. A strong link between class background and risk of poverty is demonstrated. The elements giving rise to that link are then examined.

The influence of class background on educational participation is of central importance. Such features as early school leaving and participation in third-level education are still strongly related to class background, despite the expansion of the educational system. The consequences of leaving school without a qualification have become increasingly serious. They include a much increased likelihood of unemployment over a prolonged period, and much lower earnings even when employed. The implications for policy are again taken up in part VI.

7 Unemployment and Poverty

TIM CALLAN AND BRIAN NOLAN

The description of the profile of poor households in chapter 5 made clear the extent to which the dramatic increase in the level of unemployment in the 1980s has been the dominant influence on the way poverty has evolved over that period. By the late 1980s, unemployment was the most important single cause of low incomes and poverty. In this chapter we probe more deeply into the impact of unemployment on individual and household incomes and living standards.

Section 7.1 describes the background in terms of the trends in the level of unemployment and in the duration of unemployment during the 1970s and 1980s. This draws on available data from the annual Labour Force Surveys and the live register of unemployed. The data obtained in the 1987 Economic and Social Research Institute survey on the characteristics of the unemployed is described and is used to look at levels of educational attainment and previous labour market history.

Section 7.2 uses the same data-base to examine the impact of unemployment on the incomes of those experiencing it. Replacement rates—incomes when unemployed compared with those when in work—for this sample are contrasted with those often constructed for 'typical' hypothetical cases and used in discussion of the impact of unemployment and the incentive to work. Section 7.3 looks at household rather than individual incomes and shows how the impact of unemployment differs depending on the role of the unemployed person in the household—particularly whether he or she is the main earner—and the number of dependants. It also draws on the indicators of life-style and deprivation available for the sample to assess the impact of unemployment on living standards. This shows the importance of the duration of unemployment, as well as the role of the unemployed person in the household, in determining the extent to which unemployment is associated with deprivation and exclusion from ordinary living patterns.

97

Section 7.4 looks at how the situation has developed since the 1987 survey, at prospects for unemployment through the 1990s, and at the particular difficulties facing the long-term unemployed in seeking employment. Finally, section 7.5 brings together the key conclusions.

7.1 TRENDS IN UNEMPLOYMENT AND THE CHARACTERISTICS OF THE UNEMPLOYED

As background to the picture of unemployment provided by the 1987 ESRI survey, table 7.1 shows how the numbers unemployed changed over the period from 1971 to 1987, and also the levels of employment and emigration, which are essential to understanding the evolution of unemployment. (These figures are based on the annual labour force surveys rather than the live register.) Total employment rose by over 100,000 between 1971 and 1980, but with a dramatic turn-around to net immigration the labour force expanded more rapidly. Unemployment therefore also increased, from 61,000 to 91,000 or from 5.5 per cent to over 7 per cent of the labour force. From 1980 to 1987, however, the total at work fell by 76,000 and, despite high levels of emigration, the numbers unemployed soared to 230,000 or almost 18 per cent of the work force.

This dramatic increase in unemployment from 1980 to 1987 was accompanied by a steady increase in the proportion who were long-term unemployed. Statistics on the registered unemployed show that in April 1980, 35 per cent of those on the live register had been registering continuously for over a year. By April 1987 this figure had reached 44 per cent. While the overall unemployment rate was well above average for those aged under twenty-five, most of the long-term unemployed were aged twenty-five or over, and 80 per cent were men (compared with 72 per cent of the total unemployed).

The increasing importance of long-term unemployment was accompanied by a shift in the pattern of social welfare support. Whereas in 1980, 47 per cent of those on the live register were receiving insurance-based unemployment benefit and 48 per cent receiving the means-tested unemployment assistance, by 1987 only 37 per cent were on benefit and the proportion on assistance had risen to 58 per cent. (About 5 per cent of those on the register in each year received neither, generally having exhausted entitlement to unemployment benefit but failing to qualify for unemployment assistance.)

The 1987 ESRI survey obtained data on the current labour force status of respondents and on their educational and labour market histories. About 18 per cent of those in the labour force were unemployed when sampled (including those seeking their first job), the same rate as shown by the labour force survey, and a further 1.5 per cent were on a state employment or training scheme. Unemployment is defined in the survey as the person reporting himself or herself to be unemployed and available for work (similar to the definition employed in the labour force surveys). Not all such people are currently receiving unemployment benefit or assistance or on the live register, and not all those on the register classify themselves as unemployed and available for work (see Sexton, 1988, and Garvey, 1988). In fact about 20 per cent of those in the sample who state that they are unemployed and available for work are not receiving unemployment benefit or assistance—mostly first-job seekers who qualify for neither—and about the same percentage of recipients do not classify themselves as unemployed—most saying they were at work as farmers or in home duties.

TABLE 7.1   *Annual numbers at work and unemployed and net migration, 1971–87*

	At work ('000)	Unemployed ('000)	Labour force ('000)	Net external migration ('000)
1971	1,049	61	1,110	–5
1972	1,052	69	1,121	+11
1973	1,067	64	1,132	+13
1974	1,082	62	1,144	+16
1975	1,073	85	1,158	+20
1976	1,064	105	1,169	+16
1977	1,083	105	1,188	+10
1978	1,110	99	1,209	+7
1979	1,145	88	1,233	+16
1980	1,156	91	1,247	–8
1981	1,146	126	1,272	+2
1982	1,146	147	1,293	–1
1983	1,124	183	1,307	–14
1984	1,103	204	1,307	–9
1985	1,079	226	1,305	–20
1986	1,081	227	1,308	–28
1987	1,080	232	1,312	–27

Source: Central Statistics Office (1988, 1991).

The numbers in the sample receiving unemployment benefit and unemployment assistance, when grossed up to the implied population totals, are close to the actual numbers receiving each at the time (Callan, 1991b). Information on how long the unemployed have been away from work was obtained for those completing a full questionnaire. Those away from work for over a year may be taken as the long-term unemployed. Again this will not correspond exactly to the definition used in the live register analyses, which relate to those continuously registering for more than a year, since some people may have been away from work for over a year but had their registration interrupted by a period out of the labour force or on a training scheme.

Comparing the long-term and short-term unemployed in the sample, the former are again older and have a higher proportion of men. Over half the long-term unemployed are married. The educational profile of the unemployed is of particular interest, given the relationship between educational attainment and labour market outcomes. About 35 per cent of the short-term unemployed and 60 per cent of the long-term unemployed had not obtained the Intermediate or Group Certificate or higher qualification, and most had only primary education. This can be compared with the educational attainment of those currently in employment, where only 20 per cent had such low qualifications. (Even those in low-paid employment had significantly higher levels of education, as documented in the next chapter.) Recent entrants to the labour market tend to have higher levels of educational qualifications than those in older age groups, so it is also relevant to make comparisons within age groups. Focusing, for example. on the under-25s, the risk of long-term unemployment for those with no educational qualification beyond Group Certificate is about twice the average risk, while for those with the Leaving Certificate or higher the risk is half the average.

The information obtained in the ESRI survey about labour force histories (for those completing full individual questionnaires) shows that the currently unemployed also tend to have spent much longer out of work during their careers than those currently at work, even where the latter have had some unemployment. Only 29 per cent of employees reported any unemployment since leaving full-time education, and the total time spent in unemployment (often involving a number of different spells) on average for those who did have some was two years. The currently unemployed had an average total of over four years of unemployment in their careers. Obviously the 'potential' for having spent time in unemployment varies with the person's current age; however, similar comparisons within age groups between those currently in employment and unemployed show very much the same picture. For example, for employees aged between 45 and 54 who spent some time in unemployment, the average length of unemployment was under three years, whereas the unemployed in the same age group had spent an average of six years in unemployment during their careers.

It is striking that the relatively small number of people who have spent long periods in unemployment have particularly low levels of educational attainment and account for much of the overall unemployment experienced. Taking current employees and unemployed together, about 40 per cent have spent some time unemployed since leaving education. Only 6 per cent report having spent more than five years in unemployment in total, but the average for this group was ten years. Over half these people do not even have the Primary Certificate, and 84 per cent did not obtain the Group or Intermediate Certificate. Because of their very long durations, this small group experienced half of all the years of unemployment reported by current employees and unemployed in the sample. The links between low levels of education, current unemployment and prolonged experience of unemployment are very clear.

7.2 UNEMPLOYMENT AND INDIVIDUAL INCOMES

Having looked at the unemployed in the sample, we now begin tracing the way unemployment produces poverty, focusing in this section on the impact on the income of the person experiencing it. As Atkinson and Micklewright (1985) point out, the relationship between a person's income when in and out of work is of interest from two quite different perspectives: adequacy and incentives. The extent to which earnings are replaced by social welfare payments obviously has a major bearing on the extent to which the unemployed are able to maintain a minimally 'acceptable' standard of living and avoid poverty. The replacement rate is also central to assessing the financial incentives facing the unemployed, which some argue are an important element in understanding the causes of unemployment itself.

In the next section we go on to look at the incomes and living standards of households headed by or containing an unemployed person, which will also be relevant to assessing the adequacy of social welfare support rates for the unemployed, and to a lesser extent to analysing incentives. In this section we concentrate on the individual.

There has been a great deal of research on replacement rates in OECD countries in the 1970s and 1980s, largely a product of heated debates—especially in Britain and the United States—about the extent to which social welfare payments (together with the tax system) act as a disincentive to taking up work, and thus contribute to raising the level of unemployment. In Ireland, as elsewhere, much of the discussion of incentive effects has been on the basis of hypothetical 'typical' cases. For example, the social welfare payment that a married man with dependent spouse and two children would receive when unemployed, as a percentage of the after-tax earnings of such a person on the average industrial wage, is taken as the illustrative replacement rate for this family type. Rates can be calculated in the same way for other family types, such as a single man or a married man with dependent wife and four children. In the Irish situation it is necessary to make separate calculations for those receiving unemployment benefit versus unemployment assistance. In addition to the payment received, the impact of other factors, such as income-related rents for local authority tenants and means-tested entitlements to health services, can also be taken into account. For particular types of household, particularly with four or more children and in local authority housing, these illustrative replacement rates can be very high, sometimes approaching or even exceeding 100 per cent, although for single people they are usually much lower.

There are a number of difficulties with taking such 'typical' cases as representative of the situation of the unemployed at a particular time. In the UK, comparisons with information provided by actual samples of households suggest that these hypothetical calculations do not accurately represent the position of the majority of the unemployed (Atkinson and Micklewright, 1985). This is because of the great diversity in the family and other circumstances of the unemployed and the complexity of the social welfare system. Many of the unemployed do not fit neatly into one of the composition categories chosen, and many are not receiving the amounts attributed to them by the simplifying assumptions used in constructing the hypothetical cases. Thus, for example, only a minority of the unemployed are in households consisting of a man with non-working wife and children living in local authority housing and receiving full insurance-related (including pay-related) benefits or full means-tested assistance.

In looking at the changes in replacement rates over time, one can look at a number of different family types and schemes, or an average across family types and schemes can be constructed. For example, Walsh (1978) and Hughes and Walsh (1985) use such an average in their analysis of the effects of Irish social welfare support for the unemployed during the 1970s, with weights based on the number of recipients in each category or scheme at the beginning of the period. The hypothetical cases, and particularly such an average, are likely to be a more satisfactory indicator of trends in replacement rates than of the situation of most of the unemployed at a particular time. However, even here the simplifying assumptions can mislead, producing an over-statement of the impact of the introduction of pay-related benefit in 1974 on the actual payments to recipients (Nolan, 1987).

The only available evidence for Ireland on actual replacement rates for a sample of recipients has been from O'Mahony (1983). This study obtained data for a sample of those registering as unemployed at a particular labour exchange in 1982, including both social welfare receipts and previous earnings, and compared the reported replace-ment rates of different categories with hypothetical ones constructed using the usual assumptions. While the overall average hypothetical rate was close to the actual sample average, the differences between categories are not reflected very accurately (see Nolan, 1987). In addi-tion, the results suggested that previous wages for the unemployed were generally well below the average industrial wage, which is used in the hypothetical calculations, so their benefits on average must also have been lower than those attributed in the hypothetical cases (since the average replacement rate was about the same).

To be able to assess the impact of unemployment and the variation in benefit receipt and replacement rates across the unemployed, one wants to be able to look at evidence on actual social welfare receipts and to compare this with income when in work for a representative sample. The 1987 ESRI survey provides a basis on which to do this, for two distinct groups: those who were unemployed when sampled but had been in work during the past year, and those in work when sam-pled who had some experience of unemployment during the past year. For the former, in addition to detailed information on current social welfare receipts and other income, the level of previous earnings when in work was sought. For the latter, in addition to current earnings, the social welfare received when unemployed was sought. The relationship between earnings when in work and social welfare received when unemployed can therefore be analysed for each group. For the long-term unemployed, i.e. those who when sampled had been away from work for more than a year, the previous wage begins to lose relevance and was not sought. It would be possible to estimate the wage that they would have received if employed, given their age, education, etc., on the basis of the relationship between earnings and such charac-teristics for the rest of the sample. (Similarly, for those who have been employed throughout the previous year it would be possible to attribute social welfare receipts during unemployment.) It is of primary interest, though, to look at those for whom information is directly available on both earnings and social welfare receipts, so we confine our attention to those who have experienced both employment and unemployment in the previous year.

It is important to stress that one cannot meaningfully talk about 'the' replacement rate: there is no unique definition suitable for all purposes. While take-home pay in work and benefit when out of work are the central elements, items such as income from other sources (such as interest), income of other household members and work expenses (e.g. travel and child-minding) may or may not be included in the calculation. Similarly, other entitlements etc. linked to income, such as local authority rents, eligibility for free health services, free fuel, and so on, may or may not be taken into account. Furthermore, the period being considered may also be critical, since benefit entitlements may change over time and previous earnings become less relevant as a guide to prospective earnings. Nonetheless Atkinson and Micklewright argue that the figure that is most directly relevant to the incentive to seek work is the ratio of social welfare benefits to last net earnings, and it is on this we concentrate.

There were 147 people in the 1987 survey who were unemployed when sampled but had been in work in the previous year and who provided full details of their previous earnings. A significant number of these (40) were not in fact currently receiving *any* unemployment-related social welfare payment: some had applied but were waiting for payment, but the majority were aged twenty-one or under and may not have been eligible. For the remaining 107 people the average replacement rate—defined as unemployment benefit or assistance as a percentage of previous take-home pay—was 58 per cent. (If one included those not currently receiving benefit, the mean would of course be much lower, at 43 per cent.) The average for those currently in receipt is heavily influenced by the small number (15) who had been working part time and therefore have low previous earnings and very high replacement rates. Excluding these, the average for those who had been full-time employees was 53 per cent, and table 7.2 shows that there was a great deal of variation around that mean. About 45 per cent have replacement rates below 50 per cent, 28 per cent are between 50 and 70 per cent, 17 per cent are between 70 and 100 per cent, and 4 per cent have rates of over 100 per cent.

About two-thirds of the recipients are on unemployment benefit rather than unemployment assistance, which is not surprising, since

TABLE 7.2   *Replacement rates for short-term unemployed and currently*
              employed with recent unemployment spell (full-time only)

Replacement rate %	Currently unemployed %	Currently employed %
<30	21.7	17.9
30–50	22.8	33.0
50–60	16.3	14.2
60–70	16.3	15.1
70–90	14.1	16.0
90–100	4.3	1.9
>100	4.3	1.9
Total	100.0	100.0
Number of cases	92	106

they are short-term rather than long-term unemployed. Recipients of unemployment benefit had slightly higher average replacement rates than those on assistance, at 55 per cent compared with 50 per cent, because benefit payments were higher on average and there was little difference in mean wages. The individuals with particularly high replacement rates were more likely to be on benefit than assistance, and received higher amounts than average (generally because of the number of dependants involved); but the most striking feature was their low previous wage. Recipients of unemployment benefit with replacement rates above 70 per cent were getting benefits that were 15 per cent higher on average than all benefit recipients, but their last pay was only 63 per cent of the group mean. Similarly recipients of benefit with very low replacement rates, of under 30 per cent, were receiving benefits not very much lower than the rest of the group, but had mean wages well above average (134 per cent of the group mean).

Turning to those in the sample who were employed when sampled but had had a recent spell of unemployment, 203 people fall into this group in total. However, 80 report no receipt of unemployment benefit or assistance (or supplementary welfare allowance) when unemployed, the majority of these again being aged twenty-one or under. The average replacement rate for the 123 who do report receipt was 55 per cent, very similar to the mean for the short-term unemployed group. (In this case, if those who were not in receipt are included the mean falls even further, to 33 per cent.) Again a small number of part-time workers (17) report very high replacement rates. Concentrating on those in full-time employment, the mean is 51 per cent, and table

7.2 again shows the considerable variation observed around that mean. About 51 per cent of these full-time employees have rates below 50 per cent, 31 per cent are between 50 and 70 per cent, 19 per cent are between 70 and 100 per cent, and 2 per cent are over 100 per cent.

As was the case for the short-term unemployed, about two-thirds of the employed who had a spell of unemployment were receiving unemployment benefit rather than assistance. There was little difference between recipients of benefit and assistance in the average replacement rate, with the latter having both lower earnings and lower social welfare support. Variations in the level of benefit appear to play a larger part in distinguishing those on high versus low replacement rates for the currently employed group, with differences in the level of earnings less important than they were for the short-term unemployed. Such variation in the level of benefits relates primarily to the number of dependants and whether the additional pay-related benefit was received.

The similarity in the pattern of replacement rates seen for the short-term unemployed and the currently employed with recent unemployment experience provides some basis for confidence in the findings, despite the relatively small number of cases involved. They suggest that most of these people experience a substantial fall in income during unemployment. Only about 20 per cent of those with recent experience of both employment and unemployment had replacement rates of over 70 per cent, and about 6 per cent had rates of over 90 per cent. While additional factors such as the possible loss of entitlement to a medical card and the impact on local authority rents may be important for some, they do not appear likely to alter the overall pattern revealed by the comparison between earnings and social welfare receipts. The fact that it was frequently low earnings rather than high social welfare payments that produced high replacement rates also has clear implications for the living standards of the unemployed, which will be addressed when we turn in the next section from an incentives to an adequacy perspective.

Finally, the implications of the fact that some of those with high replacement rates are nonetheless in employment also merit consideration. The time factor may again be important: the impact of unemployment on income will change over time, particularly as entitlement to benefit is exhausted, so even from the point of view of a simple job search or reservation wage model the individual should take the expected evolution of the replacement rate as well as its current level into account. In addition, of course, factors other than financial incentives play a part in attitudes to work and to any specific job.

7.3 UNEMPLOYMENT AND HOUSEHOLD POVERTY

We now move from the impact of unemployment on individual incomes to its effects on the income and living standards of the household, and thus on household poverty. In chapter 5, households with an unemployed head were seen to have a particularly high risk of being in poverty, whether this was measured using relative income poverty lines or income plus direct indicators of basic deprivation. With about 60 per cent of the households headed by an unemployed person falling below half average equivalent income, such households faced a higher risk of income poverty than any other labour force status category. When combined low income and basic deprivation criteria were applied, it was seen that households headed by an unemployed person remained the largest group. It was also noted that higher proportions were below the income poverty lines where the head of the household was receiving unemployment assistance than where unemployment benefit was being received.

We now explore the situation of such households in more detail, with the key findings presented in table 7.3. With the 60 per cent income line the risk for households with an unemployed head reaches 74 per cent, while 54 per cent are both below that income line and experiencing basic deprivation (as defined in chapter 4). The higher risk facing those receiving unemployment assistance rather than unemployment benefit persists across the income lines and when the combined income and deprivation criteria are used. About 64 per cent of households with an unemployed head receiving unemployment benefit are below the 60 per cent line, compared with 81 per cent of those receiving unemployment assistance. The gap is wider when focusing on the combined income and deprivation criteria, with 40 per cent of the households with an unemployed head receiving unemployment benefit compared with 65 per cent of those receiving unemployment assistance both below the 60 per cent line and experiencing basic deprivation. This relates partly to the level of the payment received under the two schemes: unemployment benefit levels (flat rate) were 15 to 25 per cent higher than short-term unemployment assistance and 7 to 15 per cent higher than long-term unemployment assistance in 1987. Also, those receiving them have higher levels of savings, which will have helped to cushion the effects of unemployment on living standards so far.

The main reason why some of the households with an unemployed head are not below the relative income poverty lines is the presence of other earners in the household. About 70 per cent of households with

TABLE 7.3   *Risk of poverty for households with an unemployed head*

Type of household	50% income line %	60% income line %	60% line + basic deprivation %	Percentage of all unemployed heads
All with unemployed head	59.6	74.0	54.2	100.0
Head in receipt of UB	46.1	63.6	39.5	34.2
Head in receipt of UA	70.0	80.7	64.9	56.9
Head on UB & no-one working	63.3	84.9	55.8	23.8
Head on UA & no-one working	86.7	95.6	79.3	44.0
Head on UA, no-one working, children	87.8	98.6	85.2	36.1

UB: unemployment benefit; UA: unemployment assistance.

an unemployed head receiving unemployment benefit and yet above the 60 per cent line contain someone at work, most often the spouse, and the figure for recipients of unemployment assistance is even higher, at 82 per cent. Focusing on those who are below the line, one difference between those who are experiencing basic deprivation and those who are not is that a considerably higher proportion of the latter do not contain children. In terms of the level of savings, those who are below the line and experiencing deprivation have virtually no savings to draw on, while even those who are below the line on unemployment assistance but are avoiding basic deprivation still have £200–300 on average—much less than most households where the head is at work or retired, or than unemployment benefit recipients on average, but still some indication that the household has not yet totally exhausted its resources.

It is worth noting just how high the risk of poverty is for households with an unemployed head and no-one at work. In such a situation, table 7.3 shows that where the head is receiving unemployment benefit, 85 per cent are below the 60 per cent line and 56 per cent are also experiencing basic deprivation. Again, where the household is relying on unemployment assistance the risk is higher, with 96 per cent below the 60 per cent line and almost 80 per cent also experiencing basic deprivation. If in addition there are children in the household, the risk of being below the 60 per cent line reaches almost 100 per cent, and 85 per cent are also experiencing basic deprivation.

While significant numbers of households with an unemployed head are not below the income poverty lines, therefore, this is generally because there are other sources of income. Where the household is relying on unemployment assistance, and particularly where there are children, the risk of not only being below the 60 per cent line but also of experiencing basic deprivation is extremely high indeed.

So far we have focused on unemployment of the head of the household. Just under half the unemployed in the ESRI sample were household heads, and it is also of interest to look at the situation of the 'non-household-heads'. Unsurprisingly, the impact on the household of unemployment of someone other than the head is much less, so the risk of household poverty is much lower. Only 39 per cent of the unemployed who are not household heads are in households below the 60 per cent income poverty line, and 24 per cent are in households meeting both the income and deprivation criteria. Here once again it is the presence of other earners or income sources that plays the major role in determining the household's income level. This means that when all the unemployed in the sample, whether household heads or not, are considered, 55 per cent are in households below the 60 per cent income line and 37 per cent are in households below that line and experiencing basic deprivation.

The importance of a dynamic perspective can be illustrated by examining how these risks vary depending on the total amount of time the person spent in unemployment in the past year. Table 7.4 shows poverty risks for both the currently unemployed by length of unemployment in the year (not all of which need have been in the current spell) and, for comparative purposes, those who are currently working as employees and did or did not have some unemployment in the year. We see that current employees who had no unemployment face a very low risk. Employees who did have some unemployment face a higher risk, but still very much lower than the currently unemployed. Among the latter, though, there is a considerable difference between those who spent some of the year in work and those who have been out of work all year. Particularly focusing on the combined income and deprivation criteria, the risk rises steadily from 23 per cent for the unemployed with 26 weeks or less and 33 per cent for those with 27 to 51 weeks to 47 per cent of the 'fully unemployed'.

Thus the more unemployment has been experienced in the previous year, the higher the risk of current basic deprivation because of lack of resources. This may primarily reflect the progressive run-down of savings and/or accumulation of debt as unemployment experience

TABLE 7.4   *Risk of poverty for those experiencing or not experiencing*
unemployment in previous year

Type of individual	Below 50% income line	Below 60% income line	Below 60% line + basic deprivation	Percentage of all employees plus
	%	%	%	unemployed
Employee with no unemployment	2.6	7.5	3.4	74.8
Employee with some unemployment	6.1	14.9	8.0	8.0
Unemployed <27 weeks in year	30.5	44.3	22.6	2.7
Unemployed 27–51 weeks in year	32.1	44.6	32.9	3.0
Unemployed all year	48.2	65.4	46.6	11.5

lengthens, so that those who have been unemployed all year have little or no other resources to draw on, as can be seen in the level of bank and building society deposits reported by households. Controlling for effect of age on savings by focusing on those aged 35 to 54, employees with no unemployment experience in the year were in households with average deposits of £2,150, whereas employees with some unemployment had £1,180. Among the currently unemployed with 26 weeks' unemployment or less, average savings were £1,050; for those who had been unemployed for 27 to 51 weeks the average was only £510, and for those unemployed all year it was even lower, at £258. As would be expected, this relationship between risk and extent of unemployment is repeated but at higher risk levels if one focuses on household heads.

It is also interesting to take a longer-term perspective, using the information obtained in the survey on the number of years respondents spent in unemployment since first entering the labour force. Looking at the currently unemployed, table 7.5 shows that having controlled for length of unemployment in the past year, the risk of *current* poverty rises with the extent of career unemployment experienced. Those currently unemployed but with no more than two years' unemployment in their career face considerably lower risks than those with more than two years. Between 60 and 70 per cent of those who have been unemployed for over half the current year and for more than two years in their careers are below the 60 per cent income line, and it is also remarkable that a very high proportion of these are also experiencing basic deprivation.

TABLE 7.5   *Risk of poverty for currently unemployed, categorised by unemployment in career*

Annual & career unemployment	Below 50% income	Below 60% income	Below 60% line + basic deprivation	Percentage of all unemployed	Percentage aged <25
	%	%	%		
≤26 weeks in year, ≤2 years in career	28.1	42.4	20.3	13.1	39.1
≤26 weeks in year, >2 years in career	45.2	55.2	39.0	3.1	15.6
27–51 weeks in year, ≤2 years in career	23.8	38.1	22.5	12.0	54.0
27–51 weeks in year, >2 years in career	51.3	59.5	56.5	5.3	6.7
52 weeks in year, ≤2 years in career	37.9	54.9	35.1	22.9	37.1
52 weeks in year, >2 years in career	53.6	70.9	52.6	43.6	13.5

There are differences across the groups shown in age profile and the position of the individual in the household, with those having two years or less in unemployment being more likely to be aged under twenty-five and less likely to be heads of households than the other groups. Those among the currently unemployed who are most in need are seen to be not simply those who have been unemployed for all the current year but rather those with substantial career unemployment experience, even if they have spent some of the past year in work, who face the highest risk of current household poverty. This is partly because those among the current unemployed who have substantial unemployment experience are more likely to be household heads with dependent families. It also reflects the impact of sustained previous unemployment on the household's resources *other than* current income. Clearly, a very high proportion of those with more than two years' unemployment experience are entirely reliant on current income, per-haps being eaten into by debt repayments, and find it exceptionally difficult to avoid basic deprivation.

It is also worth mentioning the relatively high risk of current poverty facing those who, although currently employed, have experienced more than two years' unemployment in their careers. Among employees who had no unemployment in the past year but had more than two years in their career, the risk of being below the 60 per cent line and experiencing basic deprivation is a not insignificant 12 per cent. Where the person has had more than two years of unemployment in his or her career and has spent much of the past year out of work, the risk is close to 30 per cent. This points to the impact of pervasive labour market disadvantage throughout the career for certain groups, making itself felt first through the likelihood that those experiencing significant unemployment will be concentrated in low-wage jobs when employed. (The strength of this relationship is taken up in the next chapter.)

Secondly, spells in unemployment will themselves have a detrimental effect on the household's savings and ability to accumulate household durables and other assets. This means that, even when receiving employment income, the household may not be able to avoid basic forms of deprivation because it has no additional resources or has a carry-over of debt.

7.4 RECENT DEVELOPMENTS AND PROSPECTS FOR UNEMPLOYMENT AND THE LONG-TERM UNEMPLOYED

In the period since the ESRI survey was carried out in 1987, the numbers unemployed first fell and then rose again, as shown in table 7.6. While the numbers at work rose, very substantial emigration in 1988, 1989 and 1990 played as large a part in the decline in unemployment in those years. With net emigration virtually ceasing in 1991, the numbers unemployed soared and by 1992 were back to their 1987 levels. (These figures are based on the labour force survey: the numbers on the live register by 1992 were substantially higher than in 1987.) Those out of work for more than a year still constitute about 42 per cent of the registered unemployed, and a more detailed breakdown now published shows that about one-fifth, or 50,000 people, have been unemployed for three years or more.

The prospects for a substantial fall in the numbers unemployed, and particularly in long-term unemployment, over the next five years or so do not appear to be good. The projections to 1996 carried out on the basis of the ESRI's medium-term macro-economic model in 1991 suggested that even with significant growth in total employment, the unemployment rate would still be as high as 16 per cent in 1996 (Bradley et al., 1991). This is because rapid growth in the labour force will continue, and net emigration is expected to be limited by the depressed state of other economies and of the British labour market in particular.

TABLE 7.6   *Annual numbers at work and unemployed and net migration,*
1987–92

	At work (’000)	Unemployed (’000)	Labour force (’000)	Net external migration (’000)
1987	1,080	232	1,312	–27
1988	1,091	219	1,310	–32
1989	1,090	202	1,292	–46
1990	1,126	179	1,305	–31
1991	1,125	208	1,334	–1
1992	1,125	225	1,350	+2

Source: Central Statistics Office (1988, 1991).

Since that forecast was prepared, unemployment has in fact been higher than expected, providing no grounds for optimism. Looking beyond 1996, the model-based analysis suggested that, given present policies and relationships and with relatively benign world growth, even a modest decline in the unemployment rate to 14 per cent by the year 2000 was likely only in the context of a resumption of high levels of emigration.

In such an environment, the long-term unemployed in particular face a bleak future, given the handicaps they face in trying to find employment. We have seen that the long-term unemployed have low levels of educational attainment. In addition, a specially designed survey of employers on their attitudes to the long-term unemployed carried out by the ESRI has shown the obstacles faced by the long-term unemployed in competing for jobs (Whelan et al., 1992). Educational qualifications were seen as important even when recruiting for semi-skilled or unskilled manual jobs; but motivation and reliability were even more important, and a significant proportion of employers felt that the long-term unemployed lack motivation and have bad work habits. The factors seen as most likely to encourage firms to hire long-term unemployed (apart from an increase in business) were recent training or work experience, or evidence of improved skills and motivation. It is worth mentioning that very few employers felt that a willingness on the part of the long-term unemployed to work for lower wages would have much effect on recruitment.

7.5 CONCLUSIONS

Unemployment is now the dominant influence on poverty in Ireland. In this chapter we have focused on those affected by unemployment and on its impact on individual and household incomes and living standards. The unemployed in the 1987 survey were seen to have particularly low levels of educational qualifications: 60 per cent of those unemployed for more than a year had not attained the Intermediate or Group Certificate, and most of those had only primary education. The relatively small number of people who had spent more than five years unemployed during their careers were even more likely to have low levels of education and accounted for half of all the years of unemployment experienced by those currently in the labour force.

Incomes and living standards when unemployed, compared with those attainable when in work, are of central importance both to the adequacy of social welfare support levels and to incentives to work rather than become or stay unemployed. The extensive discussion on this topic has generally been on the basis of hypothetical illustrative cases or anecdotal evidence rather than analysis of representative samples. Comparing reported income when in work with benefits when unemployed, for those in the 1987 sample who had experienced both employment and unemployment in the past year, it was found that most people experienced a substantial fall in income during unemployment. Where benefit levels were close to reported earnings, this was frequently because these earnings were well below average, rather than because benefits were substantially above average.

A high proportion of households with an unemployed head were found to be below relative income poverty lines or a combined income plus basic deprivation standard. Households where the head is in work but that are not below the poverty lines generally have some other member at work. The risk of poverty for household heads was higher when unemployment assistance rather than unemployment benefit was being received. Households headed by someone on unemployment assistance and with no-one else at work had a very high probability of being in poverty: almost 80 per cent were below the 60 per cent relative income line and experiencing basic deprivation. On the other hand, only a minority of the unemployed who are not household heads were in poor households. The probability of being in poverty was seen to be related to the duration of unemployment in the previous twelve months and the extent of unemployment experienced over one's career.

The prospects for a substantial fall in unemployment over the next five years or so, from current very high levels, do not appear to be good. In such an environment, the long-term unemployed face a particularly bleak future, with low levels of education and skills and often also being perceived by employers as unreliable and lacking in motivation. The implications for anti-poverty policy, that special measures to assist the long-term unemployed should be accorded priority, are taken up in later chapters.

8 Low Pay and Poverty

BRIAN NOLAN

It has been shown in previous chapters that unemployment is the most important cause of poverty in Ireland. Nonetheless, it was seen in chapter 5 that a significant proportion of the households falling below relative-income poverty lines, or below combined income and deprivation criteria, are headed by someone currently working as an employee. In this chapter we explore the links between employee pay, in particular low pay, and poverty. This first involves an analysis of the extent of low pay, using the types of benchmark commonly applied elsewhere to define what constitutes 'low' in this context. The characteristics of those falling below these pay thresholds are then described, and the extent to which they are concentrated in particular occupations or industries is examined. Focusing on the relationship between low pay and poverty, the overlap between the two is shown to be rather weaker than is often assumed. Most low-paid individuals are not in poor households, and a substantial proportion of the employees heading poor households are not low-paid. Household size and composition and the presence or otherwise of other income earners is shown to be central to understanding how this comes about.

The implications for the design of policy, and particularly the likely effectiveness of a minimum wage strategy, for combating poverty among the 'working poor' are considered. Finally, the analysis of the position of the low-paid at a point in time is extended to an examination of the links between low pay and persistent labour market disadvantage over time.

The chapter is organised as follows. Section 8.1 deals with the extent and nature of low pay. Section 8.2 looks at the extent to which the low-paid are in poor households. This is then compared with the extent to which poor households are headed by an employee or have significant income from employment. The roles of the household head's

116

earnings, income of other members and household composition are disentangled, and the links between low pay and poverty are spelt out. Section 8.3 looks at the implications for the impact of a minimum wage on poverty. Section 8.4 looks at the links between low pay and labour market disadvantage over the career, while section 8.5 summarises the key findings.

8.1 LOW PAY IN IRELAND

What is 'low pay', and how is it to be measured? Low pay is conventionally measured in terms of the gross earnings of the employee compared with benchmarks derived either from the distribution of earnings itself, i.e. relative to others' earnings, or from external points of comparison, such as social welfare rates. Examples of benchmarks of the first kind would be the bottom decile cut-off (i.e. the earnings level below which 10 per cent of employees fall) or two-thirds of the median (i.e. two-thirds of the level above or below which half the employees fall), where the point of reference is generally the distribution of earnings of full-time adult earners, often male earners only.

Benchmarks of the second kind could be derived from the rate of payment of, for example, supplementary welfare allowance for a couple with two dependent children. Both approaches have been used in previous research on low pay in Ireland (e.g. Blackwell, 1986; McMahon, 1987) and elsewhere, though most studies for other countries rely on the distribution-based benchmarks. Although previous Irish studies have focused on weekly earnings, it is more usual elsewhere to look at hourly earnings, which allows the effects of hours worked per week and of hourly earnings on weekly earnings to be distinguished. It must be emphasised, then, that the choice of method for the construction of a low-pay threshold is necessarily rather arbitrary.

The data used to examine the extent of low pay and its relationship with poverty is once again that obtained in the 1987 Economic and Social Research Institute survey. The survey, described in detail in earlier chapters, included about 2,800 individuals currently working as employees, and sought detailed information on their earnings as well as their age, sex, occupation, industry, and education. Comparisons with information available from other sources on the age, sex, occupation and industry of employees suggest that the sample represents employees in the population well (Nolan, 1993a). Unlike the data previously available for the study of low pay, which was limited to particular sectors of industry, the ESRI survey includes employees across all sectors. The fact that it is a household survey rather than a survey of employees also means that it provides a suitable basis for analysis of the relationship between the earnings of employees and the situation of the households in which they live.

The distribution of weekly earnings among employees in the ESRI sample can be compared with corresponding figures for Great Britain and for Northern Ireland, which show that for full-time male adult employees the three distributions are remarkably similar in shape. Focusing on weekly earnings of all full-time employees, the extent of low pay in Ireland can be compared with other EC countries using the results of a study applying distribution-based thresholds calculated with a common methodology (Centre d'Études des Revenus et des Coûtes, 1991). This shows that the proportion below, for example, 60 per cent of median earnings in Ireland was greater than in the Netherlands, Belgium, Italy, Germany, or France, and slightly lower than in Spain and the UK.

Here we want to cover both full-time and part-time employees, so the focus is on hourly earnings. Given that quite different low-pay thresholds could be produced depending on the precise derivation method chosen, we use two thresholds, a 'higher' and a 'lower' one, which allows the sensitivity of the results to the threshold chosen to be assessed. Calculating usual hourly earnings for employees in the sample, the average was £4.90 and the median was £4.30 (in 1987 terms). We apply two low-pay thresholds, namely £2.50 and £3.25 per hour, corresponding to £100 and £130 per week, respectively, for a person working forty hours per week (all in 1987 terms). This range encompasses the low-pay benchmarks that would be produced by most of the commonly used distributional or social welfare-based approaches. About 27 per cent of employees earned less than the higher threshold, and 15 per cent earned less than the lower one.

The risk of earning below these hourly thresholds was considerably higher for part-time than for full-time employees, and for women than for men; but the most pronounced relationship is with age. Over 50 per cent of those below the lower threshold and 59 per cent of those below the higher one were aged under twenty-five, and this meant that 36 per cent of the employees aged under twenty-five earned less than £2.50 while fully 57 per cent earned less than £3.25.

Interestingly, for these 'young' workers there was little difference between men and women in the risk of being low-paid. For older employees, though, there was a very substantial difference, so that overall the percentage of women below the thresholds was twice as high as the percentage of men (for example, 40 per cent of women versus 20 per cent of men were below the higher threshold). Most of those working part-time are women, and more part-timers are low-paid in hourly terms, but this in fact accounts for little of the gap. Most female employees work full time, and they face a much higher risk of being low-paid than men (39 per cent of full-time female employees versus 19 per cent of full-time male employees are below £3.25 per hour). It is worth noting, though, that because women only account for a minority of employees, almost half the low-paid are men.

Looking at occupation, men earning below the thresholds are predominantly labourers or unskilled workers or employed in production, whereas women are predominantly service workers, clerical workers, or shop assistants. In terms of industrial sector, low-paid men are spread over sectors, but the greatest concentrations are in agriculture, building and construction, production, retailing, and personal services. Low-paid women are much more concentrated in specific sectors, with retailing and personal services accounting for well over half the women earning below the lower threshold. Part-time low-paid employees, mostly being women, are also heavily concentrated in these sectors.

What is also striking about the low-paid is the low levels of educational attainment among those aged twenty-five or over. For those aged between thirty-five and forty-four, for example, two-thirds of those earning less than £3.25 per hour have no second-level qualification, twice the figure for those earning above that threshold.

The relationship between marital status and low pay is also of interest. As is the case for all employees, few of the low-paid aged under twenty-five are married. For those aged twenty-five or over, a majority of the low-paid, whether male or female, are married: among full-time employees the low-paid are less likely to be married than those earning above the thresholds, whereas part-timers are mostly married women.

Regression analysis confirms that age and educational attainment are the crucial factors affecting the likelihood of an employee being low-paid, with sex and marital status also having substantial effects. Such analysis suggests, for example, that a single man aged thirty-five who had not attained Group or Intermediate Certificate qualifications had a one-in-three chance of earning less than £3.25 per hour, whereas a woman with the same age and education had a one-in-two chance. Higher levels of educational attainment dramatically reduced the probability of being low-paid.

Finally, bringing together age, sex, and marital status, it is worth noting that 55 per cent of those falling below the £3.25 hourly earnings threshold are aged under twenty-five, 13 per cent are single and aged twenty-five or over, 16 per cent are married women aged over twenty-five, and only 15 per cent are married men aged twenty-five or over. The fact that most low-paid people are either young, single or married women has major implications for the relationship between low pay and household poverty, as explored in the next section.

8.2 LOW PAY AND POVERTY

If those employees falling below the 'lower' or 'higher' hourly earnings thresholds are taken to be the low-paid, to what extent do low pay and household poverty overlap? To examine the relationship between earnings and poverty, we must first specify how 'the poor' are to be defined and measured.

We first use the relative-income poverty lines calculated as 40, 50 and 60 per cent of mean household equivalent income in the sample, whose construction has been described in detail in chapter 3. The equivalence scales employed are those (broadly) implicit in the social welfare system's rates of support in 1987: where the household head is 1, each extra adult is 0.66 and each child is 0.33. The alternative scales discussed in chapter 3 were also tried but made little difference to the results presented here. The recipient unit used is primarily the household, but the narrower nuclear family or tax unit was also employed; and where the results appear to be affected significantly by the choice of unit, this will be highlighted.

Using these relative-income poverty lines to distinguish 'poor' households, the degree of overlap between low pay and poverty is seen to be quite limited. Only about 2–3 per cent of low-paid employees are in households below the 40 per cent relative line, about 9 per cent are below the 50 per cent line, and about 20 per cent are below the 60 per cent line, whether the £2.50 or £3.25 figure is used as the low-pay threshold. Using the combined income and deprivation criteria described in chapter 4 to distinguish 'poor' households leads to very much the same result.

A limited overlap between low pay and poverty is in fact a common finding in British and American studies. For example, Layard, Piachaud and Stewart (1978) and Bazen (1988) found that between 10 and 22 per cent of low-paid workers were in families below conventionally used poverty lines in the UK, while Burkhauser and Finnegan (1989) report about 8–18 per cent for the United States. The precise extent of the overlap depends on the way in which low pay and poverty are measured (which differs across these studies), but the broad message is consistent with our findings for Ireland.

If the low-paid are not predominantly in households below the relative income lines, where are they located in terms of household income? Table 8.1 shows that over 60 per cent of the employees earning less than £3.25 per hour are in households in the top half of the equivalent income distribution. Though the low-paid are more likely to be towards the bottom of the distribution than are employees taken as a group, only about 20 per cent (compared with 9 per cent of all employees) are in the bottom 30 per cent of the distribution. Even if one uses the narrower recipient unit of a single adult or a couple with dependent children, if any, the proportion of low-paid employees in families or tax units below relative income poverty lines is little different from the pattern already described for households.

TABLE 8.1 *Low-paid employees in household equivalent income distribution*

Equivalent income decile	Percentage of low-paid employees (<£3.25/hour)	Percentage of all employees
Bottom	3.1	1.1
2	9.0	3.6
3	7.4	3.9
4	5.7	4.6
5	11.9	8.8
6	14.2	11.2
7	15.2	14.5
8	16.0	15.8
9	12.1	17.5
Top	5.3	19.0

Most low-paid employees are not in 'poor' households, for two main reasons. The first is that the take-home pay produced by gross weekly earnings of £100 or £130 per week, corresponding to the hourly thresholds for a person working forty hours per week, will be substantially higher than the relative poverty lines for a single adult, for whom even the 60 per cent relative line was only £48. For a couple the poverty line was about £80; but such a household may not be below the poverty lines even if relying entirely on the earnings of a

Poverty and Policy in Ireland

low-paid individual. The second reason is that many households containing a low-paid person are not depending on his or her earnings as the main income source. Many of the low-paid are young adults living in the parental home, or married women, and the household generally has other earners or other income sources.

Because the size of the family is taken into account in the level of the poverty line, for households with dependent children and relying on the earnings of a low-paid employee the situation can be quite different. Indeed, earnings above the low-pay thresholds may not be sufficient to keep a large family above the poverty line if that is the only income source. Family size and the extent to which the employee's earnings are the main or sole source of income are thus central to understanding the relationship between low pay and poverty. What distinguishes the minority of low-paid employees who are in poor households is not that they have lower earnings than the majority of low-paid employees: rather it is the extent to which the household depends on their earnings, and the number of children in the family who must be supported. In particular, where the low-paid employee is the household head, usually a married man, the probability that the household is below the poverty line is substantially increased.

So far we have concentrated on the position of the employees themselves, but it is also interesting to take a household perspective and to ask how important earnings are, and low pay in particular, for poor households. Here we may refer back to the analysis in chapter 3 of the composition of households below the relative-income poverty lines classified by the labour force status of the household head. This showed that very few of the households below the 40 per cent line, about 10 per cent of those below half mean income and about 15 per cent of those below the 60 per cent line are headed by an employee—the precise figure depended on the equivalence scale chosen. (Unsurprisingly, the risk of being in poverty was also seen to be much lower for households headed by an employee than for other households: only 4 per cent of these households are below half mean income and 11 per cent are below the 60 per cent line.)

Focusing on the household head could understate the importance of earnings if other members are employees. In fact about 14 per cent of households below half mean income and 20 per cent of those below the 60 per cent line contain an employee (whether the head of the household or not). Even at the highest income poverty line, then, only one-fifth of households below the line are receiving employee earnings. Using the family rather than the household as the recipient unit does not significantly increase the importance of earnings from employment for those below relative income lines. The low-income population is dominated by households relying primarily on social welfare transfers or income from self-employment, mostly farming, rather than employees' earnings.

Since income from self-employment is difficult to measure accurately in household surveys, and is more variable from year to year than other income sources, so that those relying on it may tend to smooth consumption from one year to another, focusing on current income might give a misleading picture of the living standards of households relying on income from different sources. Comparisons simply on the basis of current disposable income could then underestimate the importance among the poor of households relying on employee earnings. The more general conceptual and analytical issues relating to the measurement of poverty using income alone, given the importance not just of current income but of wider resources and experiences over a longer period in determining current living standards, were discussed in detail in chapter 4. That chapter looked at the composition of households that are both below relative income lines and experiencing deprivation on one or more of what were identified there as basic deprivation indicators. This showed that farm households do make up a considerably smaller proportion of those experiencing basic deprivation and below income lines than of those simply below the income lines. The groups that are now a more substantial proportion of 'the poor', however, are mainly households headed by a person who is ill or engaged in home duties. Households headed by an employee do not increase much in significance, accounting for only about 12 per cent of households meeting the joint income and deprivation criteria (with the 60 per cent income line).

Likewise, broadening the focus beyond the head of the household, only 18 per cent of households below the 60 per cent income line and experiencing basic deprivation contain an employee. (Even using a higher income line, 70 per cent of mean equivalent household income, with the deprivation criterion does not alter this pattern.) Whether current income or income plus deprivation is used in measuring poverty, therefore, the 'working poor' receiving or relying on income from employment constitute at most about 15 to 20 per cent of 'the poor'. This is not to devalue the importance of the problem, reflecting rather the scale of poverty related to other factors in the Irish situation—in particular unemployment. The 'working poor' still make up a sizable group, accounting for up to perhaps 4–5 per cent of the population.

It is also worth noting that some policies aimed at assisting the 'working poor' would also help others, such as the unemployed, either directly or by reducing poverty and unemployment 'traps'. This discussion is, however, necessary to set the 'working poor' within the broader context of the overall profile of the causes of poverty.

How does it come about that some households with an employed head or receiving other earnings are at relatively low income levels, and how important is low pay per se in bringing this about? While we saw that 20 per cent of households below the 60 per cent income line contained an employee, only about 55 per cent of these in fact contain a low-paid employee. Similarly, while only 8 per cent of the employees in the sample are in households below the 60 per cent relative line, about 60 per cent of these employees are themselves low-paid. This pattern is not altered by using the combined income and deprivation criteria described above rather than purely income poverty lines, nor by the use of the family or tax unit rather than the household.

Concentrating on households below the 60 per cent income line that contain an employee, the role of low pay and family size is explored in more detail in table 8.2. We see that 85 per cent of these households have children, and more than three-quarters have two or more children. While 45 per cent do not contain a low-paid person, 20 per cent have a low-paid earner who is neither head of the household nor the spouse, 11 per cent have a low-paid spouse of the head, and only 23 per cent have a low-paid head.

For many of these households containing an employee, he or she—often a young person still in the parental household—is not central to the economic status of the household. It may then be preferable to concentrate on the households headed by an employee, constituting 63 per cent of all poor households with an employee. Table 8.2 (B) shows the same cross-classification for this smaller group, and we see that an even higher percentage contain children—87 per cent have two or more children. By contrast, only 40 per cent of these households contain a low-paid employee, in most cases the household head, and most of those households also have two or more children.

The role played by child dependants is illustrated by the fact that 74 per cent of the employee-headed households below the 60 per cent poverty line would be above it if they did not contain children. Only a small minority of poor households with or headed by an employee are poor because of low pay alone. However, the need to support children is not the entire story: 10 per cent of poor households headed by an employee have no children, and 24 per cent would still be below the poverty line even if there were no children.

TABLE 8.2 *The 'working poor': low pay and child dependants*

	No children %	1 child %	2 children %	3 or more children %	All %
(A) Households below 60% income poverty line that contain an employee					
Low-paid head	4.5	0.7	7.7	10.3	23.2
Low-paid spouse	0.5	2.2	2.0	6.2	10.9
Low-paid—other	3.8	4.4	3.8	7.8	19.8
No low-paid	5.8	1.3	6.5	32.5	46.1
All	14.6	8.6	20.0	56.7	100.0
(B) Households below 60% line with an employee head					
Low-paid head	7.0	1.1	12.1	16.2	36.5
Low-paid spouse	—	—	—	1.8	1.8
Low-paid—other	—	—	0.5	1.1	1.6
No low-paid	2.7	1.8	6.6	49.1	60.1
All	9.7	2.9	19.3	68.1	100.0

8.3 LOW PAY, POVERTY, AND THE MINIMUM WAGE

While consideration of policies to combat poverty is for the most part left to the final parts of this book, it is worth drawing out the implications of the findings of this chapter for the likely effectiveness of focusing on low pay per se and aiming to eliminate it via a national minimum wage. Ireland at present does not have a national minimum wage, with only certain sectors or occupations covered by a legal minimum set by joint labour committees. The introduction of a national minimum wage has been advocated by, among others, the Irish Congress of Trade Unions, and most of the debate about this proposal has focused on the possible effects on employment. This has also been the dominant theme both in the heated debates and the academic research elsewhere on the impact of minimum wages, and is clearly a crucial issue. However, it is also worth highlighting the implications of the limited overlap between low pay and poverty for the role a minimum wage could play in an anti-poverty strategy, even if there were no disemployment effects.

To explore these implications, a simulation exercise was carried out with the 1987 sample, which abstracted from possible employment effects and looked simply at the 'first-round' impact a minimum wage would have on poor households. (The results of similar exercises for the UK have been presented by Johnson and Stark (1991) and Sutherland (1991).) A simple formulation for the national minimum wage is assumed, whereby all employees aged twenty-one or over are brought up to the higher threshold of £3.25 per hour, with lower minimums for younger workers (for example £2.25 for eighteen-year olds). The net addition to take-home pay that would result is then estimated for each person.

Table 8.3 shows the distribution of the 'gainers' and gains by household equivalent disposable income decile. The top half of the distribution contains 61 per cent of the employees affected, and they receive 56 per cent of the total gains. This directly reflects the distribution of low-paid employees, and is, on that basis, hardly surprising. A similar distributive pattern, with much of the gain from a minimum wage going to the middle and upper parts of the distribution, is shown in the UK analyses by Johnson and Stark (1991) and Sutherland (1991). (It is worth pointing out, as Sutherland does for the UK, that since women workers are more likely to be low-paid, they would also receive a substantial proportion of the 'gains' from a minimum wage— although others have suggested that disemployment effects would also be likely to be concentrated among women and younger workers.)

TABLE 8.3 *Distribution of gains from a national minimum wage*

Equivalent income decile	Percentage of gainers	Average gain (£/week)	Percentage of total gains
Bottom	3.3	32.7	4.8
2	8.9	23.0	9.0
3	8.3	26.8	9.9
4	6.8	24.8	7.5
5	11.3	26.3	13.1
6	15.4	20.2	13.7
7	14.3	20.3	12.8
8	14.8	22.3	14.5
9	11.3	19.5	9.7
Top	5.6	20.4	5.0

However, while the benefits from the 'simulated' national minimum wage in the exercise appear poorly targeted, it could still be having a significant effect on those below the poverty line: it could be an effective if not an efficient strategy for assisting the working poor. In fact the results show that 27 per cent of households below the 60 per cent income line and containing an employee, and 24 per cent of those below the line and headed by an employee, would be lifted above that line by the additional income associated with the minimum wage. A further substantial proportion are helped, though not by enough to bring them above the poverty line.

In all, then, about 50 per cent of all poor households with an employee, and almost 40 per cent of those headed by an employee, benefit from the first-round effects of a national minimum wage. The contribution that an effective strategy for combating low pay could make is not to be ignored, then, but it would not in itself suffice as a strategy to assist the 'working poor'. Tax and transfer policy therefore have to be directed towards assisting this group. Three main elements of tax and transfer policy may be identified: universal child-related transfers (child benefit), family allowances conditional on employment (family income supplement), and favourable treatment for families with children in the income tax system. The effectiveness and efficiency of these strategies are assessed in chapters 15 and 16.

8.4 LOW PAY AND THE PERSISTENCE OF DISADVANTAGE

So far we have been concentrating on the position of those who are low-paid at a particular time, and we have seen the rather limited extent to which low pay is directly responsible for producing household poverty. However, it is also important to consider the relationship between low pay and poverty over time to get a more complete picture of the implications of low pay. As Atkinson (1973) pointed out, low pay may be an indirect as well as a direct cause of poverty. For example, someone working in a low-paid job for much of his or her working life will be less likely to have accumulated assets and pension rights by the time they retire than those in well-paid employment, and may therefore have a higher probability of being poor at that stage. Further, low pay may in some cases be part of a more extended pattern of labour market advantage, with spells of low-paid work alternating with spells of unemployment or illness. Where this is the case, the individual may also fail to build up full entitlement to insurance-based benefits, having to rely on means-tested social assistance when out of work and perhaps also in retirement, with an increased risk of poverty.

It is possible to assess the strength of these links between low pay and other aspects of labour market disadvantage with information in the ESRI survey on career histories, pension entitlements, and fringe benefits. The data on labour force histories has been discussed in previous chapters, and shows that within each age group, those who are currently in low-paid employment have indeed experienced more years of both unemployment and illness since leaving full-time education than other employees. For example, in the 35–44 age group those below the higher earnings threshold had on average spent one year in unemployment and one year out of work through illness, compared with half that time for employees above the threshold. The low-paid had also spent more of the previous year out of work on average.

Information on whether employees receive a range of fringe benefits shows that the low-paid are much less likely to be getting benefits such as free or subsidised health insurance, a subsidised loan, or subsidised life assurance, though the low-paid were as likely as others to be getting free or subsidised meals or luncheon vouchers, or help with education fees. The link between low pay and occupational pension entitlements is a good deal more pronounced. Overall, only 10 per cent of employees earning less than £3.25 per hour said they would be entitled to a pension from their work when they retired, compared with fully 65 per cent of employees earning above that threshold. The low-paid include a high proportion of younger workers and part-timers, both groups with relatively low pension coverage, but the contrast is only a little less stark for full-time older employees. For example, in the 35–44 age range only 13 per cent of full-time employees earning below the threshold, compared with 71 per cent of those above it, report entitlement to a pension.

Although the overall percentage with pension entitlement is low for young workers, the differential between the low-paid and others is also present at that stage: only 6 per cent of full-time workers aged under twenty-five and earning below £3.25 per hour are entitled to a pension, compared with 38 per cent for those above the threshold. This differential persists consistently across the age groups.

Low earnings when employed are thus likely to be highly correlated with low income for that person when retired. In tracing through the implications for the living standards of their households, the income of other members would have to be taken into account, as they have been in assessing the current situation of the low-paid.

8.5 CONCLUSIONS

Analysis of the 1987 ESRI survey in this chapter has shown that between about 15 and 25 per cent of employees would be counted as low-paid on the basis of thresholds derived in the manner commonly employed elsewhere. Over half these employees were aged under twenty-five, while women were heavily overrepresented among the low-paid aged twenty-five and over. Low levels of educational attainment were seen to be the best predictor, together with age, of the probability of being low-paid. Low pay appeared to be more prevalent in Ireland than in some other EC members, such as Belgium, the Netherlands, France, and Germany, though not the UK or Spain.

The extent of overlap between low pay and household poverty was found to be quite limited: only at most about 20 per cent of low-paid individuals were living in 'poor' households, whether poverty was measured on the basis of income or combined income and deprivation indicators. Up to about 20 per cent of 'poor' households contain an employee, with up to about 15 per cent headed by an employee, a conclusion that again holds whether relative-income poverty lines alone or in combination with life-style or deprivation indicators are used in measuring poverty status. While most employees below conventional low-pay thresholds are not in poor households, a majority of the employees in poor households are low-paid.

Most of the 'working poor'—poor households headed by or containing an employee—contain children, though the assumption that poverty affects those in work only where there are children is not entirely valid. While the first-round effects of a national minimum wage—that is, abstracting from any effects on employment—would assist up to half the 'working poor', most of the hypothetical 'gains' would go to non-poor households. Tax and benefit strategies to assist this group are required, and the alternative approaches are evaluated in part V.

In addition to the direct effects of low pay, the links between low pay and poverty over time need to be taken into account. In particular, those currently in low-paid employment had spent more time away from work in their careers because of unemployment and illness, had fewer fringe benefits and were much less likely to be entitled to a retirement pension from their present employer than other employees, taking differences in age profile into account.

9 Poverty, Social Class, Education, and Intergenerational Mobility

CHRISTOPHER T. WHELAN

Chapter 6 has analysed movements into and out of poverty from 1987 to 1989 and shown that there is some, albeit limited, mobility. However, the types of household to be found in poverty are still quite predictable. In this chapter the focus is on the longer-term structural transmission mechanisms that contribute to such predictability. In particular, attention is directed to the impact of social class and class origins on the risk of being in poverty, and the manner in which such relationships are mediated by educational qualifications and labour market experiences.

We begin by looking at the relationship in the Economic and Social Research Institute sample between current social class and poverty, and then at class background—parental social class—and social mobility. The central relationships between class, class origins and education, and then between these and labour market experiences, are analysed. Finally, there is a broader discussion of the ways in which dramatic increases in educational participation by those from the lower social classes have not eroded class inequalities in life chances and in the experience of poverty.

9.1 SOCIAL CLASS AND POVERTY

Chapter 5 provided a relatively brief treatment of the relationship between social class and poverty in the 1987 ESRI sample using the Central Statistics Office class categories. Here we provide a more comprehensive treatment of the issue, using an internationally standardised class schema developed in the Comparative Analysis of Social Mobility in Industrial Society (CASMIN) project.

This schema is operationalised through a threefold procedure. First, occupations are placed in occupational groups according to the content

130

of their jobs; second, they are given an employment status that reflects their social relationships at work (in both cases the categories and definitions used are those adopted in Britain by the Registrar-General for the analysis of official statistics); finally, a social class position is obtained for each person by cross-classifying the relevant occupational title and employment status (Marshall, 1990, 55).

The basic purpose of the class schema is to differentiate positions within labour markets and production units according to the employment relationships they entail. Employers, self-employed and employees are distinguished, but it is also recognised that employer-employee relationships are based on quite heterogeneous principles (Erikson and Goldthorpe, 1992; Evans, 1993). The classification is based on an understanding of the development of class relations within large-scale industrial capitalist organisations and the nature of control in such organisations. Employees may be differentiated by their conditions of employment, degree of occupational security, and promotion prospects.

There is a basic difference in the relationship between employers and higher-level employees and that between employers and working-class employees. The key feature of the relationship is the way in which commitment is obtained from the work force. A much greater degree of trust is reposed in higher-level, white-collar employees than in working-class members of the organisation. There is a direct link between the nature of these employees' tasks and the typical form of their conditions of employment. Such conditions can be seen to reflect the need for creating and sustaining organisational commitment. 'It is not so much that reward is being offered in return for work done but rather "compensation" and "consideration" in return for an acceptance of an obligation to discharge trust faithfully' (Goldthorpe, 1982, 169). What is central to the logic of high-trust relationships, it is suggested, is the significance of prospective rewards, as embodied in incremental salary arrangements, security, and, most particularly, career opportunities.

Combining these distinctions between types of employment status and employer-employee relationships and adding a degree of differentiation in acreage for farmers gives us a detailed fourteen-category class schema. It is particularly interesting to assess the impact of class because of recent claims that its explanatory power is waning in modern societies (R.E. Pahl, 1989).

In conducting class analysis it is necessary to decide whether the individual, the family or the household is the unit of analysis. This issue has been a matter of considerable controversy among sociologists (Dex, 1990; McRae, 1990; Breen and Whelan, 1993). In this case, since poverty is defined in household terms, we have assigned a class position to the household on the basis of the information relating to the head of household. Employing this fourteen-class schema, and measuring poverty using the combined 60 per cent relative-income line plus basic deprivation criterion, the risk of poverty by class in the ESRI sample was analysed.

An important distinction emerges between the impact of class for those aged under and over sixty-five. For the latter, variation in risk of poverty by class is modest. The success of the welfare state in sharply reducing poverty among the elderly in recent times is directly reflected in the attenuation of the class-poverty relationship. Among those under sixty-five the position is radically different, as we can see from table 9.1; and throughout this chapter the analysis concentrates on this group. The risk of poverty ranges from one per hundred among the professional and managerial groups to close to one in two among the unskilled manual group.

Looking in detail at the results, four broad groups emerge in terms of risk of poverty. The groups—cutting to some extent across the distinction between self-employed and employees—are as follows:

(1) The professional and managerial class, with a poverty risk of less than 2 per cent.
(2) The intermediate non-manual and higher petit-bourgeois group, which comprises
   (*a*) higher-grade routine white-collar workers;
   (*b*) technicians and supervisors of manual workers;
   (*c*) self-employed with employees;
   (*d*) farmers with more than fifty acres.
   Of this group 9 per cent fall below the poverty line.
(3) The upper working class and lower petit-bourgeois categories, as follows:
   (*a*) skilled manual;
   (*b*) semi-skilled manual;
   (*c*) lower-grade white-collar;
   (*d*) farmers with less than fifty acres;
   (*e*) self-employed without employees.
   For this group the risk of poverty rises to 21 per cent.
(4) The lower working class, made up of
   (*a*) unskilled manual workers;
   (*b*) agricultural workers.
   Among this group the poverty rate reaches 46 per cent.

TABLE 9.1   *Risk of poverty by class of head of household where head of household is under 65: combined 60% income and life-style line*

	Percentage poor	
Higher professional & managerial	1.0 ⎫	1.6
Lower professional & managerial	2.0 ⎭	
Higher-grade routine white-collar	8.9 ⎫	
Technicians & supervisors of manual workers	7.3	
Self-employed with employees	7.1	9.2
Farmers 100+ acres	7.6 ⎭	
Farmers 50–100 acres	14.9 ⎫	
Self-employed without employees	21.5	
Skilled manual	22.6	
Semi-skilled manual	17.9	22.7
Lower-grade white-collar	26.7	
Farmers less than 50 acres	28.4 ⎭	
Agricultural workers	38.5 ⎫	46.0
Unskilled manual	47.9 ⎭	

While our ability to predict poverty from class position is impressive, in fact, simply concentrating on this relationship fails to make sufficiently clear the extent to which poverty is a structured phenomenon. To develop such an understanding it is necessary for us to examine the extent to which class position is itself predictable.

9.2 SOCIAL CLASS, SOCIAL MOBILITY, AND POVERTY

Modern industrial societies are characterised by substantial levels of social mobility. Industrialisation affects the set of positions that are available for economic participation—the 'empty places' that people can fill—and the mechanisms by which people are recruited or allocated to places within that set of positions.

Increases in absolute mobility associated with economic development are primarily an outcome of structural change. It is possible to think of a great deal of social mobility as being forced by such change. Since 1960 the Irish class structure has changed dramatically. The numbers in the professional-managerial and skilled manual classes have grown markedly, and the number of lower middle-class workers has also increased significantly. On the other hand, the numbers in agriculture and in non-skilled manual work have declined dramatically.

Information obtained in the ESRI survey on the occupation etc. of respondents' parents now allows the extent of intergenerational mobility to be analysed in depth (see for example Whelan et al., 1992; Breen and Whelan, 1992). According to the aggregated four-class schema that we have identified, it is found that 54 per cent of household heads under sixty-five have been intergenerationally mobile, i.e. their current class is not the same as their parents' class. Such mobility is in large part a consequence of changes in the shape of class structure. Some indication of this is provided in table 9.2, where the composition of each of our four broad social classes by class origin is set out. Thus, while almost one in five of household heads under sixty-five come from lower working-class backgrounds, fewer than one in eight were currently in that class. Correspondingly, while only one in twelve originated in the professional-managerial class, one in five were currently members of that class.

Economic change, no matter how deep, may not be associated with alteration in relative advantages. It is possible that the creation of increased room 'at the top' and a contraction of places at the bottom will lead to a general shift upwards without necessarily reducing the relative advantages enjoyed by those families that enjoyed privileged positions in the old class structure. This can be illustrated by a simple example. If at point A 40 per cent of those from a professional or managerial background are themselves to be found in that class, compared with 4 per cent of the working class, while at point B the respective figures are 60 and 6 per cent, then the following points hold:

(1) More upward mobility is experienced at point B.
(2) The relative advantages enjoyed by the professional and managerial class over the working class remains unchanged, with the former enjoying a 10:1 advantage.

We could obviously look at a whole range of such comparisons. Reduction in inequality of opportunity, as opposed to increases in mobility, requires that these underlying odds move nearer to 1:1.

In fact there is general agreement that when one allows for mobility 'forced' by structural change, the underlying inequalities of opportunity have remained relatively unchanged. There is also a consensus that such inequalities are more substantial in Ireland than in other industrial societies (Hout, 1989; Erikson and Goldthorpe, 1992; Breen and Whelan, 1992). In international comparisons the most striking finding with regard to social mobility in Ireland is the extent of the barriers to entry into the professional and managerial class from the working class. These barriers are of a scale that marks out Ireland as an exceptional case (Whelan et al., 1992).

A further distinctive feature of the Irish situation is that families at the bottom of the old class hierarchy have, if anything, seen the gap between themselves and others widen as they have become primarily dependent on state income maintenance for their livelihood. The swiftness of the transformation of the class structure meant that decline in opportunities in traditional sectors was not compensated for by gradual expansion of alternative opportunities.

Class mobility can be viewed according to the relative chances of mobility available from different class origins, or according to the composition of current classes in the sense of the heterogeneity of the classes from which they are drawn. The latter is determined by changes in the class structure and the pattern of inequalities of opportunity, and is of particular interest in relation to poverty. From table 9.2 we can see that the two classes with relatively low rates of poverty have a relatively heterogeneous composition according to class origin, while the working classes, with high poverty rates, are drawn

TABLE 9.2 *Class origins of head of household by social class (percentage by column)*

	Social class				
Class origins	Professional & managerial	Intermediate non-manual & petit-bourgeois	Upper working class & lower petit-bourgeois	Lower working class	Total
Professional & managerial	27.2	7.5	3.0	0.0	8.3
Intermediate non-manual & upper petit-bourgeois	27.9	36.9	16.8	9.9	22.4
Upper working class & lower petit-bourgeois	36.1	42.0	55.8	38.5	47.0
Lower working class	8.8	13.6	24.4	51.6	22.2
Total	19.5	21.1	47.4	12.1	

predominantly from working-class origins. The proportion originating in the working class and lower petit-bourgeoisie rises from 45 per cent in the professional and managerial class to 56 per cent among the intermediate non-manual and upper petit-bourgeois class, and reaches 80 per cent for the upper working class and lower petit-bourgeoisie and 90 per cent in the case of the lower working class. Variation in the proportions coming from the lower working class is even more dramatic, rising from less than one in ten in the professional and managerial class to one in two at the bottom of the class hierarchy.

While it is now clear that poverty is predictable from class position, which is in turn strongly related to class origin, the question remains whether class origin has an independent impact on poverty once we allow for its influence on current class position. It is this question that is addressed in table 9.3. Here, for class origins, the two highest classes are combined into a 'middle-class' group and the remaining classes into a 'working-class' group. In every case except the intermediate non-manual and upper petit-bourgeoisie, those from working-class origins have substantially higher risks of poverty. Among the professional and managerial class the risk still remains very low. For the working-class groups, however, origin has a significant influence. For the upper working class and lower petit-bourgeoisie, the poverty rate rises from one in eight of those with middle-class origins to one in four of those originating in the working class. For the lower working class the corresponding figures are one in six and almost one in two.

TABLE 9.3   *Risk of poverty by class origins, controlling for social class*

	Class origins	
Social class	Middle class Percentage poor	Working class Percentage poor
Professional & managerial	0.9	2.1
Intermediate non-manual & upper petit-bourgeois	8.1	8.6
Upper working class & lower petit-bourgeois	12.1	23.9
Lower working class	16.9	48.8

In table 9.4 we set out the composition of the poor by class and class origin. Over eight out of ten of the poor have been intergenerationally stable in the working class; 50 per cent are located in the upper working class and lower petit-bourgeoisie, and 30 per cent in the lower working class. In contrast, fewer than one in twenty of the poor have been intergenerationally stable in the middle class.

TABLE 9.4 *Composition of the poor by social class and class origin*

Social class	Class origin	
	Middle class Percentage of the poor	Working class Percentage of the poor
Professional & managerial	0.5	1.0
Intermediate non-manual & upper petit-bourgeois	4.3	5.7
Upper working class & lower petit-bourgeois	6.5	51.5
Lower working class	1.0	29.3

9.3 CLASS, EDUCATION, AND POVERTY

It can of course be argued that simply demonstrating that associations exist between poverty and class position and class origins 'conflates a number of distinct processes which should be kept analytically distinct' (R.E. Pahl, 1989, 710). The process of unpacking the class-poverty relationship is begun by examining the role of education. In table 9.5 the educational profiles of each of our four broad social classes are shown. The proportion with no qualifications varies from 7 per cent in the professional and managerial classes to almost 80 per cent in the lower working class. Correspondingly, the proportion with the Leaving Certificate or third-level education rises from 2 per cent of the lower working class to 82 per cent of the professional and managerial class.

Education is of course the most important mechanism by which advantages associated with class origin are translated into access to desirable class locations. Given the operation of meritocratic principles, there is nothing either surprising or undesirable about the close relationship between educational qualifications and current class position. The relationship between class origin and educational qualifications, on the other hand, is in no sense artefactual. The strength of this association, shown in table 9.6, although inevitably lower than that between education and current class, is nonetheless striking. Almost seven out of

TABLE 9.5 *Educational qualifications by social class (percentage by column)*

	Professional & managerial	Intermediate non-manual & upper petit-bourgeois	Upper working class & lower petit-bourgeois	Lower & working class	Total
No qualifications	6.5	46.7	63.9	79.3	50.9
Intermediate or Group Certificate	11.4	27.3	23.7	18.6	21.4
Leaving Certificate	35.7	17.6	8.9	1.9	15.2
Third level	46.4	8.3	3.5	0.2	12.5

ten of those from lower working-class origins attained no educational qualifications, compared with fewer than one in ten of those from professional and managerial backgrounds. Correspondingly, 40 per cent of the latter obtained third-level qualifications, compared with only 3 per cent of the former. (The influence that the recent substantial increase in educational participation rates may have had on this relationship is discussed later in this chapter.)

TABLE 9.6 *Educational qualifications by class origin (percentage by column)*

	Professional & managerial	Intermediate non-manual & upper petit-bourgeois	Upper working class & lower petit-bourgeois	Lower working class
No qualifications	9.0	40.0	55.8	68.2
Intermediate or Group Certificate	13.8	19.9	22.5	23.2
Leaving Certificate	38.1	21.0	12.4	5.1
Third level	39.1	19.1	9.2	3.4

Not surprisingly, in view of the strength of the relationship between current class and education, the risk of poverty varies sharply by level of educational qualification, as we can see from table 9.7. Only 4 per cent of those with the Leaving Certificate or better are in poverty; this rises to just less than one in six for those with the Intermediate or Group Certificate and to just over one in four for those with no qualification. In composition, we find that three out of four poor households are headed by a person with no qualification; a mere 6 per cent had the Leaving Certificate or better. The poor are predominantly poorly educated.

TABLE 9.7 *Risk of poverty by educational qualifications of household head*

Education	Percentage poor	Composition of the poor
No qualifications	26.1	75.1
Intermediate or Group Certificate	15.6	18.9
Leaving Certificate	4.6	3.9
Third level	3.0	2.1

9.4 CLASS, LABOUR MARKET EXPERIENCE, AND POVERTY

In this section the relationship between class position and labour market experiences is examined, again concentrating on household heads. In particular, the focus is on three distinct elements of such experience: (*a*) unemployment, (*b*) percentage of potential labour market time spent unemployed, and (*c*) illness or disability.

From table 9.8 it is clear that each of these elements varies sharply by social class. Thus the proportion currently unemployed is less than 1 per cent in the professional and managerial class; this figure rises to a still modest 4 per cent in the intermediate class. It is, however, among the working class that the risk increases dramatically, reaching one out of five in the upper working class and two out of five in the lower working class. A similar situation pertains with regard to the proportion of potential labour market time (i.e. since leaving full-time education) spent unemployed, with the figure rising from 1 to 15 per cent as one ascends the class hierarchy.

Finally, class turns out to be an excellent predictor of illness or disability, although the scale of variation is now less sharp, rising from 9 per cent in the case of the professional and managerial class to 27 per cent among the lower working class.

9.5 MULTIVARIATE ANALYSIS OF THE RISK OF POVERTY

At this point we want to consider the net effects of class origins, social class, education and labour market experience on the risk of poverty. Attention is also directed to the cumulative effects of these factors.

TABLE 9.8 *Labour market experience by social class (percentage by column)*

	Percentage unemployed	Percentage of time unemployed	Percentage ill/disabled
Professional & managerial	0.8	1.0	9.1
Intermediate & non-manual & upper petit-bourgeois	4.1	2.3	12.5
Upper working class & lower petit-bourgeois	19.1	7.2	17.9
Lower working class	40.0	15.5	26.5

In pursuing this investigation, use was made of a statistical procedure known as logistic regression. Rather than attempting to present the detailed results from this analysis, we concentrate here on communicating the major findings, which are as follows.

(1) The net effect of social class on the probability of being in poverty, having controlled for the other variables in the analysis, is a good deal weaker than the gross effect, but remains substantial. Education and labour market experience are important factors mediating the impact of social class but are by no means the only influences involved.

(2) Education operates primarily through its influence on current class position, but a complete absence of qualifications continues to have an independent if relatively modest additional effect on the risk of poverty.

(3) Class background operates primarily through its influence on educational qualifications and current class situation, but, even having allowed for such factors and labour market experience, where the head of household has working-class origins, the risk of poverty is increased.

(4) The cumulative effect of the variables in our analysis is such that a household headed by a person currently in the

professional-managerial class and in employment, with no previous experience of unemployment and with some educational qualification, has a zero probability of being in poverty. On the other hand, where the head of household is an unemployed, lower-working-class person with no qualifications, from a working-class background and having been unemployed for 15 per cent of his or her potential time in the labour market, the probability of the household being poor approaches 1.

Some indication of the independent impact of class background and absence of educational qualifications is given by the fact that a household headed by a person currently in the lower working class who is in employment and possesses some educational qualification and comes from a non-working-class background has one chance in twenty-five of falling below the poverty line; where the qualification is lacking and working-class origins are involved, the risk rises to one in eight.

9.6 EDUCATION, MOBILITY, AND POVERTY

With regard to education, the evidence presented indicates that its relationship to poverty is primarily a consequence of the manner in which it predicts current class situation; although a complete absence of qualification does impose additional independent disadvantages. Concern with equality of educational opportunity stems to some extent from the fact that education is a desirable consumption good. In this context, however, our focus is on education as an investment good: the higher one's level of education, the greater one's chances of achieving a secure and well-paid job and avoiding unemployment and poverty (Heath et al., 1992).

To understand how changes in the distribution of educational qualifications may affect the distribution of the risk of being poor, we must focus on the manner in which education provides the link between class origin and current class situation. It is also necessary to examine the changing significance of the presence or absence of qualifications.

The Irish situation provides a useful testing ground for theories that seek to relate social change to economic development. Perhaps the most influential, the liberal theory of industrialisation, provides a specific set of predictions regarding the role of education:

(1) Class origins are expected to become less closely linked to class destinations as direct inheritance and ascribed status, in the sense of what family one comes from, become less important than achievement; but it remains a significant factor.

(2) Educational outcomes become less closely related to class origins.

(3) Educational qualifications are increasingly used to recruit people to occupational positions as the competitive pressures of modern businesses make the recruitment of inferior applicants increasingly costly and as educational achievement comes to be seen as the prime indicator of merit.

The society emerging from such processes could be termed, following Jonsson (1989), 'neo-liberal', since it entails equality of educational opportunity and the right to pass on legitimately acquired assets to children. One expectation would be that such changes would lead to a situation where class background would show a declining effect in relation to the risk of being poor, and this effect would be little affected by whether we controlled for education or not.

In fact the situation turns out to be a good deal more complicated, partly as a consequence of the need to take into account the particular dynamics of the supply and demand for qualified labour associated with substantial changes in both the educational and occupational distributions. With regard to the relationship between class background and education, the Irish experience confirms evidence from elsewhere that 'reform is better at changing totals than relationships' (Heath et al., 1992).

The Irish educational system has expanded dramatically over the past thirty years, and it might appear inevitable that such expansion would be associated with reductions in inequality of educational opportunities. In fact what appears to have occurred is that everyone, regardless of class, has benefited more or less equally, leaving class differentials relatively unaffected (Breen, 1989; Breen et al., 1990). Put another way, the available evidence suggests that the reduction in class differentials that did occur was the outcome of expansion and increases in the numbers participating rather than diminution in the influence of class in the selection processes (Breen, 1984; Hout, 1989; Raferty and Hout, 1990; Whelan and Whelan, 1984). Children from working-class origins tend to benefit from educational expansion as the take-up from higher classes moves towards saturation level (Halsey et al., 1980; Heath and Clifford, 1990). Through expansion, the educational system became less selective, with consequent benefits for those from less-advantaged backgrounds; but where selection continued to be important, class effects remained undiminished (Goldthorpe, 1992, 421; Hannan, 1986).

The consequences of expansion in participation rates for class inequalities in life chances and, in particular, for poverty depend not just on the relationship between class origins and education but also on the relationship between education and class. In one sense it is obvious that education has become increasingly important, in that a minimum level of education is increasingly a prerequisite for successful participation in the labour market. Industrialisation has been associated with substantial changes in both educational and occupational distributions. One consequence is that while the number failing to acquire any educational qualification has declined dramatically, the consequences of such failure are now much greater. Changes in the occupational structure leave little in the way of employment opportunities for those lacking in credentials.

In a series of studies, Breen and Hannan have shown that the consequences of educational failure have become more serious, while at the same time very young school leavers are now drawn almost exclusively from lower-working-class backgrounds. In 1980 around 9 per cent of the relevant age group left school before the Group or Intermediate Certificate; this declined to almost 6 per cent at the beginning of the 1990s. In recent years unemployment rates among those who left school without any qualification have been over three times greater than among those who left after sitting their Leaving Certificate. Following up and interviewing school leavers five years later, around one in two of those leaving without any qualifications, or with poor Junior Certificate qualifications, have been found to be unemployed; 'class inequalities in educational failure are now so pronounced and so serious that a gross injustice exists in the educational provision for such children' (Hannan, 1992, 7).

The complete absence of educational qualifications increases the risk of exposure to poverty, both because it condemns those experiencing such failure to unskilled working-class occupations and because, within the lower working class, those without qualifications have less satisfactory labour market experiences. This polarisation in life chances between those with and without qualifications is a consequence of changes both in educational and occupational distributions. This also turns out to be true for the significance of the possession of particular levels of educational qualifications. Thus the evidence increasingly suggests that industrialisation and expansion of the educational system, rather than producing an inevitable strengthening of the association between education and class, produce outcomes that depend on the particular dynamics of the supply and demand for qualified labour.

In particular, evidence is now available from a number of countries, including Ireland, that in an important sense, education has become less influential in shaping inequalities in social fluidity. British evidence points to a devaluation of intermediate qualifications (Heath et al., 1992, 232–3). Similarly Breen and Whelan (1993) have shown that with regard to the relationship between education and first job, the advantages of having a junior cycle certificate diminish over time, as does the difference between a Leaving Certificate and a junior cycle qualification. In contrast, the gap between third level and Leaving Certificate has remained stable.

As Boudon (1974) pointed out, the rational decision of individuals to acquire more education has an unforeseen aggregate effect: as qualifications become less scarce, they lose their relative value. In attempting to understand this process, it is necessary to take into account, as Heath et al. (1992, 234) note, that the occupational payoffs of particular qualifications may depend as much on employers' beliefs about their value as on their intrinsic educational worth.

The results of Breen and Whelan's (1993) analysis, however, unlike those reported by Heath et al. for Britain, do not point to the increasing importance of luck relative to merit. The available evidence suggests, rather, that the direct impact of property and inheritance on current class position is increasingly mediated by educational qualifications. The overall effect of class background, however, remains constant over time. The changing relationship between education and class directs attention to the role of class background influences other than those mediated by property or education. The Irish evidence suggests that, in circumstances of a substantial excess supply of labour, many employers may find it unnecessary, or indeed too costly, to recruit through formal competition; or it may be that where such competition occurs, other qualities come to count. These results suggest that as the game changes, not only are the players most motivated to succeed able to adapt their strategies but the advantages associated with traditional strategies, relating to the use of social networks and specialised knowledge of the labour market, may indeed become relatively more important (Halsey, 1977).

The changing pattern of relationships between class origins, education and class destination provides an instructive example of the ability of those in positions of power and privilege to maintain their position against the encroachment of outsiders, even in the face of the functional requirements of industrial society and of specific state policies that might threaten them (Breen and Whelan, 1992, 1993). The increasing tendency of those without educational qualifications to be drawn from the lower working class and the increasing risks of unemployment associated with that status, the persistence of class-related educational inequalities, the devaluation of intermediate qualifications and the evidence for the continued significance of other class-related resources all contribute to the preservation of class difference in life chances and, in particular, in exposure to poverty.

9.7 CONCLUSIONS

The results we have set out in this chapter show that it is possible to predict poverty with considerable success from the current class situation of the head of household. In turn, despite the existence of large-scale social mobility associated with structural change, current class situation is strongly related to class origins. In particular, the working-class groups that experience the highest risks of poverty are drawn predominantly from working-class origins. Over eight out of ten households in poverty (according to combined income and deprivation criteria) have a household head who has been intergenerationally stable in the working class or lower petit-bourgeoisie.

In attempting to explain these associations, the roles of educational qualifications and labour market experience have been explored. Consideration of the latter element forces recognition of the fact that class situation serves as an indicator for a variety of advantages and disadvantages that are experienced over the life cycle. In summarising our position regarding the consequences of changes in the class structure and educational participation rates, it is important once again to stress the distinction between absolute and relative outcomes. Structural change has been associated with large-scale and desirable mobility. The professional and managerial class is not a closed elite but a relatively heterogeneous group by class origins. However, in the absence of change in the underlying pattern of inequality of opportunities, the lower working class, in particular, has come to be drawn almost exclusively from those with working-class origins.

Similarly, large numbers have benefited from expansion of the educational system, and these benefits are by no means illusory. Higher levels of educational qualifications are desirable in themselves, constitute a prerequisite for further economic development, and produce an absolute increase in life chances for those who emigrate. It remains true, though, that increases in participation rates do not necessarily produce a reduction in inequality of outcomes; and since educational qualifications have their predominant effect on life chances through the manner in which they determine one's relative position in the class hierarchy, the underlying pattern of social fluidity may remain unchanged.

Politicians shared with many social scientists a sanguine view of the relationship between economic growth and mobility opportunities; hence the significance of the catchphrase 'The rising tide lifts all boats.' In fact a remarkable stability has pertained in relation to mobility chances at the extremes of the Irish class system. The lower working class experiences particularly severe obstacles to upward mobility. This class also displays a distinctive homogeneity, with over 90 per cent of its members being drawn from working-class or small farm backgrounds. With opportunities in unskilled work becoming increasingly scarce in Ireland and elsewhere, there is at the same time no adequate provision for intragenerational or intergenerational mobility out of the marginalised working class. Furthermore, those households that are exposed to the highest risks of unemployment and poverty are also the source of those school leavers who come on the labour market each year totally lacking qualifications.

It is worth noting here that since such households are not concentrated in a limited set of areas, then, as Hannan (1992) emphasises, educational policies couched solely in terms of deprived areas cannot hope to reach more than a small proportion of such students. As he suggests, targeting disadvantaged schools might be a great deal more productive, although remedying inequality of opportunities is likely to require a direct attack on inequalities of condition.

The immediate causes of the range of factors that have been identified as contributing to poverty—education, unemployment, and health—are obviously not identical. However, to the extent that such causes can be traced to the location of certain households at the bottom of the class hierarchy, the importance of class as an explanatory factor is demonstrated. The Irish experience is in line with an accumulating body of research findings that demonstrate the persistence of class-linked inequalities even within periods of rapid economic change (Goldthorpe and Marshall, 1992).

PART IV

ASPECTS OF DISADVANTAGE

How does poverty affect the physical and mental health of those experiencing it? Are women at higher risk from poverty than men? Do problems of making ends meet on a low income bear especially heavily on women? Is poverty concentrated in particular areas or is it widely dispersed across the country? These are some of the specific aspects of disadvantage addressed in part IV.

The relationships between unemployment, poverty and 'psychological distress' are examined in chapter 11. While attention is often paid to the stress brought about by work situations, research evidence shows that the mental health of unemployed people is put under much greater strain. The links between unemployment and psychological distress have long been recognised, but the processes at work are poorly understood Here the distinction is made between the direct effect of being unemployed per se—affecting feelings of self-worth, for example—and the indirect effects through the drop in living standard it produces. Factors that can reduce the stress normally associated with unemployment and poverty are discussed—in particular, networks of social support and psychological dispositions that encourage positive coping responses.

Poverty is associated with greater risks of physical as well as mental ill health. Chapter 12 shows the extent to which illness and early death are related to socio-economic status. Those in the lower social classes and those experiencing poverty and deprivation are shown to experience greater ill health than others. Likewise, as in other countries, mortality and life expectancy in Ireland are seen to be strongly related to socio-economic position. The mechanisms that could lie behind such patterns are discussed, and the role of long-term and deep-seated inequalities in living conditions across the social classes is highlighted. Access to and utilisation of the health services could also play a part, though probably only a relatively minor one. Patterns of utilisation in Ireland by income group and social class are discussed, and the extent to which the distribution of service usage and need across income distribution corresponds is analysed. Chapters 13 and 14 focus on different aspects of poverty and sex inequality. In the United States, rapid growth in the proportion of poor families headed by a woman gave rise to concerns about the 'feminisation of poverty'. Growth in the numbers of lone-parent families has also been seen in many other countries. In Ireland, unlike many other countries, widows account for a high proportion of female-headed families. The relative income position of this group has improved during the 1970s and 1980s; this has led to a decline in the risk of poverty for female-headed households, while risks for households headed by a man or a couple have risen. Some sub-groups do face particularly high risks of poverty: for example, lone parents, the great majority of whom are women, are at very high risk.

The assumption implicit in most analysis of poverty—including most of this book—is that all members of a particular household or family share a common standard of living. This assumption is generally made because so little is known about the distribution of resources and welfare within the family or household, and because it is so difficult for research to open up the 'black box'. Chapter 14 describes what has been discovered about the allocation of resources within the household and the management of household finances from analysis of data obtained for a large sample of households. The various ways in which households organise their finances are described. These range from situations where the main earner (usually the husband) turns over all the wages or benefits, or a fixed allowance, to the household manager (usually the wife), to independent management by two-earner couples. The 'whole wage' and 'allowance' system, common in low-income households, tend to maximise problems of stress associated with family finance and make the distribution of resources within families less equal. The way in which the burden of juggling family needs against limited financial resources tends to fall disproportionately on women is also shown. The separate question of whether unequal division of resources within households leads to a substantial amount of 'hidden poverty' is also discussed.

Spatial aspects of poverty are considered in chapter 15. It is well known that some geographical areas have very high rates of unemployment and poverty. How might such areas be systematically identified using information available from the census? And how many of the poor live in such areas? Are special policy measures required to combat poverty in such areas, and if so, what should be their focus? Questions such as these are raised and discussed in this chapter.

10 Poverty, Unemployment, and Psychological Distress

CHRISTOPHER T. WHELAN

This chapter looks at the impact of unemployment on the psychological health of those affected by it. The most striking feature of the current literature on the psychological consequences of unemployment is its remarkable lack of emphasis on poverty as a crucial intervening factor (Whelan, 1992a). The failure to deal with material deprivation is made all the more surprising by the fact that the classic studies of the 1930s overwhelmingly focused on poverty in attempting to explain the psychological effects of unemployment.

10.1 UNEMPLOYMENT AND PSYCHOLOGICAL DISTRESS

In cross-sectional comparisons of people who are at the time unemployed with similar people who are in paid work, higher levels of psychological distress are generally found among the unemployed. The possibility arises that psychological problems, or factors associated with such problems, may have led to unemployment. This interpretation is a great deal more credible during periods of very low unemployment, where personal characteristics might be thought to impede job-getting. When unemployment rates are high, however, it is more likely that the observed differences arise primarily from deterioration in mental health occurring after job loss: that is, unemployment is causing the psychological distress (Warr, 1985, 1987).

Support for this argument is provided by evidence from the Dutch study by Spruit et al. (1985), which excluded respondents who were identified as having previous health problems that might have led to their unemployment and which, despite this control, found significant mental health differences between the unemployed and a control group of employees. Similarly, there is considerable evidence that unemployed

149

people who regain a job show a rapid and substantial improvement in mental health (Jackson et al., 1983; Payne and Jones, 1987). Furthermore, a recent study has provided evidence that, far from impeding job-seeking efforts, high distress was actually associated with a slightly increased likelihood of finding a new job over the one-year follow-up period (Kessler et al., 1989, 654).

Longitudinal studies in which individuals are followed up over time make particularly clear the causal impact of unemployment, and a variety of such studies has now confirmed this effect (Liem, 1987; Warr, 1987). One of the few studies to fail to observe a substantial effect was that of Kasl and Cobb's (1979) follow-up of two plant closings. In this research, blue-collar workers often reported their greatest level of psychological strain before the actual lay-off. Some of the strongest effects appeared to result from anticipation of being laid off rather than the actual lay-off. However, median unemployment for the first year was five-and-a-half weeks, and a substantial number of workers were re-employed immediately following the closure. Thus, rather than contradicting the other findings, this study simply highlights the importance of the economic environment in which job losses occur.

Kelvin and Jarrett (1985) note that while there is widespread recognition that unemployment brings both economic and psychological problems, consideration of the relationship between them is remarkably rare. Similarly Fryer, in a number of recent publications, has drawn attention to the fact that while financial hardship is repeatedly mentioned in the literature, it is not allocated a central role. The neglect of poverty is made more surprising by the fact that the seminal 1930s field study of Marienthal, an Austrian village stricken by mass unemployment, showed that there was a clear connection between a family's attitude and their economic situation (Jahoda et al., 1933).

Subsequently, however, the classic studies were interpreted in a particularly one-sided fashion. Jahoda's own subsequent explanatory emphasis (1982) was on the latent, non-economic consequences of unemployment, involving the loss of social contact, activity, status, purposefulness, and time structure. Others followed Jahoda in making psychological rather than material deprivation theoretically central (Warr, 1987). As a consequence, despite the evidence that unemployment in the 1980s still involved the manifest consequence of a substantial reduction in income, sight was lost of the impact of declining resources on capacity to cope (Whelan, 1994).

The data available to us in the Irish case from the 1987 survey is cross-sectional, and we do not wish to deny that there are limitations associated with such data. The information available, however, does offer significant advantages. We are in a position to take into account the effects not only of unemployment but also of income, life-style, and the manner in which personal and social resources mediate between such factors and mental health. This allows us to explore the way in which the acute stress associated with being made unemployed can lead to the chronic stress arising from hardship in basic enduring economic and social circumstances. It is possible to study these issues not just for the unemployed individuals but also for other family members. Such analysis can also make a significant contribution to our ability to choose between competing explanations of the nature of the relationship between unemployment and mental health.

The main measure of psychological distress we employ is the 'general health questionnaire' (GHQ) in its twelve-item format. The GHQ was designed by Goldberg (1972) as a screening test for detecting minor psychiatric disorders in the community. The items included in the measure are designed to give information about the respondent's current mental state. It is neither a measure of long-standing personality attributes nor an assessment of the likelihood of falling ill in the near future. It is most definitely not, on the other hand, a mere complaints inventory. It consists only of items that have been chosen from a substantial battery of those shown to discriminate between groups of respondents in terms of their likelihood of being assessed as non-psychotic psychiatric cases.

If the results of a set of GHQ scores are compared with an independent psychiatric assessment, it is possible to state the number of symptoms at which the probability that an individual will be thought to be a psychiatric case exceeds one-half. In the case of the twelve-item version the threshold score is 2, and all respondents scoring above this level will be classified as suffering from psychological distress. Since the conclusions we wish to draw remain true irrespective of whether a dichotomous or continuous measure is employed, we will present our results in terms of the former, not just because of their intrinsic interest but also because this facilitates the communication of our most important results.

Using the GHQ measure, we find that, as shown in fig. 10.1, just over one in three of the unemployed come above the psychological distress threshold, compared with one in fourteen of employees. The differentials between these groups on the individual items are documented in table 10.1. It is necessary to note that only departures from usual functioning are scored as pathological, and not responses such as 'no

TABLE 10.1 *Comparison of level of negative responses on general health questionnaire (GHQ) for unemployed and employees*

	Unemployed %	Employees %		Unemployed %	Employees %
Been feeling unhappy & depressed	34.2	9.5	Felt capable about decisions about things	10.2	2.6
Felt you couldn't overcome your difficulties	22.8	5.7	Been feeling reasonably happy, all things considered	17.9	5.5
Been thinking of yourself as a worthless person	13.8	0.8	Been able to face up to your problems	13.8	3.6
Lost much sleep over worry	19.5	5.7			
Felt constantly under strain	23.5	11.3	Felt able to enjoy your day-to-day activities	13.0	2.8
Been losing confidence in yourself	20.0	3.6	Felt that you are playing a useful part in things	20.1	2.4
			Been able to concentrate on what you are doing	6.0	1.1

more than usual.' Despite this, almost 36 per cent of unemployed men give a response in the pathological category to the question regarding feeling unhappy and depressed. Over 20 per cent or more *in each case* indicate that they have (*a*) felt they couldn't overcome their difficulties, (*b*) lost much sleep over worry, (*c*) felt constantly under strain, or (*d*) been losing confidence in themselves.

The disparities between the unemployed and the employees on such items range from 2:1 to 4:1. On perhaps the most extreme negative item in the set, 'been thinking of yourself as a worthless person,' the level of pathological response is lower for the unemployed than on the other negative items, at 14 per cent. The differential, however, between the unemployed and employees of 17:1 is the highest on any of the items. The results provide a dramatic demonstration of the mental health consequences of unemployment. The unemployed have major difficulties in coping with day-to-day problems and social difficulties and in preserving self-esteem.

In examining the relationship between poverty and psychological distress, we have chosen as our poverty line the combined income and life-style deprivation threshold, which involves an average disposable household income adjusted for household size of below 70 per cent of average and the enforced absence of at least one of the basic deprivation items discussed earlier. Using this cut-off point, we find that over one in three of those in poor households come above the psychological distress threshold, compared with one in eight of those outside such households. For the poor, mental health problems are not an unusual phenomenon.

The issue of the relative importance of unemployment and poverty must, to some extent, be an artificial one, since unemployment is one of the major causes of poverty. The evidence, though, is clearly relevant to the issue of the relative significance of manifest and latent functions of employment. Jahoda (1982) argues that over and above the manifest function of providing income and security, employment serves a variety of latent functions, by embedding the individual in a web of social relations. Our empirical analysis does indeed show, as set out in fig. 10.2, that unemployment has a significant effect even among the non-poor, with those who are unemployed being five times more likely to come above the psychological threshold than those who are at work or retired. However, our results clearly indicate that the impact of unemployment is mediated, to a significant extent, by exposure to poverty. The cumulative impact of unemployment and poverty is illustrated by the fact that while fewer than one in fourteen of those at work or retired and non-poor exhibited mental health problems, the figure rose to well over four out of ten for those who suffer both poverty and unemployment.

Those concerned with the psychology of work have long stressed that work provides much more than merely money. Those concerned with unemployment need to stress that to be unemployed is frequently to be poor (Kelvin and Jarrett, 1985; Fryer, 1992).

10.2 IMPACT OF LENGTH OF UNEMPLOYMENT

The notion of stages of unemployment, which emerged in the literature of the 1930s, has become a basic concept in accounts of the psychological effects of unemployment. Once again, however, the role of poverty has been neglected. Eisenberg and Lazarfield (1938, 378) describe a series of stages going from shock combined with an optimistic attitude to pessimism and distress and finally fatalism. Studies relating length of unemployment to mental health have, however, been far from consistent. Jackson et al. (1984) suggest that the failure of early studies to find a relationship may have been due to the fact that the age range of respondents or the length of unemployment were too restricted. More recent studies suggest that the newly unemployed experience a deterioration in psychological health within weeks, and that by three months this has become worse, but it then remains stable for long periods and might even improve (Fryer, 1992).

Our own results, set out in fig. 10.3, show little difference between those unemployed for less than one year and those unemployed for more than a year. These results are consistent with the findings in the literature. However, this contrast conceals some interesting differences. If we exclude those seeking their first job and those on state training schemes, we find that levels of mental health decline beyond the second year of unemployment, with the level of psychological distress increasing from 37 per cent above the threshold for those unemployed for less than two years to 43 per cent for those between two and three years and to 54 per cent for those above three to four years; at this point it drops dramatically to 25 per cent for those unemployed more than four years. With the exception of this final result, our findings are consistent with the hypothesis of a gradual decline in psychological well-being.

To understand these findings it is necessary to turn our attention to the relationship between unemployment and poverty. Despite the attention devoted to stages, there have been very few attempts to trace the interaction of the economic and psychological effects of unemployment and to move beyond description to examine the systematic relationship between increasing poverty and changing reactions to unemployment.

The limited extent to which such issues have been explored appears to be related to the tendency to view the unemployed as passively enduring movement through a series of stages. Understanding the consequence of unemployment requires that we emphasise not just the constructive aspects of employment but also the destructive aspects of unemployment. It is also necessary to see the unemployed person as an active, interpreting, striving, questioning agent. From this perspective it becomes possible to see how the erosion of economic resources undermines such coping capacities (Fryer, 1986).

If one again excludes those seeking their first job and those on state schemes, the proportion falling below the poverty line rises steadily from one in three of those unemployed for less than one year to over half those unemployed for more than three years. This result makes the previous finding regarding the relatively low levels of distress displayed by those unemployed for more than four years even more perplexing. It tends to undermine an explanation of the 'deviant' result in terms of participation in the 'black economy'. An alternative explanation could be offered in terms of coping adjustments. Two particularly important mechanisms are adaptation to a new role and reduced commitment to finding a new job. This interpretation takes into account the fact that the initial period of unemployment may be a traumatic time. Gradually, adaptation may take place. A further adjustment arises from the calculation that the probability of obtaining paid work is low, with a consequent reduction in employment commitment and job-seeking.

Set against such possibilities is the increased probability of poverty. It seems doubtful in view of this that such coping strategies could account for the results we have observed. It is necessary, therefore, to consider the further possibility that the type of response alternative used in our measure of psychological distress may lead to an underestimation of levels of distress of those in long-term unemployment (Warr and Jackson, 1985). The GHQ may miss chronic disorders, because it asks respondents for an assessment of symptoms in terms of categories such as 'same as usual'. This seems to occur less than might be expected on theoretical grounds, because people cling rather stubbornly to the concept of their 'usual self'. It seems likely, though, that those unemployed for more than four years may have great difficulty in preserving such a concept.

10.3 THE IMPACT ON WIVES OF HUSBANDS' UNEMPLOYMENT AND POVERTY

It is clear that while the risk of poverty that is associated with unemployment is one of the important ways in which job loss is translated into psychological distress, a great deal more is involved. Unemployment involves exclusion from a range of experiences and associated psychological benefits and exposure to the potentially stressful demands of the new role of being unemployed.

For the wives of unemployed men, the situation is rather different. While their husbands' altered role can clearly have implications for their pattern of activities, any alterations in their own roles are likely to be marginal in comparison with those to which their husbands must accommodate. In view of this, one might expect economic factors to loom large. Indeed, husband's unemployment has very little effect when allowance is made for poverty. Where a husband's unemployment does not result in a household being pushed into poverty, it does not appear to have any impact on the wife's level of psychological distress. In non-poor households, 13 per cent of married women with husbands at work or retired were above the distress threshold, while for those whose husbands were unemployed the figure was 14 per cent. By contrast, 40 per cent of the wives of unemployed men in poor households are above the threshold.

These results do not necessarily imply that a wife's response to her husband's unemployment takes an entirely economic form. However, whatever the emotional aspects of the response are, in non-poor households they do not seem to involve a heightened probability of psychiatric morbidity. In poor households, however, it is often the wives who have to live on their wits, make and mend and deprive themselves in order to provide for other family members (McKee and Bell, 1985; Pahl, 1980, 1983).

10.4 THE BUFFERING EFFECT OF SOCIAL SUPPORT

People confront stress-provoking conditions with a variety of behaviours, perceptions and evaluations that are often capable of mediating the different conditions. Among the elements having a crucial place in the stress process, therefore, are those that can be invoked by people in their own defence. They are referred to collectively as 'mediators'. Here we are particularly concerned with the role of social support, and in particular with the impact of economic and emotional support.

Not surprisingly, social support of either form contributes to improved levels of mental health (Whelan et al., 1991). The question arises, though, whether support enhances health and well-being irrespective of level of stress or whether its effect operates by buffering the effect of stressful experiences. The direct hypothesis argues that support enhances mental health at each level of stress. This could come about through the perception that others will provide aid in the event of stressful occurrences. The buffering hypothesis, on the other hand, argues that support exerts its beneficial effects by protecting people from the effects of stress on health. Support may provide the resources that allow one to redefine the potential for harm posed by a situation and/or augment one's ability to cope with increased demands (Cohen and Syme, 1985).

Our findings provide strong support for the buffering hypothesis. Both support variables have substantial effects, but to be understood they must be considered jointly with the role of poverty. Among the non-poor, when we have allowed for the effects of other variables, those lacking social support are more likely to be distressed; but the most substantial effects occur for those below the poverty line (Whelan, 1993).

10.5 FATALISM AND PSYCHOLOGICAL DISTRESS

Powerlessness and fatalism, or, alternatively, mastery, has consistently been identified as the most important belief in affecting an individual's level of distress. Most importantly, the expectation is that lower class positions socialise individuals to be more fatalistic in their causal perceptions, and that fatalism increases vulnerability to disorder, primarily because it undermines persistence and effort in existing situations.

In measuring fatalism, we have drawn on a set of items that have been fairly widely employed (Pearlin et al., 1981):

(1) I can do just about anything I set my mind to.
(2) I have little control over the things that happen to me.
(3) What happens in the future depends on me.
(4) I often feel helpless in dealing with the problems of life.
(5) Sometimes I feel I am being pushed around in life.
(6) There is a lot I can do to change my life if I want to.
(7) There is really no way I can solve some of the problems I have.

Not surprisingly, a high level of sense of control is associated with a low level of psychological distress. A belief that one is, at least to some extent, master of one's own fate leads to a search of the environment for potentially distressing conditions, to taking preventive steps, and to accumulating resources or developing skills or habits that will reduce the impact of the unavoidable. In contrast, fatalism—the belief that important events in one's life are predetermined by external circumstances—leads to ignoring problems until they actually happen, and will, in the long run, be more pervasively harmful. In consequence there is a magnification of differences, with the fatalists suffering an increasing number of problems, which reinforces a feeling of lack of control. This in turn produces passivity in the face of subsequent difficulties. Lower-class people may then carry a triple burden. They have more problems to deal with; their personal histories are likely to have left them with a deep sense of powerlessness; and that sense of powerlessness discourages them from marshalling whatever energy and resources they have in order to solve their problems. The result for many is a multiplication of despair (Wheaton, 1983).

Of course, it is possible to argue that for many deprived respondents, feelings of fatalism are simply an accurate reflection of their environment. They might even be taken as simply reflecting an accurate understanding that their deprivation arises from wider structural factors over which they have no control. Fortunately, a number of items in the Irish survey dealt with perceptions of the causes of poverty. Respondents were asked to indicate the extent of their agreement or disagreement with the following statements.

(1) When people are poor it is usually their own fault.
(2) By and large, the reason people are poor is that society does not give them a chance.
(3) Lack of ambition is the root cause of poverty.
(4) Only by completely changing the way the country is run can we reduce the number of people in poverty.

Our analysis shows that there is no significant relationship between fatalism and perceptions of the causes of poverty. This finding suggests that it is possible to facilitate people in developing feelings of personal efficacy without encouraging the tendency to make scapegoats of the deprived, or deny the importance of structural factors.

It has also been suggested that the impact of sense of control on emotional well-being depends on the nature of the typical outcomes in one's life. Claiming responsibility for good outcomes enhances self-esteem, while accepting responsibility for negative outcomes has the opposite effect. Thus for those at the bottom of the class hierarchy, rejecting the role of choice, effort and ability as determinants of life outcomes reduces distress (Hyman, 1986). Despite the intuitive appeal of the theory, the empirical evidence does not support it (Mirowsky and Ross, 1990). Our own results confirm the finding that feelings of control have their most dramatic effect among those with *low status* and *limited resources* (Whelan, 1992b).

Our analysis does provide support for the notion of a threshold of dysfunction, beyond which increased feelings of control are actually detrimental to one's well-being. It is necessary to strike a balance between realism and optimism. The optimum level of sense of control is directly related to power and command over resources. The sense of control that is most beneficial to young professional workers who experience little in the way of life-style deprivation would be completely inappropriate for an unemployed manual worker living in a household in which basic items of food, heat and clothing are gone without.

Our results, however, do support the view that most people at all levels of status are likely to benefit from enhanced feelings of control: 'Fatalism and alienation are the recognition of a harmful reality and in no way soothe the discomforts' (Mirowsky and Ross, 1990, 1531). Furthermore, a sense of control and the availability of social support can substitute for each other. Those who feel in control of their lives are less dependent on supportive relationships to maintain their sense of emotional well-being. Similarly, those who enjoy such support will not feel the need for such high levels of control (Whelan, 1992c).

10.6 CONCLUSIONS

The evidence we have presented demonstrates the substantial effect of both unemployment and poverty on psychological distress. In combination they produce a situation where acute and chronic stress converge to produce an impact on psychological health that stems from hardship in basic enduring economic circumstances and the experience of what has been described as 'economic brinkmanship', in which resources are persistently insufficient to permit the development of adequate coping strategies. The original Marienthal conclusion that the deterioration in mental health among members of households affected by unemployment is intimately related to the erosion of economic resources appears to be no less true today.

Economic factors are important for all groups, but for married women in particular the unemployment of their spouses has its major effect on their mental health through the grinding consequences of poverty. For others, such effects are compounded by the damage to their self-esteem brought about by the fact that they are denied the opportunity to undertake roles that are deemed appropriate by society, and are excluded from valued categories of experience that are associated with employment. The results we have presented demonstrate clearly the role of poverty in mediating the impact of unemployment, not only for the individuals affected but for other members of their families.

It is important, however, not to replace a one-sided emphasis on the latent functions of employment with claims for the exclusive importance of economic deprivation. Unemployment continues to have a substantial and damaging effect on the psychological health of the unemployed individual even when we control for poverty. Employment does indeed provide more than money. The great majority of those in employment can enjoy those benefits while at the same time being fortunate enough to escape the psychological damage associated with exclusion from the customary life-style of their society.

Psychological distress arises from the loss of the employment role and/or the experience of a level of deprivation that, by any reasonable standards, must be judged to be extreme. The evidence clearly shows that a great deal of psychological distress could be ameliorated, in principle, by remedial action arising from social policy. Those who experience re-employment or are removed from poverty will regain their mental health. There is a great deal to be said for stressing that what is involved is 'mental health' rather than 'mental illness', in that remedial action must take the form of changing the social circumstances of those affected rather than the provision of individual treatment or therapy (Jahoda, 1988).

The fact that high levels of unemployment are likely to persist for the foreseeable future has led to the view that there is strong need not only for the highest possible rate of job-creating growth 'but also for a rapid development of new forms of employment and for a strengthening of the social fabric by providing as many citizens as possible with an active role in society, both as a means of income and of self-identity' (OECD, 1987, 7). Increasingly, attention is being focused on the need to devise systems of income support that would allow recipients the possibility of perceiving themselves, and being perceived, as making a useful contribution to economic and social life.

Recent examples of moves in that direction include schemes allowing certain categories of unemployed people to take up a paid part-time job for under twenty-four hours a week and continue to receive an income supplement; pre-retirement allowances for the long-term unemployed aged sixty and over; and a scheme to encourage the unemployed to take an active part in voluntary and community work.

While the role of factors other than poverty and unemployment is clearly secondary, our results do support the view that social support can play an important buffering role. Furthermore, the evidence on the relationship of distress to feelings of fatalism suggests the possibility of intervention that could ameliorate psychological distress through increasing self-esteem and altering fatalistic attitudes. Our findings also suggest that this could be achieved without the need to impose on the participants an oversimplified view of their situation.

Those who have been concerned to avoid 'blaming the victim' have often been reluctant to discuss motivational factors. The battle lines have been drawn, so that restricted opportunities or attitudes and values have been seen as competing rather than complementary explanations. It is possible, however, to view motivation as the outcome of a complex set of interactions in which restricted opportunity plays a central role. Psychological theory predicts that when faced with uncontrollable circumstances, people ultimately respond with learnt helplessness.

There are three such basic messages to be derived from such an analysis (Kane, 1987, 410):

First any motivational deficit observed among the persistent poor should not be thought of as an immutable personal pathology. Second, at the same time, someone who has been conditioned with a lack of control will not necessarily respond immediately to any new opportunities for control. Third, government can play a role, first in making real options available—in the way of jobs and education— and just as important in making voluntarism salient as an opportunity for control.

This analysis is consistent with the view that while local action cannot in itself solve problems of poverty and disadvantage, it can make a significant contribution to strategies to combat disadvantage (Chanan and Vos, 1990). The difficulties of successful intervention, however, must not be underestimated, and can be illustrated by a consideration of the potential role of social support.

While our results show that social support can play an important buffering role, even spatial or social concentration of problems does not necessarily encourage collective rather than individual solutions to problems. For many unemployed people, unemployment is perceived as a transitory state, and 'the unemployed' may be seen as a reference group in which membership is both unwilling and temporary. The unemployed are defined by what they are not. Thus, mobilising the unemployed in a manner that allows them to provide support for each other is no easy task.

More generally, it is important that social support not come to be seen as a panacea. In the first place, not all networks are socially supportive. In other circumstances the costs involved in social support transactions may outweigh the benefits (Schilling, 1987). Furthermore, our knowledge of which specific aspects of social support are crucial, and under what conditions, is restricted by the limited number of systematic evaluations of support interventions. Important strategies of intervention, such as community work, have tended to focus on the process 'to the point of excluding a proper concern with results' (Chanan and Vos, 1990, 55).

Finally, it must be stressed that many supporting ties depend on adequate funding of basic social and income maintenance programmes. Social networks do not exist in a vacuum: they need resources. The balance of research findings suggests that the poor have weaker networks than others. Reciprocity is a central factor in informal networks, and when exchange is perceived as being unequal, withdrawal tends to occur. Many aspects of communal life are linked to work-place characteristics and may exclude the unemployed. Most mutual aid and support appears to occur between households experiencing unemployment (Morris, 1987). Schilling (1987) concludes that while many current policy trends assume the existence of a vast reservoir of social support, to emphasise the influence of social supports while ignoring their broader context is a political abuse of the positive findings on social support.

Despite such reservations, it is worth while noting, as Ronayne et al. (1986) conclude in their view of locally based responses to unemployment, that (*a*) most employment schemes achieve little in terms of reduction of unemployment, and (*b*) many initiatives are not oriented towards job creation but are in fact responses to a broader range of social needs in areas that carry multiple burdens. There would appear to be value in an explicit recognition of this reality and in encouraging community development responses that recognise the relevance of resource and support issues and that have the potential to give the unemployed access to categories of experience previously denied to them. This approach recognises that 'people in poor conditions tend to be overwhelmed and isolated by the weight of their problems. They are often diminished by their conditions and need a period of encouragement, confidence and practice in order to realise their own untapped talents' (Chanan and Vos, 1990, 52).

The cost of financing such interventions must be set against the costs currently associated with the consequences of unemployment and poverty, not just in terms of the scale of human misery generated but also of the extent of employment of health services (Whelan et al., 1991).

Despite the potential value of local initiatives, it is necessary, at the risk of repetition, to stress that the major factors involved in raising levels of psychological distress are the absence of jobs and a minimally acceptable standard of living. The issues involved are clearly national rather than local. The most effective ways to increase self-esteem and feelings of mastery and to improve mental health are to create jobs and remove people from poverty.

11 Poverty and Health Inequalities

BRIAN NOLAN

Health is fundamental to quality of life, and differences across socio-economic groups in experience of ill health and in life expectancy constitute a basic yardstick of underlying social inequalities. Poverty manifests itself not only in psychological distress, as detailed in the previous chapter, but in physical ill health and reduced life expectancy. This chapter presents evidence that the incidence of ill health and the pattern of mortality in Ireland, as in other countries, is related to socio-economic background. Complex and dynamic causal processes are at work, with health affecting socio-economic status as well as vice versa; but the relationship between material deprivation and health outcomes appears to be crucial.

In the international research literature on health and socio-economic background, a great deal of emphasis has been placed on age of death, involving comparisons across socio-economic groups of mortality rates for particular age groups. This is where we begin, setting out in section 11.1 evidence from the analysis of mortality rates by socio-economic group for men aged fifteen to sixty-four, using information from the registration of deaths and the census of population.

The incidence of (self-reported) chronic illness across income groups and social classes is then examined in section 11.2, using information obtained in the 1987 household survey carried out by the Economic and Social Research Institute described in earlier chapters. This also facilitates analysis of the extent to which those currently experiencing basic deprivation suffer more ill health than others, as well as the relationship with longer-term background characteristics such as parents' social class. Both in the case of mortality and morbidity, the findings of studies for other countries are employed to put the Irish pattern in context and in particular to help tease out the importance of the different relationships involved.

Section 11.3 looks at the role of the health services. The patterns of use of health services are analysed in the light of the differences in morbidity across socio-economic groups, and the evidence on morbidity and utilisation is used to tentatively assess whether at an overall, system-wide level the objective of providing 'equal treatment for equal need' is being attained. Finally, section 11.4 brings together the main conclusions.

11.1 SOCIO-ECONOMIC MORTALITY DIFFERENTIALS

The fact that there are differences across occupations, occupational groups and social classes in death rates for men of working age has been known for many years, and analysis of such differences has served as the foundation stone of research on health inequalities internationally. In Britain these differentials have been studied for over a century, and interest in the topic was given new impetus by the Black Report (Department of Health and Social Security, 1980). It not only pointed to very large differences in death rates between occupational classes at the beginning of the 1970s but also suggested that these had increased rather than decreased since the early 1930s.

A follow-up report by the Health Education Council (Whitehead, 1987) further fuelled the debate, suggesting that mortality differentials between manual and non-manual groups had widened from 1971 to 1981. Provoked by the Black Report, a substantial body of research on the interpretation of the available British data and its limitations, and on the causal factors at work, has been produced. Important new types of data have also been produced, providing valuable insights into these processes. A great deal of research on mortality differentials has also been carried out in other developed countries, notably Sweden, and comparisons across countries of the extent of these differentials, though fraught with difficulty, have recently been attempted.

Until recently, little has been known about mortality differentials in Ireland at national level, though some small-scale local studies had been done. This was despite the fact that, as elsewhere, information on occupation has been routinely gathered at time of death. The British procedure, widely followed internationally, has been to calculate death rates by occupation using the number of deaths of people in each occupation, as revealed by this death registration information, and the total number in the occupation at the time as shown by the census of population. Comparison of mortality rates across occupations and broader occupational groups, socio-economic groups or social classes can then be made.

In Ireland this type of analysis has recently been carried out using data for 1981 (Nolan, 1990). In processing the information from the deaths registration process, the Central Statistics Office classifies it into socio-economic groups (SEGs), and so the analysis was carried out on the basis of SEGs rather than narrower occupational breakdowns or the conceptually somewhat different categorisation by social class. The analysis looks at deaths in 1981 of men aged between fifteen and sixty-four, classified by SEG, compared with the total number of men in this age range in each SEG in the 1981 census. Women and older men were not included at this stage, because of the nature of the information on their occupations. Married women are classified by the occupation of their husbands, which may or may not be most appropriate in this context; and the occupational data for the retired is thought to be less reliable than for those in work.

Since the death rate for each SEG for the entire 15–64 age group will be influenced by its age composition—the proportion who are between 55 and 64, for example—it is useful first to look at death rates within narrower age groups. Table 11.1 shows that there are marked differences between SEGs. For example, in the 55–64 age range the death rate for the higher professional group is 13 per 1,000, compared with 22 for the semi-skilled and 32 for the unskilled manual groups. Similarly, in the 45–54 range the rate per 1,000 for unskilled manual workers is 11, compared with 4 for higher professionals.

Alternatively, summary measures for the entire 15–64 age range that *standardise* for the differing age compositions of the SEGs can be calculated. Standardised mortality ratios (SMRs) designed to do this are commonly used in the literature in this context. These involve calculating what the expected number of deaths for a particular SEG would be if the population in that SEG in each age range—25 to 34, 35 to 44, etc.—experienced the average death rate over all SEGs for that age range. The actual total of deaths for the SEG is then expressed as a percentage of the expected deaths. An SMR over 100 thus means that the SEG had more deaths than would be expected on the basis of the SEG's age composition and average age-specific death rates for the entire population.

SMRs calculated in this way for men aged fifteen to sixty-four are also shown in table 11.1. Higher and lower professionals, employers and managers and salaried employees have SMRs well below 100. For farmers, farm relatives assisting, and farm workers, the SMRs are also well below 100. Skilled manual workers have an SMR closer to 100, and for the 'intermediate' groups of non-manual wage-earners they are about 100. For semi-skilled and particularly unskilled manual workers SMRs are substantially above 100, which is also the case for the 'unknown' group. SMRs thus range from 55 for the higher professional group to 163 for the unskilled manual one; actual deaths for higher professionals are only about half the figure we would expect on the basis of average age-specific death rates, but for unskilled manual workers they are over one-and-a-half times the expected figure.

TABLE 11.1 *Mortality rates for men aged 15–64 by socio-economic group, 1981*

Socio-economic group	15–24	25–34	35–44	45–54	55–64	Standardised mortality rate
			Death rate per 1,000			
Farmers	0.9	0.8	1.4	5.6	14.8	79
Farm labourers	1.6	1.3	3.1	4.6	15.2	86
Higher professional	0.2	0.3	0.8	3.5	12.8	55
Lower professional	1.5	0.5	1.4	5.5	16.0	79
Employers & managers	0.9	0.5	1.2	4.5	11.6	62
Salaried employees	1.0	0.6	1.5	3.6	15.2	71
Non-manual white-collar	1.0	1.1	2.4	7.8	20.2	105
Non-manual other	1.8	1.2	2.0	6.2	20.1	104
Skilled manual	0.9	0.7	1.9	6.2	18.7	91
Semi-skilled manual	1.7	1.1	3.0	7.2	22.1	117
Unskilled manual	1.9	1.5	3.4	10.7	31.6	163
Unknown	3.0	6.8	6.8	13.4	25.9	174

These differences in SMRs across socio-economic groups are statistically significant, using statistical tests commonly applied in this context. It must be noted, though, that the 'unknown' group has a particularly high SMR, higher even than the unskilled manual SEG. This group comprises those individuals who could not be assigned to an identified SEG on the basis of the information supplied in registering the death (in deriving the number of deaths for each SEG) or in the census (in deriving the total in each SEG). The SMR is so high because, while 6.5 per cent of men aged 15–64 were classified in the unknown SEG in the census, this was the case for 14 per cent of deaths. This could reflect problems with the data, a relatively high death rate for the type of people most likely to be classified as unknown (such as those not gainfully occupied), or, most probably, both.

This problem highlights the general issue of the reliability of the data used to derive these mortality rates. The possibility that bringing together information from two different sources could give rise to substantial 'numerator-denominator biases', with the same individual classified differently in the census and the death registration records, has long been recognised. However, the longitudinal study being carried out by the UK Office of Population Censuses and Surveys, which has followed a sample of about 1 per cent from the 1971 census for England and Wales through the 1970s and 1980s, has allowed mortality differentials based entirely on census occupational classifications to be derived. Although a substantial number were in fact classified differently by the census and death registration records, there was no consistent tendency to either 'promote' or 'demote' when registering deaths for men aged 15–64, and so the differentials between the social classes produced by the conventional matching of death registration and census data were not subject to substantial bias. While this is helpful, the need for further validation of the Irish data must be noted, particularly since a higher proportion of the Irish deaths fall into the 'unknown' category.

One of the main obstacles to comparisons of socio-economic mortality differentials across countries is the fact that there are usually significant differences in the way occupations and socio-economic positions are classified. However, a necessarily suggestive rather than exact comparison can be made with differentials across socio-economic groups for the same date for England and Wales. This shows the patterns for Ireland and for England and Wales to be broadly similar, with if anything a steeper gradient—i.e. a wider differential—between professional-managerial and unskilled manual socio-economic groups in Ireland.

The differentials in England and Wales appear to be wider than in Sweden but narrower than in France. What is most interesting, though, is that for many European countries major differences in mortality rates across social classes, socio-economic groups or educational levels have been observed. This suggests that deep-seated factors common to all these countries produce such health inequalities.

How then are these mortality differentials across socio-economic groups to be interpreted, and what do they tell us about the relationship between poverty and health? The causes of these differentials have been debated for as long as they have been recognised, with attention focusing initially on health risks associated with particular occupations. The role of social circumstances and environment has always been a central theme, however, and was emphasised in the Black Report. This distinguished four types of explanation: artefact, social selection, cultural-behavioural, and 'materialist'.

Artefact explanations suggest that the relationship is produced or trends are distorted by the process of measurement, because of, for example, numerator-denominator biases, the way in which categorisation into social classes is carried out, or the fact that focusing on differentials across classes ignores major changes over time in the class composition of the population. Explanations in terms of selection suggest that health itself plays a major part in determining socio-economic position, with the unhealthy being downwardly mobile, leading to a concentration in lower socio-economic groups of people with a high risk of dying early. The British Longitudinal Study mentioned earlier, which was able to follow a sample classified in terms of their occupation etc. in the 1971 census through the 1970s and 1980s, shows that neither artefact nor selection processes account for the observed differentials there.

Cultural-behavioural explanations focus on health-related behaviour that differs across social classes and could produce inequalities in health or mortality, notably cigarette smoking, alcohol consumption, diet, and exercise. The links between life-style and health outcomes are often rather loose and poorly understood, though such factors may contribute to the observed differentials. As a general explanation, however, it is undermined by longitudinal studies showing that differences in mortality from, for example, coronary heart disease could not be accounted for by differences in behaviour, and the fact that risk of death from most causes, including those not apparently related to such 'life-style' factors, tends to be higher in less privileged groups.

Almost by a process of elimination, then, one is led to focus—as the Black Report was—on 'materialist' explanations, emphasising the importance of differences in material circumstances and the impact of poverty and deprivation on health and mortality. This has in addition the merit of accounting for the existence and persistence of socio-economic mortality differentials in countries that vary widely in cultural and behavioural patterns, degrees of social mobility, and methods of collecting and producing information on mortality differentials. The channels through which life circumstances could have an impact on health are many, ranging from the links between damp housing and respiratory disease, those between nutrition and ill health, the interactions between psychological and psychosocial factors and physical ill health, and greater risk of accident and exposure to environmental hazards for lower socio-economic groups.

The complex relationship between material circumstances over one's lifetime and ill health is further discussed in the next section, where we turn from mortality differentials to the pattern of morbidity across socio-economic groups in Ireland.

11.2 MORBIDITY, CLASS, AND POVERTY

Evidence from other countries suggests that the incidence of ill health, like premature mortality, is highest in the lower social classes and socio-economic groups. For Ireland, until recently this relationship had only been studied for small samples or particular illnesses. However, information obtained in the 1987 household survey carried out by the ESRI allows the incidence of self-reported physical illness among a nationally representative sample to be examined (Nolan, 1991c).

The survey asked adults whether they had 'any major illness, physical disability or infirmity that has troubled you for at least the past year or that is likely to go on troubling you in the future.' This type of question on chronic illness has been widely used elsewhere, for example in the British General Household Survey and regular health surveys carried out in France and the Scandinavian countries. While self-reporting might be thought likely to be problematic, where comparisons have been made with doctors' assessments or medical records the level of agreement has been high. Substantially higher rates of self-reported chronic illness in the lower than the higher social classes have been found in various countries, the gap generally being particularly pronounced in the middle age ranges.

About 17 per cent of adults in the ESRI survey reported chronic illness in response to this question. Table 11.2 shows the way in which this varied by age range and social class, using the CSO's six-category social class scale. Overall, the proportion reporting such illness rises steadily from 10.5 per cent for the higher professional class to 25 per cent for the unskilled manual one. The incidence of illness rises markedly with age, as one would expect, so differences in the age composition of the classes could affect this overall comparison. However, the table shows that within age ranges a very substantial differential across the classes persists, with the gap being widest for the middle age groups. For those between 45 and 54, the proportion reporting chronic illness rises from 11 per cent for the higher professional class to 27 per cent for the unskilled manual one.

When current income rather than social class is used to categorise people, the pattern is very much less marked, although, controlling for age, those living in households towards the bottom of the (equivalent) income distribution are more likely to report chronic illness than those towards the top of the distribution. Table 11.3 shows that within each age group, the percentage reporting chronic illness is significantly higher for those in households below the 60 per cent relative-income poverty line than for those in households above that line.

TABLE 11.2 *Chronic physical illness by age and social class, 1987*

Age range	Percentage reporting chronic illness by social class					
	Higher professional	Lower professional	Other non-manual	Skilled manual	Semi-skilled manual	Unskilled manual
15–34	5.1	2.9	5.3	9.2	7.9	10.0
35–44	5.6	5.8	9.4	11.2	15.4	12.3
45–54	11.0	13.0	16.7	19.2	23.5	27.0
55–64	23.5	22.0	28.2	28.9	32.6	44.7
65 & over	21.8	33.6	30.8	37.6	36.3	33.4
All	10.5	10.5	13.9	17.0	19.0	24.6

Nonetheless, the relationship over the income distribution between ill health and current income is not as pronounced as that with social class, which is not particularly surprising, since (*a*) current income is not in itself a comprehensive measure of current economic resources and living standards, for a variety of reasons, discussed in earlier chapters, and (*b*) experiences and living patterns over a long period, rather than simply current economic status, affect health outcomes, and one would expect these long-term factors to be better captured by social class.

Each of these aspects can be explored using data in the ESRI survey. Focusing first on current economic status, the combined income and deprivation criteria developed in chapter 4 can be used to distinguish those who are currently both on low incomes (below the 60 per cent line) and experiencing basic forms of deprivation. Table 11.3 then shows that adults in these households have a much higher probability of reporting chronic illness than the remainder of the sample, the gap being considerably wider than that between people above and below the income poverty line alone. More precise measurement of current living standards and deprivation levels thus produces a wider differential in reported ill health between the 'poor' and the 'non-poor'.

TABLE 11.3 *Percentage of 'poor' versus 'non-poor' reporting chronic illness*

Age group	60% income poverty line		60% income plus basic deprivation	
	Below	Above	Below	Above
15–34	9.6	6.4	11.5	6.3
35–44	17.7	8.9	21.5	9.3
45–54	24.0	17.0	26.8	17.6
55–64	28.1	37.4	47.7	27.6
65 & over	42.5	32.6	53.7	32.9
All				

Turning to the role of life circumstances over a long period, categorisation by social class is essentially based on occupation, together with farm size or size of business for farmers and the self-employed. This is likely to be a better indicator of differences across groups in income over many years or 'permanent income' than current weekly or annual income, which may be quite variable. As shown in earlier chapters, weekly income may fluctuate through the year because of illness, unemployment, hours worked, or other factors, and can therefore differ significantly from annual income, while, particularly for farmers and other self-employed people, annual incomes can also fluctuate a good deal from year to year.

The level of financial assets held by households is seen to relate more consistently to position in the social class scale than to ranking in the current income distribution, controlling for age, lending support to the notion that class is a more reliable indicator of longer-term economic position. Thus the strength of the relationship between class and current reported chronic ill health is entirely consistent with an emphasis on 'materialist' explanations.

There has been particular interest elsewhere in the possible consequences of deprivation in early life for health in adulthood. In this light it is worth exploiting the fact that the 1987 survey obtained information not only on current social class but also on the occupation etc. of the principal breadwinner in the family when the respondent was growing up, allowing the social class of origin to be identified. When we control for an individual's own current social class (and age), those whose parents were in the unskilled manual social class have a higher probability of reporting chronic illness than others in the same social class (and age group). The same is true of those who say that when they were growing up their family was able to manage financially 'with great difficulty': they are now more likely to be reporting chronic ill health than others currently in the same class and age group. This is again suggestive of the importance of material circumstances throughout one's life for health outcomes, though the channels through which these effects operate cannot be identified with the data available to us. Further information obtained in the 1987 survey on labour force histories also suggests that downward social mobility for those away from work for substantial periods because of ill health is of quite limited importance, so once again selection-type effects do not appear to be a major contributor to the observed differentials in health across the social classes.

11.3 HEALTH INEQUALITIES AND HEALTH SERVICES UTILISATION

Given the differentials across socio-economic groups in mortality and morbidity documented in this chapter, the role of the health services in addressing health inequalities merits discussion. In the Department of Health's consultative document *Health: the Wider Dimensions* (1986), the stated aims of health policy include the promotion of equity, seen as including the distribution of available health services over the population on the basis of need. Noting the existence of inequalities in health between age or sex and socio-economic groups, a basic objective 'should be to frame policy responses on a broad front ... which promote equality in health,' the health services being only one element in such a response. It is worth considering then whether the health services as they are now structured do deliver health care on the basis of need and contribute to alleviating inequalities in health.

The structure of eligibility to state-financed health care is seen as helping to meet these objectives by discriminating in favour of the less well off, in that only those meeting the means test for medical card cover are entitled to free general practitioner care and prescription medicines from the state. Those with medical card cover visit the GP more often than the rest of the population, and even when age and sex are taken into account their visiting rates are considerably higher on average than those without cover. This was seen as a source of concern through the 1980s, given the implications for state expenditure not only on GP fees but also on prescription medicines, since prescriptions and visits tend to be closely associated. Research by Tussing (1985) suggested that the high visiting rate for those with medical card cover was heavily influenced by the combination of services provided free to users and a GP remuneration system based on a fee for each visit. This meant that doctors had a financial incentive to encourage utilisation, while medical card patients were less resistant than those who had to pay for visits.

To control state expenditure on providing this service, the method of remuneration for GPs treating medical card patients was changed in 1989 to one based principally on capitation: that is, doctors were paid for the number of patients on their panel rather than per visit. Despite this, expenditure on the service, and particularly on the pre-scription medicines element, has continued to grow rapidly.

However, one reason for the relatively high visiting rate of those with medical card cover that was not taken into account explicitly in pre-vious research is the higher incidence of ill health among the lower socio-economic groups, documented in this chapter. In the 1987 survey the average number of GP visits in the previous year reported by those with medical card cover was over five, compared with about two for the rest of the population. While the former include more elderly people, who tend to have more visits, even when age composition is taken into account those with medical card cover have about twice as many visits on average as those without cover. Regression analysis confirms that, controlling for age, sex and location and even including income and social class as explanatory variables, the presence of medical card cover is a significant and positive influence on visiting rates. However, this takes no account of differences between those with and without cover in 'need' for health care.

The data obtained in the survey on self-reported physical health status described in the previous section, and the general health ques-tionnaire on psychological health described in chapter 10, allows such differences to be included in the analysis, albeit in a rather crude way. When additional variables for presence or absence of chronic physical illness or psychological distress (above the GHQ threshold) are includ-ed in the regression predicting the number of visits to the GP (and controlling for age, sex, etc.), they are seen to be highly significant and account for a considerable proportion of the difference between those with or without medical card cover (Nolan, 1991c, 1993c). The likely impact of medical card cover itself, then, and of the financial incentives to patients and doctors involved, is less than it appeared to be when differences in morbidity were not taken into account.

More refined measures of health status would be needed to assess whether the remaining significant and positive impact of medical card cover on the predicted number of visits is primarily attributable to the effects of such incentives or to differences in the incidence and severity of illness and therefore 'need' for care not fully reflected in the measures available in the survey. The importance of taking differences across socio-economic groups in morbidity and therefore in health 'needs' in framing policy and evaluating its impact is to be emphasised.

More broadly, measures of health status and the incidence of ill health are clearly needed if one is to assess whether the health services are in fact structured so as to ensure that health care is delivered on the basis of need. The definition and measurement of 'need' in this context is highly problematic, but a start can be made by comparing the distribution of health care delivery—of utilisation—with that of reported ill health. It is then of interest to see whether utilisation varies systematically with income in a way that is not simply a reflection of differences in health needs—whether the poor get more or less care than the rich, controlling for differences in needs.

A collaborative international study sponsored by the EC Commission and applying a common methodology has recently addressed this issue (van Doorslaer et al., 1993), the Irish element being based on analysis of the 1987 ESRI survey data. This involved attributing expenditure on health care (whether by the state or households) to those who benefit from it on the basis of their reported utilisation of different types of care over the previous year and estimated unit costs (per GP visit, night in hospital, etc.). The distribution of health care expenditure among individuals could then be compared with that of reported ill health.

The results for Ireland (Nolan, 1993b) showed that when people were simply classified by (equivalent household) income, a very high proportion of expenditure went to those towards the bottom of the income distribution; about 53 per cent of health care expenditure went to the bottom 40 per cent. However, those towards the bottom were also more likely to report chronic physical illness, with the bottom 40 per cent containing 54 per cent of those who reported such illness. Thus the distribution of expenditure over the income distribution was in fact seen to mirror rather closely the distribution of the chronically ill.

Health care needs may also vary over the income distribution with the proportion of elderly people or women, over and above the impact of the numbers reporting chronic illness (since both the elderly and women are more likely to require care even if not chronically ill). When the distribution is standardised for these differences, it is seen that, if anything, those at the bottom of the income distribution received a higher proportion of health care expenditure than would be expected on the basis of age and sex composition and the proportion reporting chronic illness. Regression analysis also suggested a similar conclusion, though the hypothesis of no income-related inequity is in fact only weakly rejected statistically. Results for other countries covered by the study identified inequity favouring the rich in the United States, the UK, and Spain, perhaps because of above-average private expenditure on health care by the better-off. Once again, more refined measures of health status are needed before strong conclusions can be reached. This is illustrated by results for countries that had a range of indicators of health status, where it was found that the distribution of expenditures favoured the poor less when several indicators were included simultaneously than when only one was included in the analysis.

It will also be necessary to take into account the fact that in assessing the distribution of expenditure relative to 'need' one may be primarily concerned with capacity to benefit from health care, which will not always be the same as the presence of ill health or severity of illness.

11.4 CONCLUSIONS

In Ireland, as in other developed countries, the poor and disadvantaged experience more ill health and have lower life expectancy than those from higher socio-economic groups. Analysis of data from death certificates reveals marked differentials across socio-economic groups in mortality rates for men between the ages of fifteen and sixty-four, those in the unskilled manual group having rates well above average. The pattern for Ireland is broadly similar to that for England and Wales; and the fact that such differentials are found for many different countries suggests that they are produced by deep-seated factors: research elsewhere suggests that differences in material circumstances and the impact of poverty and deprivation on health are an important part of the explanation.

Differences across social classes and socio-economic groups in morbidity are also commonly found elsewhere. Respondents in the ESRI survey were asked about their health, and the percentage reporting chronic physical illness rises steadily as one moves down the social class scale, from 10 per cent for the higher professional class to 25 per cent for the unskilled manual one. Those currently on low incomes and experiencing basic deprivation were also much more likely than the remainder of the sample to report such illness.

The fact that those experiencing poverty and deprivation often have greater 'need' for health care than others has to be taken into account in analysing the utilisation of health services and assessing whether health care is delivered on the basis of need, irrespective of socio-economic status. Thus, for example, the fact that GP visiting rates are considerably higher for those with medical card cover, who do not have to pay for this service, is partly attributable to differences in health status rather than the financial incentives facing patients and doctors. More broadly, when health care expenditure is allocated among those using the health services, a relatively high proportion goes to lower-income groups, but this appeared to mirror quite closely the distribution of those experiencing chronic illness. More refined measures of health status and health care 'needs' are required to see in more depth the relationships between socio-economic status, 'needs', and availability of care.

In conclusion, it is particularly relevant in a book about poverty to emphasise that the persistent marked differences across socio-economic groups in health and life expectancy found in Ireland and elsewhere are not likely to be amenable to 'treatment' through the health services. While the structure and design of the health services must take them into account and direct care where it is most needed, health inequalities reflect wider inequalities in material circumstances, and alleviating poverty may be the most effective way of narrowing differentials in health and life expectancy.

12 Poverty and Gender Inequality

TIM CALLAN

The impact of poverty on women has become a focus of considerable interest in recent years. There are many reasons why women's poverty has attracted increasing attention. In the United States the term 'feminisation of poverty' was coined to highlight the fact that despite women's increased participation in the labour market, poverty among women had increased while poverty among men had declined (Pearce, 1978). The growth of lone-parent families, mostly headed by women, was also a focus of concern in many other countries, as they have generally been found to be at a particularly high risk of poverty.

Feminist critiques of social research methods have also pointed to the danger of assumptions of equal sharing of resources within house-holds and to the possible extent of 'hidden poverty' among women in households with total resources above the poverty thresholds. They have also pointed to the importance of the division of paid and unpaid work within families in determining women's economic position and wider access to resources (Glendinning and Millar, 1987).

The issues arising from these debates are addressed and the available evidence for Ireland is explored in this chapter and the succeeding one. The present chapter begins by reviewing briefly some of the major themes from the international literature on the impact of poverty on women and the hypothesis of the 'feminisation of poverty'. It then turns to the evidence on risks of poverty for men and women, and the potential hidden poverty of female-headed families within multi-family households. The issue of unequal sharing of resources within marriage, and the potential 'hidden poverty' among women arising from this, is explored in the next chapter.

Taken together, this evidence provides a fuller picture of the sex-specific impact of poverty in Ireland than has been possible heretofore. But in order to understand why this picture arises it is necessary to consider the factors structuring women's economic opportunities. Thus, the present chapter draws together evidence on the structure of the incentives facing women in making decisions about participation in the labour market and the impact of the division of labour in child care and other family responsibilities on their current participation and potential future earnings in the labour market.

12.1 POVERTY AND GENDER: A REVIEW OF THE ISSUES

Much of the recent interest in poverty and gender has centred on the concept of the 'feminisation of poverty'. This term was used by Pearce (1978) to highlight a tendency for women to form an increasing proportion of the poor population in the United States. The main reason for this trend has been a growth in lone-parent families headed by women. Risks of poverty for such families have tended to be high but relatively stable in the United States: it has been growth in the number of such families, as a proportion of all family types, that has given rise to an increased concentration of poverty among women (Rodgers, 1990).

Growth in the number of lone-parent families, mainly headed by women, has also been observed in many other OECD countries. A natural question, therefore, is whether a similar 'feminisation of poverty' has occurred in these countries. There have been few empirical studies of this question. In the UK, Wright (1992) finds that there has been little change in the female share of poverty between 1968 and 1986. From a longer-term perspective, Lewis and Piachaud (1987) find indications that women's share of poverty at the turn of the century appears to have been little different from its current level.

Such results have given rise to an alternative argument: that women are overrepresented among the poor, but that this overrepresentation has become increasingly visible. Glendinning and Millar (1987) argue that in the UK context the rise in the number of female-headed households has been one factor making women's poverty more visible. But they also contend that the feminist focus on women's experience within the household and family has uncovered hidden poverty—poverty within marriage or perhaps lone mothers experiencing poverty in a household that has an average income above the poverty line. Poverty studies using the traditional household level of analysis, with its implicit assumption of equal sharing of resources between members of each household, cannot address these issues.

There are, therefore, two key questions that must be addressed by an empirical investigation of the Irish situation. First, are women overrepresented among the poor in Ireland? And second, has the burden of poverty shifted towards women, so that they now form an increased proportion of the poor?

There are strengths and weaknesses in the types of answer that the Economic and Social Research Institute data, and the methods used in analysing it, can provide to these questions. Obvious advantages include the fact that the ESRI survey provides a nationally representative picture, and that the relative income poverty lines allow an exploration of how answers change with the level of the poverty cut-off and the nature of the allowances made for the needs of children (the 'equivalence scale'). As seen in chapter 4, it is also possible to go beyond the usual income-based measures of poverty and include a measure that also takes direct evidence of deprivation into account.

The ESRI survey has also been used to provide much richer analyses of poverty at sub-household level than have been possible heretofore in Ireland, and indeed in many other countries. In this chapter we consider analyses at what has been termed 'tax unit' level. This helps to identify lone parents, usually women, living as part of larger household units, and also distinguishes as separate units young adults who have finished full-time education. In this way we can take account of the possibility that, for example, lone parents do not share equally in the resources of households with an average income above the poverty line. (In the next chapter, more detailed evidence from the follow-up ESRI survey on the nature of income sharing and financial management within households, and particularly between couples, is considered.) The major limitation of the ESRI survey, and the analysis based on it, is that it is not possible in a large-scale household survey to conduct the sort of intensive investigation of intra-household and intra-marriage financial arrangements that some qualitative studies have undertaken. Such studies can provide valuable insights into the nature of financial management and control within households; but the small and highly selective samples used in such studies do not allow reliable generalisations to national level.

12.2 POVERTY AND GENDER IN IRELAND

How then can we address the question of whether women are overrepresented among the poor in Ireland? A first attempt, which follows the lines of the literature on the feminisation of poverty in the United States, is to consider the risks faced by men and women of living in a poor household (see table 12.1).

TABLE 12.1 *Risks of income poverty for adult men and women, 1987*

Income cut-off	Men	Women
40% line	8.0	6.2
50% line	18.3	16.0
60% line	28.3	27.5

Using these relative poverty lines, the risks of being in a poor household are found to be very similar for men and women. Women face very slightly lower risks than men at each income cut-off, and therefore are, if anything, slightly underrepresented amongst the poor in 1987. Almost equal numbers of men and women are found to be in households below half average income, with slightly more women in households below 60 per cent of average income; but this reflects the fact that there are more women than men in the general adult population.

Given that a large majority of adults are married, and that consideration of possible differences in poverty status within marriage are deferred until the next chapter, it is unsurprising that risks of poverty for men and women in this analysis should be relatively close. It may be of more interest to focus on households headed by a woman as against households headed by a man or by a couple, where greater differences might be expected. Table 12.2 shows the results of such analysis, using both the standard income poverty lines and the income-cum-deprivation standard described in chapter 4.

TABLE 12.2 *Risks of poverty for households headed by man or couple or by woman, 1987*

	Below income line		Also experiencing basic deprivation	
	Man/couple	Woman	Man/couple	Woman
40% line	8.3	5.5	3.3	2.6
50% line	19.4	10.6	10.4	5.1
60% line	29.8	32.8	15.5	16.2

Female-headed households faced a lower risk of income poverty at the 40 per cent and 50 per cent lines than households headed by a man or couple. Male or couple-headed households were almost twice as likely to be found below half average income as female-headed households. A much smaller difference in risk was found at the highest income poverty line, with female-headed households slightly more likely to be below 60 per cent of average income. The introduction of direct evidence on deprivation alters this pattern only in one respect: the differences in risk at the lowest income cut-off are greatly reduced. Male or couple-headed households are still found to be at about twice the risk of poverty at the intermediate income cut-off, with almost equal risks at the highest income cut-off.

The relatively low risk for female-headed households in this analysis partly reflects the fact that many of these households are headed by elderly women, who have benefited from the substantial increases in social welfare rates for the elderly during the 1970s and 1980s. Some would also have benefited from private occupational pension schemes with provision for spouses; the coverage of such schemes would also have increased over this period. An age-related analysis confirms that this factor is important. Other results in this age-related analysis are sensitive to the level of the poverty line, and the allowances made for the needs of children (the 'equivalence scale').

Comparing households headed by young (aged less than 35), middle-aged (35 to 64) and elderly (65 or over) women with households headed by a man or couple of similar age, we find that women were not at much greater risk of being below half average income; in fact the reverse was true for middle-aged and elderly women. At the higher (60 per cent) income cut-off the small group of households headed by a young woman were found to be at higher risk than households headed by a man or couple of similar age. The results for middle-aged and elderly women depend on the equivalence scale. A scale that is more generous to children suggests that male or couple-headed households were at greater risk of poverty, but a scale that is closer to that implicit in social welfare rates suggests that female-headed households were at higher risk. This is partly caused by the fact that the non-contributory old age and widows' pensions were close to the 60 per cent income cut-off, with the precise relationship depending on the equivalence scale.

To allow for the possibility that lone-parent families and single people in larger households may not share fully in the resources available to these households, an analysis was also undertaken at the level of the 'tax unit': an individual or married couple, together with any dependent children. The implicit assumption in this analysis, as discussed in chapter 3, is that income is shared fully within the tax unit but no income is shared between tax units in the same household. Thus, analysis at this level helps to tell us how many tax units would be poor by relative income standards if their resources were not supplemented or their needs reduced in any way by being part of a larger household. This may not be a realistic assumption: tax units may benefit either from explicit cash transfers from other tax units within the household or from not having to pay a proportionate share of housing, heating, food or other costs. But it is a useful assumption in identifying the possible importance of a lack of full sharing of resources between tax units in a household, which is the implicit assumption in household-level analysis.

TABLE 12.3 *Risks of poverty for tax units headed by man or couple or by woman, 1987*

	Tax unit head by	
Below income line	Man/couple	Woman
40% line	11.0	11.9
50% line	22.0	18.1
60% line	32.3	33.8

On this basis, table 12.3 shows that the risks of income poverty facing tax units headed by a woman are very similar to those facing tax units headed by a man or a couple. Whereas female-headed households were at a relatively low risk of being below half average income, female-headed tax units are at a risk close to the average. When the analysis is extended to control for the age of the head of the tax unit, the male-female differentials in the risk of poverty remain small. The tax units classified as 'poor' in this analysis would include not only lone-parent families in larger households but also some young single men and women engaged in very low-paid employment.

A more direct insight into the risks of poverty for lone parents can be achieved by focusing on households with children aged under eighteen but headed by a person who is single, widowed, or separated. There is a substantial difference between the risks of poverty for such households, depending on whether they are headed by men or women. Women heading such households are at a very high risk of poverty, with 30 per cent being below half average income and almost three out of five below the 60 per cent income cut-off. This is, therefore, a high-risk group; but in calculations of the overall risk of poverty for men and women its influence is limited, because fewer than 5 per cent of households fall into this category.

TABLE 12.4 *Trends in risk of poverty for households headed by man or couple or by woman, 1973–87*

	Household head by	
	Man/couple	Woman
	Percentage of households below half average income	
Household budget survey, 1973	14.5	30.4
Household budget survey, 1980	15.6	22.4
ESRI survey, 1987	19.4	10.6

Growth in the size of this high-risk group was the main cause of the 'feminisation of poverty' in the United States. There has been rapid growth in the number of lone mothers (including widows) in Ireland. A detailed study of this growth is provided by McCashin (1993), who shows the difficulties in arriving at precise measures that are comparable over time. Some idea of the growth can be gleaned from census figures, which show that between 1979 and 1986, for example, the number of lone mothers increased by almost 17 per cent, about three times the rate of growth of the population. Almost 95 per cent of these were in one-family households and thus were heads of household. Analysis of trends in the risk of poverty for female-headed households as against other households should therefore help to show whether poverty has become more concentrated on women in Ireland as it has in the United States.

As shown in table 12.4, however, the risk of income poverty for female-headed households has fallen, while the risk of poverty for other households has risen. The same trend is found for higher and lower income cut-offs and alternative equivalence scales. Improvements in the relative income position of old age pensioners and widows have been the main contributory factors to this trend. The small group of households headed by a woman aged under thirty-five fared less well than households headed by a man or couple in that age group; but the risks for other female-headed households fell.

In 1987 most women in poor households were married women. Almost four out of every five women in households below half average income were married—many of them to unemployed men or to farmers. The numbers of lone mothers, who were at particularly high risk of poverty, had grown; but they still represented a rather small proportion of the population. The relative income position of elderly women and widows improved during the 1970s and 1980s, tending to reduce their risk of poverty to below average levels.

12.3 WOMEN'S POSITION IN THE LABOUR MARKET

In analysing the relationship between women's work and poverty, Daly (1989) points to two key dimensions: the extent to which women work full time in the home rather than for pay, and the extent to which women in paid employment receive lower pay than men. A paid job may help to lift a woman out of poverty either by raising the couple's total income above the poverty line, if income is adequately shared, or, if a woman's poverty is caused by lack of income-sharing, by raising her independent income sufficiently. But most Irish women do not have a paid job; and those who are in employment tend to have lower wages than their male counterparts.

In this section we review recent trends in each of these areas, in order to understand the current extent and nature of women's participation in the labour market. This information will be used to assess policies to equalise opportunities between the sexes and the potential role of increased employment for women as part of a strategy for tackling poverty.

Overall participation rates for Irish women have been relatively constant since the 1960s, at about 30 per cent. But there have been substantial structural changes behind this overall constancy. Labour market participation by young women and men has tended to decline, as they spent longer periods in full-time education. Participation has also declined among elderly women and men, as pensions for widows and the elderly improved and the agricultural sector contracted. These factors have led to a decline in the overall participation rate for men, to about 70 per cent. But women have come to form an increased share of the paid work force, because of a striking increase in the employment rate for married women. In the early 1960s only one out of twenty married women was at work in the paid labour force; by 1989 this figure had risen to something closer to one in four.

Such increases in married women's participation rates reflected a widespread international trend. However, Irish married women are still much less likely than their foreign counterparts to participate in the paid labour market. In most EC countries the participation rate for married women would be close to 50 per cent; in the Scandinavian countries rates of over 70 per cent are common. Differences in typical family size go some way towards explaining this difference; but participation rates for women with equal numbers of children are also lower in Ireland than in many other countries.

Why has married women's participation in the Irish labour market grown so rapidly? And why is it still so much below the rates in other countries? There is a tendency to look towards social attitudes for answers to these questions. Changes in attitudes and differences in attitudes across countries do undoubtedly have a role to play. But international studies (for example those reviewed by Mincer, 1985) have shown a clear role for economic influences in explaining the growth in married women's labour force participation. The study by Callan and Farrell (1991) for the National Economic and Social Council, based on the ESRI data, suggests that economic factors are of considerable importance in the Irish context.[1]

The starting point for that analysis is that, other things being equal, a married woman is more likely to work in the paid labour market if she can command a high wage rate, and less likely to do so the higher the value she places on time spent at home and the higher the costs (such as child care) associated with employment. An inherent problem facing the analysis is that wage rates are observed only for women who do become employees. But it is possible to predict the wage rates that could be obtained by women who are not currently employed. This is done by estimating the relationship between wage rates for those who are employed and relevant characteristics, such as their level of education and the extent of their past labour market experience. Since these variables are known for all women, predicted wage rates can be obtained even for those who are not currently employees. Because different women face different wage rates and place differing values on time spent at home, it is possible to estimate the extent to which an increase in the wage rate would make it more likely that women would take up employment outside the home than work in the home.

The analysis suggests that in 1987 Irish women's participation in the labour market was very responsive to wage rates by international standards. Looking back at the rise in married women's participation since the 1960s, it seems that over half, and perhaps two-thirds, of the increase could be due to increases in the real wage. Rising real wages have made working in the paid labour market more attractive than unpaid work in the home, and for that reason increasing numbers of married women have chosen to take up paid employment.

Fig. 12.1.   *Labour market activity rates of married women classified by age and number of children*

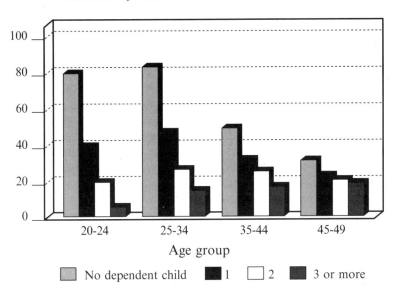

The differences between participation rates for women with children and those without children are strikingly illustrated in fig. 12.1. For women in each age group an additional child reduces the rate of participation in the paid labour market. The effect is particularly strong, however, in the two younger age groups, where the age of the children would also tend to be younger. The econometric modelling by Callan and Farrell (1991), which takes account of the many factors influencing married women's decisions on participation in the labour market, also shows a strong influence from the number of young children. In particular, there is strong evidence that the presence of a pre-school child makes it much less likely that a woman will participate in the paid labour market. There is no similar effect in the case of men. Similarly, caring for family members with special needs tends to be done predominantly by women and has a much stronger effect on their labour market participation than on men.

Social norms and personal preferences obviously play a role in giving rise to these patterns. But financial considerations also enter into the decision process. Thus the availability and cost of child care, and the degree to which state financial support depends on a mother's work status, are also relevant.

The rapid growth in married women's participation in the Irish labour market can be explained largely by growth in real wages, and the fall in average family size in the past twenty years. Some of the growth in real wages has been brought about by legislative change, such as equal pay provisions and the removal of the marriage bar in the public service; but a substantial part is due to widespread wage growth in the economy, reflecting increased investment in physical capital and in human capital, through education and training. The fact that participation rates are still low by international standards partly reflects the fact that Irish family sizes are still somewhat larger, but also the fact that real wages are lower in Ireland than in the United States, Scandinavia, and most EC countries.

The income tax system also tends to discourage participation by married women in the labour market. There has been something of an international trend towards more independent taxation of husbands and wives. But the Irish system, like that in Germany, provides for what is termed 'income-splitting': a married couple's total income tax bill depends basically on their total income and not on the division of earnings between the spouses. Alternatively, the system can be seen as providing tax-free allowances and rate bands that are 'fully transferable' between husband and wife. This means that the effective tax rate on a second earner is particularly high, since the only additional allowances that may be received are the PAYE and PRSI allowances. At an income approximately equal to the average industrial wage, the average effective tax rate in 1991 was 33 per cent. For the first earner in a married couple, the tax rate was 22 per cent, because of the benefit from transferable allowances. But for a potential second earner in a married couple, typically the woman, the average tax rate on earnings from that job would be 42 per cent if her husband was already in a similar job. Similar disparities exist at other income levels, as shown by Callan and Farrell (1991).

Why do women who are in the labour market earn less than men? Women's lower average working hours explain part of the difference, but a substantial gap in hourly wage rates remains. Time series evidence is limited to that on production workers in industry, from the Central Statistics Office's industrial inquiry. This shows that the ratio of female to male hourly wage rates was roughly constant for much of the 1950s and 1960s. Between 1970 and 1974 the ratio rose from 56 to 60 per cent. It rose by seven percentage points between 1974 and 1980 following the implementation of equal pay legislation (1975) and anti-discrimination legislation (1977). Since then, however, the hourly pay of women industrial workers has remained at about two-thirds of that received by men.

This statistic is often interpreted as meaning that women, on average, earn two-thirds of the pay received by men. But this statistic is based on industrial workers, a group that covers less than one-third of all employees and only about a quarter of all women employees. A more comprehensive picture is provided by the ESRI's 1987 survey, which covers employees in all occupations and industries. Table 12.5, drawn from Callan and Wren's analysis (1994), shows that the average hourly pay of all women is about 19 per cent higher than for female production workers in industry, but that the average wage of men in other industries and occupations is about equal to that of men employed as industrial workers. Thus, women's average hourly pay is about 20 per cent below that of men, rather than the 33 per cent commonly quoted.

TABLE 12.5 *Average hourly earnings of men and women: industrial workers and all employees, 1987*

| | (1) | (2) | (3) |
| | Average hourly earnings | | Ratio (1/2) |
	Women	Men	
Industrial workers in industry (CSO)	£3.59	£5.31	67.6
All employees (ESRI)	£4.27	£5.33	80.1

Source: Callan and Wren (1994).

A gap of twenty percentage points between men's and women's pay is, nevertheless, a substantial one. There is a general tendency for wages to rise with age and/or labour market experience, which may provide part of the explanation. Table 12.6 provides a relatively simple perspective on this, showing how men's and women's wages vary with age, and how male and female employees are distributed over the age categories. A striking feature of the table is that the gap between men's and women's wages is much lower when age is taken into account. For the two youngest age groups, which include about 70 per cent of women employees, the average gap between men's and women's wages is less than 8 per cent. The higher gap in the statistics for all ages taken together arises from the fact that female employees are concentrated in the youngest age groups, who tend to have lower wage rates, irrespective of sex. These younger age groups will, therefore, be more heavily weighted in calculating the average female than the average male wage rate. In effect, the overall wage gap includes a comparison of the wages of younger women with those of older men.

TABLE 12.6 *Average hourly earnings of men and women by age, 1987*

	(1)	(2)			(3)
	Average hourly earnings		Percentage in age category		Ratio 1/2
	Women	Men	Women	Men	
15–24	£3.03	£3.25	36.1	17.8	93.2
25–34	£4.79	£5.16	34.8	34.8	92.8
35–44	£5.36	£6.26	13.4	21.7	85.6
45–54	£4.84	£6.22	9.4	16.1	77.8
55–64	£5.89	£6.20	5.0	9.2	95.0
All ages	£4.27	£5.34	100.0	100.0	80.0

Source: Callan and Wren (1994).

This evidence suggests that it may be fruitful to break down the gap between men's and women's average wages, along the lines of many international studies, into two parts: one part that is attributable to differences in the characteristics of the average male and female employees (such as age, experience, or educational qualifications) and a 'residual', which cannot be explained in this way and may be due to discrimination. The results of such analyses must be interpreted with caution. To the extent that there is or has been direct discrimination in pay, this will also have reduced women's investment in human capital (via education, training, and labour market experience); so some of the 'explained' gap in wages may reflect the indirect effects of discrimination. On the other hand, it is possible that the 'residual' can overestimate the degree of *direct* discrimination, because, as a residual, it may reflect the influence of factors not included in the analysis. Nevertheless, the analysis is useful in pointing to the sources of the gap between men's and women's wages.

About half the gap between the wage of the average male and female employee can be attributed to differences in their characteristics. The most important differences are in length of labour market experience. Thus a large part of the gap in wages is related to the fact that women tend to withdraw from the labour market during the child-bearing and child-rearing years. However, this still leaves half the gap that cannot be explained in these terms. Women's wage rates would be about 10 per cent higher, on average, if their 'human capital' attributes—mainly educational qualifications and labour market experience—were rewarded in the labour market to exactly the same extent as men's. This figure is not greatly affected by the inclusion or exclusion of variables that control for the fact that women and men tend to be concentrated in certain occupations and industries.

The role of child-related interruptions to women's labour market careers in reducing women's wages relative to men's is very clear. It seems equally clear that equality of labour market *outcomes* cannot be achieved without policy intervention in this area. But does this mean that equality of labour market *opportunity* cannot be achieved without state support for child care? This question is addressed in some depth by Callan and Wren (1994), who conclude that intervention to achieve equality of opportunity is justified. A key consideration here is that the internal division of labour in the household cannot realistically be regarded as simply the outcome of an equal bargain between husbands and wives. The weight of social norms—which give women the right to choose a labour market career as long as it is not to the detriment of their caring role, but do not question men's absolute right to such a labour market career—also influences the internal division of labour. State support for child care could help to offset such pressures.

12.4 CONCLUSIONS

When analysing poverty on either a household or tax-unit basis, women were not found to be at high risk of poverty relative to men. Lone-parent families, particularly those headed by younger women, were found to be at very high risk of poverty. But despite the rapid growth in the number of such families, they still remain a small proportion of the overall population. The growth in their number did not result in a 'feminisation of poverty' such as was seen in the United States. In fact the risks of poverty for female-headed households fell significantly, while risks for male or couple-headed households rose between 1973 and 1987. This largely reflected the fact that most female-headed households and families are headed by widows or elderly women, who benefited from improvements in social welfare rates during the 1970s and 1980s.

Married women's participation in the labour market has grown rapidly in the past thirty years, and is likely to continue to grow over the next decade. But this growth may have a limited impact on poverty at household level, as much of it may arise from women in non-poor households. Most women in poor households are married, and most, whether married or not, have children. This makes it less likely that they will be employed in the paid labour force, partly because of personal preferences and partly because take-home pay, allowing for the costs of child care, would often be very low. Even if their husbands are unemployed, and thus potentially available to take over the child-rearing role, the nature of the means tests used for unemployment assistance and the fact that part of the unemployment benefit is withdrawn if a spouse's earnings exceed a certain limit tend to discourage or reduce women's labour market participation.

For women whose husbands are in low-paid employment, the effective tax rates on taking up a job can be particularly high, as will be seen in part V of this book. Women married to farmers may already be working on the family farm, or face greater difficulties than urban women in finding employment relatively close to home.

A general form of assistance with child care costs can be seen as an effective strategy for equalising labour market opportunities between the sexes. But for similar reasons to those discussed above, it may have limited impact on poverty, unless combined with reforms of the social welfare and income tax system. Policy packages that involve substantial increases in child benefit (some of which are considered in part V) may offer greater assistance to women in poverty.

A separate and strong thread in the analysis of women's poverty is concerned with the potential for 'hidden poverty' within marriages. This theme is taken up in the next chapter, which provides new evidence on this topic. Here it is sufficient to note that increased labour market participation could have a greater impact on this phenomenon. In the longer term, a tendency towards greater participation by women in the labour market could also have a broader impact on household poverty. At present many women tend to be financially dependent on men, and if their husbands become unemployed, the combination of low labour market opportunities for women who have been out of the labour market for many years and the structure of social welfare payments makes it difficult for a woman to take up employment that will keep the family income above the poverty line. A higher participation profile for women, together with a concentration of child income support on child benefit that is unrelated to either parent's work status, could make it more likely that a family would remain above the poverty line despite the loss of a job by one partner.

13 Allocating Money Within Households: Better Off Poorer?

DAVID B. ROTTMAN

This chapter focuses the discussion about poverty and public policy to include the distribution of resources within families. Previous chapters took as their point of departure the idea that a household or nuclear family should be treated as a single unit. Doing so carries with it a host of assumptions about what happens within families, the most important being that income received by earners and social welfare recipients is being shared and that consequently either all a household's members are poor or none of them are poor.

What if that is not so? Important pockets of poverty are possibly being overlooked, a possibility supported by evidence that married women raising children on their own after separation or divorce sometimes report an improvement in their financial circumstances. 'Fewer resources but increased access to them' translates into a healthier financial situation than the one the women had experienced as part of a married couple with a far higher total income (Graham, 1987, 235; see also J. Pahl, 1989). In short, they are 'better off poorer'. Conventional analyses of poverty, however, would have ignored their plight while part of a married couple.

Sharing, managing and control of money within families are all examined in this chapter to broaden the consideration of where poverty is located. Detailed information on the finances of 625 married couples provides the empirical foundation for the discussion.[1] The couples responded to a series of questions asked in a survey conducted in late 1989. But before resorting to numbers and statistics from that survey to describe how families manage their finances, the next section sets the context by outlining why such numbers matter and why they belong in a book about poverty and policy.

13.1 HIDDEN POVERTY

Nineteenth-century poverty researchers noted the existence of households that were made poor not by a lack of income but through irresponsible spending on the part of the main earner. A more structural perspective, linking sex inequality in society to the incidence and consequences of poverty, emerged in the 1980s (e.g. Glendinning and Millar, 1987).

Here it is argued that poverty is being hidden from view when it is assumed that all individuals in a household share equally in the income that is received. If money is withheld by the husband for his own use, it is possible for households to accrue incomes sufficient to place them significantly above the poverty line but for wives and dependent children to live in penury. Further, who takes responsibility for what types of purchase is also of great consequence for the standard of living of people within households. Individuals in households with moderate to high disposable incomes may experience deprivation if income is not being spent in an equitable manner. Consequently, the full income spectrum is potentially of interest rather than the contrast between the situation of households above and those below particular poverty lines.

These more recent approaches to poverty give prominence to the management and control of family finances. The core idea is that management is distinct from control of family money. Managers take day-to-day responsibility; controllers set priorities and policies for spending. Management and control can be held by one spouse or be undertaken jointly, but typically wives manage and husbands control family finances. Women's economic dependence on their husbands leads, it is argued, to poverty that is hidden from conventional studies of poverty.

How does this occur? The argument is that sharing, management and control of money within families is a product of the structure of power and of financial relationships between men and women in society. The sharing of income and expenditure responsibilities thus touches on other important aspects of family and individual well-being. Specifically, women work as unpaid carers in virtually all families. That work is unrecognised for the purpose of establishing entitlement to social insurance or even social assistance.

Participation in the labour force by married women in Ireland is the lowest in the EC (Blackwell, 1989). Those women who do work tend to earn less than men, and thus their contribution to family finances is typically of less consequence than that of their husbands. Where women's earnings do approach or exceed that of their spouses, their income still tends not to translate into the prerogatives afforded the equivalent sum if earned by the husband.

So far these ideas have been pursued through studies that focus on relatively small numbers of selected types of family. Efforts are now being made to incorporate intra-family inequalities in the mainstream of poverty research (e.g. Jenkins, 1991), but concrete results are probably some years away. So the aims of this chapter are more modest. One aim is factual: to indicate how much income is currently being shared within families and how those families make spending decisions. A second aim is more speculative: to ask whether the portrait of family finances that emerges is consistent with a society in which there is a reservoir of hidden poverty untapped by poverty researchers. This is based on a comparison of the circumstances experienced by husbands and wives, on consideration of the uses made of a specific type of income such as child benefit, and on whether these aspects of family finance differ by income level and by social class.

The first step is to establish how much is shared, both of income and of expenditure responsibility, in Irish families.

13.2 FINANCIAL MANAGEMENT IN IRISH FAMILIES

Income sharing
Do Irish families share their incomes? Some form of income sharing can be found in the overwhelming majority of families. One or more household members pay an allowance or contribute to a household 'kitty' in 85 per cent of families. Members of families, on average, share an estimated 55 per cent of their incomes. Most of that shared income is used to pay for basic costs of living. In the average family the weekly grocery bill (defined as 'food and household essentials') accounts for 59 per cent of the amount being shared.

Financial allocation mechanisms
How is the money that is shared managed? Research in other countries suggests that there are four main methods of family financial management: *whole wage* (in which the chief income earner turns over their full wages or benefits to the household manager); *allowance systems* (where each spouse takes responsibility for their own spending spheres); *shared management* (with pooled finances); and *independent management* by two-earner couples. Generally, if there is room for discretionary family expenditure the responsibility for consumption tends to confer power

on wives. Where such discretionary income is lacking, consumption responsibility becomes an additional burden for wives. Therefore wives' control over consumption tends to translate into power and greater equality in middle-class families but acts to the detriment of the position of wives in low-income households. Power relationships within families are also such that the husband serves as the senior partner in households using shared management (Pahl, 1991; Vogler, 1989).

To determine the types of allocation system used in Irish families, a classification was developed by looking at which spouse takes responsibility for specific areas of expenditure. The designated 'household manager' in each household was asked, 'How are the following items usually paid for?', with ten specific items listed. The responses are shown in table 13.1.[2]

In most households the wife takes responsibility for 'food and household essentials': purchasing food and providing for children's needs from the household kitty or from an allowance. Wives with incomes take responsibility for children's clothing and school expenses as well as their own clothing. The clearest distinction is in major recurring bills for housing and fuel, which are paid directly by the main earner in between a fifth and a third of households. Still, for all expenditure items the typical situation, describing more than one-half of the married couples, is for the wife to be responsible, relying on an allowance or a joint kitty that she manages. Clearly, traditional divisions of labour within the family are paralleled in divisions of responsibility for expenditure spheres.

The division of expenditure responsibilities leads to the following classification of Irish married couples in 1989:

One-person management: One household member, usually the wife, is responsible for all routine purchases (practised by 48 per cent).

Main earner control: The main earner, usually the husband, is responsible for all routine purchases (practised by 5 per cent)[3].

Shared management: Some routine purchases are made from allowance or kitty; other purchases are made directly by main earner (practised by 38 per cent).

Independent management: Routine purchases are made by both spouses from their own incomes *and* from a joint kitty (practised by 10 per cent).

Most Irish families allocate their finances in ways that are very different from what is reported in British studies. In the middle 1980s, whole-wage systems were scarce in Britain, present in about one out of every six households. Allowance-based systems were more common but represented only one out of every four households. One-half of British households used a shared-management system, and one out of twelve practised independent management (Pahl, 1983, 245–9).

TABLE 13.1 *Spheres of expenditure responsibility*

	How the following items are usually paid for:				
	Household manager from 'kitty'	Household manager from own income	Directly by main earner	Other member	Total
	%	%	%	%	%
Food	92.0	2.8	5.2	0.0	100 (623)
Rent/mortgage	62.7	3.4	33.6	0.3	100 (422)
ESB	69.4	2.3	27.8	0.4	100 (614)
Coal or gas	72.5	1.9	25.1	0.5	100 (616)
Wife's clothes	78.6	6.7	13.7	1.0	100 (610)
Husband's clothes	59.2	2.0	38.1	0.7	100 (608)
Child's clothes	78.6	5.7	13.7	2.0	100 (437)
School expenses	73.6	3.7	22.3	0.4	100 (351)
Child's recreation	82.6	2.5	14.0	0.9	100 (387)
Child's money	75.2	3.1	20.9	0.8	100 (310)

Note: Percentages exclude households for which an item of expenditure is not applicable, as where a home is owned outright or where dependent children are not present. Figures in parentheses indicate the number of households included in each preceding percentage.

13.3 HUSBAND AND WIFE DIFFERENCES

Thus far the concern has been to describe how Irish families share and manage their money. The theme now becomes more exploratory, to use what we know about family financial management to assess the consequences that alternative allocation systems have for the standard of living enjoyed by family members. We look first at whether husbands and wives have different views and priorities for how money should be used. Once the degree of consensus is established, we look at access to personal spending money and to leisure time.

Views on family finances
Both spouses were asked to assess their household's economic situation
in five questions. How much divergence is there between husbands and
wives, and is there a tendency for wives to be more optimistic or more
pessimistic than their spouses?

Spouses tend to agree in their description of the recent state of their
household's finances, as shown in table 13.2. Agreement is likely when
a dichotomy is presented and when one of those choices describes
acute deprivation. But the level of agreement is also very high when
spouses are asked to use a five-point scale to describe their financial
circumstances. There is a slight, but only slight, tendency for husbands
to be the more pessimistic about the household's economic circumstances.

Agreement on who would make a 'major' financial decision moves
the consideration to how money is being spent. Both spouses were
asked: 'If an unforeseen medical bill of, say, £100 were to arise, who
do you think would decide how to meet it?' Overwhelmingly couples
claim that it would be a joint decision. In nearly two-thirds of the
families (64 per cent), husband and wife agree that it would be a
joint decision. There is agreement in a further 11 per cent of households that the husband would decide and in 5 per cent that the wife
would do so. The spouses in 80 per cent of the households therefore
agree on who would make the decision. This leaves a minority of
families in which the wife believes that the decision would be made
jointly but the husband claims that he would decide (7 per cent of
the households) or where the husband says it would be a joint decision
and the wife replies that her husband would decide (4 per cent). Disagreements in which each spouse claims that the other would be the
one to decide characterise fewer than 2 per cent of the households.

Apparent consensus also prevails when couples are asked to identify
the most likely source of the money to meet an emergency bill. The
choices include income, savings, cutting back on other expenditure, and
borrowing from relatives, a bank, or a moneylender. Provision was
made for 'other' replies. This creates 49 possible pairings of responses
by husbands and wives—a formidable obstacle to consensus. However,
in 70 per cent of the couples spouses agreed on where the £100 would
be found. There are, however, differences between the views husbands
and wives express about the likely source of financial help. Wives are
more likely than husbands to expect requesting help from relatives: 12
per cent of the husbands and 19 per cent of the wives cited relatives
as the likely source. A narrower difference is present in the stated

TABLE 13.2 *Patterns of agreement and of pessimism in financial assessments*

	Agreement	Pessimistic	
		Wives	Husbands
	%	%	%
1. Has your overall financial situation ... ? (five choices)	63.9	35.2	39.3
2. Unable to pay mortgage, rent, gas, or ESB (yes/no)	94.8	14.5	15.2
3. Gone into debt to pay mortgage, rent, gas, or ESB (yes/no)	95.2	13.0	13.2
4. Gone into debt to pay other ordinary living expenses (yes/no)	94.5	13.5	12.5
5. Had to do without things that you feel are necessary to pay mortgage, rent, gas, or ESB (five choices)	71.9	27.2	28.9

likelihood that borrowing would provide the money: 26 per cent of the husbands and 30 per cent of the wives gave that response.

This leads to consideration of household spending priorities. The priorities selected by husbands and wives from the same list can be seen in table 13.3. They were responding to the question of what would be the first priority in spending an increase of, say, £20 a week in household income: 'on what would you be most likely to spend it?' With eight possible responses, husbands and wives still agree in 43 per cent of the households. Wives, however, are substantially more likely to cite children's clothing as the first priority: 18 per cent of wives made that choice, compared with 10 per cent of husbands. The reverse is true for the choice of savings, selected by 13 per cent of husbands and 8 per cent of wives. Overall, the similarities in the patterns of response tend to overwhelm the differences in what is given emphasis.

Personal expenditure and leisure

Do husbands and wives enjoy equal access to personal spending money and to leisure-time pursuits? Both spouses were asked: 'Most weeks, do you have some money to spend on yourself for your own pleasure of recreation?' In reply, 76 per cent of husbands and 61 per cent of wives say that they do. In nearly one of every five households the husband has personal spending money and the wife has not. The reverse is true in only one household out of twenty.

TABLE 13.3 *First spending priority if there is an increase of, say, £20 per week in total household income*

Husband's response	Wife's response								Row total
	More/ better food	Child clothes/ shoes	Adult clothes/ shoes	Regular bills	School expenses	Clear debts	Save	Home repairs	
More/better food	11.7	1.9	1.7	2.1	0.0	0.9	0.9	0.7	20.1
Children's clothes/ shoes	1.1	5.6	0.9	0.8	0.1	0.5	0.3	0.4	9.6
Adults' clothes/ shoes	0.9	0.7	2.3	0.4	0.0	0.1	0.4	0.5	5.2
Regular bills	3.1	4.2	0.8	7.9	0.4	1.1	0.8	0.0	18.6
School expenses	1.3	1.1	0.2	0.0	0.7	0.1	0.1	0.1	4.0
Clear debts	0.7	0.6	0.3	2.7	0.2	6.9	0.8	0.8	13.0
Save	2.1	1.6	1.3	0.9	0.2	0.8	4.0	1.0	13.3
Home repairs	0.6	1.0	0.0	0.8	0.1	0.6	0.5	4.0	8.1
Column total	21.6	17.8	9.0	15.7	1.7	11.5	8.4	9.5	*n* = 610

Note: Column totals refer to the choices made by wives and row totals to those made by husbands. The row and column totals do not add to 100% because some categories are omitted.

Fig. 13.1. *Personal spending money: equity between spouses*

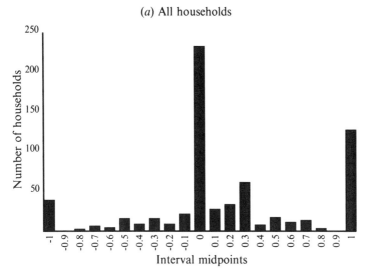

(*a*) All households

(*b*) All households in which at least one spouse has personal spending money

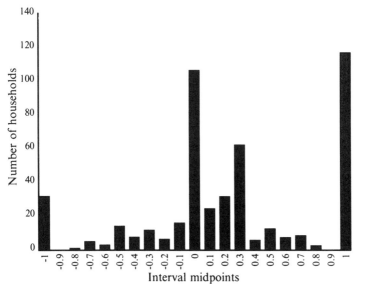

Note: Based on an index that scores 1 if the husband controls all the personal spending money, 0 where both spouses have equal amounts of personal spending money, and –1 if the wife has access to all the personal spending money.

But have husbands and wives access to equal amounts of money for personal spending? This can be addressed both in terms of the absolute amounts being spent and as proportions of personal and household incomes. On average, husbands report having £11.20 weekly for personal spending, while wives report access to £7.66.

A simple index of equity in access to personal spending money can be constructed by subtracting the wife's personal spending money from that of the husband and dividing the result by the sum of both spouses' personal spending money. This yields a score of +1 when the husband has access to all the money, 0 when there are exactly equal shares, and −1 when the wife has access to all the personal spending money. The range of situations can be seen in fig. 13.1, which uses histograms to display the concentration of households found at various points along the equity index. The top histogram includes with a score of 0 those couples reporting that neither has personal spending money. In the bottom histogram those couples are omitted, and a score of 0 indicates that the spouses have equal amounts of spending money.

Two strong patterns can be seen in how personal money is distributed. Approximately one-third of all couples have access to equal amounts of spending money. Even when the histogram omits those couples in which neither has access to personal spending money, equality describes nearly one-fifth of the remaining couples. There is a second pattern in which the husband receives the bulk of the personal money. This is anchored by the 118 households in which the husband is the only spouse with personal spending money. However, the typical situation is for the husband's share to exceed that of the wife.

Another aspect of intra-family equality is the ability to enjoy leisure pursuits and to socialise with one's friends and relations. Overall, 62 per cent of the husbands and 56 per cent of the wives report that they had 'an afternoon or evening out in the last fortnight, for your entertainment, something that cost money.' In nearly one-half of the households with a married couple (47 per cent) both spouses had an afternoon or evening out. Neither spouse reports such an excursion in a further 28 per cent of the married couples. Couples gave the same response, therefore, in three-quarters of the households. Instances where the wife did have time out and the husband did not (10 per cent of the couples) were rarer than examples where the husband went out and the wife did not (16 per cent). In sum, there is again a considerable degree of agreement and equity in the pattern of responses, but a layer of inequality in favour of the husband remains.

13.4 THE NEXUS OF INCOME AND SOCIAL CLASS

Thus far, a picture of broad consensus and equality characterises Irish families. Does that apply across all levels of society? Research in other countries suggests that such uniformity is unlikely, so attention now turns to establishing the prevalence of different forms of financial management and degrees of income sharing by income level and social class. Access to personal spending money and to leisure are also considered.

In studies done elsewhere, chiefly in Britain, low household income is associated with whole-wage and wife-control allocation systems, in which the husband is responsible only for his personal recreational spending; high incomes encourage husband control through an allowance system in which he is responsible for major expenditure items, such as rent and major purchases of consumer durables, particularly if the husband is the sole income earner. Sharing is more common where the wife has an income, with wife-controlled pooling being the norm at medium income levels and husband-controlled pooling at higher income levels. However, where wives make a substantial contribution to household incomes, independent management prevails. There is evidence that where the wife makes the largest contribution to household income, household finances are managed jointly without additional control accruing to the wife (McRae, 1987).

Husbands' earnings appear more likely than wives' earnings to confer ownership rights that translate into control. Consequently, where the husband is the main income earner, husband control may obtain in households that our classification treats as 'joint' financial management (Burgoyne, 1990). Wife management, in contrast, is common where income is primarily or entirely in the form of social welfare payments (Morris, 1984).

We can explore these relationships in the Irish setting by reference to the 1989 survey data. Five income quintiles provide a reasonable map of household financial means. To create the quintiles, households were ranked from the one reporting the lowest disposable income to the one with the highest income. After the first fifth of all households are included, the bottom quintile is defined.[4] Expenditure responsibilities are divided differently in each income quintile. The bottom and the top quintiles provide a strong contrast. Wife-managed households are most common at the bottom of the income distribution, used in 59 per cent of households in the bottom quintile and 36 per cent of those in the top quintile. Main-earner control is twice as common in the bottom as in the top quintile. Independent management is found in only 7 per cent of the bottom-quintile households and 18 per cent of the top. The top and the bottom of the income distribution are therefore distinctive in the degree to which independent management is practised in the former and wife management in the latter. The second-lowest quintile also is more likely to use wife management. However, there is little to differentiate the top four quintiles in the prevalence of shared management.

Social class refers to differences in the economic resources that can be used to generate income that are sufficiently strong to persist from one generation in a family to the next. Social classes represent categories of families that experience similar life chances: the likelihood of obtaining an adequate education, of finding secure employment, of remaining healthy. Social class thus represents more durable inequalities than income levels, and is of particular importance in Ireland because, compared with other western democracies, the prospect of a child born into a class transferring into another through educational, occupational or marriage mobility is low (Goldthorpe, 1987, chapter 11; Erikson and Goldthorpe, 1992; Breen and Whelan, 1992). Six social classes are distinguished here, following a census-based definition (see O'Hare et al., 1991).[5]

The social classes and their respective expenditure arrangements can be seen in table 13.4. Social classes 1 and 2, with their concentration of professional and managerial households, tend to be distinctive. Both are particularly likely to use independent management, an arrangement that presupposes two incomes. Wife management accounts for fewer than one in five households in social class 1, compared with nearly one-half in all other categories. Shared management is practised in 55 per cent of that class's households, compared with about one-third in the other social classes. The fact that shared management is present to roughly the same degree in social classes 2 to 6 indicates the diversity of ways that households in similar income and other circumstances organise their finances.

Social class differences tend to persist when comparisons are restricted to households in which either the wife is or is not in employment. For example, households in social class 1 are substantially more likely than those in any of the other classes to use shared management, even if only one spouse is in employment. Independent management is common in social classes 1 and 2 if the wife is employed (describing 44 per cent and 47 per cent of households, respectively); but the only other substantial presence of independent management is in social class 4, where it accounts for 26 per cent of the households with a working wife.

The extent of income sharing also differs according to a household's socio-economic standing. Income level is the obvious point at which to

TABLE 13.4 *Division of expenditure responsibilities: differences by social class*

Social class	Division of expenditure responsibilities				
	One-person management	Main-earner management	Shared	Independent	Row total*
	%	%	%	%	%
Higher professional	18.3	7.3	54.6	19.8	100
Lower professional	47.7	1.0	34.3	17.1	100
Intermediate non-manual	58.5	1.0	30.3	10.2	100
Skilled manual	47.8	5.7	36.9	9.6	100
Semi-skilled manual	57.2	6.9	35.2	0.6	100
Unskilled manual	56.3	2.3	38.0	3.4	100

*Rows will not always add up to exactly 100 per cent, because of rounding errors.

start. The proportion of income that is shared, either through allowances or contributions to a kitty, tells us how much of the income accruing to household members is made available for common consumption. In fact there is a curvilinear relationship between the amount of household disposable income and the percentage of income that household members share. This means that sharing is least prevalent at the top quintile (where 50 per cent of household income is made available for common use) and at the bottom (40 per cent is shared, on average). Sharing is most prevalent in the middle quintile, where, on average, household members share 70 per cent of their combined incomes.

The source of income is also important. Households with income derived mainly from social welfare payments typically share 33 per cent of their income, compared with the average of 63 per cent in other households. The extent of sharing is slightly higher in households where the wife is in paid employment and in farm households.

13.5 THE CONSEQUENCES OF FINANCIAL ALLOCATION SYSTEMS

Overall, then, we can predict the type of financial management system and extent of income sharing that will be found at particular income levels and in particular social classes. Does the type of financial management system being followed matter for the well-being of individuals within the household?

The survey data can be adapted to offer a meaningful answer. The first point of assessment is whether spouses agree on who would decide how to meet an unforeseen emergency expense: the husband, the wife, or both partners jointly. Table 13.5 compares the responses given by husbands and wives in the four 'division of expenditure responsibility' categories. Shared decision-making is the predominant and agreed choice in all but the 'main-earner control' households, where in nearly one-half of households there is disagreement. The husband is most likely to make the decision in either a 'main-earner control' household or where 'independent management' prevails. Shared and independent provision for expenditure do not preclude responses suggestive of husband control of household finances. (The co-existence of 'independent' management and husband control is also present in the British studies by J. Pahl, 1989, and Vogler, 1989.)

Husband control, as indexed by agreement that the husband would decide how to meet an emergency expense, is also promoted where either very little or most of the household's income is shared. Sharing of money or expenditure responsibilities within families does not inexorably erode sex inequalities in the distribution of power within marriages. However, this study, like most previous forays into the topic of family finances, is heavily weighted towards material describing what Pahl and others regard as financial management;

TABLE 13.5 *Who would decide how to resolve financial emergency: husband and wife responses by allocation mechanism*

| | Division of expenditure responsibility | | | |
Who decides	One-person management	Main-earner control	Shared	Independent
	%	%	%	%
Husband	7.8	24.0	10.1	18.4
Wife	5.8	8.7	4.2	3.8
Joint	70.6	27.3	59.8	60.2
Disagree	15.8	40.0	25.9	17.6
Total	100.0	100.0	100.0	100.0
	$n = 290$	$n = 17$	$n = 142$	$n = 61$

only one question (on emergency expenses) can be considered an indicator of 'control' over finances.[6]

How important are financial allocation systems for the well-being of individual family members? In Irish families the answer appears to be that allocation systems are of considerable importance. This emerges when we look at the distribution within households of personal spending money and opportunities for personal leisure. A simple index of the degree of inequality that is present between the spouses compares instances where only one partner or both have access to personal spending money. Equity in that regard is greatest in households with 'independent expenditure systems' and least where the main earner controls all expenditure. For example, where responsibility for expenditure is 'independent', in 6 per cent of households the husbands have personal spending money but their wives have not; in 5 per cent this is reversed; in nearly three-quarters both have personal spending money; and in a further 16 per cent neither spouse has access to money for their own use.

Differences between spouses tend in all situations except 'independent' expenditure management to favour the husband, with the husband being the sole possessor of personal spending money in one household out of five. It should be noted, however, that in the majority of households husbands and wives are equally situated: either both have personal spending money or neither has.

When income sharing is considered, the similarity between households with low and high levels of sharing emerges once again. Equity in the circumstances of the spouses is maximised at those points. The underlying reasons may be quite different, however. A high level of income sharing is characteristic of working-class households practising the 'whole-wage system'. Low levels of sharing tend to be characteristic of two-earner households that do not pool their incomes or only pool an amount to cover the essentials. Limited or no sharing is also found in husband-management systems in which little or no money is made available for common consumption needs; the groceries, rather than the money for purchasing food and other essentials, are provided to the household manager.

The practical consequences for the well-being of wives do vary, therefore, according to the way in which household finances are managed. Wives' personal spending money is the lowest in 'main-earner control' households (on average, £6 per week) and the highest in independent-management households (£22 per week). On average, wives in one-person-management households have £11 per week, while those in shared-management households have £12. The extent of income sharing, however, does not predict the amount of personal spending money to which wives have access. So wives often have low levels of personal spending money in households in which much of the total available income is being shared.

The relationship between the allocation of family finances and access to leisure is particularly strong. Here, 'main-earner control' households can set a benchmark for comparing the other categories. In one-third, the husband but not the wife reported having had 'an afternoon or evening out in the last fortnight,' compared with 63 per cent of households in that category where both spouses either had or had not had such leisure time. In the other categories, the inequity between husbands and wives is less pronounced. Approximately 15 per cent of the husbands had an afternoon or evening out while the wife had not; in a smaller percentage of households that was reversed. Where responsibility for expenditures is independent, 82 per cent of couples gave the same response. This compares with 75 per cent in 'one-person management' households and a virtually identical 74 per cent in shared-responsibility households.

Overall, then, financial allocation arrangements are related to the relative access that husbands and wives have to personal spending money and to leisure. The differences that emerge are rarely dramatic, but they are clear and consistent. The pattern of differences offers some of the first support from large-scale survey data for the general perspective tying levels of well-being enjoyed by household members to the nature of the allocation system being used. The next section looks at whether consideration of financial allocation systems can provide insight into the use of a particularly important source of income, child benefit.

13.6 CHILDREN AND CHILD BENEFIT

The control and the use of child benefit payments are of particular interest, because they are the only source of state income support that is paid directly to the mother. One way to gauge the importance of child benefit payments is to estimate the number of families with dependent children in which these payments are the largest source of income received directly by the wife. Among the 414 families receiving child benefit, the wives in 58 per cent have no other source of income; in 10 per cent there is income from employment or interest that on a weekly basis is less than what child benefit provides; and wives' earnings in 32 per cent of households exceed the amount that is derived through child benefit.

How does the role of child benefit vary by income level and social class? Table 13.6 gives a profile of wives' earnings in each social class. Earnings in excess of the money the wife receives through child benefit are not typically found in any of the categories. However, social class and income levels are both strongly related to the percentage of households in which the wife has either a small independent income (relative to what child benefit provides) or earns a sum greater than what child benefit makes available.[7] Among families in the unskilled manual category, 80 per cent of wives have no independent income other than child benefit; in about nine of every ten households in the bottom three income quintiles either the wife has no independent income or that income falls below what child benefit provides.

TABLE 13.6 *Households with dependent children: wives' income status by social class*

	No independent income	Earnings less than child benefit	Earnings greater than child benefit	Total	*n*
Social class:	%	%	%	%	
1	42.2	13.5	44.3	100	63
2	59.7	9.5	30.8	100	49
3	53.8	13.0	33.2	100	56
4	57.1	12.5	30.3	100	143
5	64.4	0.7	34.9	100	62
6	80.4	3.8	15.8	100	40

Where a household was receiving child benefit, the household manager was asked who decides how it is spent: (*a*) 'usually the wife,' (*b*) 'usually the husband,' or (*c*) 'usually a joint decision.' Responses from 367 households receiving child benefit are available for consideration (the question was not answered in four of the households). In most households the wife controls the use of child benefit (77 per cent). Decisions are made jointly in 22 per cent of households. Husbands make the decision in only one out of every 200 households.

How is child benefit used? Households tend to divide fairly evenly into those that usually spend it on general costs of living and those spending it on child-specific purchases (most of the 'other' uses supplied by respondents fall into the latter category). That balance seems, however, to differ between households where the decision on spending the money is joint and where it is taken by the wife. Where the wife makes the decision, 46 per cent of the households claim that the money goes for general housekeeping and regular bills and 44 per cent for child-specific expenses. The corresponding breakdown for 'joint decision' households is 75 per cent and 18 per cent (a statistically significant difference). Such differences suggest that the policy of directly channelling child benefits through the mother does affect the manner in which that money is spent.

Information on how child benefit is spent in families offers an opportunity to better understand the meaning of the four financial allocation systems. When households are categorised according to how they divide expenditure responsibility, the pervasive nature of 'main-earner control' becomes apparent (see table 13.7). Wives are less likely in this than in other categories to decide on the use of child benefit. Wife control over child benefit is greatest in households with 'shared' expenditure responsibility. Income sharing is also related to who decides on the use made of child benefit, with the decision most clearly in the hands of the wife when there are lower levels of sharing. The sharing of income in households apparently extends to child benefit payments. At low levels of sharing, having control over child benefit may be of particular importance for the wife. Child benefit may be the only money whose use she can direct towards her child care priorities.[8]

The use made of child benefit also varies according to the financial allocation system used. Where one person, usually the wife, is the sole manager, the tendency is to use the money for general housekeeping and regular bills. In those households the manager lacks an independent source of income, although they may have access to an allowance or a kitty contributed by other earners. Child benefit augments the money available from other sources to cover essential living expenses, a use fully in keeping with the objectives underlying the introduction of the benefit (see Lee, 1989, 277–85). Purchases of children's clothing represent a far larger share in households that make expenditures jointly or independently. The manner in which money is channelled into and distributed within the household, then, does affect the spending priorities of household managers. In some arrangements, child benefit can be targeted for use for children's clothing or schooling; in others, day-to-day necessities have the first call.

TABLE 13.7 *Control and use of child benefit by allocation system*

	Division of expenditure responsibility			
	One-person management	Main-earner control	Shared	Independent
(i) Decided by:	%	%	%	%
Usually wife	74.5	59.5	85.6	70.8
Usually joint	25.5	40.5	14.4	29.2
	100.0	100.0	100.0	100.0
	n = 165	n = 18	n = 144	n = 32
(ii) Use:	%	%	%	%
General housekeeping	31.9	24.0	25.7	11.8
Regular bills	28.2	58.0	18.0	14.9
Children's clothing	25.5	14.3	44.2	54.2
School	2.4	0.0	2.7	8.5
Other	12.0	3.6	9.3	10.6
Total	100.0	100.0	100.0	100.0
	n = 163	n = 18	n = 144	n = 32

13.7 CONCLUSION: EARNING, CONTROLLING, MANAGING, AND SPENDING

In weighing the evidence on how much money and expenditure responsibility is shared, on consensus on finances and equity in personal spending money and recreation, the first conclusion relates directly to social policy. The Irish social insurance and social welfare system, like that in most western European countries, divides payments between a fixed sum for the individual recipient and smaller amounts for each adult or child who is dependent on the recipient. In the Beveridge Report tradition, which had a major impact on Ireland, there remains the vestige of the belief that a husband's secure employment is a married woman's 'first line of defence' against poverty and other contingencies (quoted by Kennedy, 1989, 88). That recipients may share varying proportions of their individual entitlement is not, for the most part, regarded as the state's business, nor is the use made of money provided for dependent spouses or children. Yet child benefit emerges as carrying great significance because it is the sole independent income available to most married women.

Money that women earn or that they receive by right appears to confer greater power to control its use. Policies for allocating entitlements to social insurance and social assistance between spouses could usefully be reconsidered in the light of that finding. Arguably, married women not in the labour force should be entitled to direct payment of allowances for dependants under various social welfare programmes.

A second conclusion is that how families make financial decisions does affect the well-being of individual family members. The equity with which members of households enjoy access to personal spending money and to leisure is related to the financial management system being used. The division of personal expenditure and of access to leisure tends to favour husbands, unless independent management is used for family finances. The consequences of how household finances are managed are quite significant for the well-being of individual members.

Access to leisure and to personal spending money was used to indicate the material inequalities present within families. As in other countries, wives tend to have greater access to personal spending money if they have an independent source of income. Also, whole-wage or one-person management does involve a price for the wife or manager: full responsibility for makings ends meet on a day-to-day basis. There are also implications for the psychological well-being of family members (Rottman, 1993). Higher incomes, multiple earners and low levels of dependence in households all tend to make more equitable forms of financial management possible. Selecting a financial management system is a luxury beyond the means of families receiving a single low income and raising young children.

A third conclusion is more tentative. The survey results do not lend credence to claims that substantial numbers of women and children live in 'hidden poverty'—hidden because conventional studies of poverty attribute a household's income to all its members. That conclusion is tentative because the available evidence is so indirect: the apparent consensus between spouses on spending priorities, the extent of income sharing, and the moderate inequalities in access to leisure. But it is difficult to reconcile this observable pattern of differences with the image of a significant reservoir of individual poverty hidden among the notional affluence of households. In other words, it is unlikely that women and children in households located substantially above conventional poverty lines live in conditions comparable to those experienced by women and children in households below those lines.

To be clear, the presence of pervasive sex inequality is not in dispute. It is manifest in the division of expenditure responsibilities between husbands and wives, the concentration among husbands of the power to make major financial decisions, and in the various measures of access to leisure and personal spending money. However, the shift in focus made by this chapter to look inside families suggests that differences in the standards of living experienced by husbands on the one hand and wives and children on the other are insufficient to confirm claims that studies based on individuals rather than on households will uncover a massive lode of what is currently called 'hidden poverty'. It follows that public policy on poverty should concentrate on the plight of people living in households that are poor.

14 Spatial Aspects of Poverty and Disadvantage

BRIAN NOLAN, CHRISTOPHER T. WHELAN,
AND JAMES WILLIAMS

In this chapter we adopt a spatial perspective on poverty to address such questions as whether 'poor areas' or 'black-spots' can be identified and how this can best be done, and to what extent the poor are in fact clustered together in particular geographical areas.

Such issues have obvious relevance both to understanding the causes of poverty and to designing policies to combat it. For example, if the poor were largely concentrated in a limited number of inner-city areas, this would be central to understanding the processes at work in creating poverty, and to the types of policy that would be effective in tackling poverty. The data available for Ireland does not allow these issues to be fully explored, but does provide a basis for analysis producing some tentative but interesting conclusions. This is particularly relevant to assessing the role of area-based strategies, which have formed the major element in the European Community's programmes to combat poverty and to which expanded resources are now being devoted in Ireland.

Two sources of data are employed. The first is, once again, the survey carried out by the Economic and Social Research Institute in 1987 on income distribution, poverty, and the usage of state services. Given the numbers in this sample and the sampling design, the extent to which the results can be disaggregated by geographical area is very limited. However, some analysis at the level of the planning region can be carried out, and information on the type of area in which households live—e.g. whether rural, town, or city—can also provide insights into some of the issues of interest. Since the survey information on responding households allows those on low incomes and/or experiencing deprivation to be identified directly, it is possible to see the variation in poverty rates and the extent to which poor households are concentrated by type of area, and to compare poverty rates across the regions, which we do in sections 14.1 and 14.2, respectively.

214

The second data source, employed in section 14.3, is the small area population statistics from the 1986 census of population. Rather than information on households, this contains information on areas: counties or smaller electoral districts. The numbers in poverty in an area cannot be derived directly, since the information required is not collected in the census, but the prevalence of characteristics that are known to be correlated with poverty and were measured—such as unemployment and social class—can be seen. These characteristics may act as surrogates for a direct measure of poverty and allow one to draw some tentative conclusions about the spatial distribution of poverty and the areas and types of area that are most disadvantaged. The main findings are brought together in section 14.4.

14.1 POVERTY AND AREA IN THE 1987 ESRI SURVEY

The 1987 ESRI survey was designed to produce a national sample (of the population resident in private households), the sampling frame being the register of electors. The sampling incorporated both stratification and clustering, using the RANSAM programme (see Whelan, 1979). The target sample was selected as 225 clusters of 26 households each. While the number of households in the achieved sample for analysis, at 3,294, is relatively large, the extent to which the results can be disaggregated by geographical area is limited by both sample size and sampling design. This means, for example, that one would expect the unemployment rate for the state as a whole to be measured well in the sample, as it is, but the sample estimate of the unemployment rate for a particular county or smaller area would in statistical terms have a much wider confidence interval, and so one could place much less reliance on it. This means that while it would be possible to derive poverty rates by county from the sample (the electoral district in which each household is located is known) it would not be productive to do so. Analysis at the level of the planning region, each consisting of a number of counties, is more reliable, and is pursued in the next section.

First, however, we make use of a household location variable, also obtained in the survey, relating to the *type* of area, which provides a basis for some interesting analysis. This allows the location to be identified as falling into one of the following categories:

(1) open country;
(2) village or town with population of less than 3,000;
(3) town with population of 3,000 or over;

(4)　Cork, Limerick, Waterford or Galway city;
(5)　Dublin city or county.[1]

We now examine how the risk of poverty for sample households varies across these area types, and how poor households in the sample are distributed by area. Table 14.1 shows the risk and incidence of poverty by area, using three different measures of poverty described in earlier chapters: the 50 and 60 per cent income poverty lines, and the combined income and deprivation criterion identifying those both below the 60 per cent income line and experiencing basic deprivation (see chapter 4).

The poverty rate or risk of poverty does vary substantially by area type with all three poverty measures. The highest rate is for households in small towns or villages, and the lowest is for those in Dublin, with the former about twice as high as the latter. There are some differences across the poverty measures in the ranking of open country, towns of 3,000 and over, and the four cities other than Dublin, but in each case these have rates lower than villages and small towns and a good deal higher than Dublin. The most notable difference between the income lines and the combined income and deprivation criterion is that with the former the poverty rate for households in 'open country' is above average, whereas for the combined income and deprivation measure it is slightly below average.

TABLE 14.1 *Risk and incidence of poverty by type of area, ESRI survey, 1987*

Area	50% income line		60% income line		60% line + basic deprivation		Percentage of all households
	Risk	Incidence	Risk	Incidence	Risk	Incidence	
Open country	21.6	46.5	34.7	42.7	15.5	33.9	35.8
Village/town <3,000	25.2	16.7	36.9	14.3	23.6	16.2	11.2
Town >3,000	14.2	15.1	31.5	19.5	18.1	19.8	18.0
Waterford, Galway, Limerick, Cork cities	18.0	9.1	28.0	8.3	21.0	11.0	8.6
Dublin city & county	8.7	13.5	16.7	15.1	12.0	19.2	26.3
All	17.0	100.0	29.1	100.0	16.4	100.0	100.0

Focusing on the distribution of poor households, the table also shows that about 60 per cent of those falling below the income poverty lines live in open country or in villages and small towns. With the combined income and deprivation measure this figure is lower, primarily because, as seen in chapter 5, farm households are a higher proportion of those below the income lines than of those meeting the combined income and deprivation criteria. However, even with that measure, half the poor households are in open country or in villages and small towns, not very different from the 47 per cent of all households in the sample living in these areas. Dublin, although it has a poverty rate well below average, contains 26 per cent of all sample households, and has 15 per cent of those below the 60 per cent income line and 19 per cent of those below that line and experiencing basic deprivation. Poor households are thus not highly concentrated in particular types of area using these categories.

It is useful to complement this analysis by also categorising households by tenure type, since this allows us to examine how poverty rates vary between public and private housing—which tend to be spatially segregated—and to see whether poor households are highly concentrated in public housing in particular areas. Table 14.2 shows poverty risk and incidence by tenure type for sample households using the same three poverty measures. Households renting local authority housing are seen to face much higher risks of poverty than others: 59 per cent of these households are below the 60 per cent income line and 47 per cent are below that line and experiencing basic deprivation. Those in local authority housing but on a tenant purchase scheme have poverty rates close to the average.

Those who own their house outright or rent privately have poverty rates that are about the average using the income poverty lines. Using the combined income and deprivation criteria, outright owners have a below-average rate, while those renting privately are above average. Owner-occupiers with a mortgage, however, face a much lower risk of being in poverty than any other group at all three poverty standards.

In terms of incidence, the high risk facing local authority tenants translates into a significant degree of concentration of the poor in public housing. About 40 per cent of those below the income poverty lines, and almost half those below the 60 per cent line and experiencing basic deprivation, are in local authority housing, mostly rented rather than tenant purchase. This arises even though only 22 per cent of all households are in such housing. Nonetheless, when combined with the area categorisation, this is still seen to imply only a limited degree of concentration in, for example, public housing in Dublin and the four other cities.

TABLE 14.2 *Risk and incidence of poverty by tenure type, ESRI survey, 1987*

Tenure	50% income line		60% income line		60% line + basic deprivation		Percentage of all households
	Risk	Incidence	Risk	Incidence	Risk	Incidence	
Owned outright	16.8	44.2	30.0	45.9	12.6	34.0	44.4
Owned with mortgage	6.7	11.1	12.5	12.2	6.3	10.8	28.1
Local authority tenant purchase	17.8	8.1	27.5	7.3	15.1	7.1	7.7
Local authority rented	37.4	32.1	59.1	29.6	46.8	41.3	14.5
Other rented	14.4	4.5	27.7	5.0	21.3	6.8	5.2
All	17.0	100.0	29.1	100.0	16.4	100.0	100.0

Table 14.3 shows that only 21 per cent of the households meeting the combined 60 per cent income line and basic deprivation criteria are in local authority housing in the cities of Dublin, Cork, Limerick, Waterford, and Galway. Households living in public authority housing in these cities do face a much higher risk of poverty than those in private housing in the same areas—though the risk facing those in public housing outside these cities is just as high, as the table also shows. With only 10 per cent of all households living in local authority housing in the cities, these households are heavily overrepresented among the poor but still only constitute about one-fifth of all poor households, measured in this way.

This pattern of risk and incidence has major implications for our understanding of the nature of poverty and for policy design. For example, whatever relevance such concepts as an urban underclass may have for particular sub-groups, the fact that most poor households are not in public housing in the cities means that such concepts are not central to the understanding of poverty in Ireland. In terms of policy design, the evidence suggests that 'black-spots' with very high poverty rates can indeed be identified, and we discuss later in this chapter how this might be done with available information.

However, since most poor households are not to be found in such places, policies targeting specific locations, however effective, can be expected to reach only a minority. Policy issues such as the role of area-based strategies to combat poverty are considered in more detail in the light of these results in the final parts of this book.

TABLE 14.3 *Risk and incidence of poverty using 60% income line plus basic deprivation by area and tenure type, ESRI survey, 1987*

	Risk of poverty (%)		Percentage of poor		Percentage of all households	
	Local authority	Other	Local authority	Other	Local authority	Other
Open country	32.8	14.0	5.9	28.0	2.9	32.9
Village/town <3,000	52.0	12.0	10.3	5.8	3.3	8.0
Town >3,000	31.2	11.8	11.1	8.7	5.8	12.1
Waterford, Galway, Limerick, Cork cities	37.0	11.2	7.3	3.6	3.3	5.4
Dublin city & county	32.9	4.4	14.0	5.1	7.0	19.3
All	35.8	10.9	48.7	51.3	22.2	77.8

It is worth recording that very much the same conclusions arise from analysis of the distribution in the sample of unemployed household heads and of heads in the unskilled manual social class (using the Central Statistics Office scale), both of which have been shown in earlier chapters to be strongly associated with risk of poverty. Table 14.4 presents the distribution of both by area type, showing that the unemployment rate for household heads is highest in villages and small towns and in Cork, Limerick, Waterford, and Galway, and lowest in open country and in Dublin. The percentage of heads who are unskilled manual workers is also highest in villages or small towns and lowest in Dublin, and is much higher than the unemployment rate in open country. In terms of concentration, though, unemployed heads are spread across the area types rather evenly, and over half those in the unskilled manual class are in open country or small towns and villages.

Table 14.5 shows that households in local authority housing have a much higher proportion of unemployed or unskilled manual heads than those in private housing. One-third of all local authority renters have an

TABLE 14.4 *Probability and incidence of household head being unemployed or in unskilled manual social class by type of area, ESRI survey, 1987*

	Percentage of heads of households in area unemployed	Percentage of unemployed heads of household	Percentage of heads of households in area unskilled	Percentage of unskilled heads of household	Percentage of all households
Open country	6.5	21.3	15.6	37.1	35.8
Village/town <3,000	21.1	21.8	21.6	16.1	11.2
Town >3,000	12.7	21.0	15.2	18.2	18.0
Waterford, Galway, Limerick, Cork cities	18.5	14.7	16.8	9.6	8.6
Dublin city & county	8.8	21.2	10.9	19.0	26.3
All	10.9	100.0	15.1	100.0	100.0

unemployed head, compared with only 6 per cent of owner-occupiers. This gives rise to a substantial degree of concentration: over half of all households with an unemployed head, and about 44 per cent of those with an unskilled manual head, are in public housing (rented or tenant-purchasers). However, taking both area and tenure type into account, this still means that only 23 per cent of households with an unemployed head, and 18 per cent of those where the head is in the unskilled manual social class, are in local authority housing in Dublin, Cork, Limerick, Galway, or Waterford. Indicators such as unemployment or social class can be used to identify areas with particularly high levels of poverty and deprivation, in the manner to be discussed in section 14.3; but the limited extent of concentration of the poor in specific areas or types of area must be kept in mind in making use of such indicators.

14.2 POVERTY IN THE ESRI SURVEY BY PLANNING REGION

As already made clear, the numbers in the 1987 ESRI sample would not allow a reliable disaggregation of poverty rates or incidence to county level or below. However, it is possible to look at a higher level of aggregation, namely the planning regions, which group counties as follows:

East   Dublin, Kildare, Meath, Wicklow
South-West   Cork, Kerry
South-East   Carlow, Kilkenny, South Tipperary, Waterford, Wexford
North-East   Cavan, Louth, Monaghan
Mid-West   Clare, Limerick, North Tipperary
Donegal   Donegal
Midlands   Laois, Longford, Offaly, Roscommon, Westmeath
West   Galway, Mayo
North-West   Leitrim, Sligo

TABLE 14.5 *Probability and incidence of household head unemployed or in unskilled manual social class by tenure type, ESRI survey, 1987*

	Percentage of heads of household in type unemployed	Percentage of unemployed heads of household	Percentage of heads of household in type unskilled	Percentage of unskilled heads of household	Percentage of all households
Owned outright	5.7	23.2	14.9	44.1	44.4
Owned with mortgage	5.8	15.1	4.8	9.0	28.1
Local authority tenant purchase	12.5	8.9	26.7	13.7	7.7
Local authority rented	33.6	44.9	29.8	28.9	14.5
Private rented	16.5	7.9	12.6	4.4	5.2
All	10.9	100.0	15.0	100.0	100.0

Combining Donegal with the North-West, there are sufficient numbers in the sample in each of the eight regions to permit analysis, though the results must be treated with caution. (There are at least 200 households in the sample in each region.) The distribution of sample households (after reweighting) over the regions is shown in table 14.6, and is similar to that in the 1986 census, though the survey has slightly too few in the East and too many in the West and North-West.

Table 14.6 also shows the risk and incidence of poverty by region in the sample, again using the 50 per cent and 60 per cent income poverty lines and the combined 60 per cent line and basic deprivation. The East region has the lowest poverty rate and the North-West has the highest with all three poverty standards. The ranking of regions in income poverty rates using the 60 per cent line is the inverse of their ranking by average household income or equivalent income, with the East having higher income and lower poverty rate and the Midlands and

TABLE 14.6 *Risk and incidence of poverty by planning region, ESRI survey, 1987*

Planning region	50% income line		60% income line		60% line + basic deprivation		Percentage of all households
	Risk	Incidence	Risk	Incidence	Risk	Incidence	
East	9.6	20.2	19.3	23.7	13.6	29.5	35.6
South-West	17.7	16.1	31.0	16.5	16.3	15.3	15.4
South-East	20.8	11.0	33.3	10.2	16.9	9.2	8.9
North-East	24.6	8.6	35.7	7.3	20.6	7.4	5.9
Mid-West	20.5	13.2	32.9	12.4	19.7	13.0	10.9
Midlands	21.7	8.6	41.1	9.5	19.4	7.9	6.7
West	19.6	11.0	31.0	10.2	13.8	8.0	9.5
North-West + Donegal	27.3	11.3	42.6	10.3	22.9	9.8	7.0
All	16.9	100.0	29.0	100.0	16.4	100.0	100.0

North-West lower income and higher poverty rates than the other regions. There is less variation in poverty rates across the regions using the combined 60 per cent income and basic deprivation criteria, though the East still has a lower rate than other regions.

The overall pattern is quite similar to that derived by Roche (1984) from analysis of the 1973 and 1980 household budget surveys using income poverty lines, in that he also found the East to have the lowest poverty rate and the North-West to have the highest each year. The regions with the highest poverty rates have relatively small populations, while the East, with the lowest poverty rate, is by far the largest in population. Thus poor households in the sample are seen to be distributed across the regions rather than concentrated in particular ones.

To take a more disaggregated spatial perspective on poverty and deprivation it is necessary to use sources of information other than the 1987 survey—indeed, other than household surveys. We now examine the way in which the wealth of information in the small area population statistics of the census of population can be used to study the characteristics of specific areas and relate these to the likely extent of poverty and deprivation.

14.3 DEPRIVATION SURROGATES FROM THE CENSUS OF POPULATION

The small area population statistics provide a detailed breakdown by geographical area of the information collected in the census of population. While no direct measure of poverty is available, research using the 1987 survey and earlier ESRI studies such as that of Rottman et al. (1982) have shown that characteristics measured in the census, notably social class, agricultural employment and farm size, and unemployment, are highly correlated with the risk of poverty. It is therefore possible to learn a good deal from the analysis of variations across areas in these poverty 'proxies' or surrogates.

The most recent small area statistics relate to 1986. We first concentrate on risk, in terms of the variation across areas in rates—the percentage in an area in a particular social class or farming or unemployed—and then focus on incidence, the spatial distribution of the high-risk population. The results are presented in the form of tables and maps. The tables cover the eight planning regions (with Donegal included in the North-West), while the maps are drawn at a more disaggregated level. The country is divided into 217 rural and urban districts, with each urban district wholly contained within one rural district. For convenience and clarity of presentation we have incorporated these urban districts with their relevant rural district. The maps are thus based on 159 units, to which we refer throughout (somewhat loosely) as rural districts. A reference map identifying these areas is given at the end of the chapter.

The maps use a quintile interval system, so that each of the five categories shown in the legend contains exactly 20 per cent of rural districts, and the areas with the densest shading are the 20 per cent with the highest rates for the variable in question. For example, in mapping unemployment (fig. 14.6) the 159 rural districts are all ranked from the one with the highest to the one with the lowest unemployment rate, and the 20 per cent of districts with the highest rates make up the top quintile and have the densest shading in the map.

One of the most direct proxies of income, poverty or disadvantage available from the census data is social class. The strength of the relationship between class and vulnerability to poverty has been demonstrated in chapters 5 and 9, where it was seen that those from the professional and managerial classes were very much underrepresented and those from the unskilled manual class very much overrepresented among the poor (with a variety of poverty measures). The census classifies people into the CSO's six class categories, described in chapter 5, on the basis of current or former occupation of the family head.

Table 14.7 and figs. 14.1 to 14.3 look at the spatial variation in the percentage of the area's population in the two highest classes—i.e. the higher and lower professional-managerial ones—and in the two lowest, the semi-skilled and unskilled manual classes.

TABLE 14.7 *Class profile of planning regions, 1986*

Planning region	Higher & lower professional %	Semi-skilled manual %	Unskilled manual %
East	27.3	13.9	9.7
South-West	24.1	15.1	9.8
South-East	23.4	14.5	12.3
North-East	19.1	19.4	10.1
Mid-West	23.1	14.5	10.3
North-West	18.8	19.2	11.9
Midlands	21.0	16.7	11.0
West	20.3	18.0	8.8
State	24.0	15.4	10.2

Table 14.7 shows that even at the highly aggregated planning region level there is a good deal of variation in class structure. The North-West, North-East and West regions have a relatively low percentage in the professional classes, about 19–20 per cent, compared with 24 per cent in the country as a whole. The East region, by contrast, is relatively advantaged, with 27 per cent in the professional-managerial classes. There is less variation in the percentage in each region in the unskilled manual class. The South-East and North-West regions have an above-average percentage of their populations in this class, while the West has a below-average figure.

Caution is required in assessing the implications for the incidence of poverty, however, because those operating small farms are categorised in the CSO's schema as semi-skilled or skilled rather than unskilled manual. Thus the table also shows that the West, with the lowest percentage of unskilled manual, has a relatively high percentage in the semi-skilled manual class; the North-West and North-East regions have particularly high percentages in these two classes taken together. We return to the distribution of small farms shortly, but look first at the sub-regional class structure.

Fig. 14.1 shows the extent of class advantage and disadvantage in terms of the percentage in the professional and managerial classes at the rural district level. Belmullet is at one end of the spectrum, with only 10 per cent of its population in the two professional groups; and other rural districts having particularly low levels include Glennamaddy, Mullaghoran, Kinlough, and Mohill. In contrast, the most class-advantaged district in the country in these terms is Dún Laoghaire-Rathdown, with 46 per cent professional and managerial, while Dublin-Fingal, Rathdown No. 2, Celbridge No. 1 and Dunshaughlin also have particularly high percentages in those classes.

Fig. 14.2 shows that areas with a relatively high proportion in the semi-skilled manual class are concentrated in the West, North-West and North-East regions, notably Belmullet, Oughterard, Swinford, Naas no. 1, and Clifden. Districts in the East, South-East and South-West, on the other hand, are characterised by a below-average percentage in the semi-skilled category. Fig. 14.3 shows that the percentage in the unskilled manual class is particularly high in parts of Cos. Donegal, Limerick, Galway, and Mayo, as well as Cos. Meath, Kildare, Wicklow, and Wexford.

As the regional class structure is heavily influenced by the importance of farming, it is worth looking separately at the spatial pattern of farming and of small farming in particular. The census allocates

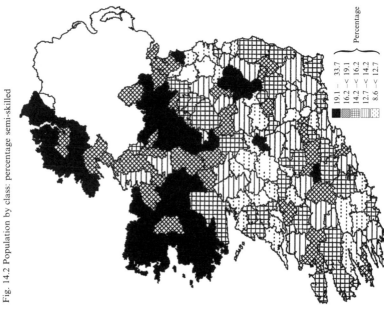

Fig. 14.2 Population by class: percentage semi-skilled

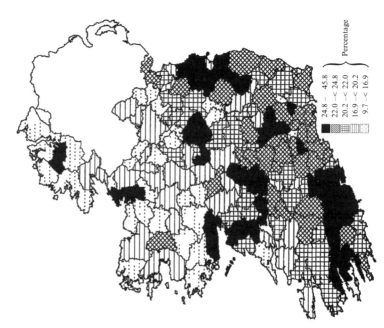

Fig. 14.1 Population by class: percentage professional (higher and lower)

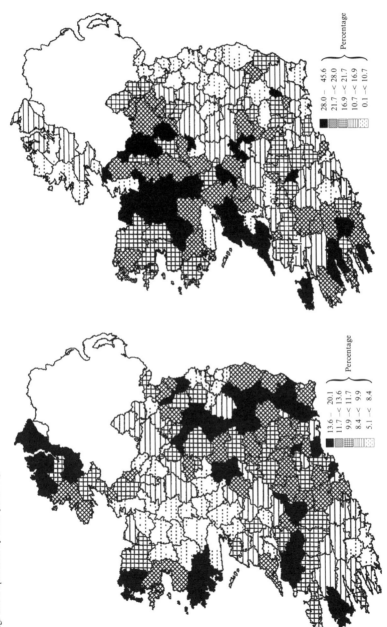

Fig. 14.4 Farmers as a percentage of all occupations

Fig. 14.3 Population by class: percentage unskilled manual

those defined as farmers (and their families) to social classes on the basis of farm size, with those operating farms of under 30 acres classified as semi-skilled manual, those with 30–49 acres as skilled manual, 50–99 acres as other non-manual, 100–199 acres as lower professional and managerial, and those farming 200 acres or more as higher professional and managerial. Table 14.8 shows the importance of farmers in the labour force in each region and the breakdown of their farms by size. There is very wide variation across the regions in the importance of farming, from the West, where farmers make up 21 per cent of the labour force, to the East region—very much an oütlier—where farmers account for only 1 per cent. Fig. 14.4 shows that, at rural district level, farming is most important in areas to the north and west of a line drawn from Co. Louth to Kilrush in Co. Clare. The most densely shaded rural districts on the map have farm employment rates ranging from 28 to almost 46 per cent.

TABLE 14.8 *Importance of farming and farm size by region, 1986*

Planning region	Farmers as percentage of all occupations	Percentage of farmers <30 acres	Percentage of farmers 30–49 acres	Percentage of farmers 50+ acres
East	1.7	14.8	18.4	66.9
South-West	11.6	13.8	21.9	64.3
South-East	11.8	8.1	15.7	76.2
North-East	14.0	32.7	30.8	36.5
Mid-West	13.7	12.7	23.2	64.2
North-West	15.4	37.4	29.6	33.0
Midlands	18.1	19.6	26.5	53.9
West	20.8	37.5	34.4	28.2
Total	9.4	21.6	25.2	53.1

The size of farm worked is of particular relevance in the context of disadvantage and deprivation. Table 14.8 also shows that at a national level almost half of all farmers operate less than 50 acres, with 22 per cent under 30 acres. There are substantial variations in scale of operation between one planning region and another. Small-scale farming clearly predominates in the West, North-West and North-East regions, whereas the South-East, South-West and Mid-West have a relatively high proportion operating 50 acres or more. Fig. 14.5 shows the percentage of farmers operating less than 50 acres at rural district level. There are clear-cut regional variations between large-scale and small-scale operators. The former predominate in Cos. Kildare, Wicklow, Carlow, Wexford and Kilkenny as well as in a rough belt extending through Cos.

Laois, Tipperary (North), Waterford, and Cork. Areas with a relatively high percentage of small-scale farmers, on the other hand, are Cos. Mayo, Donegal, Leitrim, Monaghan, and Cavan.

Earlier chapters have demonstrated the strength of the relationship between unemployment and poverty. Using the small area census data, unemployment rates by area can be derived. The national unemployment rate recorded in the 1986 census was 17.9 per cent. Regional unemployment rates ranged from 16 per cent in the West and Midlands to 22 per cent in the North-West, the other regions having rates of between 17 and 19 per cent. At county level the highest rate was in Donegal (27 per cent), followed by Louth and four of the five cities (the exception being Galway), where the rates were 22–23 per cent. Counties with the lowest level of unemployment (between 12 and 15 per cent) were Roscommon, Clare, Cavan, Leitrim, Cork, and Westmeath.

Unemployment rates at rural district level are shown in fig. 14.6. In general, rural districts with the highest levels of unemployment were in Co. Donegal, north and west Co. Mayo, parts of north and west Co. Kerry, and a long tract through parts of Cos. Offaly, Kildare, Wicklow, Wexford, and Waterford. The highest rate was experienced by Dunfanaghy, Co. Donegal, where 39 per cent of the labour force were classified as unemployed. This was followed by Belmullet, Carrick-on-Suir, Inishowen, and Millford, each at over 30 per cent.

In view of the clearly established link between unemployment and poverty, it might be tempting to focus on regional unemployment rates as an all-encompassing proxy for disadvantage. It is important, however, to consider the influence of other factors, again most importantly the role played by farming, in determining regional unemployment rates. People classified in the census as employed in farming are, by definition, not counted among the unemployed, but a significant proportion may be *underemployed*. Many of the counties with the highest proportion of their labour force engaged in farming are also those with the lowest rate of unemployment. Co. Roscommon, for example, has the highest proportion classified as employed in farming, at 28 per cent, and also the lowest unemployment rate in the country. Other counties in a similar situation include Cavan, Leitrim, and Monaghan. The overall negative relationship between the rate of unemployment and the proportion employed in farming is shown by the correlation coefficient, which at the county level is –0.58.[2] Since, as we have seen, farming in these counties is often characterised as small-scale—65 to 70 per cent of farmers in Cos. Leitrim, Cavan and Roscommon farmed less than 50 acres—underemployment may be common.[3]

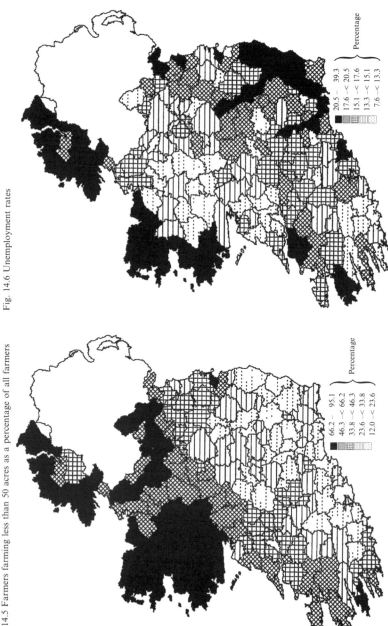

Fig. 14.6 Unemployment rates

Fig. 14.5 Farmers farming less than 50 acres as a percentage of all farmers

Analysis of the spatial variation in the age and class structures, the rate of unemployment and the extent of small farming allows particular areas to be identified as disadvantaged in terms of one or more of these variables. Ideally, of course, a single summary measure that allowed areas to be ranked from the most to the least disadvantaged would be easier to use, but this might involve a loss of significant information. Factor analysis provides one method of analysing the relationship between the different characteristics and distilling the information they contain into the most important factors or dimensions. The results of such an analysis, fully reported by Williams (1993), suggest that it is useful to distinguish between different aspects of deprivation even in such summary measures, with disadvantage in the North-West and West being associated with educational disadvantage, small-scale farming, and an aging population, whereas in the East and South-East disadvantage is primarily associated with adverse labour market conditions, as reflected in unemployment rates and the proportion in the unskilled manual class.

While the identification of the 'most disadvantaged areas' is a valuable exercise, in using this information for policy purposes the implications of the key distinction between risk and incidence must be emphasised. Identifying areas with very high poverty or unemployment rates, for example, is valuable in that such areas are likely to have particular problems on which resources may need to be targeted. However, most of the poor or the unemployed may not be found in such areas. To see the extent to which the census characteristics associated with poverty are in fact spatially concentrated, we turn to incidence rather than risk. We look at how people who are unemployed, in lower social classes etc. are distributed by rural district across the five quintiles formed by the distribution of the rates of the census variable in question. In other words we consider, for example, the proportion of the unemployed contained in each of the quintiles presented in fig. 14.6: the 20 per cent of rural districts with the highest unemployment rates, the second-highest quintile, etc. Table 14.9 presents the results for the proportion of the population who are (*a*) from the two professional class categories, (*b*) from the unskilled manual class category, (*c*) unemployed, and (*d*) small farmers (i.e. operating holdings of less than 30 acres). For comparative purposes it also shows in each case the distribution of either all persons or all persons aged fifteen and over.[4]

This provides an overall picture of the extent of clustering of *people* within the areas defined by the quintile distribution of *rates*. For example, the first two columns show that 6 per cent of people in the professional and managerial social classes are in the 20 per cent of rural

TABLE 14.9 *Distribution of professional and managerial classes, unskilled manual class, unemployed and small farmers by respective quintile distribution of rural districts, 1986*

Quintile distribution of relevant population by rate	Higher & lower professional		Unskilled manual		Unemployed		Small farmers	
	% profes-sional	% total popu-lation	% Unskilled manual	% total popu-lation	% unem-ployed	% popu-lation aged 15+	% small farmers	% popu-lation aged 15+
Quintile 1 (low rate)	5.7	8.8	19.5	27.6	10.2	15.1	6.7	54.9
Quintile 2	20.2	25.4	19.1	21.6	12.7	15.9	8.5	12.9
Quintile 3	10.6	12.1	29.9	27.9	10.8	12.4	16.0	13.3
Quintile 4	18.7	18.8	15.6	12.5	28.6	27.1	24.1	9.6
Quintile 5 (high rate)	44.9	34.9	15.9	10.3	37.7	29.4	44.6	9.2

districts with the lowest proportion in these two classes, and that these contain 9 per cent of the total population. At the other end of the distribution, the 20 per cent of rural districts with the *highest* proportion of people from these two classes contain 45 per cent of all people in these classes and 35 per cent of the total population. This means that the most densely shaded areas of fig. 14.1 contain 29 per cent more people from the professional and managerial classes than they would if these two class groups were distributed across the rural districts in the same way as the total population. Turning to the unskilled manual class, 16 per cent of all people in this class are in rural districts in the top quintile of the distribution for this characteristic (i.e. in the most densely shaded districts in fig. 14.3), compared with 10 per cent of the total population, representing a 55 per cent overconcentration of the unskilled manual class in these areas.

For the unemployed, the table shows that the quintile of rural districts with the highest unemployment rates (the most densely shaded regions of fig. 14.6) contains 38 per cent of all those who were classified as unemployed in the 1986 census. This compares with 29 per cent of all people aged fifteen and over, and so represents an overconcentration of the order of 28 per cent. The top 40 per cent of rural districts in terms of unemployment rate contain two-thirds of all unemployed people, compared with 56 per cent of the labour force.

The distribution of farmers operating 30 acres or less is more striking. The table shows that 45 per cent of these farmers are in the quintile of rural districts where small farming activity is most important,[5] which contain only 9 per cent of the population aged fifteen and over. This means that there are almost five times as many small farmers in this top quintile as there would be if the small farm population was spatially distributed on the same basis as the total population aged fifteen and over.

The degree of concentration in the five cities of Dublin, Cork, Galway, Waterford and Limerick is also of interest. Thirty per cent of the unemployed are in these areas, compared with 24 per cent of the population aged fifteen and over, so these urban centres have about 24 per cent more of the unemployed than they would if the distribution was the same as that of the population aged fifteen and over. Similarly, 23 per cent of all unskilled manual workers are in these five cities, compared with 22 per cent of the total population. This confirms the tentative findings from the ESRI survey discussed in section 14.2, that neither the unemployed nor the unskilled manual groups were heavily concentrated in these five cities.

Both the rural district and county borough (city) levels are relatively aggregated areal units. The level of aggregation may be masking clusters of disadvantage that manifest themselves at a more disaggregated level. We therefore briefly consider the most spatially disaggregated units available from the small area census data, namely the district electoral divisions (DEDs), of which there are 3,438 (including the wards within the five county boroughs).

There is enormous variation across DEDs in area and population, the smallest containing only 28 people and the largest 26,669, the mean population being 1,033. District electoral divisions are therefore not uniform regions, and there are hazards in analysis at this level. For example, two DEDs (Newgrove in Granard, Co. Longford, and Sheskin in Belmullet, Co. Mayo) had a zero unemployment rate, but their total labour force was only 19 and 13, respectively. At the other extreme, in Inishbofin 68 per cent of the labour force was unemployed, representing 50 out of a total labour force of 74. In all, 101 DEDs had unemployment rates of more than 35 per cent (i.e. twice the national average in that year). Some of these were in Dublin, notably Tallaght-Fettercairn, Priorswood B, North Dock C, Usher's B, Blanchardstown-Mulhuddart, and Tallaght-Killinardan, all of which had rates of over 50 per cent.

On the basis of DEDs one can therefore identify localities (subject to the caveat about the extent of variation in size) with particularly high unemployment rates. How many of the unemployed would be in such localities? Table 14.10 classifies the DEDs in terms of unemployment rate decile; i.e. the lowest decile contains the 10 per cent of DEDs with the lowest unemployment rates, the top decile contains the 10 per cent with the highest rates, etc. The DEDs in the top decile had unemployment rates in the range 27–68 per cent, and the table shows that these contained 28 per cent of all unemployed people, compared with 15 per cent of the population aged fifteen and over. This means that there was almost a 100 per cent overrepresentation of the unemployed in this group of DEDs compared with a situation where the unemployed had the same distribution as the population aged fifteen and over. The 30 per cent of DEDs with highest unemployment rates contained 56 per cent of the unemployed and 38 per cent of the total population aged fifteen and over, an overrepresentation of the unemployed in these DEDs of approximately 47 per cent. Once again, analysis at DED level illustrates the importance of the distinction between areas with high rates of unemployment or poverty and the spatial distribution of the unemployed or poor.

TABLE 14.10 *Distribution of the unemployed classified by decile of unemployment rate at district electoral division level*

Unemployment rate decile	Percentage of unemployed	Percentage of population aged 15+
Decile 1 (low rate)	2.7	7.1
Decile 2	4.3	8.4
Decile 3	5.6	9.0
Decile 4	6.5	9.2
Decile 5	6.4	8.3
Decile 6	8.0	9.2
Decile 7	10.0	10.3
Decile 8	13.1	11.8
Decile 9	15.0	11.6
Decile 10 (high rate)	28.4	14.9
All	100.0	100.0

14.4 CONCLUSIONS

This chapter has focused on what can be learnt from taking a spatial perspective on disadvantage and deprivation, using both the 1987 ESRI survey and the small area statistics from the 1986 census. The aim was to see what types of area had particularly high rates of poverty or disadvantage, and the extent to which the poor and disadvantaged were concentrated in such areas. This is of particular relevance to policy, given the recent focus on area-based strategies in combating poverty. It also provides important insights into the nature of poverty, and in particular the relevance or otherwise for Ireland of the emphasis in recent poverty research on the notion of an urban 'underclass'.

Given the numbers in the sample, the ESRI survey, like other household surveys, does not provide a suitable basis for the analysis of poverty in specific localities. However, information on the type of area in which households were located, and on tenure type, can provide some interesting insights. With a variety of poverty measures, the proportion in poverty was lowest for households in Dublin (city and county) and highest for households in villages or small towns (rather than in urban areas or open country). Given the distribution of the population, these differences in risk mean that about half of the poor households were in open country or in villages and small towns (where 47 per cent of all households lived). About 15–20 per cent of households in poverty lived in Dublin, compared with 26 per cent of the sample as a whole.

The circumstances of those in local authority versus private housing are of particular interest, as these tend to be spatially segregated. Households in local authority housing had a much higher risk of poverty than other households, and thus were substantially overrepresented among the poor: only 22 per cent of all households, but half those meeting the combined income and basic deprivation poverty criteria, were in local authority housing. Many of these poor households in local authority housing were not in the major urban areas, however. Combining the area and tenure classifications, at most about one-fifth of poor households were in local authority housing in Dublin, Cork, Limerick, Galway, or Waterford, where 10 per cent of all households lived. Households in public sector housing in the cities are therefore heavily overrepresented among the poor, but this high risk does not mean that a majority of poor households live in such areas.

While the ESRI survey does not provide a reliable basis for analysis at county level or below, poverty rates across the planning regions can usefully be compared. Poverty rates were highest in the North-West, followed by the North-East and Midlands, and lowest in the East. Regional differentiation in risk was less when a combined relative income and basic deprivation poverty measure was used rather than one based solely on relative income. The overall regional pattern was quite similar to that found by Roche (1984) using the 1973 and 1980 household budget surveys.

To examine variations in disadvantage at a more disaggregated spatial level, indirect measures available from the 1986 small area statistics of the census of population were employed. The census contains no information on income, but it does have detailed information on important aspects of the socio-demographic structure of different areas that are related to disadvantage. Variations across regions and rural districts (including the urban districts they contain) in social class structure, in the importance of farming (and farm size) and in unemployment were analysed. Areas in the East, South-East and South-West were relatively advantaged in class structure, with above-average proportions in the two professional and managerial classes, while areas in the North-West and North-East and parts of the West region were relatively disadvantaged, having below-average proportions of their populations in the professional and managerial classes and above-average proportions in the semi-skilled manual class.

While the importance of farming varied considerably across the regions, being greatest in the West, Midlands, North-West, and North-East, there were also clear-cut regional variations between large-scale and small-scale operators. In general, large-scale farming predominated in the East, South-East and South-West regions, whereas areas in the North, North-East and West are characterised by small-scale operators. In terms of unemployment rates the North-West was also clearly disadvantaged, with a rate of 22 per cent, compared with the national average at the time of 18 per cent. Unemployment was particularly high in parts of Cos. Donegal, Mayo, Kerry, Kildare, Wicklow, Wexford, and Waterford. Cos. Roscommon, Clare, Cavan and Leitrim were among the counties with relatively low levels of unemployment, but the relationship between unemployment and level of farming activity must be taken into account. Those classified in the census as farmers are by definition not counted as unemployed, and districts with a high level of small farming were often those with low unemployment rates, and vice versa. This underlines the problems of using any single, unidimensional surrogate for regional deprivation.

Analysis of these 'proxies' or surrogates for deprivation in the census allows specific geographical areas to be identified as relatively disadvantaged, which is valuable for policy purposes. However, most of the disadvantaged are seen not to be located in highly disadvantaged areas. For example, the 20 per cent of rural districts with the highest unemployment rates contained 38 per cent of the unemployed, compared with 29 per cent of all those aged fifteen or over. Nor are the unemployed concentrated in the five cities: they contain about 30 per cent of the unemployed, compared with 24 per cent of those aged fifteen or over. Similar results were found for the distribution of people in the unskilled manual class. Farmers operating smallholdings were more clustered, however.

Moving to the lowest level of disaggregation available from the census, the district electoral division, localities with very high unemployment rates can be identified, including some in Cos. Donegal and Mayo as well as Dublin district electoral divisions such as Fettercairn, Priorswood B and Killinardan in Tallaght, the central city areas of North Dock C and Usher's B, and Blanchardstown-Mulhuddart, all of which had rates of over 50 per cent. If one selects the 10 per cent of DEDs with the highest unemployment rates, these contain 28 per cent of the unemployed, compared with 15 per cent of all those aged fifteen and over. In one sense, clearly this represents a high degree of concentration of unemployment, in that there are almost twice as many unemployed in these areas as there would be if the unemployed were distributed in the same way as the adult population. In terms of the potential of a policy targeting specific areas, though, the implication is that a policy concentrating on a relatively small number of areas with very high unemployment rates could reach perhaps one-quarter of the unemployed. Widening the focus of such a policy, the 30 per cent of DEDs with the highest unemployment rates would contain a majority of the unemployed, but also almost 40 per cent of the population.

The evidence from both the ESRI survey and the census indicates that poverty and unemployment are spatially pervasive phenomena, which affect virtually every area in the country. The poor or the unemployed are not clustered in the urban centres, and most poor households are not in public housing in the cities. This means that the reality is more complex than the stereotypical notions that see 'the poor' as necessarily living in public housing in inner-city areas or peripheral housing estates would allow. It also suggests that, whatever relevance concepts such as that of an urban underclass may have for particular sub-groups, such concepts are not central to the understanding of poverty in Ireland. While policies targeting highly disadvantaged areas can be expected to reach only a minority of those in need, they may still serve an important function in helping people in such areas to overcome what may be cumulative disadvantages. There may also be important variations in the nature of poverty across areas, so that it represents a qualitatively different experience in particularly disadvantaged areas. This is something that would repay detailed investigation.

The findings of this chapter are not, then, to be seen as taking away from the need for targeted assistance to those in unemployment and poverty 'black-spots', or attempting to play down their needs. Rather the central message is that such policies can form only one element of an overall strategy to combat poverty, not a replacement for such a strategy.

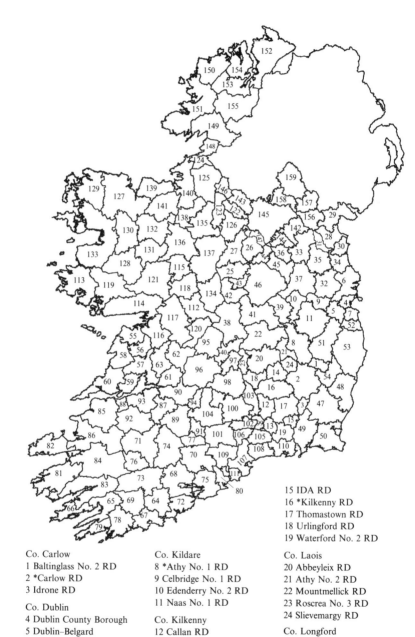

15 IDA RD
16 *Kilkenny RD
17 Thomastown RD
18 Urlingford RD
19 Waterford No. 2 RD

Co. Carlow
1 Baltinglass No. 2 RD
2 *Carlow RD
3 Idrone RD

Co. Dublin
4 Dublin County Borough
5 Dublin–Belgard
6 Dublin–Fingal
7 Dún Laoghaire–Rathdown

Co. Kildare
8 *Athy No. 1 RD
9 Celbridge No. 1 RD
10 Edenderry No. 2 RD
11 Naas No. 1 RD

Co. Kilkenny
12 Callan RD
13 Carrick-on-Suir No. 3 RD
14 Castlecomer RD

Co. Laois
20 Abbeyleix RD
21 Athy No. 2 RD
22 Mountmellick RD
23 Roscrea No. 3 RD
24 Slievemargy RD

Co. Longford
25 Ballymahon RD
26 Granard No. 1 RD
27 *Longford RD

Co. Louth
28 Ardee No. 1 RD
29 *Dundalk RD
30 Louth RD
31 Ardee No. 2 RD

Co. Meath
32 Dunshaughlin RD
33 *Kells RD
34 Meath RD
35 *Navan RD
36 Oldcastle RD
37 Trim RD

Co. Offaly
38 Birr No. 1 RD
39 Edenderry No. 1 RD
40 Roscrea No. 2 RD
41 *Tullamore RD

Co. Westmeath
42 *Athlone No. 1 RD
43 Ballymore RD
44 Coole RD
45 Delvin RD
46 Mullingar RD

Co. Wexford
47 *Enniscorthy RD
48 Gorey RD
49 *New Ross RD
50 *Wexford RD

Co. Wicklow
51 Baltinglass No. 1 RD
52 *Rathdown No. 2 RD
53 *Rathdrum RD
54 Shillelagh RD

Co. Clare
55 Ballyvaghan RD
56 Corrofin RD
57 *Ennis
58 Ennistimon RD
59 Killadysert RD
60 *Kilrush RD
61 Meelick RD
62 Scarriff RD
63 Tulla RD

Co. Cork
64 Bandon RD
65 Bantry RD
66 Castletown RD
67 *Clonakilty
68 *Cork RD
69 Dunmanway RD
70 *Fermoy RD

71 Kanturk RD
72 *Kinsale RD
73 *Macroom RD
74 *Mallow RD
75 *Midleton RD
76 Millstreet RD
77 Mitchelstown No. 1 RD
78 *Skibbereen RD
79 Schull RD
80 *Youghal No. 1 RD

Co. Kerry
81 Cahersiveen RD
82 Dingle RD
83 Kenmare RD
84 *Killarney
85 *Listowel RD
86 *Tralee RD

Co. Limerick
87 Croom RD
88 Glin RD
89 Kilmallock RD
90 *Limerick No. 1 RD
91 Mithchelstown No. 2 RD
92 Newcastle RD
93 Rathkeale RD

Co. Tipperary (North)
94 Tipperary No. 2 RD
95 Borrisokane RD
96 *Nenagh RD
97 Roscrea No. 1 RD
98 *Thurles RD

Co. Tipperary (South)
99 *Carrick-on-Suir No. 1 RD
100 *Cashel RD
101 Clogheen RD
102 *Clonmel No. 1 RD
103 Slievardagh RD
104 *Tipperary No. 1 RD

Co. Waterford
105 Carrick-on-Suir No. 2 RD
106 Clonmel No. 2 RD
107 *Dungarvan RD
108 Kilmacthomas RD
109 Lismore RD
110 Waterford No. 1 RD
111 Youghal No. 2 RD

Co. Galway
112 *Ballinasloe No. 1 RD
113 Clifden RD
114 *Galway RD
115 Glennamaddy RD
116 Gort RD

117 Loughrea RD
118 Mount Bellew RD
119 Oughterard RD
120 Portumna RD
121 Tuam RD

Co. Leitrim
122 Ballinamore RD
123 Carrick-on-Shannon No. 1
   RD
124 Kinlough RD
125 Manorhamilton RD
126 Mohill RD

Co. Mayo
127 *Ballina RD
128 Ballinrobe RD
129 Belmullet RD
130 *Castlebar RD
131 Claremorris RD
132 Swinford RD
133 *Westport RD

Co. Roscommon
134 Athlone No. 2 RD
135 Boyle No. 1 RD
136 Castlereagh RD
137 Roscommon RD

Co. Sligo
138 Boyle No. 2 RD
139 Dromore West RD
140 *Sligo RD
141 Tobercurry RD

Co. Cavan
142 Bailieborough RD
143 Bawnboy RD
144 Castlerahan RD
145 *Cavan RD
146 Enniskillen No. 2 RD
147 Mullaghoran RD

Co. Donegal
148 *Ballyshannon RD
149 Donegal RD
150 Dunfanaghy RD
151 Glenties RD
152 *Inishowen RD
153 *Letterkenny RD
154 Millford RD
155 Stranorlar RD

Co. Monaghan
156 *Carrickmacross RD
157 *Castleblaney RD
158 *Clones No. 1 RD
159 *Monaghan RD

* An asterisk denotes that the relevant district contains an urban district, municipal borough, or county borough.

PART V

TACKLING POVERTY

The analysis in earlier chapters has helped to clarify the nature, extent and causes of poverty in Ireland. Now policy responses to the problems of poverty are examined. For a number of key policy areas—including social welfare, income taxation, and labour market policies—the effectiveness of existing policies in tackling poverty is considered. Where possible, the analysis also offers guidance on which public policy initiatives offer the best prospects of reducing poverty in future.

Much of the state's redistribution from high-income to low-income families takes place through the income tax and social welfare system. Chapter 15 examines the effectiveness of these taxes and transfers in providing support to those on low incomes and in alleviating poverty. Compared with other countries, the Irish social welfare system is seen to be quite efficient in concentrating resources on those with low incomes. It is not as effective in reducing the numbers on low incomes, largely because Ireland has a relatively high number of such families. In extreme cases, the interaction of the tax and social welfare systems can create 'traps' that leave an individual or family with little or no incentive to take up employment or to try to increase their earnings. More generally, changes in social welfare rates and/or income tax provisions can alter the balance between income in work and income when unemployed, and the effective financial reward for an increase in earnings. Irish and international evidence on the likely responses to such incentives is discussed, and the impact of recent changes in policy outlined.

Chapter 16 goes on to look at the options for reform of the tax and benefit systems, bearing these problems in mind. Various strategies that could be adopted are assessed on the basis of the direct redistribution of income involved—the extent of gains and losses and who would win or lose—and their likely effects, including those implied by financing of the costs involved, on growth and employment. Proposals investigated include those of the Commission on Taxation, the Commission on Social Welfare, and the National Economic and Social Council. More radical strategies that aim to integrate the tax and benefit systems and/or provide a guaranteed 'basic income' to all citizens are also considered.

Income transfers through the social welfare system play a vital role in alleviating poverty, but cannot provide a complete solution, particularly given the scale of the unemployment problem. Labour market policy aimed at promoting employment and facilitating the reintegration of the long-term unemployed offers another avenue for intervention. Chapter 17 assesses the effectiveness of schemes that have been intended to promote employment and assist the long-term unemployed, and points to their weaknesses. The contribution such schemes can make, and how they might become more effective, are discussed. More broadly, the role of training and the scope for effective labour market intervention through education and training are considered.

The EC in its limited programmes explicitly aimed at 'combating poverty' had concentrated on pilot development projects in specific localities. Such an area-based strategy has also been a focus of attention for Irish anti-poverty policy and was adopted as an important element of the Programme for Economic and Social Progress. Chapter 18 looks at this and other aspects of the EC dimension to tackling poverty in Ireland. Community development initiatives can be particularly valuable in increasing the involvement of people in decisions affecting their lives and futures, which should not be undervalued. Expecting a substantial impact in terms of job creation appears much less reasonable, given the constraints within which such local action must operate. The role of EC social policy and the potential of the transfers to Ireland from the structural funds in combating poverty are also discussed.

15 The Role of the Tax and Social Welfare Systems

TIM CALLAN AND BRIAN NOLAN

The Irish state devotes considerable resources to the alleviation of poverty through the social welfare system. In 1993 expenditure on social welfare schemes is expected to be close to £3,500 million. How effective is this expenditure in reducing poverty? Could it be made more effective? To answer questions such as these we must obviously examine its direct impact, to see the extent to which social welfare payments provide assistance to those on low incomes. But it is also necessary to examine the incentives created by the social welfare system in order to gauge their likely impact on economic behaviour. Furthermore, we must consider the implications of the taxes and social insurance contributions required to finance this expenditure.

This chapter begins by examining the direct impact of cash transfers on incomes, in the absence of behavioural responses. Does the system meet its own objectives in the provision of a safety-net income level? Does most of the expenditure go to those on low incomes? How great an impact has it on the incomes of recipients? These are the questions analysed in this initial framework. Where possible, we draw on comparable results for other countries in order to put the Irish system into perspective.

In the context of high unemployment, there are strong concerns that the tax and transfer system should not pose obstacles to people seeking employment, or make it unduly expensive for employers to take on additional workers. The structure of social welfare schemes, and their interaction with aspects of the income tax system, are of particular relevance here. Section 15.2 draws together the available evidence on these issues from international and Irish sources.

Much of the empirical analysis in this chapter, as in others, is based on the Economic and Social Research Institute's 1987 survey. There have been significant changes to both the social welfare and income tax codes since then. A brief summary of these changes, and their implications for the role of the tax and transfer system in tackling poverty, is given in section 15.3. This provides the necessary backdrop for a consideration in the next chapter of options for reform of the system.

15.1 EFFECTIVENESS AND EFFICIENCY OF THE SOCIAL WELFARE SYSTEM

The social welfare safety net
We noted in chapter 2 that safety-net income standards have often been used, both in Ireland and internationally, as the basis for poverty lines. That approach has been rejected here, because of its inherent disadvantages: a rise in the safety-net income leads, other things being equal, to a rise in poverty measured in this way, although it tends to increase the incomes of some of the poorest members of society. For the measurement of poverty we prefer to use an independently defined standard, such as those used elsewhere in this volume. But measurement of the numbers falling below the safety-net income does provide information about the performance of the social welfare system in meeting its own objective of providing such a safety net.

The purposes of the supplementary welfare allowance (SWA) scheme, as stated at the time of its introduction, included guaranteeing a 'standard basic minimum income' and the provision of a 'residual and support role in the income maintenance structure.' Thus the rates of payment under that scheme, which are the lowest in the social welfare system, can be regarded as an official safety-net income level. The payment rate for most of the period covered by the ESRI survey was £33 per week for a single person. This was also the rate for short-term (rural) unemployment assistance. The performance of the system in providing at least this safety-net income level depends not just on these schemes but on the coverage of low-income groups by all other schemes in the system as well.

The SWA scheme works with a unit of assessment similar to what we have termed earlier a 'tax unit': a single person or married couple together with any dependent children (under the age of eighteen). To gauge the system's performance in providing a safety-net income it is necessary to establish what each unit in the survey would receive if they were being paid SWA and had no other income. For most families this is determined simply by the maximum rates of payment under the scheme; but for children aged over eighteen who are unemployed or in full-time education the 'benefit and privilege' rules impute a certain amount of income support from their parents, which is taken into account in assessing their potential entitlement.

About 10 per cent of individuals were found to have incomes below the SWA rate of payment. The precise number depends on the extent of any allowance made for housing costs, and the treatment of students. But even the most conservative estimates—which exclude all full-time students and make no allowance for possible additions to SWA payments in respect of housing costs (or heating or dietary needs)—suggest that about 8 per cent of individuals had incomes below this official standard. Additional payments under the SWA scheme could also be made for housing costs (rent or mortgage interest) over £1.50 per week; when this is taken into account, 11 per cent of individuals are found to be below the standard. The numbers falling below safety-net schemes in the UK (supplementary benefit or, more recently, income support), estimated in a similar way, have been relatively stable at around 5 per cent for the 1970s and 1980s. Despite the uncertainties that surround such estimates (see, for example, Duclos, 1992) it seems that Irish families are more likely to fall below safety-net incomes than their British counterparts.

To examine why this might be so, we must consider how individuals and families can fall below the safety-net income levels. Two main reasons can be distinguished: some are in circumstances that are simply not covered by a social welfare scheme, while others are covered but are apparently not receiving the benefits to which they are entitled. The main groups excluded from support under the SWA scheme were students in full-time education and those in full-time employment. We find that quite large numbers of full-time students fell below the safety-net standard, even when account is taken of their own earnings and an imputed parental contribution along the lines of the SWA means test. The numbers of full-time employees falling below the safety-net standard were much smaller. In part this reflects the fact that full-time employees with children were covered by the family income supplement, which provided income support at a higher level than the SWA. Larger numbers of farm families and self-employed people are found with extremely low measured incomes. There are considerable difficulties in measuring their incomes precisely and deciding on their eligibility and possible entitlement to income support.

But even apart from these groups there are many people with an apparent entitlement to income support who do not receive it. A small proportion of those apparently entitled to but not receiving social welfare payments were waiting for a decision on a claim. But most of these people had not made a claim—either for SWA or for other benefits, such as unemployment assistance or old age non-contributory pension, to which they might have been entitled. This phenomenon of *non-take-up* of benefit appears, therefore, to account for a significant proportion of people below the safety-net income standard. There are many potential causes of non-take-up, with widely varying implications. Potential recipients must, of course, be aware of the existence of the benefit to which they may be entitled. But basic information of this type is far from being enough to ensure that all those entitled *will* apply. There may be costs attached to claiming a benefit, in time, effort, and money; some benefits may also be seen as having a stigma attached, which reduces the value of the assistance given. Such costs may affect those who receive the benefit as well as those who forgo it.

Research evidence in the UK suggests that non-take-up is linked to the amount of the potential entitlement: those whose potential entitlement is small are less likely to expend time and energy in applying for it. This means that measures of take-up that are based on the amount of actual expenditure (divided by the amount of potential expenditure) tend to show higher levels than measures based on 'case load' (the number of actual recipients divided by the number of potential recipients). Analysis of the family income supplement (FIS) in Ireland shows a similar pattern. Less than a quarter of families potentially eligible for FIS appear to receive it; but a somewhat higher proportion of potential expenditure, up to about 40 per cent, appears to reach its target. This means that small entitlements are less likely to be taken up; but non-take-up is by no means confined to those with small entitlements. Take-up rates for similar schemes in the UK (FIS and its replacement, family credit) were substantially higher—between 50 and 60 per cent on a case load basis.

Poverty reduction effectiveness and efficiency
Having examined the effectiveness of the system on its own terms, we turn now to assess its poverty reduction performance in terms of independently defined relative-income poverty lines.

Alleviating poverty is not, of course, the sole objective of the social welfare system: other objectives may include the redistribution of income above the poverty line and the redistribution of income across the life cycle, as well as the provision of a temporary replacement income for those experiencing illness or unemployment. But it is widely regarded as a primary goal of the system, and it is of interest to assess its performance on this crucial dimension. Recent studies in the UK, for example, have concluded that most of those on low incomes do not benefit from social insurance schemes (as against means-tested benefits) and that most of the expenditure on such schemes does not go to those on low incomes (Webb, 1992). This has led to the conclusion that, as far as poverty is concerned, such schemes may be relatively inefficient and ineffective. Here we will attempt to establish whether similar conclusions hold for Ireland.

The analysis pioneered by Beckerman (1979) provides a useful starting point. It is based on two central concepts: the aggregate poverty gap, and pre-transfer income. The poverty gap for an individual family with an income below the poverty line is the gap between its income and that line. The 'aggregate poverty gap' is simply the sum of these gaps for all households below the poverty line. It provides a measure of poverty that takes into account not only the numbers in poverty but the depth of poverty, and can be related to the poverty indices used in chapter 3. Because it provides a measure of poverty in aggregate money terms, it can be related easily to the analysis of social welfare expenditure.

Pre-transfer income is defined as actual net income less actual social welfare transfers received. It is a simple first approximation to income in the absence of social welfare payments. It ignores the possible reductions in tax liability that might be associated with a lower total income; but its most important drawback is that it does not take account of the fact that economic behaviour would be very different in a world without social welfare. Despite these drawbacks, this initial analysis can provide a useful overview of the structure of the system. While the levels of effectiveness and efficiency may be sensitive to these considerations, comparisons at different poverty lines or across countries may be more robust. (Issues concerning potential behavioural responses to social security are considered in section 15.2 of this chapter.)

Households or families can be classified into three types, depending on the relationship between their pre-transfer and post-transfer incomes and the poverty line:

(1) those with incomes below the poverty line even after social welfare transfers;
(2) those with pre-transfer incomes below the poverty line but post-transfer incomes above the line;
(3) those with pre-transfer incomes above the poverty line.

Fig. 15.1.   *Classification of households for analysis of effectiveness and efficiency of transfers*

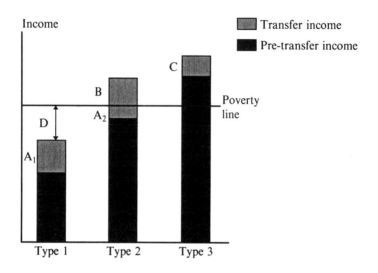

Note: Adapted from Dilnot et al. (1984).

The *effectiveness* of social welfare expenditure can be measured in this schema by the reduction in the pre-transfer aggregate poverty gap brought about by the addition of transfers. The total poverty gap before transfers is the sum of the gaps for households of type 1 ($A_1 + D$ in fig. 15.1) and of type 2 (A_2 in fig. 15.1). The total poverty gap after transfers is given by the sum of the gaps for households of type 1 (D in fig. 15.1). Beckerman's effectiveness measure is the percentage reduction in the pre-transfer gap, which is simply the difference between the pre-transfer and post-transfer poverty gaps, divided by the pre-transfer gap.

Beckerman's measure of *efficiency* is the percentage of total social welfare spending that goes towards the reduction of the pre-transfer poverty gap. All social welfare benefits received by type 1 households and a part of the benefits (denoted by A_2) going to type 2 households are going towards the reduction of the poverty gap. Total expenditure includes these payments and the 'spillover' payments that raise those initially below the line to a position above the poverty line (denoted by B), as well as payments going to those with pre-transfer incomes above the poverty line.

TABLE 15.1 *Poverty reduction effectiveness and poverty reduction efficiency at different income standards*

Cut-off as a proportion of mean equivalent disposable income	40%	50%	60%
Percentage of tax units below the standard	12	22	31
Poverty reduction effectiveness	79	76	70
Poverty reduction efficiency	54	67	77

These measures were applied to the Irish situation, as shown by the ESRI's 1987 survey. The analysis was conducted at 'tax unit' level, which is close to the level at which the social welfare system tends to operate, with an equivalence scale of 1 for the head of the tax unit, 0.66 for the spouse of the head, and 0.33 for dependent children. A similar pattern of results was found for the household level of analysis—though the levels of effectiveness and efficiency were lower—and for other equivalence scales. The basic results are presented in table 15.1. They show that poverty reduction effectiveness is close to 80 per cent at the lowest poverty line and is about ten percentage points lower at the highest poverty line. Poverty reduction efficiency, on the other hand, is some twenty-three percentage points higher at the highest poverty line than at the lowest.

These results are heavily influenced by differences in payment levels within the social welfare structure. Payment rates in 1987 varied considerably between contributory and non-contributory schemes, and between the elderly, widows, and the unemployed. The lowest rates of payment were close to the levels of the lowest poverty line, while the highest rates were close to the highest (60 per cent) relative-income poverty line. Lower efficiency at the lowest poverty line largely reflects the fact that the payment rates for many schemes were sufficient, even if the recipients had no other income, to raise incomes above that poverty standard. Lower effectiveness at the highest relative poverty line reflects, in turn, the fact that several important schemes had a rate of payment well below that level.

International comparisons of analyses of this type are dogged by problems of comparability. Evidence from the international project for which the ESRI provided the Irish element suggests that the Irish social welfare system is markedly more efficient than those of the Benelux countries over a wide range of poverty lines (Deleeck et al., 1992). The

Irish system is, however, somewhat less effective. The size of the pre-transfer poverty gap is relatively large in Ireland: it forms over 15 per cent of aggregate household income, as against about 10 per cent in the Netherlands. This means that a given proportion of national income devoted to social welfare, at any given level of efficiency, will tend to be less effective in Ireland than in countries, such as Belgium and the Netherlands, with a lower pre-transfer poverty gap.

Limited comparisons are possible with published analyses for other countries (Britain, the United States, and Australia). These analyses are based simply on the measures of effectiveness and efficiency at safety-net income levels. In Ireland such analysis produces similar results to those at the 40 per cent relative-income cut-off. These confirm the picture of the Irish system as relatively efficient but not so effective, because of the size of the problem faced.

These results can be used to shed some light on the scope for greater targeting of social welfare payments towards those in poverty. In the UK context, Dilnot et al. (1984) suggest that efficiency levels of close to 50 per cent mean that if the principal objective is to boost low incomes to an acceptable level, this could be done more cheaply, or the support provided could be increased, if payments to those who do not strictly 'need' the money were curtailed. But our analysis shows much less scope for such reallocation of resources at higher poverty lines: at the 60 per cent relative poverty line, 77 per cent of social welfare expenditure is found to be already going towards the reduction of the poverty gap, i.e. bringing recipients up to the line. It also highlights the extremely differentiated nature of the payment structure in 1987. From the point of view of poverty reduction, such differences can only be justified in terms of differences in needs; differences in payment rates between contributory and non-contributory schemes could not be justified on these grounds.

Several methods of targeting payments on those in greatest need are available, and indeed are already used. Some would argue that means-testing is the surest way of directing resources efficiently to those with the lowest incomes. Others, such as the Commission on Social Welfare (1986, 181), argue that contingency-based schemes 'are an effective means of directing social security payments to persons in need of an income without actually undertaking means tests.' Table 15.2 provides evidence relevant to this debate: it shows the distribution of expenditure under means-tested and contingency-based schemes over tax units arranged in order of their pre-transfer income, based on the 1987 survey.

TABLE 15.2 *Distribution of social welfare expenditure by equivalent pre-transfer income decile*

Decile	Total social welfare benefits	Means-tested benefits	Contributory benefits	Child benefits
Bottom 30%	58	70	58	22
Fourth	20	20	23	8
Fifth	9	7	8	17
Sixth	5	2	4	16
Seventh	3	1	2	14
Eighth	2	0	2	9
Ninth	2	0	1	8
Tenth	1	0	1	6
All	100	100	100	100

These results show that contributory benefits were in fact quite selective, even relative to means-tested payments. About 58 per cent of contributory benefits got to tax units with little or no other income; the corresponding figure for means-tested benefits is 70 per cent. Around 10 per cent of contributory benefits goes to tax units in the top half of the distribution, as against 3 per cent of means-tested benefits. It is true that non-means-tested benefits tend to raise recipients higher up the income scale than the corresponding means-tested payments. This involves greater 'spillover' of benefits, raising recipients above the poverty line. But the evidence suggests that this is due in large part to the higher payment rates for contributory benefits rather than the failure to adjust contributory benefits for incomes from other sources by means-testing. On balance, therefore, contingency-based payments can be quite selective. They do have the disadvantage, however, of increasing the incentive to be classified as meeting the contingency: means-testing is not necessarily a solution to this problem, which is discussed in more general terms in the next section.

Table 15.2 also provides evidence on the distribution of child benefit payments. Child benefit payments in 1987 did not seem to be very selective. Further analysis shows that only 34 per cent of expenditure on child benefit went to the poorest 30 per cent of the population, classified by post-transfer income. Results for an equivalence scale with a more generous provision for the needs of children suggest that the scheme is somewhat more progressive; but over one-third of the expenditure still goes to the top half of the income distribution.

An alternative way of targeting resources is to have contingent or universal benefits withdrawn selectively through the income tax system.

Long-term social welfare benefits (such as pensions) were subject to tax in 1987. Budget statements have indicated that a move towards the taxing of short-term benefits is envisaged, though not yet implemented except for disability benefit. Taxing of an increased child benefit has also been discussed by the National Economic and Social Council (1990). The implications of such proposals are examined in the next chapter.

15.2 INCENTIVE ISSUES

Economic responses to the existence of social welfare benefits and the taxes required to finance them can potentially play an important role in determining the total effect of anti-poverty policy. In terms of the analysis in the preceding section, the essential point is that individual and aggregate pre-transfer incomes may respond to the incentives posed by the tax and transfer systems. The design of anti-poverty policies should therefore take such responses into account.

In general, the existence of income support that is either means-tested or contingent on the claimant being unemployed or out of the labour force creates a financial disincentive towards employment. Income taxes and income-related social insurance contributions, which may be increased to finance increases in social welfare payments, also reduce the financial rewards from additional work effort. The responses to these labour supply disincentives may lead to increases in unemployment by a number of routes. A direct effect could arise on decisions influencing the entry to or duration of unemployment: a higher unemployment benefit might lead individuals to reduce their search effort, or to raise their 'reservation wage' (the minimum wage at which they would accept a job). Such incentive effects could lead to an increase in the numbers unemployed and measured as poor. Taxes required to finance social welfare expenditure also have broader labour market and macro-economic effects on output and employment. Taxes on labour incomes tend to increase the cost of labour to employers; and other taxes may also reduce the level of economic activity.

Considerable research effort has been devoted in many countries to the estimation of the incentive effects of taxes and welfare expenditure. Often there appears to be considerable variation between estimates of the same effect within a given country, as well as variation between countries. Nevertheless, recent reviews of the incentive effects of welfare systems have come to quite similar conclusions. Atkinson (1992) suggests that 'there is broad agreement that, to the extent that disincentive effects exist, they are modest in size.' In the United States, Moffitt (1992) finds that there is unequivocal evidence for an effect of the welfare system on labour supply, but that 'the importance of these effects is limited in many respects.' Geary (1989), reviewing the evidence on incentive effects and broader macro-economic effects of anti-poverty policies, concludes that 'these effects exist but there is not strong evidence that they are quantitatively large.'

The available evidence on these issues is more limited in the Irish situation. Public attention has been focused in recent debate on two distinct 'traps': an 'unemployment trap', which arises if the net income available to a person when employed is less than that available to him or her when unemployed, and a 'poverty trap', which arises if an increase in his or her gross earnings gives rise to a fall in disposable income. These 'traps' represent extreme forms of disincentive. More generally the financial incentive to taking up employment can be measured by the balance between income in work and income when unemployed; and the financial reward for additional earned income is measured by the increase in disposable income it gives rise to. Two types of evidence are relevant to the assessment of incentive effects: measures of the incentives faced by individuals, and estimates of the response of individuals to those incentives.

The issues involved in measuring the balance between income in work and income when unemployed were discussed in chapter 7. Replacement rates relevant to the incentive to work, measured by the ratio of benefits received when unemployed to after-tax income in work, were calculated for the short-term unemployed and for those who had recently moved from unemployment to employment. At the time of the ESRI's 1987 survey, the personal rate of unemployment benefit for the short-term unemployed was about 12 per cent higher than the unemployment assistance rate for the long-term unemployed. Furthermore, pay-related benefit of up to £40 could be paid with unemployment benefit. Thus, replacement rates for the short-term unemployed were at that time likely to be above those for the long-term unemployed. While the calculations shown in chapter 7 do not include allowance for possible differences in non-cash benefits (such as a medical card) or travel-to-work costs, they do make it clear that there is considerable variation in replacement rates, with a rather small proportion of individuals facing the highest rates.

Estimation of responses to replacement rates also pose considerable difficulties. In the international literature, cross-section studies have tended to find that effects, if significant, are quantitatively small

(Chiplin, 1992; Atkinson and Micklewright, 1985). Time-series studies have produced mixed results, some of which would suggest larger effects; but there are particular difficulties in disentangling the effects of benefits from a range of highly correlated regressors (Narendranathan et al., 1985).

Panel studies seem to offer the greatest opportunities for more precise information on these issues; but suitable panel data is not available for Ireland. Walsh and Hughes's time series study (1983) found a significant influence from unemployment compensation—as measured by an average replacement ratio and the length of the period of entitlement to benefit—on the probability of remaining unemployed. They found that small changes in this probability can have a substantial impact on the level of unemployment and the share of unemployment that is long-term. Breen and Honohan (1991), however, find that it is possible to explain most of the variation in the share of long-term unemployment during the 1980s on the basis of a *constant* probability of remaining unemployed. During the longer period 1972–90 they find evidence of one sharp change in this probability, coinciding with a change in the definitions and procedures used in compiling the data in 1979, which is their preferred explanation for the shift. Thus it is not clear how strong a role changes in replacement rates have played in actual developments.

Much of the international research on labour supply has emphasised that women's participation in the labour market is particularly sensitive to the net financial incentive to work. Similar findings have been obtained for Ireland, as discussed in chapter 12. There is some evidence that unemployment compensation can affect the labour supply of wives of unemployed men. The pound-for-pound withdrawal of benefit under the unemployment assistance means test applies to the earnings of spouses; and the adult dependant and half of the child dependant additions under the unemployment benefit scheme depend on the spouse's gross earnings being below a limit of £55 per week. The structure of the income tax system also means that a woman whose husband is already employed faces a particularly high tax rate on taking up a job. Average tax rates on a job for a single person are also much higher than for a married man whose wife is not in paid employment.

This structure of taxes imposes particularly large disincentives on the most responsive groups: married women and potential migrants, most of whom are young and single. This could be expected to maximise the deleterious effect on employment of a given level of income taxes, if wage determination is affected by competitive forces.

Bargaining models of the labour market would also suggest that income taxes have a damaging impact on the level of employment. Honohan and Irvine (1987) find that a shift from income tax to property tax could therefore lead to an improvement.

Turning to the incentives faced by low-paid workers, it should be noted that a number of measures aimed specifically at this group were introduced in the middle 1980s. On the tax side, these measures included increases in general exemption limits, child additions to the income tax exemption limits, and a reduction in the tax rate applied to those just above the exemption limits (the marginal relief rate). On the welfare side, increases in family income supplement and an intensive campaign to increase take-up of entitlements to that benefit were the main features. What were the implications of the various welfare and tax measures for incomes and incentives at low incomes?

Fig. 15.2. *Gross earnings and disposable incomes, 1986 and 1992*

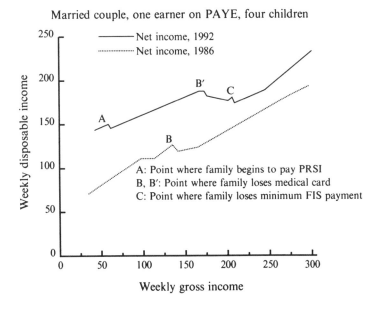

Fig. 15.2 demonstrates the relationship between gross and net incomes in 1986 and 1992 for one family type.[1] It is designed to show the incentive structure facing those in employment, rather than the replacement rates that might be relevant to a choice between

employment and unemployment. Disposable incomes are defined as gross incomes less taxes and PRSI plus FIS payments. The imputed value of a medical card is not included, but the transfer of liability for the health and employment levy and training levy from the employee to the employer, which is associated with medical card entitlement, is included in the calculations.[2]

The extreme form of 'poverty trap' phenomenon is absent from the 1986 schedule, apart from a kink relating to medical card entitlement, though the combination of FIS withdrawal, marginal income tax relief and PRSI does approximate a 100 per cent effective tax rate over a narrow range of gross incomes (about £5,300–5,700). The 1992 schedule lies above the 1986 schedule over the full range of incomes, but the upward shift is particularly marked for incomes below £10,000 per year. There is an effective marginal tax rate (from marginal income tax relief, FIS withdrawal and PRSI) of over 100 per cent on gross earnings between about £165 and £206 per week. While marginal rates decline thereafter, there is no gain in disposable income for an increase in gross earnings from about £160 to about £240 per week.

Two implications of these changes stand out. First, the band of income over which highest marginal tax-cum-benefit withdrawal rates (at or over 100 per cent) apply is wider in 1992 than in 1986. Second, the income range over which these rates apply has been shifted up the income scale.[3] This could have led to an increase in the number of families for whom such calculations are relevant; but the numbers actually in positions that involve these high effective tax rates are in fact quite limited. For the highest effective tax rates to be relevant, the family must be in receipt of FIS; but the numbers in receipt of FIS have increased only from about 5,000 in 1986 to just over 7,000 in 1991. This may be contrasted with estimates of about 20,000 families with a potential entitlement to FIS (Callan et al., 1989).

Do these relatively low numbers indicate that the poverty trap phenomenon is unimportant? As pointed out by Dilnot and Webb (1988, 40), 'the fact that there are relatively few people in the poverty trap may in fact imply that high marginal tax rates are important and that individuals have adjusted their labour supply accordingly.'

But what form would such adjustment take? Disposable income is maximised by a gross income that is just below the income tax exemption limit; it is reduced by opting out of work, since FIS improves the incentive to take up a job. Again, the administrative statistics indicate that relatively small numbers could have altered their behaviour in this way. Indeed, the fact that, even by 1991, the total number of FIS recipients was not much more than 7,000 indicates that the number of people who might face a low-income 'poverty trap' because of FIS, or who might have altered their behaviour to avoid one, is rather limited.

15.3 POLICY CHANGES SINCE 1987

Since much of our analysis, apart from consideration of the incentives for low-paid workers to increase their earnings, has been based on 1987 data, it is useful at this point to draw together information on recent changes in income tax and social welfare policy. General increases in social welfare have been in line with or slightly greater than inflation, but somewhat less than increases in average earnings over that period. Child benefit has been the major exception to this rule, with only one increase over the period up to 1992. Thus the balance of child income support has shifted away from this universal benefit towards additions to welfare payments for child dependants.

Special increases have been concentrated on the schemes for which payment rates were lowest. In particular, unemployment assistance and supplementary welfare allowance have been increased quite sharply. The personal rate for long-term unemployment assistance is now about £4 higher than flat-rate unemployment benefit. The rate and ceiling for pay-related benefit have been reduced. There has been considerable streamlining of the additions payable for child and adult dependants.

There were also significant changes in the income tax system. The 1986/87 system had three rates of tax, but these were reduced to two by 1992/93. The standard rate, which stood at 35 per cent for ten years, was reduced to 27 per cent; the top rate was reduced from 58 to 48 per cent, the same as the old 'higher' rate. The standard rate band was widened in real terms, but the basic personal allowance was increased by only 5 per cent over six years—much less than the rate of increase in prices and wages. The social insurance net was widened to cover the self-employed, and the income ceiling on the health contribution was removed. The overall burden of direct tax, measured in terms of national income, remained close to 21 per cent throughout these years.

There are considerable difficulties in identifying the effects of such policy changes on household incomes and poverty, as discussed by Callan and Nolan (1992a). It would be necessary not only to disentangle such effects from the impact of broader macro-economic developments (such as growth in world trade) but also to ascertain the extent to which tax and transfer policy changes themselves influenced growth and employment. Faced with these difficulties, and the lack of any micro-level data on household incomes since 1987, we confine our comments to two salient points. First, as regards the direct impact of social welfare policy on income poverty, it should be noted that the concentration of special increases on the schemes with the lowest rates of payment is likely to have made the system more effective in directly providing income support to those with the lowest incomes. In terms of the analysis in section 15.1 of this chapter, the system is likely to have been made more efficient and more effective by these changes than it otherwise would have been.

Second, we may note that as regards the incentives offered by the tax and transfer system, the relative and absolute movements in unemployment benefit, pay-related benefit and unemployment assistance mean that trends in replacement rates differ markedly depending on which measure is chosen. The increases in family income supplement, which, as shown in fig. 15.2, had a particularly strong effect on those with low earnings, have tended to reduce the replacement rate for those at very low levels of pay (who would have had the highest replacement rates). The highest replacement rates in 1986/87 would tend to have been for people receiving unemployment benefit, perhaps with a pay-related addition. The National Economic and Social Council (1990) found that replacement rates for recipients of unemployment benefit (calculated for a number of hypothetical cases) fell since then. Similar calculations show that replacement rates for recipients of long-term unemployment assistance, on the other hand, fell between 1986 and 1987, but have risen since then.

15.4 CONCLUSIONS

The analysis in this chapter has shown that the social welfare system plays a major role in providing income support to people whose income from other sources fell below a number of relative-income poverty lines. A significant poverty gap remains. The resources of the system seem to be more heavily concentrated on those with low incomes than those of other countries for which comparable evidence is available. The fact that poverty rates are, nonetheless, relatively high in Ireland reflects in large part the size of the problem. This serves to point up the role that growth and increased employment could play in tackling poverty.

The evidence from chapter 5 suggests that social welfare payments have been particularly effective in reducing poverty among the elderly.

But incentive effects for this group are not likely to be very strong. Greater responsiveness to work incentives can be expected from those more closely connected with the labour market, such as the unemployed and low-income employees. This suggests a need for greater co-ordination of tax and welfare policies. A number of forms of integration of the tax and welfare codes have been proposed with this in mind, and are considered in the next chapter.

16 Reform of Tax and Transfer Policy

TIM CALLAN AND CIARÁN J. O'NEILL

Many have pinned their hopes for employment growth and effective anti-poverty policies on the reform of the income tax and social welfare systems. The reasons for doing so, and the types of reform envisaged, can vary a great deal—even when all are agreed that unemployment is the most important cause of poverty in Ireland today. Some would emphasise that tax and welfare reform must aim above all at increasing employment (see, for example, McCarthy, 1993, and Tansey, 1991).[1] Others (Conference of Major Religious Superiors, 1991) would stress that while tax and welfare reform can contribute to this goal, unemployment is likely to continue at a high level; as a result, they would place considerable emphasis on the income support role of the social welfare system.

In this chapter we assess some of the major proposals for reform that have been put forward in recent years, taking into account both these perspectives. Where possible, we draw on analysis of the likely direct impact of the proposals on the overall distribution of income, paying particular attention to the impact on those at the lowest incomes, and also on the effects of the proposals on the incentives facing employers and employees to offer and to take up employment.

The Culliton Report (Industrial Policy Review Group, 1992) notes that 'the tax reform agenda has been set out clearly for several years.' Much of that agenda can be found in the first report of the Commission on Taxation (1982). We begin, in section 16.1, by briefly reviewing the commission's reform proposals, concentrating on those for a first phase of reform, which were broadly endorsed by the National Economic and Social Council (1986, 1990). Similarly, we review the proposals of the Commission on Social Welfare (1986). Several of the difficulties with the existing tax and transfer systems noted in the previous chapter arose from the lack of co-ordination between the two systems. There has been, as a result, considerable interest in integration of the tax and transfer systems. But 'integration' can mean quite different things to different people. Alternative proposals for integration of the systems, ranging from the inclusion of social welfare benefits in taxable income to fully fledged 'basic income' schemes, are also considered in section 16.1.

In subsequent sections a number of the key proposals are analysed using the Economic and Social Research Institute tax-benefit model. This model calculates the cash gain or loss a given family would experience from a change in policy before making any adjustment to their own behaviour. Applied to the nationally representative survey data, this allows calculation not only of the aggregate cost and revenue implications of a change in policy but also of the overall effects on the distribution of income, and on the tax rates faced. Section 16.2 deals with issues arising in broadening the direct tax base. Section 16.3 analyses more closely a package of measures that broaden the income tax base and cut tax rates, along the lines proposed by the Commission on Taxation. Section 16.4 concentrates on the analysis of options relating to child income support, noting the instructive parallels with issues arising in connection with basic income schemes. The main conclusions are drawn together in the final section.

16.1 MAJOR REFORM PROPOSALS

Commission on Taxation
The Commission on Taxation's first report (1982) advocated broadening of the income tax base, rate reductions, and simplification of the tax rate structure. Part of the simplification involved was the abolition of employer and employee PRSI contributions in favour of a broadly based social insurance tax at a lower rate. Ultimately the commission proposed to move to a single rate of income tax, with an individual expenditure tax aimed at the very top of the distribution. However, they also set out a package of measures that they recommended as a first phase towards this goal, involving rate reductions, base broadening, and a simplification of the rate structure, without an expenditure tax. It is this package of measures that has subsequently been given most attention and has been broadly endorsed as a strategy for tax reform by the National Economic and Social Council (1986, 1990) and the Culliton Report. Thus it is on this set of measures that we will concentrate here.

As regards the treatment of those on low incomes, the commission summed up as follows (1982, 249): 'We believe that the most effective and efficient method of helping the poor is not to exempt them from taxation, but to ensure by means of income maintenance payments that they have an adequate income ... The income tax system cannot be used to help people who have no income—those who need help most.'

Consistent with this approach, the commission advocated the abolition of income tax exemption limits (p. 246). It also proposed that tax reliefs be given in the form of tax credits (of equal value to taxpayers at different marginal rates of tax) rather than tax allowances (which are of greater value to those at higher marginal rates of tax). Responsibility for income maintenance, for those in low-paid employment as well as those without an income from employment, were placed firmly in the realm of the Department of Social Welfare.

Despite the clarity with which the commission set out the tax reform agenda, and the subsequent endorsement for its first-phase proposals by the NESC (1986, 1990), many of its recommendations remain unimplemented. A full analysis of why this is so is outside the scope of the present chapter, but some of the reluctance to implement certain proposals may have to do with fears about the extent and distribution of gains and losses involved. If this is so, it may be that analysis of the likely gains and losses arising from the change, such as is possible using the ESRI model, can clarify the nature of the options available. With this in mind, we analyse some elements of the commission's package in section 16.2 (notably the inclusion of short-term welfare benefits as taxable income, the abolition of special reliefs for mortgage interest, life assurance and medical insurance premiums, and the introduction of a general property tax), as well as providing a similar analysis in section 16.3 of an overall package based on the commission's recommendations.

Commission on Social Welfare

The Commission on Social Welfare set out a number of objectives that, in its view, should govern the development of the social welfare system. The first and most important of these was that payments must be adequate in relation to prevailing living standards. Other objectives included the attainment of a significant degree of redistribution, comprehensive coverage, consistency within the social welfare system and between social welfare and other aspects of social policy, and simplicity from the point of view of administrators and claimants. While recognising that trade-offs between these objectives would be required, the commission clearly indicated that adequacy was the most important principle.

The principal recommendation of the commission was for an increase in the basic rate of payment for a single person to a level between £50 and £60 per week, in 1985 prices.[2] The commission also recommended the streamlining of adult and child dependant rates, with adult dependant rates being set at 60 per cent of the corresponding payment for a single person. It advocated retention of the distinction between social insurance and social assistance, with social insurance payments approximately 10 per cent higher than social assistance rates. The commission viewed social insurance as 'an expression of social solidarity and citizenship' and considered that contributions helped to 'create a sense of entitlement to benefit and generate support among the public for these benefits' (Curry, 1986, 4).

As regards the financing of these higher rates, the commission proposed that the social insurance base be broadened to include the self-employed and farmers; that the ceiling on PRSI contributions be abolished; and that public servants should pay the full rate of PRSI. The commission also recommended that short-term benefits should be treated as part of total annual income for income tax purposes, and advocated the abolition of many special tax reliefs as part of a revenue-raising package.

The commission's recommendations were costed on the basis of a minimum personal rate of £50 per week for social assistance schemes and £55 per week for social insurance schemes—approximately £64 and £71, respectively, in 1993 prices. The gross cost in 1985 terms was £560 million. This excluded any increase in social insurance payments to the self-employed, but also any increase in revenue from their inclusion in the PRSI net.

The recommendations of the report have been strongly supported by the Combat Poverty Agency (1989) and the Justice Commission of the Conference of Major Religious Superiors (1991). However, the reaction of the NESC was more qualified. In its *Strategy for Development* (1986) the council 'generally endorses the analysis of the commission and accepts that the overall goal of public policy should be to provide an adequate, uniform and simple set of social welfare payments, and that in the short term there is a need to increase the lowest payments and to give priority to families.' However, the council stopped short of endorsing a large slate of the commission's recommendations. Other commentators have strongly opposed many of the commission's proposals. Dowling (1986) characterises it as proposing simply to increase social welfare payments and to pay for them by increased taxes on public servants, the self-employed, and those with incomes above the PRSI ceiling, with very limited changes to the essential structure of the system.

The main thrust of the commission's recommendations is for a levelling up of basic rates of payment towards the levels (£64–71 in 1993 prices) regarded as 'minimally adequate' by the commission. Paying for this increased expenditure does involve substantial increases in the aggregate PRSI and income tax takes. Most of the sources of revenue identified by the Commission on Social Welfare (broadening the social insurance base, abolishing the ceiling, eliminating special tax reliefs, and instituting a property tax) were also identified by the Commission on Taxation as necessary to finance reductions in income tax rates. There is, therefore, considerable tension between the basic thrust of the two reports. The report of the Commission on Taxation is generally seen as advocating a broadening of the tax base to finance lower tax rates,[3] while that of the Commission on Social Welfare proposed broadening of the tax base to finance increased social welfare payments.

In later sections we will analyse some of the elements common to the two reports—such as the inclusion of short-term welfare payments in taxable income as part of the base-broadening process—and clarify the implications of the differences. In particular we will pay attention to the different implications in terms of work incentives—noting both the balance between social welfare entitlements out of work and after-tax income from employment and the tax rates on additional earnings at higher income levels. It should be noted here, however, that at the current stage of development of the ESRI tax-benefit model it is not possible to provide a comprehensive analysis of the proposals of the Commission on Social Welfare.

'Integration' of tax and social welfare
A number of the problems identified in the previous chapter, such as the existence of a 'poverty trap' for those in low-paid employment, arise from the lack of co-ordination between the income tax and social welfare codes, which have developed in independent directions over the years. Correspondingly, 'integration' of the tax and social welfare systems is often seen as the solution. While debate on this issue sometimes proceeds as if 'integration of taxes and benefits' had a unique and unambiguous meaning, there are in fact many alternative sets of reforms that could fall under this heading. The most elementary form of integration, and one often proposed, is the inclusion of short-term social welfare payments as part of taxable income (this is analysed directly in section 16.4). The fullest form of integration would be represented by a radical alternative approach, involving a fully unified tax and transfer system. This is most commonly described as a '(guaranteed)

basic income' scheme, but similar schemes are also referred to as 'negative income tax' or 'social dividend'.[4] Such schemes have generated considerable interest in recent years. It may be useful, therefore, to outline the nature of this alternative and of some intermediate positions that may be regarded by some as stepping-stones to this 'grand design' and by others as worthwhile achievable improvements in themselves, without any necessary commitment to further change.

The purest form of basic income would comprise a single untaxed payment made to all individuals, replacing all existing social welfare schemes, with all other income being subject to tax at a single rate. The payment level in some versions would be differentiated by a small number of categories (such as age and/or health status). Such a structure has many attractions. Poverty traps created by a combination of benefit withdrawal and income taxes could not arise. The universal nature of the benefit would mean that problems of non-take-up with means-tested schemes would be overcome. The simplicity of the system would give rise to considerable administrative savings. It would also provide people with greater flexibility and certainty in movements into and out of full-time and part-time employment. The major difficulty with such schemes is the high cost involved. In effect, there is a sharp trade-off between the level of the basic payment and the taxes required to finance it.

A number of *modified basic income schemes* have been proposed to improve the trade-off that can be achieved. Some would move away from the individual basis of entitlement, making payments instead to a family unit or household. This loses some of the advantages claimed for the pure schemes in terms of the independent treatment of married people. Another modification that would reduce the net cost of the scheme is to have a high rate of benefit withdrawal at low incomes: Honohan (1987) analyses such a scheme. This reduces the net cost of providing a higher basic payment without imposing high marginal tax rates on a large proportion of the population. A third modification recognises the difficulty of paying a large enough basic income for subsistence by paying a smaller amount as a partial basic income, to be supplemented by means-tested and/or contingency-based payments for those with low or no incomes from other sources.

A full-scale basic income scheme involves as a central element a payment in respect of children. For this reason, we concentrate in section 16.4 on the options for reform of child income support, including an option that amounts to a 'basic income for children'. If this option is rejected as impossible to finance, it seems unlikely that a full-blown scheme, involving basic income payments for adults as well as children, could be acceptable and affordable. If, on the other hand, a basic income is regarded as the ultimate goal or guide to policy, a 'basic income for children' could be a useful intermediate target.

More modest changes could iron out many of the kinks and traps in the current system, by 'harmonising' or 'co-ordinating' the tax and transfer systems without fully integrating them. For example, the inclusion of unemployment benefit and unemployment assistance payments as part of taxable income would help to ameliorate the impact of the unemployment trap for some people. Similarly, the 'poverty trap' for low-income employees could be reduced or eliminated by measures short of full integration: for example assessment of family income supplement (FIS) on the basis of net rather than gross income. Increases in basic personal allowances, coupled with the abolition of the income tax exemption limits, would also help to improve incentives in the current system. Some of these measures are considered in section 16.4 below.

16.2 EFFECTS OF BASE-BROADENING OPTIONS

We have seen that a broadening of the income tax base is a common feature of many of the reform proposals in recent years. Here we use the ESRI tax-benefit model to look in some detail at the likely effects of a number of commonly mooted base-broadening options: taxing of short-term social welfare benefits, abolition of special tax reliefs such as mortgage interest tax relief and relief on medical insurance (VHI) contributions, and the introduction of a broadly based residential property tax.

Under the current income tax system, people with similar incomes may pay quite different amounts of tax, for a number of reasons. One of these is that short-term welfare benefits have not been included as part of taxable income[5]—a feature that can also create an incentive to become unemployed or ill for part of a year in order to maximise net income. The proposal to include short-term welfare benefits as part of taxable income would remedy these problems, but has aroused considerable controversy. In part this may reflect a mistaken perception that it would consist of a tax deduction or withholding tax applied to all short-term welfare payments. In fact empirical analysis using the ESRI model shows that a tax liability would not arise for the majority of short-term welfare recipients. A tax liability would only be likely to arise if the family concerned were not wholly dependent on social welfare for the relevant tax year. If a person became unemployed or ill during the year, it is likely that the increased tax liability would simply result in the reduction or elimination of tax rebates due under the current system. A reduction in the net payment of social welfare would only be likely if the recipient had a concurrent source of other income, or had a spouse in employment.

The other concern widely expressed was that the taxing of short-term benefits would tend to hit those on low incomes, because short-term welfare recipients tend to be on low incomes. Fig. 16.1 shows clearly that this would not be the case when families are ranked according to their annual income: it illustrates the average loss from the change over the income distribution, ranging from the poorest 10 per cent of families up to the richest. Those who would experience cash losses from the change are concentrated in the upper middle area of the income distribution. This applies whether families are ranked, as in the diagram, by net income per 'adult equivalent', in order to take into account differences in family size and composition, or simply by their total net income. About 70 per cent of tax units affected by the change are in the upper half of the income distribution. Less than 10 per cent of those affected are among the lowest 30 per cent of incomes (the bottom three deciles). The total cost of exempting short-term welfare benefits from tax in 1987 was close to £100 million. Less than £5 million of this amount went to the poorest 30 per cent of families, and more than £70 million went to families in the upper half of the annual income distribution.

The general message from this analysis is that the progressivity of the income tax system means that exempting short-term welfare benefits from its scope is not progressive. Concern that ending this exemption would be regressive is therefore misplaced.

The first report of the Commission on Taxation (1982) recommended abolition of special reliefs such as the deductions for mortgage interest, medical insurance, and life assurance. Such reliefs, it was argued, distorted decisions in the relevant areas and, by narrowing the tax base, required higher tax rates to achieve any given revenue. Furthermore, it was argued that the benefits from such 'tax expenditures' were concentrated on the upper end of the income distribution. That this is indeed the case is illustrated by fig. 16.2. At the top of the income distribution the tax expenditure leads to an average gain in net income of 3 per cent. For those at the bottom of the distribution, where little if any income is taxable, gains are non-existent or negligible, while

Fig. 16.1.   *Taxation of short-term welfare benefits*

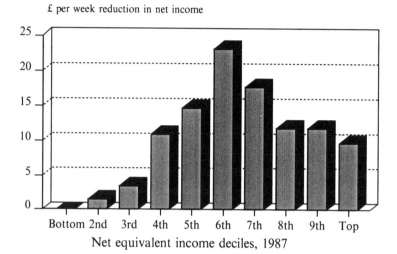

£ per week reduction in net income

Net equivalent income deciles, 1987

for others in the bottom half of the distribution the average increase is 0.5 or 1 per cent. The proportion of taxpayers benefiting from these reliefs rises with income; and the value of the relief is also particularly high for taxpayers with the highest incomes, who faced the higher marginal tax rates. As a result, over 60 per cent of the tax expenditure goes to the richest 20 per cent of families.

Substantial numbers of taxpayers in the middle of the income distribution do benefit from these reliefs, which has made it politically more difficult to remove or restrict them. Relief on life assurance premiums has been removed, but there has been no change in the treatment of medical insurance premiums. Furthermore, the restrictions on mortgage interest introduced in the late 1980s, which brought the relief down to 80 per cent of mortgage interest, with a maximum tax relief of £3,200 per couple, were relaxed in the 1993 budget in response to high interest rates arising from the devaluation (or pre-devaluation) crisis. The evidence above suggests that this relaxation will have been of most benefit to those at the top of the income distribution. This should reinforce the resolve to withdraw this temporary relaxation, now that interest rates have fallen substantially. (Indeed, an automatic mechanism for tailoring interest relief to the level of interest rates would be to limit the relief to the interest on a fixed capital sum, rather than a fixed amount of interest.)

Fig. 16.2. *Distribution of tax expenditures on mortgage interest relief, life assurance, and health insurance premiums*

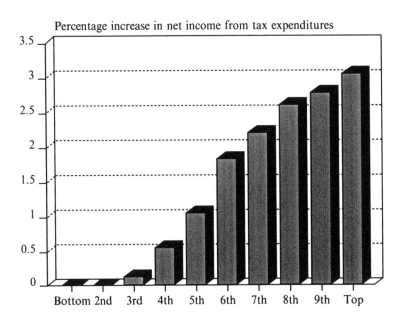

Percentage increase in net income from tax expenditures

Even the abolition of mortgage interest relief would not fully redress the basic distortion in this area: the fact that the implicit income accruing to owner-occupiers (the saving in not having to pay rent, because they own the property) is not subjected to tax. A general tax on the value of owner-occupied residential property, coupled with the retention of some form of relief for those who are paying mortgages, could be used to finance a reduction in the tax rate on earned income.

There are several reasons why this much-discussed reform proposal, endorsed by the Commission on Taxation and the NESC, has not been implemented. Here we focus on the key question of linking the amount of property tax to ability to pay.[6] The lack of such a link was one of the main factors that made domestic rates so unpopular. One merit of such a tax is that it encourages those with larger properties than they need to 'trade down', leading to a more efficient use of the housing stock. But there is a concern that elderly people living in highly valued accommodation but with low current incomes should not be forced to uproot themselves. This problem could be met in a number of ways. For example, the property tax liability could be deferred, to be paid by the inheritor. Alternatively, some form of waiver could be provided to those on low incomes. The difficulty with this is that it would, in effect, create an additional tax on the income of those just above the income level required for a full waiver. One such scheme is explored in the next section, as part of a comprehensive direct tax reform package.

16.3 BASE-WIDENING, RATE-REDUCING TAX REFORMS

The major concern of the Commission on Taxation was to design an equitable and simple tax system that would be flexible enough to permit different political choices. For example, the degree of progressivity could be altered by changes to the level of tax credits or allowances and to the standard rate of tax. The reports of the commission do not set out detailed income tax rates and bands for their first-phase reform; nevertheless it is possible to identify a revenue-neutral package that reflects the main thrust of the commission's proposals. A detailed comparison of the package modelled here with the commission's recommendations is made by Callan (1991c). In table 16.1 we set out the values for tax rates and tax bands in 1987, the time of the survey, and the values used in the reform package.

The major features of the reform package are that employee social insurance contributions are abolished, and social security is financed entirely from income tax on a broader base. The top tax rate is cut by eight percentage points, and the standard-rate tax band is widened substantially. The package results in a fall of eight percentage points in the effective marginal tax rate for a standard-rate taxpayer who is liable for full PRSI. Much of the revenue needed to finance the package comes from a property tax, set at a rate that can be seen as the product of the standard rate of tax and an assumed real rate of return of 5 per cent. Consistent with this, real interest payments are made allowable for tax. The commission also recommended a 'waiver' scheme based on income, without specifying the details: the scheme modelled here would exempt those with incomes not much more than the contributory old age pension level.

Fig. 16.3 shows the effects of the package on effective marginal tax rates, taking into account not only income tax but also employee PRSI contributions (in the unreformed system) and the withdrawal of property tax waivers (in the reformed system).[7] It is clear that the tax reform package would bring about substantial reductions in tax rates for many taxpayers. It would also lift a significant number of those

TABLE 16.1 *Comparison of policy parameters in 1987 and a 'tax reform package'*

Policy parameter		1987	'Tax reform package' (revenue-neutral)
Social insurance parameters:			
PRSI higher rate		5.5%	0
PRSI reduced rate		0.9%	0
Health contribution rate		1.25%	0
Employment and training levy		1.0%	0
Income tax parameters:			
Standard rate		35%	35%
High rate		48%	none
Top rate		58%	50%
Standard rate band	—single	4,700	9,000
	—married	9,400	18,000
High rate band	—single	2,800	nil
	—married	5,600	nil
PAYE allowance		700	0
PRSI allowance		286	0
Tax short-term social welfare?		no	yes
Qualifying percentages for income tax relief:			
Medical insurance premiums		100%	0
Life assurance premiums		50%	0
Mortgage interest		90% of nominal interest	Real interest payments only
Property tax parameters:			
Tax rate		0	1.75%
Income exemption limit	—single	not applicable	3,150
	—married	not applicable	6,300
Marginal relief rate		not applicable	20%

paying PRSI on low incomes out of the direct tax net. Almost 750,000 taxpayers were faced with effective marginal tax rates of more than 35 per cent in 1987; the revenue-neutral reform would reduce that figure to about 250,000. Most taxpayers would experience reductions of at least five percentage points, while more than 250,000 would see reductions of over ten percentage points. But some families would face higher marginal tax rates, largely because of the marginal relief provisions associated with the waiver scheme for the property tax.

The distributional effects of the reform are quite complex. There are almost equal numbers of gainers and losers. Gainers outnumber losers

Poverty and Policy in Ireland

Fig. 16.3.   *Marginal tax rates under 1987 policy and revenue-neutral reform*
              package

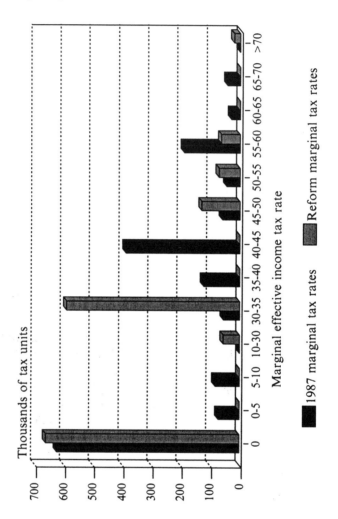

at the lowest incomes, but both the number and the size of gains and
losses are quite limited in this part of the income distribution. Losers
outnumber gainers in the middle of the income distribution, and
average losses are greater than average gains. Net gains are heavily
concentrated in the top part of the income distribution, particularly
among the top 10 per cent of tax units. This concentration of net gains

at the top end of the income distribution is not peculiar to the reform specified here: it is a common feature of many reforms that lower tax rates, even when financed by the broadening of the income tax base. Fig. 16.4 shows that even as a percentage of income, gains are greatest at the top of the income distribution, with losses for those in the middle of the distribution and more limited gains for those at the bottom.

Fig. 16.4. *Distributional effects of a base-broadening, rate-reducing income tax reform*

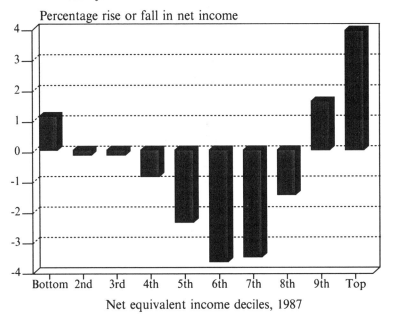

Percentage rise or fall in net income

Net equivalent income deciles, 1987

It is a commonly held belief that financing income tax reductions by base-broadening measures will maintain the progressivity of the system. For example, the National Economic and Social Council (1990, 182) came to the conclusion that 'it is generally correct that income tax rate reductions will tend to reduce progressivity, but this does not necessarily bias the Council against the proposal to flatten the income tax rate schedule since there are feasible and easily identifiable base-widening measures which, if taken in conjunction with income tax rate reductions, would preserve, or even enhance, the progressivity of the system.'

The results of our analysis run counter to this assertion. A trade-off between efficiency considerations (lower tax rates) and equity considerations (progressivity) can persist, even when tax cuts are financed by a broadening of the tax base. It should be noted in this context that the model-based calculations concentrate on 'cash' or 'first-round' effects, before any behavioural responses to the tax changes. It has been widely argued that a tax reform package of this type would lead to increased employment, which would improve the incomes of those otherwise likely to remain unemployed. The ultimate distributional consequences of the package could therefore be more favourable than those examined here. Nevertheless, the results caution against the idea that base broadening will itself offset the reduction in progressivity brought about by cuts in tax rates.

What in fact happened in the late 1980s and early 1990s was that income tax rates were cut *without* substantial broadening of the income tax base. The standard rate was cut from 35 to 27 per cent and the top rate from 58 to 48 per cent; the standard rate band was also widened significantly, but personal allowances were increased by less than the rate of inflation. Some base-widening measures were introduced, such as the abolition of relief on life assurance premiums and the restriction of mortgage interest relief to 80 per cent of the interest paid. But the revenue gained from such extensions to the tax base was small in comparison with that conceded by reductions in tax rates. These policies have had even more regressive consequences than the revenue-neutral package examined here. Furthermore, they left in place many of the undesirable features of the narrowly based income tax system, and wasted opportunities for introducing tax reform when circumstances would have permitted some compensation for those who would lose from a revenue-neutral reform.

Where should policy go from here? There is still a strong case for broadening the tax base in order to reduce tax rates on employment. But this should not mean a continued concentration on headline numbers, such as the standard and top rates of tax, which have already been reduced by eight and ten percentage points, respectively. The biggest disincentives to taking up employment will not be greatly altered by further reductions in these tax rates. The highest effective tax-cum-benefit withdrawal rates are faced by the unemployed and those in low-paid employment, as outlined in the previous chapter. A key feature here is the fact that much child income support is conditional on being out of employment or linked to a high benefit withdrawal rate for those in low-paid employment. Alternative arrangements of child income support are explored in the next section. These offer a more effective way of tackling high tax rates on low earners than the more commonly discussed methods of widening the standard rate tax band and increasing the tax exemption limits for families with children.

Very high tax rates also apply to potential second earners, most of whom are married women, and to young single people. The key feature of the tax system that gives rise to high effective tax rates on these groups is the fact that married couples are entitled to fully transferable allowances and rate bands. The rationale for this approach offered in the budget speech that introduced it was, implicitly, that it provided support to one-income families, especially where a married woman chose to care for her family on a full-time basis. Once again, therefore, the issue of how best to provide income support for families with children is critical. In the next section we discuss alternative ways of providing income support to families with children that do not involve such high tax rates on potential second earners.

16.4 CHILD INCOME SUPPORT

We have seen in earlier chapters that over time, poverty among families with children has become more prevalent, largely as a result of increased unemployment. As a result, families with children are a key group for anti-poverty policy. We have also seen (chapter 15) that the most extreme disincentives to work (the 'unemployment trap' and the 'poverty trap' for low-paid employees) also tend to be concentrated on families with children. A crucial question for anti-poverty policy is, therefore, how best to provide income support to families with children. In particular, it is desirable to provide income support in a way that does not create severe disincentives to work.

Before considering options for future policy, it is useful to review briefly the balance of policy at present. The state provides free services (such as education and some health services) and a set of cash income supports for children. In the present chapter we concentrate on the cash income supports, which are provided through a number of different mechanisms:

(1) Child benefit is paid in respect of all children in the relevant age groups. The total cost of this was around £220 million per annum before the 1993 budget increase: this could be expected to raise the annual figure to around £260 million.

(2) Adults on most social welfare schemes receive child dependant additions for their dependent children. The resources put into this mechanism are somewhat greater—closer to £300 million.

(3) Support for families in low-paid employment is provided by the family income supplement scheme. About £15 million is paid through this route.

(4) Child additions to the income tax exemption limits also benefit some families with low incomes. It is estimated that the cost of these provisions is of the order of £10 million.

Much of the income support for low-income families has been concentrated on child dependant additions for those on social welfare schemes. But this is one of the key elements in the 'unemployment trap': a substantial part of the income support for children is conditional on the claimant being unemployed and is lost on their taking up a job.

Some of the main options for reform have quite close parallels with the 'basic income' approach, discussed in section 16.1. A 'basic income for children' would concentrate all payments into an increased universal child benefit, which would not be subject to tax.[8] The advantages of this approach to child income support include the fact that it could direct additional resources towards low-income families in employment in a way that avoided the problems of non-take-up associated with family income supplement and similar schemes. The incentive to work would be improved by the fact that the same child income support would be paid in employment or out of employment. As with basic income, the major difficulty is the trade-off between the cost of the scheme and the level of support provided. The total financial support currently received by social welfare recipients for each child is approximately £17 per week. Child benefit would have to be almost quadrupled to reach this level on its own so that it could replace child dependant additions completely while leaving social welfare recipients no worse off. Consolidation of the existing child dependant additions, together with the much smaller amounts of resources involved in FIS and child additions to tax exemption limits, would only finance something over a doubling of child benefit.

This perspective again highlights the parallels with basic income schemes. There is a similar trade-off between the level of the universal payment (basic income or child benefit) and the tax rates required to finance it. But there is a crucial difference: the aggregate revenue required to finance a basic income for children at about the levels of payment currently made to those on low incomes is much lower than the aggregate revenue required to finance a basic income for all people, adults and children, at close to current social welfare support levels. Yet the 'basic income for children' would achieve major improvements in the incentive to work, while providing additional resources to low-income families in employment.

One possible source of finance for such a change in child income support would be a change in the tax treatment of married couples. At present the income tax payable by a couple is calculated in such a way that allowances (and the standard rate band) can be transferred fully from a non-earning or low-earning spouse to a higher-earning partner. This concession leads to a very substantial reduction in tax revenue. The rationale given for this approach in the 1980 budget was, in essence, to give financial support to families in which a married woman elected to care for her family on a full-time basis rather than working outside the home. It can be seen, therefore, as an implicit subsidy of married women caring for children. But this tax subsidy is not well targeted towards those who need it. It is of greatest value to high-rate taxpayers, and it applies to all married couples, not just those with children. A system that taxed husbands and wives more independently would improve the incentive to work for married women (who at present face major disincentives to work, and whose labour supply tends to be more responsive, as reported in chapter 12) while at the same time providing resources that could be used to finance a very substantial increase in child benefit.[9]

Even with these additional resources it might be difficult to finance an increase in child benefit to the level of £17 per week in current terms. Some would argue that it would not be desirable to finance such an increase, because a universal payment such as child benefit is seen as poorly targeted, with payments going to those with high incomes regarded as 'wasteful'. This takes no account of the fact that state child income support is aimed not only at helping those with low incomes but at sharing the costs of raising children more broadly, across the community and across the life cycle. However, there is an additional policy option that would help to reduce the cost of reform and meet the concerns about 'targeting' by helping to concentrate more of the resources on low-income families. This is to make child benefit a part of taxable income, while using the revenues gained to finance an increase in child benefit. It should be made clear that this does not involve a *reduced* child benefit payment to mothers: it would not be implemented as a withholding tax. In fact the direct payment to mothers in the home would be substantially increased. Nor does it mean that tax would be payable on the child benefit by every family: this would only happen if total taxable income was sufficient to bring the family into the tax net. The advantages of this approach are that it helps to withdraw some of the resources going to high-income families and redirect them towards low-income families, while retaining most of the advantages of the 'basic income for children'.

The effectiveness of this strategy can be demonstrated by analysis of a more limited option: an increase in child benefit that is just sufficient to compensate standard rate taxpayers for making the benefit taxable. The net cost of such a change was estimated to be about £20 million in 1987. The distributive effects are illustrated in fig. 16.5, which shows the average gain or loss for each successive tenth of the population, ranging from the poorest to the richest.

Fig. 16.5.   *Increased and taxable child benefit*

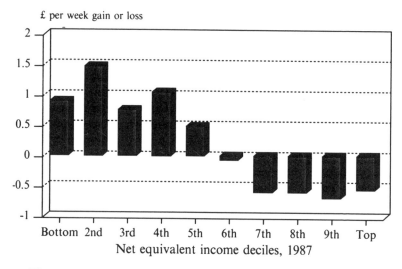

£ per week gain or loss

Net equivalent income deciles, 1987

The pattern shown is of significant average gains for those in the lower half of the income distribution, and losses for those in the upper half. More detailed analysis shows that there are no losers in the poorest decile and very few in the bottom half of the distribution. The great bulk of taxpayers face unchanged marginal tax rates.

It is important to recognise that this increased and taxable child benefit would differ substantially from the proposal in the 1989 budget to withdraw child benefit from families above a certain cut-off income. This proposal was vehemently opposed by those concerned that child benefit should reach women in the home irrespective of their income: a taxable child benefit, by contrast, would lead to an *increased* payment to mothers caring full-time for children in the home. All families with children would continue to receive some support. The proposal for a cut-off income would create new 'kinks' in the effective tax rate structure, whereby increases in earnings could lead to lower disposable income; a taxable child benefit would not give rise to such problems.

The NESC came to the conclusion that 'the fully integrated Child Benefit scheme offers a benchmark against which incremental changes in the tax and benefit system should be evaluated. Specifically, the Council recommends that CDAs should gradually diminish in scope in the child income arrangements while Child Benefit's role should be enhanced.' Our analysis supports this conclusion, and suggests that making child benefit taxable may assist in the redirection of resources towards those in greatest need. This strategy can be used to provide increased support to families with low incomes, either in or out of employment, without damaging the incentive to take up paid employment.

16.5 CONCLUSIONS

There is no shortage of proposals to reform the tax and welfare systems. In this chapter we have focused on some of the key issues. We began by reviewing three of the major sets of reform proposals that form part of the current debate on tax and welfare policy: the proposals for a first phase of direct tax reform by the Commission on Taxation, the proposals of the Commission on Social Welfare, and the proposals from a number of sources for a guaranteed 'basic income'. While each of the commissions favoured broadening the tax base, their proposals varied in the use that would be made of the revenue: the Commission on Taxation favoured reduction of tax rates, while the Commission on Social Welfare stressed the need to increase welfare payment rates.

Some of the key base-broadening measures were analysed using the ESRI tax-benefit model. This enabled us to assess the likely distribution of gains and losses from tax and welfare changes across the income distribution, something that has not been possible up to now. The inclusion of short-term welfare benefits in the income tax base has sometimes been opposed on the grounds that it would hit hardest those on low incomes. Analysis using the ESRI model shows that this would not be the case. Most short-term welfare recipients would be unaffected, and those who would lose from the change tend to have annual incomes that are above average. The losses would be heavily concentrated in the upper to middle regions of the annual income distribution.

A package of base-broadening measures combined with income tax rate reductions, along the lines of the Commission on Taxation's recommendations for a first phase of tax reform, showed that the commonly held belief that base broadening would preserve the overall progressiveness of the tax system when combined with rate reductions is highly questionable. There are significant gains and losses within each income group, but on average substantial gains are likely for the highest income groups, while middle-income groups on average lose out. What happened in the late 1980s and early 1990s was that tax rates were cut without substantial broadening of the tax base: this must have led to even greater reductions in tax progressiveness.

The arguments for broadening of the tax base in order to reduce taxes on employment are still relevant, but in our view the focus for efforts to reduce disincentives to work should shift away from headline numbers such as the standard tax rate and the top tax rate. The highest effective tax rates on employment income are now on those at the bottom of the income distribution: the unemployed and those in low-paid employment. There is a danger that the width of the standard rate band will become the new headline number by which progress will be judged. This is not desirable. The most severe disincentives arise from the way in which child income support is at present structured. Much child income support is conditional on the claimant being unemployed (via child dependant additions in the social welfare code); there is also substantial income support for a non-earning spouse in the income tax code. A reform package that concentrated child income support into a universal child benefit, partly financed by making the payment taxable and partly by making the taxing of husband and wife more independent, would have considerable merits.

17 Poverty and Labour Market Measures

RICHARD BREEN

In Ireland, as in many other western industrialised countries, the past twenty years have seen the growth of a plethora of Government programmes whose aim, direct or indirect, has been to create jobs and to improve the chances of unemployed people acquiring a job. This chapter looks at some of these programmes, namely those that involve direct Government intervention in the workings of the labour market. Our focus is on whether—and if so to what extent and how—such programmes can reduce poverty in Irish society.

17.1 POVERTY AND UNEMPLOYMENT

Unemployment is a major cause of poverty in Ireland, just as it is in many other countries. For example, in Britain the growth of poverty during the early and middle 1980s was largely due to the increasing incidence of unemployment. However, the relationship between poverty and unemployment is not wholly straightforward, not least because unemployment is not the only cause of poverty in Irish society. Equally, having a job is no guarantee against poverty. Whether or not individual unemployment causes a household to become poor depends on various other factors: for example how long the spell of unemployment lasts and whether there are other income earners in the household. The link between household poverty and individual labour force status is a complex one, as explored in previous chapters. Nevertheless, unemployment has been shown to be the most important cause of poverty in Ireland at present (see especially chapter 6 above).

Governments in many western industrialised countries have sought to combat unemployment through the use of job creation measures and training schemes. One way such programmes might be expected to

281

reduce poverty would be through creating new jobs. But while this is, by and large, a reasonable supposition, it does not necessarily follow that the success of job creation measures will imply a reduction in poverty levels. Much depends, for example, on the wages that such jobs pay: if jobs created in this way yield a take-home wage little or no higher than rates of unemployment assistance or benefit they will have little or no impact in alleviating poverty. Much also depends on the incidence of such jobs: in other words, on who benefits from the creation of new jobs. Hence, one of the important issues in Government job creation interventions in the labour market concerns who gets the jobs so created. To have the maximum possible impact on poverty, job creation programmes would not only have to create jobs, they would have to create them for specific sorts of unemployed person. Ideally, then, we might want to target such jobs on, say, long-term unemployed people living in households where no-one else is working.

In reality, it is impossible to incorporate so many criteria: job creation schemes, when they are targeted at all, tend in practice to be targeted at groups considered to be experiencing particular difficulties in the labour market, such as unqualified school leavers or the long-term unemployed. Labour market interventions often have, as a result, both an 'equity' goal and an 'economic' goal (that is, to create additional jobs). It is important to bear in mind that these can be quite distinct in their effects. For example, even if a programme does not create any new jobs, it could reduce poverty by persuading employers to hire from among the long-term unemployed (who are more likely to come from households experiencing poverty) or by providing training for (and so making more employable) people who are in such households.

In this chapter we will first examine the job creation effects of labour market measures and then assess their equity or redistributive impact.

17.2 LABOUR MARKET INTERVENTIONS: A TYPOLOGY

By labour market measures we mean those programmes that seek to intervene directly in the workings of the labour market. Such programmes are, in the main, administered by the training authorities, FÁS and CERT. Fig. 17.1 shows a typology of such labour market schemes. The main distinction made here is between the two broad types: training programmes and employment schemes. This is a somewhat arbitrary distinction, of course, not least because some training programmes—such as the Community Youth Training Programme and Alternance—contain substantial elements of temporary employment.

Fig. 17.1. *Typology of labour market measures (with participation at end of April 1991)*

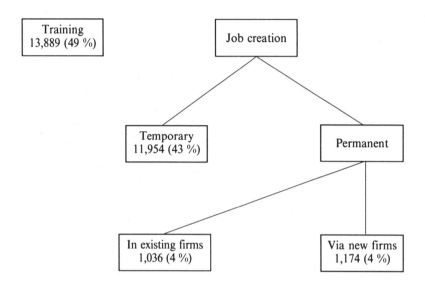

Note: Participation figures from *Labour Market Monthly*.

Furthermore, there is an obvious link between some of the training programmes and some of the employment schemes—for instance between enterprise training and the Enterprise scheme. Another way of labelling these two broad categories would be as supply-side (training) and demand-side (employment schemes) programmes. This is because training schemes attempt to alter the characteristics of the supply of labour, in an attempt, among other things, to make job seekers more 'employable', whereas job creation programmes seek directly to increase the demand for labour in the economy.

Within the employment schemes, fig. 17.1 distinguishes between temporary and permanent schemes. The former comprise the Social Employment Scheme (SES) and Teamwork, both of which offer work to unemployed people for a fixed period, with the Government paying most of the costs of such employment. Among permanent schemes, we distinguish two further kinds: those that are targeted at existing firms and employers and those that seek to help establish new businesses. The Employment Incentive Scheme (EIS) is the most significant of the former, having been in operation since 1979 (when it replaced the similar Premium Employment Programme); but this category also includes the PRSI exemption scheme (which has operated intermittently since the middle 1980s) as well as some smaller subsidy schemes that were established by the Youth Employment Agency during the early to middle 1980s. Enterprise (formerly the Enterprise Allowance Scheme) and the Community Enterprise Programme are the two main schemes whose aim is to create jobs by helping establish new businesses. 'Training programmes' in fig. 17.1 include a very wide range of schemes, ranging from apprenticeship training, through specific skills training, to Jobsearch.

Participation in April 1991 in the schemes shown in fig. 17.1 reveals an equal balance between training and job creation. Among training programmes, specific skills training, apprenticeship, the Community Youth Training Programme and Community Training Workshops are by far the largest. Within the job creation schemes the balance is overwhelmingly in favour of temporary programmes, with fewer than 10 per cent of participants in any form of permanent job creation programme.

17.3 LABOUR MARKET MEASURES AND JOB CREATION

If the effort and ingenuity devoted to instituting new labour market measures were any guide, Ireland's unemployment problem should have been solved long ago. Of course it has not been. It would be unfair, however, to suggest that this was only because of faults in the labour market measures themselves; nevertheless, each of these kinds of measure has problems associated with it that make it difficult for any of them to have an appreciable impact on the overall problem of high unemployment. As a result, there can be little doubt that they have had an insignificant effect on poverty. In this section we examine in turn each of the four broad measures identified in fig. 17.1—permanent job creation in existing and new businesses, temporary job creation, and training—and discuss the problems associated with them.

Permanent job creation in existing firms
The most important scheme in this area is the EIS, which has been in operation for over fourteen years, despite the fact that when it was introduced it was considered a temporary measure. The detailed workings of

the scheme have changed many times but the basic idea has remained constant: this is that employers are given a weekly fixed-rate subsidy for a fixed period on the pay of all additional new employees they hire.

At present the subsidy rates are £60 and £45, depending on whether the person comes from among the long-term unemployed or not. The original purpose of the scheme was twofold: to increase overall employment by encouraging employers to take on workers, and to improve the relative position of those among the unemployed who qualified for the subsidy.

The PRSI exemption scheme is also a job subsidy programme; here the subsidy takes the form of the waiving of PRSI contributions in respect of new employees for a certain period. Both this scheme and the EIS offer only a temporary subsidy; schemes of this type are therefore more correctly termed 'hiring subsidies' (rather than employment subsidies).

By and large it is difficult to find any argument to support the idea that a temporary job subsidy scheme will create permanent jobs. When the scheme began, in the late 1970s, it was argued that, as the economy came out of recession, such a job subsidy would encourage employers to hire new workers sooner than they would otherwise have done. Thus the scheme would accelerate the growth of new jobs and so create some additional 'person-years' of employment. However, during the prolonged recession that prevailed for most of the 1980s, such a justification was obviously untenable. A second argument in favour of the scheme was that by giving employers an extra employee for six months at a reduced cost it might demonstrate to them that they could in fact profitably employ an extra person in their business. But this argument rests on the assumption that employers themselves (or at any rate some employers) have a mistaken idea about their own business affairs.

The EIS was evaluated in 1986 on behalf of the Department of Labour (Breen and Halpin, 1989). It was estimated that, not surprisingly, of every 100 hirings made using the EIS, 91 would have occurred even if the scheme had not been in operation. In other words, there was a substantial 'deadweight effect'. Such deadweight (or 'windfall' effects, as they are sometimes called) is found in many programmes of public expenditure. In this context it arises because, when Governments give an incentive to change behaviour, there will always be certain actors in society who would have behaved in the way the Government was seeking to encourage them, even without the incentive. For these people it is rational to claim the incentive payment in respect of something they would have done even without it.

While the problem appears to be a simple one, it has proved impossible to design incentive schemes—such as employment or hiring subsidies—in such a way as to eradicate the problem. In the case of the EIS, for example, whether a particular subsidised hiring represents a deadweight loss or not depends on whether the firm in question would have hired an extra employee even without the subsidy. Since this can only be determined ex ante by reference to the employer's intentions, it is impossible to exclude such cases from the scheme. Even when unemployment is very high there is a great deal of hiring of new workers going on.

Breen and Halpin (1989) suggested that any additional employment generated by the EIS comes from two sources: firstly, from the 9 per cent of employers who claimed they would not have hired someone if they could not have used the scheme and, secondly, from a further 23 per cent of participating employers who, although they would have hired someone at a later date, were persuaded to take on someone at that time because of the subsidy.

The high level of deadweight in the EIS means that it has only a minor job creation effect. The same is probably true of the PRSI exemption scheme, although the take-up of this scheme among employers has been very low.[1]

Enterprise schemes

Programmes that encourage the unemployed to establish their own businesses were introduced in virtually every European country during the 1980s. The Enterprise Allowance Scheme, which began on a pilot basis in 1983, was modelled very closely on the UK scheme of the same name. In 1987 it was re-named Enterprise. The basic idea of the scheme is that it provides a weekly allowance for one year to unemployed people who are setting up a new business. The aim is therefore to encourage the founding of new businesses and thus the creation of jobs.

In schemes such as Enterprise the major difficulty is not the level of deadweight. Although there is some deadweight—in the sense that some unemployed people would have set up their business without the help of the scheme—it is almost certainly less than 50 per cent and probably much lower. Rather, the difficulties with a scheme like this concern its displacement effects. These arise because businesses that are established under the scheme tend to be in direct competition with existing firms.

In the middle 1980s a study of the Enterprise scheme was undertaken, again at the request of the Department of Labour (Breen and

Halpin, 1988). In this study, participants were interviewed roughly two years after they had joined the scheme. At that time 55 per cent of businesses established under the scheme were still in operation. For every 100 such businesses, 44 full-time employee jobs were in existence. However, this extra employment was very heavily concentrated; 83 per cent of surviving businesses had no employees at all.

Of more concern in this case, however, was the type of business the scheme helped set up. Of all entrants to Enterprise, three-quarters set up in services or in building and construction. The difficulty with this, from the point of view of net job creation, was that these firms were usually supplying a very local market and were supplying services that could not have been considered to have been in short supply. This was also true of those who set up in manufacturing: this included a large proportion of dressmakers, soft-toy makers, joiners, welders, and the like. Over 85 per cent of participants reported that they were in direct competition with one or more existing Irish firms. Only 3 per cent were engaged in exporting or import substitution.

While none of this is surprising, it places severe limitations on the job creation impact of the scheme. It is very difficult to put an exact figure on it, but Breen and Halpin estimated that around 90 per cent of the business done by firms set up under Enterprise was taken from other firms. As a result, for every 100 full-time jobs created, about 60 were lost elsewhere in the economy as a result of 'displacement effects'.

Temporary job creation schemes
The virtue of temporary job creation schemes such as the SES and Teamwork is that they suffer neither from deadweight nor displacement problems to any appreciable extent. This is because, by and large, SES and Teamwork projects either would not exist without the scheme (in the sense that the market would not fund them) or would be provided directly by the exchequer. The major difficulty with such schemes, however, lies in the fact that they are temporary.

There is plenty of evidence that long-term unemployment can in some cases bring demoralisation, psychological distress, and health problems (see Whelan et al., 1991); one important role of a scheme such as the SES is to interrupt the accumulation of such effects. Nevertheless one cannot escape the fact that these schemes are temporary, and any alleviation of distress they bring may well also only be temporary.

The main argument invoked against the expansion of such schemes into some form of permanent direct public sector employment is cost. It may be acceptable to employ people on a temporary basis at the low wage levels offered by the SES and Teamwork, but it is not sustainable—for a variety of reasons—to offer these wage levels for permanent jobs. Once this is admitted, direct job creation becomes expensive. In 1984, for example, the National Planning Board estimated that a net expenditure of £1,000,000 per annum would yield 175 jobs at a wage of £145 per week in various types of local authority and other projects similar to those that feature in the SES. By net expenditure the board meant extra expenditure that such employment would entail over and above the payment of unemployment assistance and/or unemployment benefit. Similarly, in 1984 the Department of Finance produced estimates to suggest that an expenditure of £1,000,000 annually could support 95 directly created jobs. This compares unfavourably with the numbers that could have been supported by the same expenditure on social welfare: on unemployment assistance 560 single people or 255 married people with one adult and two child dependants, or 218 equivalent families on unemployment benefit.

Training programmes

There are many good reasons for offering training to the unemployed. In particular we can point to the existence within the labour force of certain groups who lack skills and/or educational qualifications and who, as a result, spend excessively long periods unemployed. For such people training might well help them compete for jobs more effectively within the labour market.

However, as a response to the unemployment problem, training programmes have, at best, a limited effect. Ireland's problem is that the supply of labour far outstrips the demand for it. Training alters the nature of the labour supply but has little impact on the demand for labour, at least in the short term. Clearly, if the work force is more highly trained this might help attract more multinationals to Ireland, and in the long run it might well make businesses more competitive and thus help them expand and create more jobs; but these are effects at the margin. There is no way that simply training the labour force can have a major impact on levels of unemployment in the short to medium term. It is better to view training as a form of investment that will only pay in the long term.

17.4 LABOUR MARKET PROGRAMMES, EQUITY GOALS, AND POVERTY

Thus far we have examined the four main types of labour market programme in operation in Ireland over the recent past. We have sought to demonstrate why, for various reasons, none of them can be really effective in creating jobs and reducing unemployment. If we see the creation of extra employment in the economy as a way of reducing poverty, these schemes have little to offer.

This is not to argue, however, that they might not be effective in other ways. As we mentioned earlier, many such schemes may have important social or equity objectives. For example, the EIS is nowadays targeted mainly at a social goal. Under the scheme there were always differential subsidy rates for different categories of job seeker hired. Since the late 1980s the differential in rates of subsidy has been set explicitly to try to encourage employers to hire from among the long-term unemployed. The hope is not so much that the scheme will create new vacancies but that when an employer has a vacancy, he or she will be tempted by the more generous EIS subsidy to fill that vacancy using someone from the long-term unemployed. Similar equity goals are found in, for example, the SES, which is only open to those who have been on the live register for one year or more.

While the equity issue is explicit in the case of the EIS and SES, it should be considered in assessments of all labour market interventions, regardless of whether they create any extra jobs. In the case of training programmes—which, we have argued, do not create any additional employment—the equity issue arises because if training is effective it will improve the employment chances of those who receive it. But if no extra jobs are created, this improvement will occur in the context of a zero-sum game: participants' chances of getting a job, by increasing, simultaneously reduce in relative terms the labour market chances of non-participants.

The question then arises of how effective labour market measures can be in reducing poverty as a result of their redistributive effects. This question can be broken down into two parts: firstly, is the measure targeted at individuals who are likely to be experiencing poverty, and secondly, is the targeting effective?

Surprisingly little is known about the targeting of many training schemes. For a number of years criticisms were made that training schemes in the youth labour market were not being taken up by those young people most in need of training (see, for example, Breen 1984;

1988). The evidence during the early 1980s suggested that schemes such as the Work Experience Programme (WEP) were mainly availed of by young people leaving school after sitting for the Leaving Certificate and were consequently of little benefit to unqualified school leavers, who experience the greatest difficulties in the youth labour market. The Social Guarantee was an attempt to overcome this problem and to ensure that those young people who experience such difficulties receive preferential access to programmes. The Youthreach scheme is an attempt to implement such a guarantee.

In terms of combating poverty, of course, youth labour market schemes are of less importance than those in the wider labour market: here the equity goals are often difficult to attain. In the case of schemes—such as the EIS—that seek to encourage employers to hire particular categories of worker, differential incentives often seem to have surprisingly little effect.

At the time of Breen and Halpin's study (1989), firms that hired someone from the long-term unemployed under the EIS received £60 per week for 24 weeks, as against the £30 per week they would have received had they hired someone who had been on the live register for between 13 and 52 weeks. Despite this, only 15 per cent of EIS hirings were of the long-term unemployed. When asked, employers said that they would require, on average, a subsidy £65 greater for the long-term unemployed than for short-term unemployed people to be persuaded to hire the former.

A similar lesson can be learnt from the WEP. As mentioned earlier, most school leavers placed with employers under this scheme were relatively well qualified. The difficulty of targeting the scheme towards the less well qualified was that these are people whom employers are, by and large, reluctant to hire as employees and are equally reluctant to accept on WEP-type placements.

The second difficulty in this area concerns schemes such as the SES that can clearly be targeted at groups like the long-term unemployed: there is no question in this case of having to offer incentives to employers. The problem, however, concerns their temporary nature and the fact that they pay wages that are very low. Indeed, for some participants SES rates leave them worse off than they would be were they receiving unemployment assistance. As a result it is difficult to make a convincing case that a scheme like the SES can be directly effective in alleviating poverty.

Turning finally to the fourth type of labour market intervention, those that seek to stimulate the growth of new businesses, these are not targeted except insofar as they are open only to the unemployed. As noted above, a scheme like Enterprise does not add appreciably to the stock of jobs in the economy, primarily because of the high level of displacement it causes. It could, of course, be argued that Enterprise acts in a redistributive fashion as a result, with businesses started under the scheme possibly replacing (partially or even wholly) existing businesses; but it is difficult, not to say impossible, to believe that the weakening of existing businesses in such a fashion should be a legitimate goal of Government policy.

17.5 CONCLUSIONS

This chapter has examined the four main sorts of labour market programme in operation in Ireland, with the aim of trying to assess how they might alleviate poverty. We can suggest that they might do this in either or both of two ways: firstly, by creating new, additional jobs in the economy, and secondly, by redirecting jobs towards those who are most likely to be in poverty. The effectiveness of the former is not independent of the latter condition: only if job creation means that jobs are given to people from households that are experiencing poverty can such programmes directly contribute to the reduction of poverty.

In our examination of these four types of programme we concluded that none of them were particularly effective in creating employment. The exception to this is direct job creation by the Government (as in schemes like the SES); but even here the magnitude of the effect is limited both by the relatively small numbers on the schemes (when set against the total on the live register) and by the fact that participation is temporary. Of the four schemes, the equity effect (targeting) of many training programmes is difficult to establish.

In the case of schemes that are explicitly targeted at the long-term unemployed (who, of all the unemployed, are most likely to be in households experiencing poverty), their impact in alleviating poverty must be doubtful, because of the difficulty of persuading employers to hire from among this group in the case of the EIS and because of the low wage rates in a scheme like SES.

In summary, then, it is difficult to discern any effective reduction in poverty that is being brought about by such labour market measures; and indeed it is difficult to discern how this might be done within the framework of existing measures, short of a massive commitment to job creation schemes funded directly by the Government.[2] Such a commitment is unlikely to be realised in the foreseeable future.

This being said, it is important to acknowledge the limitations of such measures. Here two points are worth making. Certain labour market measures have been subjected to considerable and detailed analysis of their costs and benefits (as in the two studies by Breen and Halpin referred to earlier). One could legitimately argue that, given the lack of any comparable comprehensive evaluations of other, more expensive schemes of job creation, the emphasis on evaluating direct labour market measures has been disproportionate. There are many other programmes, and many state agencies, that have as their direct or indirect goal the creation of jobs but that have never received the kind of comprehensive evaluation to which some (but by no means all) labour market measures have been subjected.[3]

The second point is closely linked to this, and it is that expenditure on labour market measures of the kind described in this chapter is very small indeed when set against the budget devoted to job creation by the Industrial Development Authority. The labour market measures run primarily by FÁS can operate only at the margin—but unemployment and poverty are not marginal problems. The creation of jobs and training of the labour force can play a central role in combating poverty. If a serious attempt is to be made to reduce the level of poverty, then we should not confine our focus to the kind of direct labour market measures discussed here: rather, a broader view must be taken in which all forms of Government expenditure in pursuit of job creation are audited for their effects on poverty and evaluated in a comparable and comprehensive manner.

One reason why evaluation of such programmes is so important is that, in addressing the problems of unemployment and poverty, the most efficient strategy would be to adopt the most cost-effective measures and expand their provision. As things stand, we do not know which, of all forms of Government expenditure on job creation, is the most cost-effective. In other words, while combating poverty through job creation and labour market measures obviously requires the commitment of resources by the Government, it also requires a knowledge of the relative merits of different policies in order to decide how best to put such a commitment into effect.

18 The EC and Combating Poverty

Brian Nolan

In designing policies to deal with poverty in Ireland, the European Community (EC) dimension is of central importance. Membership of the EC obviously affects the socio-economic environment and the way in which poverty evolves in Ireland through many different channels. In addition, the availability of substantial resource transfers through the structural funds will continue to be a major influence on policy formation nationally. The objective of economic and social cohesion has been established in the Single European Act of 1986 as an essential counterpart to the economic freedom of movement highlighted by the 1992 programme. However, it is the narrowing of *spatial* disparities, i.e. differences between the member-states and between the various regions in the Community, that are specifically mentioned. It is towards this objective, narrowing the gap in average income between member-states and regions, that the structural funds, and the cohesion fund to be set up by the end of 1993, are primarily directed. The reduction of disparities *within* countries or regions—and for this purpose Ireland constitutes a single region—and the alleviation of poverty are not explicit objectives.

Similarly, while the Community has long operated in the area of social policy, this has had a much more restricted meaning than is usually the case, referring for the most part to the welfare, rights and working conditions of workers. Thus the Social Charter, adopted by all the member-states except the UK in 1989, is more properly the Charter of Basic Social Rights for Workers, and focuses on freedom of movement and the rights and interests of those already in employment. The section on social policy that was to have been included in the Maastricht treaty and, because of UK objections, is now a separate protocol agreed among the other eleven members incorporates a significant widening in the scope of Community objectives in this area. Up to the present, though, combating poverty has not been one of the stated objectives of social policy.

This has meant that the main Community action specifically directed towards combating poverty and social exclusion within member-states has taken the form of pilot action projects under the three Programmes to Combat Poverty. These projects have mostly been area-based, and the Irish projects under the second and third programmes have been linked with the Combat Poverty Agency set up by the Government, which is now also involved with a number of other community projects funded by the state. The Programmes to Combat Poverty have also had a research element, and the EC Commission and Eurostat (the Community's statistical agency) have had an important role in sponsoring research on poverty and related topics. This has significant potential for influencing both the ways in which such research is carried out and the perspective on poverty taken by policy-makers nationally and in an EC context.

This chapter could not and does not attempt to review comprehensively the many facets of the EC dimension to poverty and policy in Ireland. A number of recent studies have looked at different aspects of Irish membership of the Community, particularly in the context of the 1992 single market and the Maastricht treaty (see, for example, National Economic and Social Council, 1989: Foley and Mulreany, 1990; Keatinge, 1992; O'Donnell, 1991). Instead, the much more limited aim is to focus on three areas—the Programmes to Combat Poverty, EC social policy, and the structural funds—and consider their implications for Irish anti-poverty policy.

18.1 THE EC PROGRAMMES TO COMBAT POVERTY

The Projects

The initial decision to launch a programme aimed at combating poverty was taken by the Council of Ministers in 1974. The intention was to implement, in co-operation with the member-states, specific measures to combat poverty by drawing up pilot schemes. A programme was approved in 1975, and pilot projects, financed half by the Community and half by member-states, were undertaken between 1976 and 1980. In Ireland, uniquely, a National Committee on Pilot Schemes to Combat Poverty was set up to administer the projects to be jointly funded by the Government and the EC poverty programme. Twenty-four projects in different locations around the country were undertaken. Both the Irish element and the programme as a whole were the subject of some controversy, and there was something of a hiatus after the end of the First Programme in 1980, both at EC level and nationally. The EC did not continue funding for existing projects or begin new ones during a rather prolonged period of 'reflection and evaluation', and the Irish National Committee ceased operation.

From 1985 to 1989, however, the Commission, again jointly with member-states, financed ninety-one action-research projects across the member-states under the Second Programme to Combat Poverty. Unlike the First Programme, these were grouped around common themes, such as integrated action in urban or rural areas, long-term unemployed, young unemployed, etc. Co-ordination of the action-research projects was entrusted to a research institute in Cologne, with the co-operation of the Centre for Social Policy at the University of Bath.

The experimental nature of the programme was again accorded central importance, and collaboration and exchange of views across projects and countries was to be emphasised. Nine Irish projects were financed under the programme, including community development or resource groups in west Tallaght, Letterfrack, Louisburgh, Inishowen, and the south inner city area in Dublin. The Government provided 45 per cent of the funding for these projects through the Combat Poverty Agency, set up in 1986, the remaining 55 per cent coming from the EC. (A number of similar projects were fully funded by the Combat Poverty Agency, which was also given a wider role, including advising the Government on economic and social policy relating to poverty, promoting and interpreting research into poverty, and educating the public about poverty.[1])

The total budget for the Second Programme was 29 million ECU (expanded from an initial 25 million following the extension of the programme to include Spain and Portugal), a small increase on the 20 million ECU spent on the First Programme. The final report on the programme prepared by the Commission of the European Communities (1991) acknowledged that the activities of the projects were restricted in scope, rather dispersed, and varied in nature. The limited linkage between the projects and local networks and other national projects and activities was also noted. In the same vein, the Combat Poverty Agency report on the Irish projects (Cullen, 1989) also argued for the development of large-scale programmes of integrated development targeted on the most disadvantaged communities.

The Third European Poverty Programme, running from 1990 to 1994, has therefore shifted the emphasis towards a smaller number of larger-scale area-based programmes, and altered the organisational structure. Under this programme there are twenty-seven 'model action' projects and twelve smaller 'innovative projects' throughout the Community. The total amount allocated to the programme is 55 million ECU over five years. The Irish projects under this programme are two large-scale ones, People Against Unemployment, Limerick (PAUL), and FORUM Model Action in north and west Connemara, and a smaller innovatory project managed by the Dublin Travellers' Education and Development Group.

The PAUL and FORUM projects are once again financed 55 per cent by the EC and 45 per cent by the Combat Poverty Agency, and have budgets of about £350,000 per annum. This is very much larger than the budgets for the projects funded under the Second Programme, which averaged about £50,000 per annum. Poverty 3, as it is known, places a great deal of emphasis on the development of links between the projects and their localities. Management structures are to include local voluntary and community representation, statutory bodies, and possibly people from the private sector. 'Partnership' between the statutory and voluntary or community sectors is to be promoted. Ideally, this should not only allow the projects to operate more effectively but also provide channels through which their operation may influence the approach of local and central government and other statutory bodies.

Once again the projects are seen as pilot exercises, intended to provide models that could be adopted across the whole Community. In keeping with this objective, new structures (involving a co-ordinating Central Unit and national research and development units) have been put in place to promote co-ordination, evaluation, and transfer of experiences between the projects. This is all the more important in Ireland, since the Government established in 1990 a separate Community Development Programme, under which community-based resource centres in disadvantaged areas are being funded by the Department of Social Welfare. Initially fifteen centres, including some that had been projects under the Second EC Programme, were funded, and this had risen to twenty-one by 1992. The Combat Poverty Agency is responsible for supporting and monitoring these centres, and the budget for the programme in 1992 was about £1 million. In addition, the Programme for Economic and Social Progress agreed between the Government and the 'social partners' in 1991 initiated an area-based response to long-term unemployment. This has involved setting up twelve pilot area-based partnership companies, involving voluntary and statutory bodies and local community groups.

To further complicate the picture, twelve of the projects operating under the Community Development Programme and one operating under Poverty 3—the PAUL project—are participating in these PESP area-based initiatives, which are again seen as pilot exercises.

Fifteen years after the beginning of the First Programme, then, the expansion in the Community's own activities in this area has been modest. Potentially, though, the experience of the Poverty 3 pilot projects could be very influential in affecting the development of an area-based approach implemented on a much broader scale. Such an approach can clearly make an important contribution to harnessing the energies of local communities, and can be particularly helpful in promoting participation by those experiencing poverty. Its limitations as a response to poverty must also be emphasised, though, and would be clearly recognised by many of those involved (see for example Frazer, 1991). It is clear from the analysis of the causes of poverty that action at national or indeed EC level rather than local level is required to deal with many of the structural factors involved. In the case of unemployment, for example, the most important cause of poverty in Ireland, it is quite unrealistic to expect purely local initiatives to have a major impact. Areas with particularly high unemployment and poverty rates are the very ones where the obstacles to development and job creation are greatest, and so reliance on local action is even less realistic than elsewhere. In any case, we have seen in chapter 14 that while unemployment and poverty rates are very high in certain areas, most of the unemployed and poor are not to be found in such areas and so would be unaffected by action concentrated on 'black-spots'.

It is important, then, that area-based strategies, even extended beyond the 'pilot' phase, be seen not as a panacea but as only one element in a broader national and community strategy to combat poverty.[2]

The research element
In addition to action projects and the research and evaluation carried out on their activities, the EC poverty programmes have included a distinct research element. The First Programme took as starting-point the definition by the Council of Ministers in 1975 of those in poverty as 'individuals or families whose resources are so small as to exclude them from the minimum acceptable way of life of the Member State in which they live.' While 'resources' were defined as covering 'goods, cash income and services from public and private sources,' there was no attempt to set out explicitly how 'minimum acceptable way of life'

might be identified or specified. The research element of the First Programme consisted of international studies on topics such as perceptions of poverty, 'subjective' poverty lines, and the persistence of poverty, and a set of national reports on poverty in each country. (The main results are set out in the Commission's final report to the Council on the First Programme, 1981). The Irish national report (Joyce and McCashin, 1982) brought together the information then available about the extent and nature of poverty in Ireland (drawing heavily on Roche's analyses of the 1973 household budget survey) and the impact on poverty of policies in the areas of income maintenance, health, housing, education, and employment.

The 1975 Council definition saw poverty in terms of the minimum acceptable way of life within each member-state: what is acceptable in Ireland would presumably not be in Germany, and the notion of a common European standard, applying across all member-states, is implicitly rejected. Thus, in attempting in the final report to estimate the extent of poverty in the different member-states on a comparable basis, an income poverty line set at 50 per cent of average disposable income per adult equivalent unit in each country was employed. On this basis it was estimated that in the middle 1970s roughly 10 million households (11.4 per cent), containing 30 million people, were in poverty in the Community. The estimate for Ireland was that 23 per cent of households were below that line in 1973. With that of Italy, this was a much higher poverty rate than the rest of the (then) nine member-states. However, no details are given about how the figure for Ireland was derived or even the data source employed—it is not taken from the national report—and it has not been possible to replicate it by analysis of the 1973 household budget survey (see Nolan, 1991a). The data and precise methods used also differ across the countries.

In the course of the Second Poverty Programme, the EC Commission sponsored a number of research studies, with an emphasis on improving the information available and ensuring, as far as possible, that comparable data and methods were used in measuring poverty. This included part-financing the 1987 survey carried out in Ireland by the Economic and Social Research Institute (and used extensively in the rest of this book), as part of a seven-country study of methods of measuring poverty co-ordinated by the University of Antwerp (Deleeck et al., 1992). The international study of perceptions of poverty carried out in the 1970s was repeated in 1989. In addition, comparative poverty estimates for member-states and the Community as a whole were produced for the Commission by O'Higgins and Jenkins (1990) and by Eurostat (1990).

O'Higgins and Jenkins set out to measure poverty in the same way as the report on the First Programme, i.e. using half average income as the poverty line, but taking care to harmonise across countries as far as possible the data sources, definitions and methods of derivation of the estimates. They also looked at the sensitivity of the results to the equivalence scale and poverty line chosen. The 'headline' result from their exercise[3] was that by 1985 the number of poor people in the twelve countries that were then members of the Community had risen to 44 million, compared with 38 million in 1975 and 40 million in 1980. The estimates for the middle 1980s show Ireland as having about the same percentage in poverty as Spain and Greece, less than Portugal, and more than the other member-states. Their figures for the middle 1970s diverge substantially from those in the report on the First Programme, the Irish figure being 18 rather than 23 per cent and the Italian rate being 11 rather than 22 per cent! (Their total number below half average income in the middle 1970s in the then nine member-states was 28 million people, rather than the 30 million in the report, but there were offsetting differences in the figures for individual countries.)

The second study producing poverty estimates for Community countries, carried out for Eurostat (1990), again employed relative poverty lines but with household expenditure rather than income as the measure of resources. The results were that 50 million people, 15 per cent of the population of the Community, were below half the average for their country in the middle 1980s. For Ireland 17 per cent of households, 20 per cent of the people, were below that line. These estimates are based on household budget surveys, in Ireland that for 1987. Despite the difference in data sources and the use of household expenditure rather than income as the measure of resources, the estimates for Ireland are quite similar to those based on the 1987 ESRI survey, as discussed in chapter 3.

However, the final report on the Second Poverty Programme misleadingly brought together the Eurostat estimates for 1987 with the figures from the report on the First Programme for the middle 1970s. This showed a substantial fall in the percentage of households below the 50 per cent poverty standard in Ireland over the period but ignored the major differences in methodology between the two exercises, which, together with doubts about the derivation of the 1973 figure, invalidate the comparison (see Nolan, 1991a). Chapter 3 showed that when relative-income poverty lines are applied in a consistent manner, the percentage of households below the 50 per cent line between 1973 and 1987 was stable or rose (and the percentage of people in such households rose). This provides a good illustration of the need, in making poverty comparisons across countries or over time, to harmonise as far as possible data, definitions and methodology employed.

The results of the Eurostat exercise show that, in terms of the percentage of households or people below half average equivalent expenditure, Ireland in the middle 1980s had a poverty rate similar to Spain, Greece and the UK, lower than Portugal, and higher than other member-states. The Community countries with the lowest average GNP per head thus tend to have the highest poverty rates, even when poverty is measured relative to the average income of the country in question. One of the most interesting aspects of the Eurostat exercise, though, is that it also estimates poverty rates taking 50 per cent of average equivalent expenditure across the Community as a whole as the standard. On this basis the Irish poverty rate is only slightly higher than with the country-specific poverty standard, but those for Spain, Greece and Portugal are very much higher, while the richest member-states have very low poverty rates indeed.

There is thus much more variation in poverty rates across countries when a common Community-wide standard is adopted, and Ireland's position appears more favourable relative to Spain, Greece, and Portugal, though less favourable relative to the other member-states. This highlights the implications that adopting a common European standard, rather than seeing poverty purely relative to the standards of the country in question, would have for the ranking of the member-states.

The Third Programme to Combat Poverty also has a research component, though the funding is considerably lower than that originally proposed by the Commission (amounting to 9 per cent of the total budget of the programme). Eurostat is continuing to develop statistics on poverty in member-states on a comparable basis, using the household budget surveys, and is also sponsoring research on topics such as the use of non-monetary indicators in measuring poverty. A number of transnational research networks are being financed under Poverty 3, covering areas such as processes of detachment from the labour market, migration, and local development strategies. In addition, a number of 'observatories' have been established, including one on policies combating social exclusion. This observatory involves national correspondents bringing together information on relevant statistical, administrative and legislative data and the results of research in an annual report for each member-state (see Ó Cinnéide, 1992a), to be used in compiling an overall report for the Community on social exclusion.

18.2 EC SOCIAL POLICY

Social policy at Community level up to the present has had very limited scope and a rather ambiguous status. EC initiatives in this area have related for the most part to the welfare, rights and working conditions of workers, whereas the term is generally used much more broadly to encompass policies in the areas of health, education, and social protection (and perhaps housing). The Community has been active for many years in promoting equal pay between men and women, health and safety at work, freedom of movement and the rights of migrant workers, and vocational training. The Social Charter, adopted by all the member-states except the UK in 1989, also focuses primarily on freedom of movement and the rights and interests of those already in employment, as do most of the elements in the Action Programme on the charter prepared by the Commission. (The draft charter originally prepared by the Commission envisaged a broader application of the right to social protection, and was entitled the 'Charter of Fundamental Social Rights': the Council of Ministers amended this to 'of Workers').

Despite this limited scope, aspects of Community social policy have had a significant influence on developments in Ireland. For example, EC directive 79/7 on the equal treatment of men and women necessitated a change in the structure of the Irish social welfare system, fully implemented only from 1986. One result was that a married woman whose husband was receiving a social welfare payment could for the first time qualify for unemployment assistance, and women now had an equal right to claim for dependants. The implications of this change for the treatment of different household types in the social welfare code, in the light of the constitutional pledge to safeguard the institution of marriage, were examined by a Review Group on the Treatment of Households in the Social Welfare Code, whose report (1991) highlighted the complexity of the issues but failed to reach agreement on the best course of action. Suggested alternatives, in effect, were that entitlement to social assistance be assessed entirely on an individual or on a household basis.

While Community social policy has not for the most part been focused specifically on poverty, the European Council in 1989 adopted a resolution on social exclusion that stressed that combating exclusion may be regarded as an important part of the social dimension of the internal market. In 1988 the European Parliament declared itself in favour of establishing in all member-states a guaranteed minimum income to help ensure that the poorest citizens are integrated into society. Less ambitiously, the Social Charter includes the general statement that 'in a spirit of solidarity it is important to combat social exclusion,' and, in addition to social protection for workers, states that people who have been unable to enter or re-enter the labour market and the retired must be entitled to 'sufficient resources'.

In 1992 a Council recommendation recognising 'the basic right of a person to sufficient resources and social assistance to live in a manner compatible with human dignity' provided a legal basis for Community monitoring and evaluation of the minimum resources guarantee or safety net provided by national social protection systems (Nolan, 1992, is a report on the Irish system). Another recommendation on the convergence of social policy objectives and policies sets out common objectives for social protection, including guaranteeing a minimum income for all and contributing to social and economic integration of the people concerned.

This modest rate of expansion in Community involvement in the social policy sphere could accelerate as a result of the decisions taken at Maastricht in December 1991. The section on social policy in the draft treaty greatly expanded the Social Charter, and when the UK found this unacceptable the other eleven member-states agreed to these provisions in a separate protocol, the Agreement on Social Policy. This expands considerably the legal basis for EC action in relation to social policy, and sets out the objectives of Community social policy as 'the promotion of employment, improved living and working conditions, proper social protection, dialogue between management and labour, the development of human resources with a view to lasting high employment and combating of exclusion.' The EC could on this basis legislate in new areas, including social security, particularly to set minimum standards, though as with other extensions in Community competence in the treaty this is subject to the principle of subsidiarity.

The legal basis and mode of operation of the agreement using the EC institutional structure but excluding the UK remain to be clarified (if and when the treaty is ratified by all the member-states). In addition to the 'Social Chapter', the treaty itself specifically gives the EC some role in education and health policies, which could open up the possibility of much greater Community involvement in these areas.

The Maastricht agreements, if in force, would thus widen EC competence in the social policy field, and the fact that combating social exclusion is explicitly stated as an objective in the Agreement on Social Policy would provide a new impetus to policies aimed at that objective. Since the European Parliament has been to the forefront in promoting

Community involvement in social policy, the expansion in the powers of the European Parliament envisaged in the treaty could also be expected (as Ó Cinnéide, 1992b, points out) to contribute to this process.

18.3 THE STRUCTURAL FUNDS

Since its foundation, the Community has had the objective of 'harmonious development', as set out in the Treaty of Rome. This was reinforced by the introduction of the objective of 'economic and social cohesion' in the Single European Act of 1986, seen as an essential counterpart to the economic integration and freedom of movement highlighted by the 1992 programme. However, it is the narrowing of *spatial* disparities, i.e. differences between regions in the Community, that are specifically mentioned. It is towards this objective, narrowing the gap in average income between member-states and regions, that the structural funds are primarily directed. Following the Single European Act the structural funds—comprising the Social Fund, the Regional Fund, and the structural element of the Agricultural Fund—were reformed, and a doubling in their size between 1987 and 1993 was agreed.

These funds are mostly spent on operational programmes, designated the Community Support Framework (CSF), and the manner in which they are to operate is set out in the national development plan agreed between the Commission and the Government. They are seen as the main instruments for promoting economic growth in the peripheral regions and thus 'cohesion' within the Community. The Maastricht treaty envisages a further expansion in the role of the Structural Funds, and in addition a new Cohesion Fund to finance projects in the transport and environment fields, available only to member-states that have an average income per head less than 90 per cent of the Community average.

While the overall aim of the structural funds is to narrow the gap between the peripheral and core regions of the Community, the objectives specified within the CSF are as follows:

(1) promoting the development and structural adjustment of regions whose development is lagging behind—in the case of Ireland the entire country is designated an 'objective 1' region;
(2) assisting areas seriously affected by industrial decline;

(3) combating long-term unemployment;
(4) facilitating the occupational integration of young people;
(5) speeding up the adjustment of agricultural structures and promoting rural development.

The funds have to be an addition to rather than a substitute for spending by the member-state, and have to be matched by national government expenditure. The amounts involved are substantial: the CSF should comprise one-quarter of the total EC budget in 1993. Ireland should receive about 10 per cent of CSF expenditure over the period 1989–93, amounting to about £3,000 million. (Ireland also receives assistance under special Community initiatives outside the scope of the CSF, such as HORIZON and NOW, providing labour market support for the handicapped or disadvantaged and women, respectively, and the LEADER programme of rural development projects.)

A detailed description and evaluation of the overall impact of the CSF programmes in Ireland in the period 1989–93 is presented by Bradley et al. (1992), and the programme to combat long-term unemployment has been evaluated by Sexton and O'Connell (1993). It is worth bringing out some key points here in the context of anti-poverty policy. The overall conclusion of Bradley et al. was that the macro-economic impact of the structural funds expenditure between 1989 and 1993 per se would be to raise the rate of economic growth and increase employment substantially, with much of the benefit of the investment coming after 1993. By the year 2000 the level of employment could be about 30,000 higher than it would otherwise have been, but unemployment declines by significantly less, because of the impact on emigration. (The overall impact of the single market, economic and monetary union, reform of the Common Agricultural Policy and the structural funds was also analysed.) Thus, they warn, without special measures to deal with the long-term unemployed, their numbers could remain relatively unchanged over the decade.

The poor educational qualifications of the long-term unemployed and the costs to the exchequer of providing income support over the lifetime to such people is documented in one of the studies in Bradley et al., by Breen and Shortall. The high return that measures targeted at this group could have and (echoing Breen, 1991) the need to focus on education as much as training in this context are emphasised.

A related point—that most Social Fund expenditure goes on training young labour market entrants, who already possess at least Leaving Certificate qualifications, rather than the most disadvantaged in educational terms—is highlighted in the analysis of the structural funds and social exclusion by the Community Workers' Co-operative (1992). This may be effective in maximising the impact of the CSF on productivity, of course, but is not well targeted at the long-term unemployed, who are most in need of assistance.

Sexton and O'Connell (1993) point out that the way the operational programmes have actually been organised militates against achieving a co-ordinated approach to countering long-term unemployment, with the schemes that are aimed at assisting this group dispersed across three different programmes. They again emphasise the importance of what is essentially second-chance education rather than—or as a prelude to—training for many of the long-term unemployed, and suggest that the scope of the CSF be extended to cover such education. They also argue that many of the long-term unemployed can only be effectively helped by programmes involving some provision of work, that the current CSF arrangements are unduly rigid in excluding what is considered 'non-productive employment creation', and that there may be a case for supporting direct employment schemes in, for example, the social, health and environmental areas. The value of job creation in the area of social infrastructure is also emphasised in the CWC report.

Looking at the likely overall impact of the next CSF, for the period 1994–97, FitzGerald and Keegan (1993) suggest that it could add nearly 2 per cent to the level of GNP in the long term, though the full effects would not be apparent until the early years of the next decade. They emphasise that the additional resources made available through the CSF should be used to produce a permanent increase in the productive capacity of the economy rather than the temporary rise in income per head that would arise from using the resources as straight income transfers to households (even if this was permitted). The rate of return to the state, in the form of increased output and employment, should be the primary criterion. On this basis the human resources and transport infrastructure ('peripherality') programmes are considered likely to show the highest rates of return. They advocate a shift in human resources expenditure towards initial education at primary and secondary levels, designed to reduce early school leaving, and towards the long-term unemployed, away from employment subsidy schemes.

While targeted intervention to deal with potential early school leavers might not be eligible under current CSF funding criteria, they can be seen as an important element in a programme to prevent long-term unemployment in the future, and would be more effective than global reductions in pupil-teacher ratios. The study also suggests that schemes such as the Social Employment Scheme directed at the long-term unemployed should include a training element, which would increase both the return and the likelihood that the scheme would attract EC co-financing. (The Community Employment Development Programme, being piloted in PESP project areas, offers such a combination of training and community work.)

Both the CWC report and the Combat Poverty Agency's submission (1992) on the Structural Funds argue that targeting poverty and social exclusion must be made an explicit objective of the structural funds—and indeed other EC policies—if they are to be tackled effectively. Both also stress the need for much wider consultation at national level, including the participation of representatives of those experiencing poverty and exclusion, in drawing up the National Development Plan for CSF-related programmes. The effectiveness of the expenditure would then be evaluated on the basis not only of convergence between regions and member-states but also of reducing disparities and combating poverty within the states.

FitzGerald and Keegan make the point that while pursuit of goals such as rural and local development may result in some trade-off with the objective of maximising growth in output and employment, they are not incompatible objectives. The same may be true of the broader relationship between maximising growth and employment and combating poverty: many of the areas identified as priorities for CSF spending, particularly on human resources, offer the prospect both of high rates of return and a direct impact on poverty. One advantage of explicitly incorporating the tackling of poverty as a goal would be that effectiveness would be evaluated vis-à-vis this as well as other objectives: trade-offs, where they do exist, could then be identified and choices made. In such an evaluation it is the long-term impact on poverty and exclusion, as on the other objectives, that would be of central concern; nonetheless it cannot be taken for granted that maximising growth and employment would be the most effective way to combat poverty.

18.4 CONCLUSIONS

In reviewing the EC dimension to tackling poverty in Ireland, this chapter has concentrated on three aspects: the Programmes to Combat Poverty, EC social policy, and the Structural Funds. The programmes specifically directed towards combating poverty and social exclusion within member-states have taken the form of area-based pilot action projects. Expenditure on these programmes, and consequently their direct impact, have been modest, though lessons learnt could be influential in affecting the development of an area-based approach implemented on a much broader scale. Such an approach can clearly make an important contribution to harnessing the energies of local communities and promoting participation by those experiencing poverty. Its limitations as a response to poverty must also be emphasised, however: in the case of unemployment, for example, it is unrealistic to expect purely local initiatives to have a major impact. It is important then that area-based strategies, even extended beyond the 'pilot' phase, be seen not as a panacea but as one element in a broader national and Community strategy to combat poverty.

Social policy at Community level up to the present has had very limited scope and a rather ambiguous status, relating for the most part to the welfare, rights and working conditions of workers. Despite this limited scope, aspects of Community social policy have had a significant influence on developments in Ireland, notably on the equal treatment of men and women in the social welfare code. The Maastricht agreements, if and when they come into force, would significantly widen EC competence in the social policy field; and the fact that combating social exclusion is explicitly stated as an objective in the Agreement on Social Policy would provide a new impetus to policies aimed at that objective.

The very substantial resource transfers to Ireland from the Community under the structural funds have the objective of promoting economic and social cohesion, but this is seen primarily in terms of narrowing the gap in average income between member-states and regions. Particularly in the area of investment in human resources— education and training—expenditure could be better targeted towards marginalised groups such as early school leavers and the long-term unemployed, while also yielding high returns in terms of the stated objectives of increasing output and employment. More broadly, explicit recognition of the goal of combating poverty and social exclusion and evaluation of the effectiveness of structural funds expenditure in that light would be a significant shift in emphasis.

PART VI

CONCLUSIONS

19 Key Issues
Tim Callan and Brian Nolan

Our aim in this concluding chapter is to provide an overview of the most important findings of recent research at the Economic and Social Research Institute into the nature of poverty in Ireland, and to highlight the implications for the development of effective policies to tackle it. It is not intended to summarise the individual contributions in the book one by one, since each has already presented in summary form the results of detailed studies. Rather, key findings across the different contributions are brought together and linked in assessing the policy implications of the research and identifying the issues that have to be addressed. To facilitate this, we first give a brief overview of what has been learnt about the extent and nature of poverty in Ireland. We then focus in turn on major policy areas, namely education and the labour market, the tax and social welfare systems, and other aspects of antipoverty policy.

19.1 THE EXTENT AND NATURE OF POVERTY IN IRELAND

To see the extent of poverty and understand its causes, the poor must be distinguished from the 'non-poor'. This is a necessarily imprecise exercise, for a variety of reasons. Firstly, there are different ways of conceptualising poverty, and not everyone may agree on what constitutes poverty in a particular society at a specific time. Secondly, even given agreement on what constitutes poverty—*what* one is trying to measure—there are different methods of trying to identify people in that situation, none of which are entirely satisfactory. Thirdly, there is likely in any case to be a grey area where financial hardship shades into poverty, with little to distinguish the poor from the 'near-poor'. Finally, the information available on which to base the measurement exercise will always be less than ideal, so again uncertainty and imprecision are unavoidable.

Given these difficulties, the approach taken in this book has been to use a number of different poverty standards rather than attempt to identify a single one, and to examine how sensitive particular findings are to the choice of standard. Results that hold across a range—for example across different income poverty lines or equivalence scales—can then be taken as much more firmly based than those produced by concentrating on a single line. The strength of this approach has been demonstrated by the important findings about the characteristics of poor households in 1987, which were seen to hold across a wide range of income poverty lines:

(1) Households headed by an unemployed person made up a substantial proportion of the poor and faced a particularly high risk of being in poverty; the risk was considerably higher for the long-term than the short-term unemployed, and also where no-one else was at work in the household.

(2) Households with an elderly or retired head faced a below-average risk of poverty and made up a much smaller proportion of the poor than those with an unemployed head.

(3) Households headed by an employee had a much lower probability of being in poverty than other households; only a small proportion of poor households contained an employee, and most were relying on social welfare transfers or income from self-employment.

(4) Most low-paid employees were not in poor households, principally because the household was often not relying on that person's earnings as the main or only income source; where households headed by an employee were in poverty, this was as likely to be caused by the number of people depending on those earnings as by what would generally be considered low pay as such.

(5) Households with children, particularly those with three or more children, were at relatively high risk of being in poverty.

(6) Households headed by a woman did not in general face a higher risk of being in poverty than those with a male head, though households comprising a lone parent and dependent children—most of which are headed by a woman—did face a relatively high risk.

(7) Most poor households were drawn from the manual social classes, with the unskilled manual group facing a particularly high risk of being poor.

(8) The risk of poverty declined dramatically as the level of education attained by the head of household rose.

(9) During the 1970s and 1980s there were major changes in the types of household likely to be in poverty, with the elderly making up a much smaller proportion and households with children a much larger proportion by the end of the period than they had at the outset.

These findings, which do not depend on precisely where an income poverty line is drawn, are of central importance in understanding the causes of poverty and in framing policy, as we discuss shortly.

Turning to comparisons over time or across countries, even without a minimal level of agreement about how income poverty lines are to relate to overall living standards, it is still sometimes possible to identify important conclusions. In making comparisons over time, the central issue is the extent to which the poverty standard is to reflect changes in living standards generally or to remain constant (in real terms). Correspondingly, in making comparisons across countries the central issue is whether a different poverty line for each country is to be set in the light of living standards in that country or a common line applied to all the countries under consideration.

Since average income was virtually unchanged in real terms in Ireland between 1980 and 1987, it turns out that for this period income poverty lines that are held constant in real terms give very similar results to purely relative ones linked to average income: in either case the proportion of people below income poverty lines rose, except at the lowest lines. Similarly, Ireland's ranking among EC member-states is broadly similar whether poverty thresholds related to average living standards in each country or to the overall average in the Community as a whole are used: Ireland is seen to have a higher poverty rate than many of the member-states but not as high as Portugal. It is not, however, possible on this basis to rank Ireland versus Spain or Greece, to say how great the difference in poverty rates is between Ireland and other countries, or to agree on whether poverty in Ireland rose or fell over a longer period—for example 1973 to 1987—when average real incomes did rise.

Much stronger conclusions are possible if one is willing to accept that the poverty standard adopted should be directly related to average living standards in the country in question at that time. Using purely relative-income poverty lines, over the longer period between 1973 and 1987 the proportion of people in poverty in Ireland is consistently seen to have risen, across a range of poverty lines and equivalence scales. Comparing Ireland with other EC member-states using country-specific relative poverty thresholds, the Irish poverty rate is similar to that for Spain, lower than Greece and Portugal, and higher than those of the other member-states. (A common poverty threshold related to average income in the Community and applied across all the countries, on the other hand, produces much greater variation in poverty rates, with those for Greece and Portugal very much higher and those for Belgium and the Netherlands very much lower than with country-specific lines.)

The view that the poverty line should be related to ordinary living standards in the community in question is rooted in the belief that any poverty standard must reflect prevailing views about what constitutes a minimum acceptable way of life in the society, and that these views will in turn reflect the living standards, experiences and expectations of that community. Close to subsistence, there is indeed some absolute minimum necessary for survival, but apart from this an 'absolute' standard cannot meaningfully be defined. Likewise, if living standards are rising over time, a poverty standard that remains unchanged (in real terms) will become more and more detached from everyday perceptions of 'needs'. Such a fixed standard will provide valuable information about the evolution of real living standards but will become increasingly inadequate as a measure of exclusion from ordinary living patterns. Purely relative-income poverty lines are by no means the only way that poverty standards linked to ordinary living standards can be implemented, but they do have a number of advantages, particularly in that available data allows consistent measures to be produced for different years or different countries on that basis.

Focusing entirely on income has limitations, in that income is an imperfect indicator of either the resources available to a household or its standard of living. The analysis of direct measures of different aspects of deprivation is therefore a useful complement, and information in the 1987 survey allowed the complexity of the relationships between income, deprivation and wider resources to be seen. Some indicators that have been widely used elsewhere, such as housing quality and possession or absence of durables, were seen to be strongly related to urban versus rural location and to stage in the family cycle. Such factors may not in current Irish circumstances be reliable as indicators of more generalised deprivation. Concentrating instead on some rather basic types of deprivation in everyday life, such as not being able to afford new clothes or a warm overcoat, or going into arrears or debt to meet ordinary living expenses, it was seen that a substantial proportion—though by no means all—of those below the relative-income poverty lines were experiencing such deprivation. This allows a clearer identification of those most in need, and provides a more graphic and evocative picture of the actual living standards involved for many low-income households.

Households with an unemployed head were still clearly the most important group among those below the income poverty lines and experiencing basic deprivation, whereas fewer low-income farm households were experiencing such deprivation. (The year in question was a particularly poor year for farm incomes, which are in any case difficult to measure accurately). It is worth emphasising that all the key conclusions about the risk and incidence of poverty based on income poverty lines set out earlier (at 1–7 above) still held when, in addition to household income, these direct measures of deprivation were taken into account in distinguishing the poor. (Since information on the deprivation indicators is only available for the 1987 survey, it is not possible to extend this analysis to trends over time or comparisons across countries.)

All this serves to demonstrate that a great deal can be said about the types of household likely to be in poverty and about the causes of poverty, which is of central importance to the design of policies to alleviate poverty, without having to arrive at a consensus on where and how to draw a line between the poor and the 'non-poor', which would be necessary in order to agree on the *extent* of poverty. Given that there may be different perspectives on exactly what constitutes poverty in Ireland today and differences in opinion about how it is best measured, as well as the limitations in the data and methods available, we believe that this is by far the most productive approach for research to take. The scope for legitimate disagreement about the extent of poverty means that focusing simply on the question 'how many poor?' is likely to produce more heat than light, however important that question may be. The various contributions in this book provide a wealth of new information to inform people's own assessments of the extent of poverty, and the 'expert' views of researchers should not take precedence.

It may nonetheless be useful to say how we would interpret the evidence. Most importantly, it appears that there is a substantial consensus in society about what does constitute deprivation and exclusion, if that is seen as having to do without things that most people regard as necessities. Measuring the extent of such exclusion and relating it to absence of resources is inevitably problematic; the information on living standards is far from comprehensive; and any particular cut-off is likely to be rather arbitrary. However, it has been shown that between about one in six and one in five Irish households in 1987 were on relatively low incomes and experiencing deprivation of a quite basic kind. Our judgment—and it can be no more than that—is that this would constitute poverty in the eyes of most people in the society.

For a further substantial proportion of households also on low incomes, the impact on living standards had not apparently been so severe (yet), partly because resources other than current income—such as savings, help from relatives or friends, or borrowing—were used to supplement income. The deprivation criteria involved are stringent, and many of these households are having great difficulty making ends meet and are experiencing less basic forms of deprivation, though a minority have more substantial resources to fall back on (highlighting the importance of a dynamic rather than static perspective). The living standards of many of these households might be regarded by some as 'poor', by others as 'near-poor' or on the margins of poverty.

However, views about the extent of poverty depend crucially not only on just how severe deprivation and exclusion have to be before they are taken as constituting poverty but also on whether poverty is seen as necessarily relating to living standards as such rather than to the violation of a basic right to an adequate income. Precisely how such a right should be formulated requires careful examination, but our own view is that focusing entirely on current living standards is unduly restrictive: it would be commonly accepted, we believe, that avoiding poverty means not only being able to sustain minimal participation in society but also being able to do so in a way that allows one's dignity and self-respect to be maintained. Research in the United States has shown that a significant proportion of those falling below the official income poverty line have enough assets to allow them to maintain a 'non-poor' life-style for a time; they are nonetheless considered poor from a policy perspective. The social welfare system and anti-poverty policy more broadly are generally framed as a response to income inadequacy, rather than waiting until people are living in 'obvious want and squalor.'

These extremely knotty—and value-laden—issues clearly deserve a great deal of attention, but framing policy responses to poverty does not have to await their resolution. In the remainder of this chapter we highlight the implications of the most important findings of the research described in this book for policy, beginning with the key areas of education and the labour market.

19.2 EDUCATION AND THE LABOUR MARKET

Comparison of the situation in the late 1980s with the early 1970s has shown the dramatic changes in the nature of poverty in Ireland over that period. Unemployment, and its impact on household incomes and living standards, was seen to be the most important cause of poverty in the 1987 survey, and this must have become even more pronounced subsequently as unemployment has increased significantly. The contrast with the 1960s and early 1970s is marked: at that time the elderly made up a much more substantial proportion of those at low incomes, and the level of unemployment was very much lower. Anti-poverty policy in the early 1970s, following the 'rediscovery' of poverty at that time, was therefore largely framed in terms of restructuring and improving the social welfare system to increase support to the elderly and to widows, extend coverage to groups such as deserted wives, lone parents, and prisoners' wives, and improve provision for those relying on safety-net 'home assistance'.

The success of this approach, particularly in contributing to the improvement of the position of the elderly over the past twenty years, should not be undervalued or overshadowed by the emergence of new problems. However, the dominant role of unemployment means that poverty is now much less amenable to such an approach.

We turn to the particular difficulties faced by the social welfare system in dealing with those who are in the labour force, rather than the elderly, in the next section. First, though, given the greatly enhanced role that education and labour market measures must take on in tackling poverty, the lessons from the research for policy in these areas are discussed. Our limited objective must be emphasised: no attempt is made to present a general strategy for job creation, since the research described here provides no basis on which to do so. Such strategies have been recently set out both by the National Economic and Social Council and the Culliton Report on Industrial Policy. Instead we focus on the role, within an overall strategy for employment creation, of special education and labour market measures to assist those most in need and reduce inequality.

One of the most consistent findings of the research across the different contributions has been the impact of low levels of educational attainment on life chances. Failure to obtain some second-level qualification was seen to greatly increase the risk of poverty, of current unemployment and long-term unemployment, of lengthy unemployment experience over one's career, and of low pay when employed. The consequences of educational failure have become more serious over time, those without qualifications—drawn mostly from lower working-class backgrounds—being more and more limited to unskilled manual occupations at high risk of unemployment. There has thus been a sharper polarisation between those who leave school early without any qualification and their more successful peers. A priority for policy must be to address the needs of this particularly disadvantaged group.

This requires both targeting specially designed programmes at those who have already left school with little or no qualifications and introducing measures to reduce the numbers leaving school each year in that position. For those already in the labour market with few or no qualifications, the importance of what is effectively second-chance education as a prelude to training must be emphasised. Evaluations of the effectiveness of EC structural funds expenditure in the human resources area have made clear that training by itself does not address the needs of many of the long-term unemployed, and argue for the scope of the funds to be extended to cover such second-chance education (Sexton and O'Connell, 1993). As far as reducing the flow of the unqualified early leavers from education is concerned, considerable attention has recently been paid (for example in the Programme for Economic and Social Progress) to special assistance for schools in disadvantaged areas. However, as Hannan (1992) has pointed out, educational policies couched in terms of such areas cannot hope to reach more than a small proportion of the students at risk: most children who fail badly in education do not live in socially disadvantaged areas (though they are almost all from very deprived households). A strategy focusing on 'disadvantaged schools'—or, ideally, disadvantaged pupils themselves—rather than areas, on reducing selectivity between schools on the basis of social class and ability that leads to the creation of 'dump' schools, and on greatly increasing resources for home-school liaison, would be far more effective.

Such a strategy would also be an important element in tackling the more generalised inequalities in educational participation rates and outcomes across socio-economic groups and social classes. The disparities across socio-economic groups in participation in third-level education are well known, with a particularly small proportion of university students coming from working-class backgrounds. Research with the ESRI 1987 sample has shown just how marked the overall differentials across social classes in educational outcomes are: most strikingly, more than two-thirds of heads of household aged under sixty-five coming from a lower working-class background left school with no qualifications, compared with fewer than one in ten of those who were brought up in a professional or managerial household. Likewise, only 3 per cent of those coming from a lower working-class background—compared with 39 per cent of those from a professional or managerial one—obtained a third-level qualification.[1]

Like early school leaving, the root of these inequalities is to be found at primary level, and effective intervention must be concentrated there. A policy that targets substantial resources on those from disadvantaged backgrounds—not simply schools in disadvantaged areas—is required, with much greater emphasis on remedial teaching and preventive measures such as 'reading recovery'. The resources becoming available as the number of pupils at primary level falls would be much better spent on such targeted intervention than in the general reduction in pupil-teacher ratios envisaged in the 1993 programme for government: research elsewhere suggests that the impact of reducing class sizes from, say, thirty-five to thirty on the effectiveness of teaching is extremely limited.[2] Reducing social class selectivity between schools, particularly at secondary level, is also essential, but is unlikely to be achieved without a structure involving some form of local education authorities.[3]

Removing fees for third-level education, which has been the subject of some discussion recently, would have little impact on the extent of participation by those from working-class backgrounds, and would involve a substantial subsidy to middle and upper-income groups currently paying these fees.[4] The financing of third-level education could indeed be restructured to promote greater equity—perhaps by a loan scheme whereby those whose earnings capacity is enhanced repay some of the public investment; but substantially eroding social class inequalities in third-level participation rates must begin much earlier.

We now turn from education to the design of labour market measures to assist the unemployed and alleviate poverty. In evaluating the main training and employment schemes in operation up to the present, Breen argues (chapter 17) that none of them has been or can be really effective in creating jobs and reducing unemployment. Schemes like the Employment Incentive Scheme end up mostly subsidising jobs that would have been created anyway. Schemes like Enterprise that encourage the unemployed to establish their own business often simply displace other firms. Temporary job creation schemes like the Social Employment Scheme offer only a temporary respite. General training programmes can have only a limited effect on unemployment, certainly in the short to medium run. As he notes, some of these schemes also had an explicit equity objective, and could alleviate poverty without creating any new jobs by helping those most in need—for example the long-term unemployed—to get jobs. However, targeted employment subsidies like the EIS seem to have had little success in overcoming employers' reluctance to hire the long-term unemployed. Temporary employment schemes like the SES can of course be directed towards the long-term unemployed, but the problem in that case in terms of poverty alleviation is their short-term nature and the fact that the wages paid are very low.

These labour market measures can in any case operate only at the margin, but poverty and unemployment are not marginal problems. Breen also points out, though, that expenditure on this kind of labour market measure has been very small indeed compared with spending on job creation through, for example, the Industrial Development Authority. The many other programmes and incentives aimed at promoting employment have not been subjected to anything like the same comprehensive evaluation as these measures, and while little is known about the effectiveness of some much more expensive schemes, such as the Business Expansion Scheme, it must be said that the evidence is not encouraging.

Increasing expenditure on programmes aimed specifically at the long-term unemployed may still be an effective way of helping some of the most needy at a relatively low cost. Accepting that the impact on overall job creation will be very limited, offering a substantial subsidy to employers to hire someone who has been unemployed for a long time could be justified purely in terms of the social or equity objective. The evidence suggests that the level of subsidy per worker required would have to be significantly higher than that currently paid by the EIS. However, this would not necessarily involve an increase in total expenditure on the EIS if the scheme no longer offered a subsidy for hiring the short-term unemployed. A reformulated scheme targeted at the long-term unemployed with a clear and explicit equity objective could make some contribution to improving the prospects of the most disadvantaged.

It has to be recognised that this would be, for the most part, at the expense of other job-seekers, and would largely represent a more equitable sharing of the overall burden of unemployment. Given the impact that long-term unemployment has on the living standards and the morale of those affected, though, such a subsidy might be a valuable complement to efforts to improve the education and skill levels of this group. By making them more effective competitors in the jobs market it might also have some impact on the rate of increase of pay levels and, by this channel, on the numbers employed. (The notion that the exchequer could actually pay very substantial subsidies at *no* net cost, because of the social welfare payments saved and the tax paid by those taken off the live register, regularly appears in media and other discussions; it entirely ignores the fact that many of the jobs would have been created anyway.)

What about direct state job creation schemes? Schemes like the SES offering only short-term (six months') low-wage employment do little or nothing for the longer-term prospects of beneficiaries, and even in the short term they fail to alleviate poverty to any great extent. The main obstacle to direct provision of permanent employment by the state at 'normal' wage levels is of course the cost. While somewhat out of date, available estimates suggest that it might cost the state three or four times as much to employ someone on, for example, local authority projects as it does to support them in unemployment. However, given the particular problems facing the labour market over the next decade or so, there may be a role over that period for a temporary direct employment programme providing jobs for a significantly longer period than the SES and at higher wages. This could be targeted at the very long-term unemployed (for example those on the live register for two years or more), so that if other measures to improve their prospects in the market had not borne fruit, there was some safety net. While considerably more costly than simply continuing to pay unemployment assistance, the NESC report *A Strategy for the Nineties* (1990) points out that direct employment programmes are likely to be much less costly than other ways of achieving a similar reduction in unemployment, such as reducing employers' PRSI contributions, income tax cuts, or public infrastructure investment, and, unlike them, can be effectively targeted on the long-term unemployed.

The NESC then saw special employment measures as having an important role to play in achieving an early reduction in long-term unemployment; the need looks even more pressing some years later. Again, this is not to be seen as an alternative to education and training programmes aimed at improving the prospects of these people in the market—ideally there would also be a significant training element in the employment programmes themselves—nor to efforts aimed at promoting job creation in the market sector. In the long term, those are the policies that are likely to have a sustained impact: in the short to medium term, though, they are unlikely to be enough.

Some would argue, indeed, that the prospects for increasing employment sufficiently over the next decade to allow the long-term unemployed to be re-absorbed are so poor that a radical shift in focus, towards a comprehensive restructuring of the way income support is provided by the state, is required.[5] A central feature of the basic income schemes that have been proposed in Ireland and elsewhere is that the link between labour market status and entitlement to income support is broken, the payment going to everyone. This is one illustration of the more general point that the interaction between the labour market and the tax and social welfare systems has come to be seen as of critical importance. The NESC, for example, explicitly links the value of special employment measures, and the effectiveness of labour market policy generally, to the reform of the tax and social welfare systems to address disincentives. It is to tax and welfare policies that we now turn, focusing again on following through the implications of the research findings set out in this book.

19.3 THE TAX AND SOCIAL WELFARE SYSTEMS

The research has made clear the central role that the social welfare system plays in alleviating poverty. Although this is by no means its sole objective, a very high proportion of all social welfare spending goes towards reducing poverty: the Irish social welfare system is relatively efficient in these terms in allocating resources to where they are most needed. This is true not only of means-tested social assistance payments but also of expenditure on non-means-tested social insurance, demonstrating that means-testing is by no means a *sine qua non* for effective targeting. However, the system has also been seen to be less effective than those of some other EC countries in reducing poverty, largely because of the scale of the problem here. Unlike the situation in the early 1970s, when the elderly were the most important group among the poor, the impact on the labour market now has to be a major consideration in judging the appropriate response to poverty, and this also severely limits the scope for reliance on income transfers. Indeed, here as elsewhere, much of the debate about social welfare support levels has been a rather fruitless dialogue of the deaf between those who argue that the rates (in many of the schemes) are not adequate and those who argue that (in many cases) they leave little or no incentive to take up work. Both could of course be true: it is the policy implications drawn that usually distinguish those emphasising one or the other view.

Some poor households pay income tax (and/or PRSI contributions), but even those not doing so may be directly affected by the design of the income tax system, in the way in which it interacts with the social welfare code to create serious unemployment and poverty 'traps' in certain situations. In addition, of course, income tax is a major source of revenue for the state, affecting resources available for, among other things, income support. It is essential, then, that reform of the income tax and social welfare systems be assessed in the light of their impact on the overall structure rather than in isolation. The findings presented here about the extent and nature of poverty, and the way in which the tax and social welfare systems currently operate, point towards some priorities for reform as well as providing a basis for the assessment of further options. (These findings may already have played some part in highlighting the needs of those on the lowest rates of social welfare at the time of the survey, for whom rates have been increased more than other recipients since 1987, in line with the recommendations of the Commission on Social Welfare.)

We have seen that families with children, especially those with three or more children, are at particularly high risk of poverty, across a variety of poverty measures. Disincentives to taking up employment or attempting to increase earnings are also most likely to affect such families. Child dependant additions to their social welfare payments will be lost on their taking up work, they may also be most seriously affected by the loss of a medical card or other non-cash benefits, they are most likely to be receiving assistance with housing costs, and if in work on family income supplement they will face the high benefit withdrawal rate built into that scheme as earnings increase.

We have set out elsewhere (Nolan and Farrell, 1990; Callan and Wren, 1993) the arguments for and against provision of child income support by the state through various mechanisms, in the light of the different objectives that may be involved, and will not repeat that discussion here. Deciding on the best strategy involves first of all being clear about the appropriate balance between the different objectives towards which child income support might be directed. Focusing primarily on the objectives of poverty alleviation and improvement in incentives, but also having in mind the aim of contributing to horizontal equity between those with and without children throughout the income distribution, and improving the situation of women, there is a strong case for adopting a strategy focused on child benefit and involving (*a*) substantial increases in the level of child benefit, (*b*) making the benefit reckonable for income tax, and (*c*) reducing child dependant additions for social welfare recipients to offset part, though only part, of the increase in child benefit. This, in our view, should form a central element in restructuring the tax and benefit systems.

Poor families outside the tax net would see their total child income support rise significantly, even though part of the increase in child benefit would be offset by a fall in child dependant additions (CDAs). Since child benefit is a universal non-means-tested payment, shifting the balance of child income support for poor families away from CDAs would improve incentives as these means-tested payments decline, and over time this process could aim towards a level of child benefit that made possible the eventual abolition of CDAs (as recommended by the Commission on Social Welfare). If that were achieved it would be the most effective single way of attacking the unemployment trap while improving the situation of poor families. Making the payment taxable would help to finance the increase in child benefit while at the same time targeting it more towards those on low incomes.

Provided the increase in the rate of payment was large enough, middle and upper-income families would still benefit, however: this is justifiable on grounds of horizontal equity, redistributing resources between those with and without children, and would be a great deal more progressive than some of the suggested alternatives, such as reintroducing tax allowances for children for income tax purposes. It is important to be clear that the payments going to 'non-poor' households are not then simply waste and evidence of bad targeting, as is often argued. Not only is some support to such families desirable in itself, but the very fact that the payment is not restricted to the poor is central to its impact on incentives.

Continuing the current practice of paying child benefit to the mother while the tax payment generally affects the father would have a number of further advantages. It has been shown earlier[6] that child benefit is usually spent either on the children or on general household expenses from which they probably benefit, so increasing the payment would maximise the probability of directly improving the situation of children in poor households. The fact that the payment is received by the mother—and may often be her only independent source of income—and that its use is generally under her control means that this could also make a contribution towards promoting sex equality. Despite the fact that the limited evidence available here did not suggest that there was a substantial reservoir of 'hidden poverty' among women in higher-income households, an increase in child benefit would be particularly valuable to mothers who are in that situation, and their children.

Although some of the increase in expenditure on child benefit would be financed by making it taxable, and some would be clawed back by reducing CDAs over time, significant additional net expenditure would be required if the increase in child benefit is to be large enough to make a substantial impact on family poverty and produce a decisive shift in the balance between means-tested and non-means-tested elements of child income support for poor families. Once again, however, it is important to set such a policy in the context of the broad direction in which the tax and benefits systems are to be reformed. Following on the Commission on Taxation and in line with developments internationally, a clear consensus has emerged in favour of a broadening of the income tax base and a reduction in rates. A shift in the balance of the tax system away from income tax, financed by, among other things, a property tax, has also been seen as desirable from a number of points of view, not least the impact on the labour market, by the NESC and the Culliton Report among others. (The options on how such a property tax might be structured have been analysed, using the 1987 ESRI survey, by Callan, 1991a.)

A change in the income tax treatment of couples, moving towards greater independence, would be another potential source of revenue. The relatively generous tax treatment of couples in the current system is often justified by references to 'supporting the family'; a move towards independent taxation, combined with the strategy for direct child income support outlined above, would produce a much more coherent tax-cum-benefit structure of family support. In the context of wide-ranging reforms of these kinds, then, some of the revenue generated should be used to finance a substantial additional increase in child benefit, over and above the revenue-neutral rise made possible by taxing the payments themselves.[7]

Such a restructuring would not only make the system more neutral as between work and unemployment, it would also be of direct assistance to those currently supporting families on low earnings. We have seen that many people in that position would not be lifted out of poverty by alternative policies such as, for example, a national minimum wage. The overlap between low pay at an individual level and poverty at the level of the family or household was seen to be quite limited, with the numbers depending on the wage playing a crucial role. (A concern about low pay per se at an individual level could of course still be motivated by a desire to prevent exploitation and ensure 'a fair day's pay for a fair day's work.') The role of family income supplement and its effects on the effective marginal tax rate facing those receiving it could also be reduced if (net) child benefit going to those in work at low incomes increased; ideally, over time this could permit the scheme to be phased out altogether.

It is worth also spelling out the links between such an emphasis on universal child benefit and the proposals for a fundamental transformation of the income maintenance system into a basic income scheme. While there are a number of variants, the central feature of such schemes is that everyone in the population receives a payment (every week or every month), regardless of labour market status. The 'pure' version sees these payments as replacing all existing social welfare transfers—to the unemployed, the elderly, the ill, and so on. They would also replace all income tax allowances, so income tax would be payable on all income. This type of scheme can appeal to people from quite different political or ideological standpoints. The fact that the payment is received whether one is at work or unemployed is seen as the only effective way of overcoming the disincentive effects of the unemployment 'trap' created by means-tested and contingency-based schemes. However, the central obstacle that proponents of such schemes face is that financing this payment to everyone might involve what would be seen as too high a tax burden.

No comprehensive evaluation of such proposals in the Irish context is available, and attempting to quantify the costs and benefits poses a variety of complex methodological problems (see Atkinson, 1989). However, those who would wish to move the income support system in the direction of a basic income scheme might like to see increased universal payments for children as an important stage along the way. (Under a pure basic income scheme, though, these payments would not themselves be taxed, so proponents would be less happy with making child benefit taxable.) For those who are more sceptical, substantially increased child benefit may be seen as achieving some of the objectives of the more radical reform at much lower cost to the exchequer.

Basic income schemes represent one approach to achieving full integration of the income tax and social welfare systems, which could also be brought about through a negative income tax. Much of the discussion about integration of the two systems does not refer to such full-blown integration, but what different people actually mean by the term is often unclear, with a great deal of scope for confusion. The common theme underlying this discussion, however, is a concern about the poverty and unemployment traps created by the way the tax and social welfare systems currently interact.

It is worth pointing to several other reforms, in addition to the restructuring of child benefit, that would attack some or most of these traps and would therefore be valuable in themselves as well as representing progress towards more complete integration, if that is adopted as the objective. One relates to the system of PRSI contributions, which form an important part of the tax and benefit systems, of particular relevance for those on low earnings. Currently, as a response to concerns about the impact on the low-paid, those below an exemption limit pay no contributions, whereas those just above it pay contributions on their full earnings, building in a very high effective withdrawal or tax rate at that point. There is also an upper ceiling, with contributions not payable on earnings above that level. Abolishing both the exemption limit and the ceiling and reducing the contribution rate would produce a simpler and more progressive structure, without kinks. It would also make easier the eventual integration of PRSI contributions and the income tax system, which would presumably form part of a move towards full integration of the tax and benefit system.

Another area is the tax treatment of short-term social welfare benefits, which have traditionally not been subject to income tax. Disability benefit has recently been brought within the scope of income tax, and it is likely that unemployment benefit will also be included in taxable income. This, as recommended by the Commission on Taxation, both broadens the tax base and reduces the impact of income tax refunds on the unemployment trap.

As well as giving rise to specific suggestions of this type, the ESRI research programme has also had as an important objective the development of a 'model' of the income tax and social welfare systems, based on the representative sample of households obtained in the survey but updated in line with the tax and benefit structures now in operation. This permits assessment of the revenue and distributional effects of different policy options, illustrated by the analysis of the impact of increasing and taxing child benefit and of base-broadening and rate-reducing reforms of the income tax system (chapter 16). It will be particularly important in facilitating the examination of various possible reforms of the income tax and social welfare systems taken together, and providing a basis for making policy choices that has simply been absent up to the present. For example, it will be possible to see what shape a fully fledged basic income scheme might take, what levels of tax would be required to finance it, and who the gainers and losers from such a scheme might be.

As is of course the case more generally, such an empirical assessment will not determine whether or not such a radical reform is desirable, but should allow the debate to move on from discussion at the level of principle to address the concrete issues and political choices involved in determining which direction the tax and social welfare systems should take.

19.4 OTHER ELEMENTS OF ANTI-POVERTY POLICY

The research described in this book has relevance for various other aspects of anti-poverty policy in Ireland, and this concluding chapter is not intended to review these in a comprehensive fashion. However, we do want to draw out the implications for two areas that have featured prominently in the evolution of policy of late: the role of area-based strategies, and the EC dimension.

Much of the recent emphasis—at least in terms of rhetoric—in anti-poverty policy at both EC and national level has been on area-based approaches. In addition to community projects under the EC Poverty Programme and those financed by the Department of Social Welfare, area-based partnerships between voluntary and statutory bodies and local community groups have been set up under the Programme for Economic and Social Progress, as one response to long-term unemployment. Although the relationship between these locally based projects and the county enterprise boards that are also now being established is unclear, the latter are apparently also being seen as an element in an area-based strategy. The projects are currently treated as pilot exercises, the presumption being then that the lessons learnt will be applied in setting up such projects on a much wider basis in disadvantaged areas or communities throughout the country, and throughout the EC.

Such projects, when they succeed, can clearly make an important contribution to harnessing the energies of local communities and promoting participation in decision-making by those actually experiencing poverty. Drawing attention to the limitations of this approach is emphatically not to be seen as devaluing this contribution: it is very important, though, to be clear about what such projects can and cannot be expected to achieve. Their limitations as a response to poverty would be clearly recognised by many of those involved, in that the structural factors producing poverty have to be tackled primarily at national or indeed EC level rather than at local level. Purely local action can generally be expected to have little impact on unemployment in an area, and it is quite unrealistic to think otherwise. Areas with particularly high unemployment and poverty rates are the very ones where the obstacles to development and job creation are greatest, and so reliance on local action is even less realistic than elsewhere.

In addition it has been shown (chapter 14), using both the ESRI survey and the small area statistics of the census of population, that while unemployment and poverty rates are very high in certain areas or types of area, most of the unemployed and most poor households are not to be found in these areas. Those living in 'black-spot' areas are likely to face particularly severe problems for a variety of reasons, and targeted strategies can help to overcome these difficulties. Identifying in a systematic way the most disadvantaged areas—which can be done using the available data in the manner described in chapter 14—and designing policies to meet their particular needs (having first determined what these are) is of great importance. However, such strategies will affect only a minority of the unemployed or the poor. This is relevant not only to policy but also to perceptions of the extent and nature of poverty. The poor are not simply to be identified with those living in particularly disadvantaged urban public authority housing estates with high poverty rates: in fact most poor people do not live in such estates. While spatial segregation in Dublin and elsewhere is indeed pronounced, a substantial proportion of the unemployed or those in the unskilled manual working class do not live in 'poor' areas. This reinforces the point that area-based strategies targeting the most disadvantaged areas, however valuable, cannot be taken as a comprehensive response to poverty.

This applies both at national level and in considering the EC response to poverty—or, to use the term now in vogue and apparently more acceptable at EC level, 'social exclusion'. The main Community action specifically designed towards combating social exclusion within member states has been the area-based pilot action projects under the Poverty Programmes. There is some prospect that the goal of combating exclusion will come to play a more prominent part in EC policy-making in the future, since it is explicitly recognised as an objective in the Maastricht Agreement on Social Policy concluded between all the member-states except the UK. The scope for EC action in the area of social policy, which has been very limited up to the present, would also be broadened considerably.

In the short to medium term, though, what is likely to be more significant is the way in which the very substantial resource transfers to be received by Ireland from the Community through the structural funds are spent. Their potential impact on poverty is great, but major changes are required if this potential is to be realised. Although combating long-term unemployment is one of the specified objectives, in fact little of the expenditure in the human resources area has gone towards this group, and there has been no co-ordinated approach to countering long-term unemployment across the different operational programmes.

Relating back to the arguments made earlier in this chapter about policies towards the long-term unemployed, expenditure on second-chance education before training per se, and on direct employment schemes incorporating a training element, may be needed. Currently, the criteria delimiting what the structural funds may be spent on exclude both education and what is considered 'non-productive employment creation'. Widening the scope of the arrangements to include such schemes and increasing the proportion of total spending going on measures to assist the long-term unemployed would significantly increase the direct effects of structural funds expenditure on poverty. More broadly, the explicit recognition of combating social exclusion as a goal, and the evaluation of the effectiveness of the structural funds in the light of this as well as other objectives, is necessary if their potential is to be fully realised.

19.5 CONCLUDING COMMENTS

This chapter has not attempted to set out a fully articulated overall strategy to alleviate, and then eradicate, poverty in Ireland. The much more limited objective has been to point to some direct lessons for policy that we would take from the research described in this book. Perhaps the most important contribution this research can make, however, is in increasing our understanding of the nature and causes of poverty, thereby helping to inform the search for the most effective way of responding to what is now widely perceived as the most important challenge facing our society.

Indeed one of the most striking features of the present situation is just how widespread and how deeply felt the level of concern about poverty and unemployment, and the desire for a coherent and convincing strategy to address them, appear to be. Experience elsewhere has shown that when presented with such a strategy, people are often willing to make significant short-term sacrifices in the interests of national solidarity and the long-term health of the society. Research can contribute by focusing attention on the extent of deprivation and need being experienced, by trying to understand their causes, and by pointing to the costs and benefits of different policies. While there remain ideological disagreements about the type of economic strategy that should be adopted, what is remarkable is in fact the extent to which these have diminished in recent years. Views about the role of markets versus the state, for example, are very much less polarised than they were, although substantial differences across the spectrum persist. A consensus has emerged in recent years about, for example, the need to broaden the tax base and to reform both the tax and benefit systems to reduce their distortionary effects. The challenge—which is essentially a political one—is to forge a national consensus around a coherent strategy, incorporating these elements, that will harness the energies and good will of the population as a whole towards tackling poverty.

Notes

CHAPTER 3

1. These issues are reviewed in depth in Callan, Nolan, et al. (1989), chapter 10.

CHAPTER 4

1. 'Being able to save regularly', although stated to be a necessity by most people, we do not regard as a satisfactory indicator of generalised exclusion in the Irish context, because it is lacked by 57 per cent of the sample. Mack and Lansley (1985, 67), who did not include this item, found no example of an item regarded as a necessity but possessed by only a minority: in the British context, though clearly not in a Third World one, widespread ownership was a prerequisite of an item being considered a necessity. Having a hobby or leisure activity is also widely considered a necessity and is possessed by 67 per cent (and in fact loads more heavily on the basic dimension in the factor analysis). We do not include it in our preferred measure of deprivation, principally because of its vagueness and ambiguity: a hobby or leisure activity could mean quite different things to different people, involving very different commitment of resources.

CHAPTER 6

1. Morgan et al.'s results (1974, '78) are based on simultaneous multiple regression techniques, which track transitions in economic mobility. Furthermore, it should be noted that the dependent variable used is income-to-needs ratio, which should be more correctly interpreted as a measure of change in poverty status than as a measure of change in income per se.
2. In studying spell length, a problem arises because of so-called right and left censoring of the data. In other words, some spells have begun before the start of the data series, while others are still 'in progress' when

analysis takes place. There are a lot of problems (conceptual as well as methodological) in handling these 'partial spells'. For this reason it is important that we have a data-set that is sufficiently long to include a substantial number of completed spells, i.e. those that began and ended within the period covered by the series.

3. For technical reasons it is not feasible to use the data-set to study changes in farm incomes. A full discussion of the exclusion of farm households from our analysis is given by Williams and Whelan (1993).

4. The equivalence weights used are 1.0, 0.7 and 0.5 for head of household, other adult (or adults) and child (or children), respectively.

CHAPTER 12

1. Walsh (1993) comes to a similar conclusion, showing in addition the role played by increased access by women to social welfare benefits.

CHAPTER 13

1. The survey, which revisited 974 households from the 1987 ESRI survey, is described in chapter 6. This chapter looks at the 625 households in which a married couple was present and both spouses were interviewed. Questions relating to management and control of family finances were answered by both husbands and wives; there is a comprehensive analysis in Rottman (1993).

2. Generally the 'household manager' is the wife and the 'main earner' is the husband, and the generality is sufficiently strong to interpret the table on the assumption that this applies.

3. The unweighted number of households in this group is, however, larger than this percentage of the weighted sample would suggest, so there is some scope for analysing their characteristics.

4. To place the percentages in context, the income levels marking the quintiles are: bottom (up to £128 weekly), second (£128–186), third (£186–247), fourth (£247–329), and fifth (over £329).

5. The distribution of heads of household and all persons by social class in the ESRI phase 2 survey closely approximates that in the 1986 census of population. For a detailed exposition of the meaning and importance of social class in the Irish context see Breen et al. (1990, chapter 3 and 4).

6. Pahl's recent work (1991) stresses the degree to which ideologies about family life vivify the allocation systems based on who manages into gradations of domestic power and control. See the work of Vogler (1989) for a survey-based inquiry into attitudes relating to family financial management.

7. Of course dual-earner households typically, but not inevitably, will rank in the upper income quintiles. The quintile ranking, however, includes households in which the wife is the sole or main income earner (see Rottman, 1993, chapter 3, for an indication of the prevalence of such households).

8. Only one set of responses, that of the household manager, is available for the questions being used here.

CHAPTER 14

1. More detailed categories were used in the survey, but since the number of households in the sample in some of these area types is small, for the purpose of analysis we aggregate them into these five categories.
2. The corresponding figure at the rural district level is –0.37 and at DED level is –0.33 (all coefficients significant at less than the 0.01 level). This reduction in the size of the coefficient with increasing level of spatial disaggregation is a good example of the effects of modifying the areal unit of analysis. The difficulties presented by the so-called modifiable areal unit problem and related issues are discussed by, for example, Clark and Avery (1976) and Oppenshaw (1984a, 1984b).
3. The extent of underemployment among farmers is difficult to estimate, but Boyle et al. (1992) estimate that for Northern Ireland in 1987 the ratio of labour requirements to agricultural employment was 0.76, so the level of underemployment was of the order of 24 per cent.
4. The reader should note that the actual interval of each of the quintile ranges and the rural districts enclosed within them is different for each of the five variables in the table.
5. This quintile distribution is based on small farmers (less than 30 acres) as a percentage of those at work in each rural district.

CHAPTER 15

1. While the shapes and locations of the schedules vary with the number of children, the major shift in the schedule illustrated in the diagram emerges also for other family types.
2. This differs somewhat from the analysis by the National Economic and Social Council (1990), which includes an assumed value of £10 per week for a medical card and assumes that the family is in local authority accommodation paying an income-related ('differential') rent; but the main points are not sensitive to these differences.
3. Only a part of this upward shift is accounted for by indexation to deal with the effects of inflation.

CHAPTER 16

1. McCarthy (1993) argues that tax and social welfare policies are among those weakening the incentives to seek and accept job offers, and his primary prescription in this area is to 'stop levying high tax rates on low incomes.'
2. Pay-related benefit, together with the living-alone and age allowances, were to be phased out as the basic payments were increased.
3. The commission concentrated on proposals for the reform of the *structure* of the tax system that could be applied to yield different levels of revenue. However, it gave clear indications that the top rate of income tax should not exceed 50 per cent, that the standard tax rate should be lowered, and

that the numbers of individuals liable at the higher rates of tax should be reduced.

4. Each of these terms has become associated with particular—and potentially important—differences in the structure and administration of the unified tax-transfer scheme (see O'Neill, 1993). But the correspondence between the labels and the details of the schemes is not very well defined. We therefore use the term 'basic income' to encompass all such schemes, and describe alternative forms of it explicitly.

5. It was announced in the 1992 budget that disability benefit would be included as part of taxable income with effect from April 1993, and that it was intended to include all short-term welfare benefits as this became administratively feasible.

6. For a review of other issues see Callan (1991b).

7. Withdrawal of cash or non-cash benefits is not taken into account.

8. The abolition of tax allowances for children coupled with an increase in child benefit was a step in this direction.

9. For further discussion of these issues see Callan and Farrell (1991).

CHAPTER 17

1. The PRSI exemption scheme was reintroduced in October 1992, providing for two years' exemption from the employer's PRSI contributions in respect of additional workers hired who had been on the live register for at least thirteen weeks. In the previous period of the scheme's operation—from October 1989 to February 1990—it provided for one full year's exemption for employers from PRSI payments. Only 1,300 claims were made under the scheme during this period.

2. Evidence from the UK (National Economic and Social Council, 1990, 443–4) indicates that, when compared with other policies (such as reductions in employer's national insurance contributions or increased public spending), special employment schemes are a relatively cheap way to create work.

3. To take an example, consider the Business Expansion Scheme, which involved the use of tax exemptions to stimulate new business ventures and thus jobs. So far as we are aware, there have been no estimates made of its effectiveness in creating jobs (net of deadweight and displacement effects), despite the fact that the tax forgone vastly exceeds the costs of schemes such as the EIS or Enterprise.

CHAPTER 18

1. Setting up such an agency had been a central recommendation of the final report of the National Committee on Pilot Schemes to Combat Poverty (1980).

2. The role of community development initiatives is set in the context of a national strategy also involving, among other things, tax and social

welfare reform and action on unemployment in, for example, successive pre-budget submissions by the Combat Poverty Agency.
3. This was given considerable publicity and was cited by the commission in the interim report on the Second Programme.

CHAPTER 19

1. See chapter 9, table 9.6.
2. See, for example, the survey by Glass et al. (1982).
3. See Hannan (1992); Conference of Major Religious Superiors (1992b).
4. See Callan in FitzGerald and Keegan (1993).
5. See, for example, Healy and Reynolds (1990).
6. See chapter 13.
7. The NESC in *A Strategy for the Nineties* (1990, 226) shared this conclusion.

Notes on Background Studies

The objective of this book has been to bring together the most important findings from detailed studies by the contributors on poverty and related topics and to make them available to a wide audience. The following studies should be consulted for a more detailed description of many of the findings, sources and references than are presented here. Not all the findings are drawn from published studies, however—for example much of chapters 7, 9, 14, and 18.

The main studies on which each chapter draws are as follows:

Chapter 2: Callan and Nolan (1991); Callan et al. (1989); Nolan (1989).

Chapter 3: Callan et al. (1989), chapter 5; Nolan and Callan (1989).

Chapter 4: Callan et al. (1993); Callan et al. (1989), chapter 8.

Chapter 5: Callan et al. (1989), chapter 7; Nolan and Farrell (1990); Callan et al. (1993).

Chapter 6: Williams and Whelan (1993).

Chapter 7: Callan and Nolan (1990); Whelan et al. (1992).

Chapter 8: Nolan (1993a).

Chapter 9: Whelan et al. (1992); Breen and Whelan (1992, 1993); Whelan (1992a).

Chapter 10: Whelan et al. (1991); Whelan (1992a); Breen and Whelan (1993); Whelan (1993).

Chapter 11: Nolan (1990); Nolan (1991c); Nolan (1993b, 1993c).

Chapter 12: Callan (1991a); Callan and Farrell (1991); Callan and Wren (1994).

Chapter 13: Rottman (1993).

Chapter 14: Williams (1993).

Chapter 15: Callan and Nolan (1989); Callan et al. (1989), chapters 10 and 11; Callan (1991b); Callan and Nolan (1992a).

Chapter 16: Callan (1991b, 1991c); Callan and Farrell (1991); Callan and Nolan (1992b).

Chapter 17: Breen (1984, 1988); Breen and Halpin (1988, 1989).

Chapter 18: Nolan (1991a).

Chapter 19: Callan (1991b); Nolan and Farrell (1990); Callan and Farrell (1991); Callan and Nolan (1992b); Callan and Wren (1994).

References

Abel-Smith, B., and Townsend, P. (1965), *The Poor and the Poorest,* London: Bell.

Atkinson, A. B. (1973), 'Low pay and the cycle of poverty' in F. Field (ed.), *Low Pay,* London: Arrow.

Atkinson, A. B. (1987), 'On the measurement of poverty', *Econometrica,* 55 (4), 749–64.

Atkinson, A. B. (1989), *Poverty and Social Security,* Hemel Hempstead: Harvester Wheatsheaf.

Atkinson, A. B. (1992), *The Western Experience of Social Safety Nets* (discussion paper no. 80), ST/ICERD Welfare State Programme.

Atkinson, A. B. (1993), *Beveridge, the National Minimum, and its Future in a European Context* (discussion paper no. 85), ST/ICERD Welfare State Programme.

Atkinson, A. B., and Micklewright, J. (1985), *Unemployment Benefits and Unemployment Duration,* London: STICERD.

Bane, M. J., and Ellwood, D. (1986), 'Slipping into and out of poverty: the dynamics of spells', *Journal of Human Resources,* vol. 21 (1), 1–23.

Barrett, S. (1989), 'Measuring poverty in Ireland: an assessment of recent studies', *Economic and Social Review,* vol. 20 (4), 353–60.

Bazen, S. (1988), *On the Overlap Between Low Pay and Poverty* (discussion paper 120), Programme on Taxation, Incentives and the Distribution of Income, London: London School of Economics.

Beckerman, W. (1979), 'The impact of income maintenance payments on poverty in Britain', *Economic Journal,* vol. 89, 261–79.

Berghman, J., and Dirven, H. J. (1991), *Poverty, Insecurity of Subsistence and Relative Deprivation in the Netherlands,* Tilburg: Institute for Social Research, University of Tilburg.

Blackwell, J. (1986), *Low Pay: the Current Position and Policy Issues* (duplicated), Dublin: Resource and Environmental Policy Centre, University College.

Blackwell, J. (1989), *Low Pay in Ireland* (duplicated), Dublin: Resource and Environmental Policy Centre, University College.

Blau, P. M., and Duncan, O. D. (1967), *The American Occupational Structure,* New York: Wiley.

Boudon, R. (1974), *Education, Opportunity and Social Inequality,* New York: Wiley.

Boyle, G., Haase, T., et al. (1992), *Labour Adjustment and Income Developments in the Agricultural Economy of Northern Ireland, 1971–1990* (duplicated), Maynooth: Centre for Agricultural and Food Policy Research, St Patrick's College.

Bradley, J., FitzGerald, J., Kearney, I., Boyle, G., Breen, R., Shorthall, S., Durkan, J., Reynolds-Feighan, A., and O'Malley, E. (1992), *The Role of the Structural Funds: Analysis of Consequences for Ireland in the Context of 1992* (Policy Research Series, no. 13), Dublin: Economic and Social Research Institute.

Bradley, J., FitzGerald, J., and McCoy, D. (1991), *Medium-Term Review, 1991–1996,* Dublin: Economic and Social Research Institute.

Breen, R. (1984), *Education and the Labour Market: Work and Unemployment among Recent Cohorts of Irish School Leavers* (General Research Series, no. 119), Dublin: Economic and Social Research Institute.

Breen, R. (1988), 'The work experience programme in Ireland', *International Labour Review,* 127 (4), 429–44.

Breen, R. (1989), 'Social class, schools and society' in J. Mulholland (ed.), *Patrick McGill Summer School,* Donegal.

Breen, R. (1991), *Education, Employment and Training in the Youth Labour Market* (General Research Series, no. 152), Dublin: Economic and Social Research Institute.

Breen, R., with Halpin, B. (1988), *Self-Employment and the Unemployed* (General Research Series, no. 140), Dublin: Economic and Social Research Institute.

Breen, R., with Halpin, B. (1989), *Subsidising Jobs: an Evaluation of the Employment Incentive Scheme* (General Research Series, no. 144), Dublin: Economic and Social Research Institute.

Breen, R., Hannan, D., Rottman, D., and Whelan, C. (1990), *Understanding Contemporary Ireland: State, Class and Development in the Republic of Ireland,* London: Macmillan.

Breen, R., and Honohan, P. (1991), 'Trends in the share of long-term unemployment in Ireland', *Economic and Social Review,* vol. 23, 1, 73–92.

Breen, R., and Shorthall, S. (1992), 'The exchequer costs of unemployment among unqualified labour market participants' in J. Bradley et al., *The Role of the Structural Funds: Analysis of Consequences for Ireland in the Context of 1992* (Policy Research Series, no. 13), Dublin: Economic and Social Research Institute.

Breen, R., and Whelan, C. T. (1992), 'Explaining the Irish pattern of social fluidity: the role of the political' in J. H. Goldthorpe and C. T. Whelan (eds.), *The Development of Industrial Society in Ireland, Proceedings of the British Academy,* 79, Oxford: Oxford University Press.

Breen, R., and Whelan, C. T. (1993), 'From ascription to achievement?: origins, education and entry to the labour force in the Republic of Ireland during the twentieth century', *Acta Sociologica* (forthcoming).

Buhman, B., Rainwater, L., Schmaus, G., and Smeeding, T. (1988), 'Equivalence scales, well-being, inequality and poverty: sensitivity estimates across ten countries using the Luxembourg income study database', *Review of Income and Wealth,* series 33, no. 2, 115–42.

Bureau of the Census (1989), *Transitions in Income and Poverty Status, 1984–1985: Current Population Reports, Household Economic Studies* (series P-70, no. 15-RD-1), Washington: Government Printing Office.

Burgoyne, C. B. (1990), 'Money in marriage: how patterns of allocation both reflect and conceal power', *Sociological Review,* 38 (4), 634–65.

Burkhauser, R., and Finnegan, T. (1989), 'The minimum wage and the poor: the end of a relationship?', *Journal of Policy Analysis and Management,* 8 (1), 53–71.

Callan T. (1991a), 'Male-female wage differentials in Ireland', *Economic and Social Review,* vol. 23 (1), 55–72.

Callan, T. (1991b), *Property Tax: Principles and Policy Options* (Policy Research Series, no. 12), Dublin: Economic and Social Research Institute.

Callan, T. (1991c), *Income Tax and Welfare Reform: Microsimulation Modelling and Analysis* (General Research Series, no. 154), Dublin: Economic and Social Research Institute.

Callan, T., and Farrell, B. (1991), *Women's Participation in the Irish Labour Market* (report no. 91), Dublin: National Economic and Social Council.

Callan T., and Nolan, B. (1989), 'Evaluating social welfare expenditures: how well does the system perform in reducing poverty?', *Economic and Social Review,* vol. 20 (4), 329–52.

Callan, T., and Nolan, B. (1990), 'Work Incentives and Replacement Rates: Results from the ESRI Survey' (report to Inter-Departmental Working Group), Dublin: Economic and Social Research Institute.

Callan, T., and Nolan, B. (1991), 'Concepts of poverty and the poverty line: a critical survey of approaches to measuring poverty', *Journal of Economic Surveys,* vol. 5, no. 3, 243–62.

Callan, T., and Nolan, B. (1992a), 'Distributional aspects of Ireland's fiscal adjustment', *Economic and Social Review,* vol. 23 (3), 319–42.

Callan, T., and Nolan, B. (1992b), 'Low Pay, Poverty and Social Security' (paper presented to Conference on Social Security Fifty Years After Beveridge, York).

Callan, T., Nolan, B., and Whelan, C. T. (1993), 'Resources, deprivation and the measurement of poverty', *Journal of Social Policy,* vol. 22 (2), 141–72.

Callan, T., Nolan, B., Whelan, B. J., and Hannan, D. F., with Creighton, S. (1989), *Poverty, Income and Welfare in Ireland* (General Research Series, no. 146), Dublin: Economic and Social Research Institute.

Callan, T., and Wren, A. (1993), *Male-Female Wage Differentials: Analysis and Policy Issues* (General Research Series), Dublin: Economic and Social Research Institute.

Central Statistics Office (1988), *The Trend of Employment and Unemployment, 1979–85,* Dublin: Stationery Office.

Central Statistics Office (1991), *The Trend of Employment and Unemployment, 1984–91,* Dublin: Stationery Office.

Centre d'Études des Revenus et des Coûtes (1991), *Les Bas Salaires dans les Pays de la Communauté Économique Européenne,* Paris: CERC.

Chanan, G., and Vos, K. (1990), *Social Change and Local Action: Coping with Disadvantage in Urban Areas,* Dublin: European Foundation for the Improvement of Living and Working Conditions.

Chiplin, B. (1992), 'Unemployment and the labour market' in J. Creedy and B. Thomas (eds.), *The Economics of Labour Markets,* London: Butterworth.

Clark, W. A. V., and Avery, K. L. (1976), 'The effects of data aggregation in statistical analysis', *Geographical Analysis,* vol. 8, 428–38.

Coates, K., and Silburn, R. (1970), *Poverty: the Forgotten Englishmen,* Harmondsworth (Middlesex): Penguin.

Cohen, S., and Syme, S. L. (1985), 'Issues in the study and application of social support' in S. Cohen and S. L. Syme (eds.), *Social Support and Health,* London: Academic Press.

Combat Poverty Agency (1989), *Poverty: Priorities for Action,* Dublin: CPA.

Combat Poverty Agency (1991), *Tackling Poverty in the Nineties,* Dublin: CPA.

Combat Poverty Agency (1992), *Reform of the European Community's Structural Funds,* Dublin: CPA.

Commission of the European Communities (1981), *Final Report from the Commission to the Council on the First Programme of Pilot Schemes and Studies to Combat Poverty* (COM (81), 769), Brussels: Commission of the European Communities.

Commission of the European Communities (1991), *Final Report on the Second European Poverty Programme* (COM (91), 29), Luxembourg: Office for Official Publications of the European Communities.

Commission on Social Welfare (1986), *Report of the Commission on Social Welfare,* Dublin: Stationery Office.

Commission on Taxation (1982), *First Report of the Commission on Taxation: Direct Taxation,* Dublin: Stationery Office

Community Workers' Co-Operative (1992), *Structural Funds: the Challenge to Address Social Exclusion,* Dublin: CWC.

Conference of Major Religious Superiors (1991), *National Recovery For Whom?,* Dublin: CMRS.

Conference of Major Religious Superiors (1992a), *A Question of Choices,* Dublin: CMRS.

Conference of Major Religious Superiors (1992b), *Education and Poverty: Eliminating Disadvantage in the Primary School Years,* Dublin: CMRS.

Cullen, B. (1989), *Poverty, Community and Development,* Dublin: Combat Poverty Agency.

Curry, J. (1986), 'Contribution to symposium on the report of the Commission on Social Welfare', *Journal of the Statistical and Social Inquiry Society of Ireland,* vol. 25, part 4, 1–7.

Daly, M. (1989), *Women and Poverty,* Dublin: Attic.

Deleeck, H., van den Bosch, K., and de Lathouwer, L. (eds.) (1992), *Poverty and the Adequacy of Social Security in Europe,* Aldershot: Avebury.

Department of Health (1986), *Health: the Wider Dimensions,* Dublin: Stationery Office.

Department of Health and Social Security (1980), *Inequalities in Health: Report of a Research Working Group,* London: DHSS.

Dex, S. (1990), 'Goldthorpe on class and gender' in J. Clarke, C. Modgill and S. Modgill (eds.), *J. H. Goldthorpe: Consensus and Controversy,* London: Falmer.

Dilnot, A., and Webb, S. (1988), 'Reforming national insurance contributions', *Fiscal Studies,* vol. 9 (4), 1–24.

Dilnot, A., Kay, J., and Morris, N. (1984), *The Reform of Social Security,* London: Institute for Fiscal Studies.

Donnison, D. (1988), 'Defining and measuring poverty: a reply to Stein Ringen', *Journal of Social Policy*, vol. 17, part 3, 367–74.

Dowling, B. (1986), 'Contribution to symposium on the report of the Commission on Social Welfare,' *Journal of the Statistical and Social Inquiry Society of Ireland*, vol. 25, part 4, 8–20.

Duclos, J.-Y. (1992), 'Understanding the Take-up of State Benefits Using Micro Data' (paper presented to Conference on Social Security Fifty Years after Beveridge, York).

Duncan, G. (1984), *Years of Poverty, Years of Plenty*, Ann Arbor (Michigan): Institute for Social Research, University of Michigan.

Duncan, G., and Morgan, J. N. (1981), 'Persistence and change in economic status and the role of changing family composition' in M. S. Hill, D. H. Hill and J. N. Morgan (eds.), *Five Thousand American Families: Patterns of Economic Progress*, vol. 9, Ann Arbor (Michigan): Institute for Social Research, University of Michigan.

Eisenberg, P., and Lazarfield, P. F. (1938), 'The psychological effects of unemployment', *Psychological Bulletin*, 35, 358–90.

Erikson, R., and Goldthorpe, J. H. (1992), *The Constant Flux: a Study of Class Mobility in Industrial Societies*, Oxford: Oxford University Press.

Eurostat (1990), *Poverty in Figures: Europe in the Early 1980s*, Luxembourg: Eurostat.

Evans, G. (1993), 'Testing the validity of the Goldthorpe class schema', *European Sociological Review*, 8 (3), 211–32.

FitzGerald, E. (1981), 'The extent of poverty in Ireland' in S. Kennedy (ed.), *One Million Poor*, Dublin: Turoe.

FitzGerald, J., and Keegan, O. (eds.) (1993), *The Community Support Framework, 1989–1993: Evaluation and Recommendations for the 1994–1997 Framework*, Dublin: Economic and Social Research Institute.

Foley, A., and Mulreany, M. (eds.), (1990), *The Single European Market and the Irish Economy*, Dublin: Institute of Public Administration.

Foster, J. E., Greer, J., and Thorbecke, E. (1984), 'A class of decomposable poverty measures', *Econometrica*, vol. 52, 761–6.

Foster, J. E., and Shorrocks, A. F. (1988), 'Poverty orderings', *Econometrica*, vol. 56, 173–7.

Fox, A. (1976), 'The meaning of work', *Open University Occupational Categories and Cultures, I: People and Work*, Milton Keynes.

Frazer, H. (1991), 'Think Global, Act Local' (paper presented to Conference on Local Strategies to Combat Poverty in Europe and the UK, Edinburgh).

Fritzell, J. (1990), 'The dynamics of income distribution and economic mobility in Sweden in comparison with the United States', *Social Science Research,* vol. 19, 17–46.

Fryer, D. (1986), 'Employment deprivation and personal agency during unemployment', *Social Behaviour,* 1, 3–23.

Fryer, D. (1992), 'Psychological or material deprivation: why does unemployment have mental health consequences?' in E. McLaughlin (ed.), *Understanding Unemployment: New Perspectives on Active Labour Market Policies,* London: Routledge.

Garvan, T. (1989), 'Wealth, poverty and development', *Studies,* 78.

Garvey, D. (1988), 'What is the best measure of employment and unemployment in Ireland?', *Journal of the Statistical and Social Inquiry Society of Ireland,* vol. 25, part 5, 185–236.

Geary, P. (1989), 'The measurement and alleviation of poverty: a review of the issues', *Economic and Social Review,* vol. 20, 293–307.

Glass, G., Baker, L., Smith, M., and Filby, N. (1982), *School Class Size,* Beverly Hills: Sage.

Glendinning, C., and Millar, J. (1987), *Women and Poverty in Britain,* Brighton: Wheatsheaf.

Goldberg, D. P. (1972), *The Detection of Psychiatric Illness by Questionnaire,* London: Oxford University Press.

Goldthorpe, J. H. (1982), 'On the service class: its formation and future' in A. Giddens and G. McKenzie (eds.), *Classes and the Division of Labour,* Cambridge: Cambridge University Press.

Goldthorpe, J. H. (1987), *Social Mobility and Class Structure in Modern Britain* (second edition), Oxford: Oxford University Press.

Goldthorpe, J. H. (1992), 'The theory of industrialism and the Irish case' in J. H. Goldthorpe and C. T. Whelan (eds.), *The Development of Industrial Society in Ireland: Proceedings of the British Academy,* 79, Oxford: Oxford University Press.

Goldthorpe, J. H., and Marshall, G. (1992), 'The promising future of class analysis: a response to recent critiques', *Sociology,* vol. 26 (8), 381–400.

Goldthorpe, J. H., and Whelan, C. T. (eds.) (1992), *The Development of Industrial Society in Ireland: Proceedings of the British Academy,* 79, Oxford: Oxford University Press.

Gould, S. G., and Palmer, J. L. (1988), 'Outcomes, interpretations, and policy implications' in J. L. Palmer, T. Smeeding and B. B. Torrey (eds.), *The Vulnerable,* Washington: Urban Institute Press.

Graham, H. (1987), 'Women's poverty and caring' in C. Glendinning and J. Millar (eds.), *Women and Poverty in Britain,* Brighton: Wheatsheaf.

Hagenaars, A. (1986), *The Perception of Poverty,* Amsterdam: North-Holland.

Halsey, A. H. (1977), 'Towards meritocracy?: the case of Britain' in J. Karabel and A. H. Halsey (eds.), *Power and Ideology in Education,* New York: Oxford University Press.

Halsey, A. H., Heath, A. F., and Ridge, J. M., (1980), *Origins and Destinations: Family, Class and Education in Modern Britain,* Oxford: Oxford University Press.

Hannan, D. F. (1986), *Schooling and the Labour Market: Young People in Transition from School to Work,* Shannon: Shannon Curriculum Development Centre.

Hannan, D. F. (1992), 'Ending inequality in education', *Poverty Today,* July–Sept.

Hannan, D. F., with Boyle, M. (1987), *Schooling Decisions: the Origins and Consequences of Selection and Streaming in Irish Post Primary Schools* (General Research Series, no. 136), Dublin: Economic and Social Research Institute.

Hannan, D. F., and Shorthall, S. (1991), *The Quality of Their Education: School Leavers' Views of Educational Objectives and Outcomes* (General Research Series, no. 153), Dublin: Economic and Social Research Institute.

Heady, P., and Smith, M. (1989), *Living Standards During Unemployment,* vol. 1, London: HMSO.

Healy, S., and Reynolds, B. (1990), 'The future of work: a challenge to society' in B. Reynolds and S. Healy, *Work, Unemployment and Job-Creation Policy,* Dublin: Conference of Major Religious Superiors.

Heath, A. F., and Clifford, P. (1990), 'Class inequalities in education in the twentieth century', *Journal of the Royal Statistical Society,* series A, 153, 1–16.

Heath, A. F., Mills, C., and Roberts, J. (1992), 'Towards meritocracy: recent evidence on the old problem' in C. Crouch and A. Heath (eds.), *Social Research and Social Reform,* Oxford: Clarendon Press.

Hill, M. (1981), 'Some dynamic aspects of poverty' in M. Hill, D. H. Hill and J. N. Morgan (eds.), *Five Thousand American Families: Patterns in Economic Progress,* vol. 9, Ann Arbor (Michigan): Institute for Social Research, University of Michigan.

Honohan, P., and Irvine, I. (1987), 'The marginal social cost of taxation in Ireland', *Economic and Social Review,* vol. 19, 1, 15–42.

Hout, M. (1989), *Following in Father's Footsteps: Social Mobility in Ireland,* London: Harvard University Press.

Hughes, G., and Walsh, B. M. (1983), 'Unemployment duration, aggregate demand and unemployment insurance: a study of Irish live register survival probabilities, 1967–78', *Economic and Social Review,* vol. 14 (2), 93–118.

Industrial Policy Review Group (1992), *A Time for Change: Industrial Policy for the 1990s* [the Culliton Report], Dublin: Stationery Office.

Jackson, P. R., Stafford, E. M., Banks, M. H., and Warr, P. B. (1983), 'Unemployment and psychological distress in young people: the moderating role of employment commitment', *Journal of Applied Psychology,* 68, 515–26.

Jahoda, M. (1982), *Employment and Unemployment: a Socio-Psychological Analysis,* Cambridge: Cambridge University Press.

Jahoda, M. (1988), 'Economic recession and mental health: some conceptual issues', *Journal of Social Issues,* 44, 4, 13, 24.

Jahoda, M., Lazarfield, P. F., and Zeiss, H. (1933), *Marienthal: the Sociology of an Unemployed Community* [English translation, 1971], New York: Aldine Atherton.

Jenkins, S. P. (1991), 'Poverty measurement and the within-household distribution: agenda for action', *Journal of Social Policy,* 20 (part 4), 457–83.

Johnson, P., and Stark, G. (1991), 'The effects of a minimum wage on family incomes', *Fiscal Studies,* vol. 12 (1), 88–93.

Jonsson, O. (1989), *Education, Social Mobility and Social Reproduction in Sweden,* Stockholm: Swedish Institute for Social Research.

Joyce, L., and McCashin, T. (eds.) (1982), *Poverty and Social Policy in Ireland,* Dublin: Institute of Public Administration.

Kane, T. J. (1987), 'Giving back control: long-term poverty and motivation', *Social Service Review,* 405–19.

Kasl, S., and Cobb, S. (1979), 'Some mental health consequences of plant closings and job loss' in W. A. Ferman and J. P. Gordus (eds.), *Mental Health and the Economy,* Kalamazoo (Michigan): Upjohn Institute.

Keatinge, P. (ed.) (1992), *Maastricht and Ireland: What the Treaty Means,* Dublin: Institute for European Affairs.

Kelvin, P., and Jarrett, J. E. (1985), *Unemployment: Its Social Psychological Effects,* Cambridge: Cambridge University Press.

Kennedy, F. (1989), *Family, Economy and Government in Ireland* (General Research Paper no. 143), Dublin: Economic and Social Research Institute.

Kessler, R., Blake Turner, J., and House, J. S. (1989), 'Unemployment, reemployment, and emotional functioning in a community sample', *American Sociological Review*, 54, 648–57.

Layard, R., Piachaud, D., Stewart, M., et al. (1978), *The Causes of Poverty* (Royal Commission on the Distribution of Income and Wealth, background paper no. 5), London: HMSO.

Lee, J. J. (1989), *Ireland, 1912–1985: Politics and Society*, Cambridge: Cambridge University Press.

Lewis, J., and Piachaud, D. (1987), 'Women and poverty in the twentieth century' in J. Millar and C. Glendinning (eds.), *Women and Poverty in Britain*, Brighton: Wheatsheaf.

Liem, R. (1987), 'The psychological consequences of unemployment: a comparison of finding and definitions', *Social Research*, 54, 321–53.

McCarthy, C. (1993), 'A review of the crisis' in C. Keane (ed.), *The Jobs Crisis*, Dublin: Mercier.

McCashin, A. (1993), *Lone Parents in the Republic of Ireland: Enumeration, Description and Implications for Social Security*, Dublin: Economic and Social Research Institute.

McGregor, P. P. L., and Borooah, V. K. (1992), 'Is low income or low expenditure a better indicator of whether or not a household is poor?: some results from the 1985 family expenditure survey', *Journal of Social Policy*, vol. 21, part 1, 53–70.

Mack, J., and Lansley, S. (1985), *Poor Britain*, London: Allen and Unwin.

McKee, L., and Bell, C. (1985), 'Marital and family relations in times of male unemployment' in B. Roberts, R. Finnegan and D. Gallie (eds.), *New Approaches to Economic Life*, Manchester: Manchester University Press.

McMahon, G. (1987), 'Wage structure in the Republic of Ireland', *Advances in Business Studies*, vol. 1 (1), 13–27.

McRae, S. (1987), 'The allocation of money in cross-class families', *Sociological Review*, vol. 35 (1), 97–122.

McRae, S. (1990), 'Women and class analysis' in J. J. Clarke, C. Modgill and S. Modgill (eds.), *J. H. Goldthorpe: Consensus and Controversy*, London: Falmer.

Marshall, G. (1990), 'John Goldthorpe and class analysis' in J. Clarke, C. Modgill and S. Modgill (eds.), *J. H. Goldthorpe: Consensus and Controversy*, London: Falmer.

Mayer, S., and Jencks, C. (1988), 'Poverty and the distribution of material hardship', *Journal of Human Resources*, vol. 24 (1).

Mincer, J. (1985), 'Intercountry comparisons of labour force trends and of related developments: an overview', *Journal of Labour Economics*, vol. 3, no. 1, S1–S32.

Mirowsky, J., and Ross, C. (1990), 'The consolation prize theory of alienation', *American Journal of Sociology*, 95, 6, 1505–35.

Moffitt, R. (1992), 'Incentive effects of the US welfare system: a review', *Journal of Economic Literature*, vol. 30 (1), 1–61.

Morgan, J. N., et al. (1974), *Five Thousand American Families: Patterns of Economic Progress*, vol. 1, Ann Arbor (Michigan): Institute for Social Research, University of Michigan.

Morris, L. (1984), 'Redundancy and patterns of household finance', *Sociological Review*, 32 (no. 3), 492–523.

Morris, L. D. (1987), 'Local social polarisation: a case study of Hartlepool', *International Journal of Urban and Regional Research*, 11, 5, 331–50.

Narendranathan, W., Nickell, S., and Stern, N. (1985), 'Unemployment benefits revisited', *Economic Journal*, vol. 95, 307–29.

National Committee on Pilot Schemes to Combat Poverty (1980), *Final Report*, Dublin: National Committee on Pilot Schemes to Combat Poverty.

National Economic and Social Council (1986), *A Strategy for Development* (report no. 83), Dublin: NESC.

National Economic and Social Council (1990), *A Strategy for the Nineties: Economic Stability and Structural Change* (report no. 89), Dublin: NESC.

National Planning Board (1984), *Proposals for Plan, 1984–87*, Dublin: NPB.

Nolan, B. (1987), 'More on hypothetical versus actual replacement ratios in Ireland', *Economic and Social Review*, vol. 18 (3), 159–72.

Nolan, B. (1989), 'An evaluation of the new low income statistics', *Fiscal Studies*, vol. 10 (4), 53–66.

Nolan, B. (1990), 'Socio-economic mortality differentials in Ireland', *Economic and Social Review*, vol. 21 (2), 193–208.

Nolan, B. (1991a), *Recent EC Commission Statistics on Trends in Poverty*, Project on Income Distribution, Poverty and Usage of State Services working paper 22, Dublin: Economic and Social Research Institute.

Nolan, B. (1991b), *The Wealth of Irish Households: What Can We Learn from Survey Data?*, Dublin: Combat Poverty Agency.

Nolan, B. (1991c), *The Utilisation and Financing of Health Services in Ireland* (General Research Series, no. 155), Dublin: Economic and Social Research Institute.

Nolan, B. (1992), *National Social Security Provisions Guaranteeing Minimum Resources—Ireland: Report for the EC Commission,* Dublin: Economic and Social Research Institute.

Nolan, B. (1993a), *Low Pay in Ireland* (General Research Series, no. 159), Dublin: Economic and Social Research Institute.

Nolan, B. (1993b), 'Ireland' in E. van Doorslaer, A. Wagstaff and F. Rutten (eds.), *Equity in the Finance and Delivery of Health Care: an International Perspective,* Oxford: Oxford University Press.

Nolan, B. (1993c), 'Economic incentives, health status, and health services utilisation', *Journal of Health Economics,* vol. 12 (2), 151–70.

Nolan, B., and Callan, T. (1989), 'Measuring trends in poverty over time: some robust results for Ireland, 1980–1987', *Economic and Social Review,* vol. 20 (4), 309–28.

Nolan, B., and Farrell, B. (1990), *Child Poverty in Ireland,* Dublin: Combat Poverty Agency.

Ó Cinnéide, S. (1972), 'The extent of poverty in Ireland', *Social Studies,* 1 (4), 381–400.

Ó Cinnéide, S. (1992a), *Social Exclusion in Ireland, 1991–1992: the Second Annual Report for Ireland for the EC Observatory on National Policies to Combat Social Exclusion,* Maynooth: St. Patrick's College.

Ó Cinnéide, S. (1992b), 'Social policy' in P. Keatinge (ed.), *Maastricht and Ireland: What the Treaty Means,* Dublin: Institute for European Affairs.

O'Donnell, R. (ed.) (1991), *Economic and Monetary Union,* Dublin: Institute for European Affairs.

O'Hare, A., Commins, P., and Whelan, C. T. (1991), 'The development of an Irish census-based social class scale', *Economic and Social Review,* vol. 22 (2), 135–56.

O'Higgins, M., and Jenkins, S. P. (1990), 'Poverty in the EC: estimates for 1975, 1980 and 1985' in R. Teekens and B. M. S. van Praag (eds.), *Analysing Poverty in the European Community,* Luxembourg: Eurostat.

O'Mahoney, D. (1983), 'A study of replacement ratios among a sample of unemployed workers', *Economic and Social Review,* vol. 14 (2), 77–91.

O'Neill, C. (1992), *Telling It Like It Is,* Dublin: Combat Poverty Agency.

O'Neill, C. J. (1993), 'Tax/Transfer Reform in Ireland' (M.Litt. thesis, University of Dublin).

Oppenshaw, S. (1984a), 'Ecological fallacies and the analysis of areal census data', *Environment and Planning,* vol. 16, 17–31.

Oppenshaw, S. (1984b), 'The modifiable area unit problem', *Concepts and Techniques in Modern Geography,* no. 38, Norwich: Geo Books.

Organisation for Economic Co-Operation and Development (1987), *Employment Outlook,* September, part 5, Paris: OECD.

Pahl, J. (1980), 'Patterns of money management within marriage', *Journal of Social Policy,* vol. 9, 313–35.

Pahl, J. (1983), 'The allocation of money and the structuring of inequality within marriage', *Sociological Review,* 31, 235–62.

Pahl, J. (1989), *Money and Marriage,* London: Macmillan.

Pahl, J. (1991), 'Money and power in marriage' in P. Abbott and L. Wallace (eds.), *Gender, Power, and Sexuality,* London: Macmillan, 41–57.

Pahl, R. E. (1989), 'Is the emperor naked?: some comments on the adequacy of sociological theory on urban and regional research', *International Journal of Urban and Regional Research,* 13, 709, 20.

Palmer, J. L., Smeeding, T., and Torrey, B. B. (eds.) (1988), *The Vulnerable,* Washington: Urban Institute Press.

Payne, R., and Jones, J. G. (1987), 'Social class and re-employment: changes in health and perceived financial circumstances, *Journal of Occupational Behaviour,* 8, 175–84.

Payne, R., Warr, R., and Hartley, J. (1984), 'Social class and psychological ill-health during unemployment', *Sociology of Health and Illness,* vol. 6, 2, 153–75.

Pearce, D. (1978), 'The feminization of poverty: women, work and welfare', *Urban and Social Change Review,* vol. 24, 28–35.

Pearlin, L., Menaghan, E., Lieberman, M., and Mullan, J. T. (1981), 'The stress process', *Journal of Health and Social Behaviour,* 22, 337–51.

Piachaud, D. (1981), 'Peter Townsend and the holy grail', *New Society,* 10 September, 419–21.

Piachaud, D. (1987), 'Problems in the definition and measurement of poverty', *Journal of Social Policy,* vol. 16 (2), 147–64.

Raferty, H., and Hout, M. (1990), *Maximally Maintained Inequality: Expansion, Reform and Opportunity in Irish Education, 1921–1975,* Madrid: ISA Research Committee on Social Stratification and Mobility.

Rainwater, L. (1990), *Poverty and Equivalence as Social Constructions* (Luxembourg Income Study, working paper 55), Luxembourg: CEPS.

Review Group on the Treatment of Households in the Social Welfare Code (1991), *Report,* Dublin: Stationery Office.

Ringen, S. (1987), *The Possibility of Politics,* Oxford: Clarendon Press.

Ringen, S. (1988), 'Direct and indirect measures of poverty', *Journal of Social Policy,* vol. 17 (3), 351–66.

Roche, J. (1984), *Poverty and Income Maintenance Policies in Ireland,* Dublin: Institute for Public Administration

Rodgers, H. (1990), *Poor Women, Poor Families: the Economic Plight of America's Female-Headed Households* (second edition), New York: Sharpe.

Ronayne, T., Cullen, K., Wynne, L., Ryan, G., and Cullen, J. (1986), *Locally Based Responses to Long-Term Unemployment,* Dublin: European Foundation for the Improvement of Living and Working Conditions.

Rottman, D. B. (1993), *Allocating Resources Within Irish Families,* Dublin: Combat Poverty Agency.

Rottman, D. B., Hannan, D. F., Hardiman, N., and Wiley, M. (1982), *The Distribution of Income in the Republic of Ireland: a Study in Social Class and Family-Cycle Inequalities* (General Research Series, no. 109), Dublin: Economic and Social Research Institute.

Ruggles, P., and Williams, R. (1989), 'Longitudinal measures of poverty: accounting for income and assets over time', *Review of Income and Wealth,* series 35, no. 3, 225–44.

Sawhill, I. V. (1988), 'Poverty in the US: why is it so persistent?', *Journal of Economic Literature,* 26, 1037–119.

Schilling, R. F., 1987. 'Limitations of social support', *Social Service Review,* 19–31.

Sen, A. (1976), 'Poverty: an ordinal approach to measurement', *Econometrica,* 44, 219–31.

Sen, A. (1979), 'Issues in the measurement of poverty', *Scandinavian Journal of Economics,* vol. 81, 285–307.

Sen, A. (1983), 'Poor, relatively speaking', *Oxford Economic Papers,* 35 (2), 153–69.

Sexton, J. J. (1988), *Long-Term Unemployment: Its Wider Market Effects in the Countries of the European Community,* Luxembourg: Eurostat.

Sexton, J. J., and O'Connell, P. J. (1993), *Evaluation of Operational Programme to Combat Long-Term Unemployment Among Adults in Ireland: Objective 3 of the Community Support Framework,* Dublin: Economic and Social Research Institute.

Spruit, I. P., Bastiannen, J., Verkley, H., van Niewenhuizen, M. G., and Stolk, J. (1985), *Experiencing Unemployment, Financial Constraints and Health,* Leiden: Institute of Social Medicine.

Sutherland, H. (1991), *The Immediate Impact of a Minimum Wage on Family Incomes* (Microsimulation Modelling Unit, research note 1, STICERD), London: London School of Economics.

Tansey, P. (1991), *Making the Irish Labour Market Work*, Dublin: Gill and Macmillan.

Townsend, P. (1979), *Poverty in the United Kingdom*, Harmondsworth (Middlesex): Penguin.

Townsend, P., and Gordon, D. (1989), 'Memorandum submitted to Social Services Committee of the House of Commons' in *Minimum Income: Memoranda Laid before the Committee, Session 1988–89*, London: HMSO.

Tussing, A. D. (1985), *Irish Medical Care Resources: an Economic Analysis* (General Research Series, no. 126), Dublin: Economic and Social Research Institute.

van Doorslaer, E., Wagstaff, A., and Rutten, F. (eds.) (1993), *Equity in the Finance and Delivery of Health Care: an International Perspective*, Oxford: Oxford University Press.

Vogler, C. (1989), *Labour Market Change and Patterns of Financial Allocation within Households* (ESRC working paper no. 12), Social Change and Life Initiative.

Walsh, B. M. (1978), 'Unemployment compensation and the rate of unemployment: the Irish experience' in H. Grubel and M. Walker (eds.), *Unemployment Insurance: Global Evidence of its Effects on Unemployment*, Vancouver: Fraser Institute.

Walsh, B. M. (1992), 'Appropriate policy changes' in A. Gray (ed.), *Responses to Irish Unemployment*, Dublin: Indecon.

Walsh, B. M. (1993), 'Labour force participation and the growth of women's employment, Ireland, 1971–1991', *Economic and Social Review*, vol. 24 (4), 369–400.

Warr, P. B. (1985), 'Twelve questions about unemployment and health' in B. Roberts, R. Finnegan and D. Gallie (eds.), *New Approaches to Economic Life*, Manchester: Manchester University Press.

Warr, P. B. (1987), *Work, Unemployment and Mental Health*, Oxford: Clarendon Press.

Warr, P., and Jackson, P. (1985), 'Factors influencing the psychological impact of prolonged unemployment and re-employment', *Psychological Medicine*, 15, 795–817.

Webb, S. (1992), 'Social Insurance and Poverty Alleviation: an Empirical Analysis' (paper presented to Conference on Social Security Fifty Years After Beveridge, York).

Wheaton, B. (1983), 'Stress, personal coping resources and psychiatric symptoms: an investigation of interactive models', *Journal of Health and Social Behaviour*, 24, 208–29.

Whelan, B. J. (1979), 'RANSAM: a random sample design for Ireland', *Economic and Social Review*, vol. 10 (2), 169–74.

Whelan, B. J., Breen, R., Callan, T., and Nolan, B. (1992), *A Study of the Employment Possibilities of the Long-Term Unemployed* (duplicated), Dublin: Economic and Social Research Institute.

Whelan, C. T. (1992a), 'The role of income, life-style deprivation and financial strain in mediating the impact of unemployment on psychological distress: evidence from the Republic of Ireland', *Journal of Occupational and Organisational Psychology*, vol. 65, 331–44.

Whelan, C. T. (1992b), 'The impact of realistic and illusory control on psychological distress: a test of the model of instrumental realism', *Economic and Social Review*, vol. 23 (4), 439–54.

Whelan, C. T. (1992c), 'The role of sense of control and social support in mediating the impact of psychological distress: a test of the hypothesis of functional substitution', *Economic and Social Review*, vol. 23 (2), 167–82.

Whelan, C. T. (1993), 'The role of social support in mediating the psychological consequences of economic stress', *Sociology of Health and Illness*, vol. 15 (1), 86–101.

Whelan, C. T. (1994), 'Social class, unemployment, psychological distress', *European Sociological Review*.

Whelan, C. T., Breen, R., and Whelan, B. J. (1992), 'Industrialisation, class formation and social mobility in Ireland' in J. H. Goldthorpe and C. T. Whelan (eds.), *The Development of Industrial Society in Ireland: Proceedings of the British Academy*, 79, Oxford: Oxford University Press.

Whelan, C. T., Hannan, D. F., and Creighton, S. (1991) *Unemployment, Poverty and Psychological Distress* (General Research Series, no. 150), Dublin: Economic and Social Research Institute.

Whelan, C. T., and Whelan, B. J., 'Social Mobility in the Republic of Ireland: a Comparative Perspective (General Research Series, no. 116), Dublin: Economic and Social Research Institute.

Whitehead, M. (1987), *Inequalities in Health in the 1980s*, London: Health Education Council.

Williams, J. (1993), *Spatial Variations in Deprivation Surrogates* (report to the Combat Poverty Agency), Dublin: Combat Poverty Agency.

Williams, J., and Whelan, B. J. (1993), *The Dynamics of Poverty: Issues in Short-Term Poverty Transitions in Ireland,* Dublin: Combat Poverty Agency.

Wilson, F., and Ramphele, M. (1989), *Uprooting Poverty: the South African Challenge,* New York: Norton.

Wright, R. (1992), 'A feminization of poverty in Great Britain?', *Review of Income and Wealth,* vol. 38, 17–25.